ZIONISM AND THE PALESTINIANS

ZIONISM AND THE PALESTINIANS

SIMHA FLAPAN

CROOM HELM LONDON

BARNES & NOBLE BOOKS · NEW YORK
(a division of Harper & Row Publishers, Inc.)

© 1979 Simha Flapan
Croom Helm Ltd, 2-10 St John's Road, London SW11

British Library Cataloguing in Publication Data

Flapan, Simha
    Zionism and the Palestinians.
    1. Jewish-Arab relations   2. Palestinian Arabs
    – History   3. Zionists – Attitudes
    I. Title
    956.94'004'927   DS119.7

    ISBN 0-85664-499-4

Published in the U.S.A. 1979 by
HARPER & ROW PUBLISHERS, INC.
BARNES & NOBLE IMPORT DIVISION
ISBN

Library of Congress Cataloguing in Publication Data

Flapan, Simha
    Zionism and the Palestinians
    Includes index.
    1. Jewish-Arab relations – 1917-1949   2. Zionism –
History.   I. Title.
DS119.7.F6   956.94'001   78-26044
ISBN 0-06-492104-2

Printed in Great Britain by Biddles Ltd, Guildford, Surrey

CONTENTS

This book is dedicated to the memory of Louise Berman and Paul Jacobs who did not live to see the fruits of their efforts to promote Jewish-Arab understanding.

ACKNOWLEDGEMENTS

This book probably never would have been written had it not been for the encouragement of the late Mrs Louise Berman (New York), who persuaded me to engage in research. She, as well as the Institute for Policy Studies (Washington), the Foundation for National Progress (San Francisco) and Dr Nahum Goldmann provided the funds necessary for the long period of research which involved extensive travel and the aid of many assistants. I am particularly grateful to Dr Goldmann, who introduced me to the intricate problems of Zionist strategy in a series of long and fascinating interviews. In addition to her stimulating company, Mrs Sylvia Shine (London) kindly provided me with a studio, ideal for research and writing. I am indebted to my colleague David Shaham who agreed to replace me at the editorial desk of New Outlook during the year I was writing this book. I am grateful to my assistants, Yoel Blumenkrantz, Livia Rokah, Illana Cohen, Tirza Posner, Tony Klug, Abe Heiman and Daham al Attawnah, who spared me precious months of work in perusing archives, assembling documents, interviewing people, editing and translating. Most of their research-findings will be reflected in the forthcoming volume, dealing with the post-1948 period. For this volume I am particularly indebted to Stephen Schifferes who has been an indispensible collaborator. Without his diligent research and editing many chapters of this book could not have been written. I am thankful also, to Dan Gillon and Ian Black (London) for allowing me to consult their archives, and to Joseph Vashtiz and Yoram Nimrod of Givat Haviva (Israel) for making available to me their, as yet, unpublished works. While all the above mentioned influenced in one way or another the final shape of this book, this does not meant that they necessarily share the views expressed therein, which are entirely my own. Finally I owe an irredeemable debt to my wife Sara and my daughters Yael and Naama for all they had to endure and tolerate while this book was being written.

S. Flapan
October 1978

PREFACE

This book is a study of the roots of present-day Israeli policy towards the Arabs. The point of departure is that Israeli political thinking was moulded during the pre-state period and in its crystallisation made a ritual of several basic concepts: (1) gradual build-up of an economic and military potential as the basis for achievement of political aims; (2) alliance with a great power external to the Middle East; (3) non-recognition of the existence of a Palestine national entity; (4) Zionism's civilising mission in an undeveloped area; (5) economic, social and cultural segregation as prerequisites for the renaissance of Jewish national life; (6) the concept of 'peace from strength'.

Part One of the book describes the attitudes of the Zionist leaders in the pre-state period 1917-48 towards the Arab National Movement in general and towards the Palestinian Arabs in particular; Part Two deals with the application of these attitudes in a number of critical situations which constituted turning points in Jewish-Arab relations: the Arab Revolt and the Zionist struggle for Partition in 1936-8; the 'White Paper' policy 1939-45; the 1948 war in Palestine. Sketching profiles of Zionist leaders required moving forwards and backwards between political events, regardless of their sequence. Thus the description of the evolution of the conflict was made impossible – nor was it my intention – though some measure of chronological order was maintained in Part Two dealing with major events between 1936 and 1945.

The focal point of the book is the attitude of the Zionist movement towards the Palestinian Arabs and their aspirations to national independence.

The Zionist attitude towards the pan-Arab national movement has been the subject of many important studies. But little attention has been paid specifically to the Palestinian component of the problem. Even an excellent work such as Aharon Cohen's *Israel and the Arab World*, which describes in detail contacts between Arabs and Jews, subsumes the Palestinian-Zionist conflict within the framework of relations between Jews and the Arab national movement in general. Yet, it was specifically the Palestinian issue which played the decisive role in the failure to resolve the Israel-Arab conflict.[1] When former Israeli Prime Minister Golda Meir was criticised for her widely-publicised pronouncement that 'there is no such thing as a Palestinian people', it escaped the

11

notice of her critics that the view she expressed was the cornerstone of Zionist policy, initiated by Weizmann and faithfully carried out by Ben-Gurion and his successors. This policy has been pursued despite abundant proof of the tenacity with which the Palestinians have clung to their national identity in the most adverse circumstances.

Non-recognition of the Palestinians remains until the present the basic tenet of Israel's policy-makers who, like the Zionist leadership before 1948, nurture the illusion that the Palestinian national problem disappeared with the creation of the state of Jordan, leaving only the residual humanitarian problem of the refugees to be solved.

The war of 1948 was deemed to have vindicated the policy of non-recognition of the Palestinians; on the surface, the Palestinian people, dispersed as refugees all over the Middle East, had ceased to exist, and only the conflict between Israel and the Arab states remained unresolved.

Nearly 30 years had to pass before it became clear that the 1948 war did not liquidate the *national* problem of the Palestinians, but only aggravated and complicated it, changing some of its aspects and adding new ones, coming to resemble the problem of the Jews dispersed throughout the world, which the Zionist movement proposed to solve by 'ingathering of the exiles'.

This analysis was originally conceived as an introduction to the work on Israel's contemporary problems and, in particular, on the controversy following the 1956 Suez War between Ben-Gurion and his opponents Sharett and Goldmann, who opposed the policy of massive retaliation and preventive war. But while studying the pre-1948 documents, I was struck by the unbroken continuity, up to the present, of views and attitudes regarding the Arab problem, and by the relevance of pre-state debates and decisions to the situation of today. Thus, what was intended as an introductory chapter developed into a fully fledged volume, deferring execution of the original plan for a later stage.

One may doubt the wisdom of plunging into the past and reviving the bitter memory of old grievances and wrongs at a time when the focus must be on the future, and on the advance towards reconciliation. The Greeks held that even the gods are unable to change the past. However, people build their future on concepts and ideas derived from the past. Jews and Arabs in particular — and this they have in common — possess a long historical memory and suffer from the trauma of tragic experiences, unable to 'forget and forgive'. A critical review of the past may contribute to loosening the grip of prejudices that obscure the vision of the future.

The conclusions this work offers may come as a surprise and even a shock to those accustomed to accepting propaganda myths as historical truths. Unfortunately, there are many of these in both camps. In few national conflicts has propaganda become such a poisonous weapon and achieved such a powerful hold over the minds of leaders and people alike. Partisanship, emotional bias and propaganda pervade the massive literature on the Israeli-Arab conflict and have created a thick fog obscuring its real content. Arguments advanced in the heat of passionate debate and in the struggle to gain support of public opinion at home and abroad have acquired the status and force of axioms and absolute truths. While statesmen have become prisoners of their own propaganda, the peoples have become its victims.

This book deals principally with the strategy of the Zionist leadership and dwells only marginally on the attitudes and policy of the Arabs. Such asymmetry may give the impression that the book holds the Zionist movement solely responsible for the absence of peace. This is not my thesis. As the work shows, the Palestinian Arab leadership had options that were realistic and more promising, but elected to follow a course which led to perpetuation of the conflict and to national calamity.

There were important elements in the Zionist movement who placed a high priority on peace and were willing to recognise the legitimacy of Palestinian national rights. The Palestinian leadership's intransigence, which culminated in the fateful choice of collaboration with Nazi Germany during World War II, further reduced the chances of these forces to have a decisive impact on Zionist policy. But a critical reappraisal of Arab policies and tactics must be undertaken by an Arab historian if it is to be credible and effective. It is my fervent hope that this work will stimulate one to undertake it.

To dispel misunderstanding, I want to make it clear that my belief in the moral justification and historical necessity of Zionism remains unaffected by my critical reappraisal of the Zionist leadership. The history of Zionism demonstrates the extent to which the urge to create a new society, embodying the universal values of democracy and social justice, was inherent in the Zionist movement and responsible for its progress in adverse conditions. Israel's problem today lies in the disintegration of these values, due largely to the intoxication with military success and the belief that military superiority is a substitute for peace. Unless the liberal and progressive values of Zionism are restored and Palestinian rights to self-determination within a framework of peaceful coexistence are recognised, Israel's search for peace is doomed to failure. I firmly believe that these trends will ultimately become the deciding force in Israel.

Notes

1. Jon Kimche in his *Second Arab Awakening* (New York, 1970) and *Palestine or Israel* (London, 1973) was perhaps the first to throw light on this subject, using a number of hitherto unknown documents. In fact, it was Kimche's study which drew my attention to Dr Weizmann's attitude towards the Palestinian Arabs and stimulated this research.

PART ONE: ATTITUDES

The Zionist Leadership and
the Arab Question 1917-1948

1 DR WEIZMANN AND HIS LEGACY

Introduction

In his monumental work on Israeli foreign policy,[1] Professor Michael Brecher has suggested a three-fold typology of Israeli approaches to the Arabs:

Buberism — reconciliation through compromise on final aims.
Ben-Gurionism — peace resulting from superior Jewish strength.
Weizmannism and its derivative, Sharettism — a rational search for moderate and realistic solutions.

While this typology correctly describes the general attitude of the leading figures in the Zionist movement, it does not provide a frame of reference for an analysis of Zionist policy towards the Arabs, as it took shape during the period before the emergence of the state. The fact is that despite differences in outlook, both Ben-Gurion and Sharett accepted the basic tenets of Weizmann's policy.

During the Mandatory period (1917-48) the Zionist and Palestinian National Movement advanced so far along separate political trajectories that the partition of Palestine became the only realistic solution to their conflict. Inasmuch as Weizmann's strategy dominated Zionist councils, the most critical decisions of the Zionist movement *vis-à-vis* the Arab problem must be ascribed to him. Weizmann's pre-eminent position in the Zionist leadership and his decisive role in shaping pre-state Zionist policy are generally conceded. Already a legendary figure in his own time, as the architect of the Balfour Declaration, he has become known as the father of the Jewish state. This is Abba Eban's assessment of Weizmann:[2]

Few men in history have carried such a remote dream to such fulfilment . . . for three decades from the beginning of the First World War to the end of the Second, he was the dominant figure in Jewish life, recognized everywhere as the chief custodian of his people's interests . . .

There is a tendency to juxtapose Weizmannism and Ben-Gurionism as two opposing methods and ideologies. A close analysis, however,

shows that these two trends in Zionist policy are not as contradictory as they appear at first glance, and that there is substantial
continuity in Zionist strategy before and after statehood. Not only was
Ben-Gurion in full agreement with Weizmannist strategy during the
Mandatory period, differing only on questions of tactics, but some of
the basic tenets of Weizmannism have remained the guidelines for
Israeli foreign policy to the present day.

'Weizmannism is a combination of maximalist − even extreme −
aims, and a gradualist, pragmatic and flexible means to achieve them.
Weizmann's ultimate goal from which he never deviated, was a Jewish
state within frontiers even exceeding those of the "Greater Israel"
militants of today. In his view, Palestine was a Jewish and not an Arab
country.'[3] Thus, he fought for a Jewish state which would extend to
the Litani River in present-day Lebanon, to well east of the Jordan
River. However, conscious of the realities of international politics
and of the weakness of the Zionist movement, he envisaged the realisation of this aim over a long period.

Weizmann conceived the state as an entity which had to be built
up step by step, brick by brick, and settlement by settlement. This
could be accomplished only through the creation of a new productive
society, imbued with a pioneering spirit and aiming to synthesise traditional Jewish moral values with modern needs.[4] This concept of state-
building found a ready response in the Jewish labour movement of
Palestine. Over the years, Weizmann developed a close alliance with
them. Weizmann encouraged the labour movement to build a society
unique in its innovative organisation of economic activity.[5] In turn,
the labour movement acceded to Weizmann's political strategy for
achieving this aim.

So long as it was possible to continue constructive work in Palestine, Weizmann was inclined to be flexible regarding political formulations. He was ready to compromise on these in order to remove the
obstacles to practical work. He viewed the limitations imposed on
Zionist colonisation as temporary setbacks which, in due course, would
be overcome by the creative energies of the Yishuv, fuelled by the
crisis of European Jewry. Therefore, it was precisely during times of
restriction that he intensified his efforts to establish *faits accomplis*
in the form of additional Jewish settlements, industries and land
acquisitions.[6]

Weizmann's political flexibility, which led him in the 1930s to
accept the idea of political parity with the Arabs in Palestine and
then the partition of the country into two separate states, made him

the main target of the rightist elements in Zionism, the Revisionists, led by Jabotinsky, part of the General Zionists and also Religious Zionists. In the eyes of Jewish maximalists, his flexible diplomacy bordered on 'betrayal' while in the eyes of the Arabs it was regarded as hypocrisy and deception. In fact, it was neither; rather, it was a product of Weizmann's attempts to reconcile his strategic concepts — to which he remained wedded all his life — to the developing realities in Palestine.

Weizmann always had an unswerving belief in a Jewish Commonwealth; he agreed to partition only as a temporary expedient to serve for a single generation.[7] At the same time he believed that the state had to be based on justice and on an accommodation with the Arabs: 'I am certain the world will judge the Jewish state by how it will treat the Arabs.'[8] His desire for peace with the Arabs was genuine: but he conceived of it only within the framework of close collaboration with Great Britain. Weizmann's strategic concepts, which were his heritage to the Zionist movement, rested on three principles:

1. The Jewish Commonwealth would become an integral part of the British Commonwealth and guardian of Britain's strategic interests in the Middle East.

2. Under British auspices, an agreement between Zionism and the Arab National Movement would be reached which would ensure the development of the Jewish settlement in Palestine in return for substantial aid in modernising the Arab world. Zionism would serve as a link between the Arabs and the Western world.

3. The Arabs of Palestine are a tiny and unimportant fraction of the Arab Nation; their opposition to Zionism is generated by the narrow interest of feudal landlords and is not an expression of genuine nationalism. This opposition would diminish when the masses receive the economic benefits that Zionism will bring to Palestine. Some would elect to migrate to wholly Arab countries.

The events during Weizmann's period of leadership disproved all these tenets. The British never accepted the identity of their and Jewish interests. On the contrary, they regarded Zionism as an increasing liability and acted accordingly. Moreover, the 'British Connection' on which Zionist policy was based made it a target for the increasing anti-imperialist tendencies of the Arab National Movement when the thrust of this movement for independence brought it into conflict with Great Britain. But Weizmann's most serious error was his failure to give due weight to the militancy of the Palestine National Movement and its bitter opposition to the whole Zionist enterprise. In the end, it was the escalating resistance of this movement which brought about the erosion of the British commitment to a Jewish national home.

These developments in Palestine did not lead Weizmann to reassess his strategy, but rather increased his tactical flexibility in order to gain time for the Yishuv. This delayed the final break with the British, and the major clash with the Arabs until the Jewish settlement was well-organised and strong enough to weather the storm. Paradoxically, the achievement of the Jewish state was not due to Weizmann's strategic views, but to his diplomatic skill in preserving the concrete achievements of Zionism in Palestine. But the legacy that Weizmann's diplomacy left to the state was the unresolved conflict with the Arabs. In later years, this conflict reached a point where it even overshadowed the unique and spectacular achievements of practical Zionism.

The importance of analysing Weizmann's strategy derives from the fact that the assumptions on which they were based were, with slight modifications, adopted by Ben-Gurion and his successors. If one substitutes 'United States' for 'Great Britain' and the 'Hashemite Kingdom of Jordan' for the 'Arab National Movement', Weizmann's basic strategic concepts might be taken as descriptive of Israel's present foreign policy. Specifically, the non-recognition of the national rights of the Palestinian people has remained an immutable feature of Zionist orientation with respect to the Arab problem.

The 'British Connection'

I have defended the British Administration before my own people, from public platforms, at Congress in all parts of the world, often against my own better knowledge, and almost invariably to my own detriment. Why did I do so? Because to me close co-operation with Great Britain was the cornerstone of our policy in Palestine. But this co-operation remained unilateral — it was unrequited love.

(Weizmann, *Trial and Error*, pp. 783-4)

Weizmann's role in bringing about the Balfour Declaration and a British Mandate over Palestine has been the object of exhaustive scholarly research.[1] It is not our intention to tread over such familiar ground. What is less well-known is the extent to which British policy influenced Weizmann's views of the Arabs.

Weizmann staked the entire fate of Zionism on an alliance with Great Britain, as against the principle of neutrality to which the Zionist movement was committed from the days of the First Zionist Congress (1897). The principle of neutrality took into account the dispersal of Jews throughout the world. The Zionist movement felt that to mobilise the energies of the Jewish people for a national home and to gain the support of the international community it was imperative to divorce Zionist policy from Great Power rivalries. As though to give proof of this neutrality, during the First World War the Zionist movement established a bureau in Denmark, a neutral country, while the seat of the Zionist movement remained in Berlin.

Weizmann's closest associates were concerned that by his exclusive reliance on Britain, he was depriving Zionism of international levers of influence. Symbolically, Weizmann's career in the Zionist movement spanned the period which started with the Balfour Declaration in 1917 and ended with the British withdrawal from Palestine in 1948.

Weizmann's preference for the British did not come upon him suddenly. At the beginning of the war, Weizmann had a pro-Allied outlook, but did not look solely for British support. In October 1914, he wrote to Shmaryahu Levin:

> As soon as the situation is somewhat cleared up we could talk plainly to England and France with regard to the abnormal situation of the Jews, having combatants in all armies fighting everywhere and being nowhere recognized . . . We must unite the great body of conscious Jews in Great Britain, America, Italy and France. The German and Austrian Jews will understand us later.[2]

However, as early as 1914, the idea of a Jewish Palestine as a British protectorate was germinating in his mind. In the same month, he wrote to Zangwill:

> Palestine will fall within the influence of England . . . we could easily move a million Jews into Palestine within the next 50-60 years and England would have a very effective and strong barrier, and we would have a country . . .[3]

At this stage, Weizmann thought that the fate of Palestine would be decided only after the war, and that the British could offer no practical help in promoting Zionist aims 'while the guns are roaring'.[4]

Weizmann thought that Turkey's entry, in 1915, into the war, might lead to Great Power rivalry in the Middle East and that Great Britain would try to prevent an outside power establishing itself astride her empire communication routes. Weizmann suggested that Zionism could help secure Britain's position if the Jews took over the country and developed it under the aegis of a British protectorate.[5] During the next two years, Weizmann pursued with increasing fervour the idea that there was 'a providential coincidence of British and Jewish interests'.[6] He was guided along the lines of British interests by British officials, particularly Sir Mark Sykes, the Foreign Office representative for the Near East.[7] Sykes' ambition was to free Britain from the provisions of the agreement he had negotiated in 1916 with the French. The Sykes-Picot agreement had divided the Middle East between the two powers, but had left Palestine outside British control with an international administration. (The agreement had also given the Syrian coast to France and the ports of Acre-Haifa, to the British, and had allotted respective spheres of influence in the interior to the French in the northern half, and the British in the southern half.[8]) Sykes hoped to gain Palestine for Britain with the help of the Zionists, and in February 1917 he began to promote the Zionist cause. He explained:

> At present it would be dangerous to press for a British Palestine, but if the French agree to recognize Jewish nationalism and all that carries with it as a Palestinian factor, I think it will prove a step in the right direction.[9]

When Weizmann was informed of the substance of the Sykes-Picot agreement, his reaction was that Turkish government in Palestine would be better than an international regime, and that 'Zionists throughout the world would regard a French administration as a great disaster: a third destruction of the Temple.'[10] Under the influence of Sykes and the British Foreign Office, Weizmann's activities as Zionist leader became merged with the stratagems of British diplomacy. At the behest of the Foreign Office, Weizmann was instrumental in stifling an American initiative — the Morgenthau mission — looking to a separate peace with Turkey, which would have precluded any European claims on her Asiatic territories.[11]

In the spring of 1917, Weizmann was seconded from his position at the Admiralty Laboratory 'to work for a British Palestine'.[12] Throughout the year he closely co-ordinated his work with the British government, which even despatched and approved all Zionist correspondence he sent from London.[13] He was instrumental in arranging for the American and Russian Zionists to support 'the policy eventually determined on by Great Britain'.[14] He also blocked attempts by Nahum

Sokolow, formal head of the Zionist Executive, to negotiate a separate arrangement with the French concerning Palestine.[15]

In his effort to bring about a declaration in favour of a Jewish National Home, Weizmann was unquestionably the

> most gifted and fascinating envoy the Jewish people ever produced . . . There was no other Jew in whom the non-Jewish world perceived the embodiment of the Jewish people, with their will, ability and their longings . . . [He] fascinated them with his Jewish grandeur, his genius for depicting for them the deepest and most intimate emotions of the people of Israel.[16]

However, Weizmann's activities to secure a British protectorate over Palestine brought him into close co-operation with professional diplomats, administrators and military intelligence officers in the Middle East, who were weaving plans to promote British interests as they conceived them, sometimes, without the knowledge or explicit approval of London. These elements used Weizmann's singular faith in an alliance with Britain, his power of persuasion and his urbanity, to allay Arab fears and suspicions and to constrain Jewish demands. Weizmann's naivete and over-optimism blinded him to the fact that these manipulations had nothing to do with the furtherance of the Zionist objectives.

Actually, there was no necessary connection between the Balfour Declaration and the British Mandate over Palestine.[17] Many of the supporters of the Balfour Declaration seriously doubted the advisability of Britain assuming the responsibility for a Jewish national home in Palestine, among them Lord Balfour himself, who favoured an American mandate.[18] Most of the military and Foreign Office officials who for strategic and imperial reasons supported British rule in Palestine, were not specially interested in the development of Zionism. On the contrary, they feared its adverse effects on British interests in the rest of the Moslem world, and were actively hostile to it. Nevertheless, they saw it as a way to secure a British protectorate over Palestine and to gain Ameircan support against French claims for an equal interest in Palestine.

Sykes frankly proposed to 'use' Weizmann to[19] promote his favourite plan — an Arab-Jewish-Armenian entente under British auspices in the Middle East. Under the guise of this plan, Britain could revise the Sykes-Picot agreement at the peace conference without inviting American charges that Britain had annexationist designs.[20] Weizmann followed Sykes's lead and urged American Zionists to reach an accord with Arab leaders in the United States and help minimise 'one of the great disadvantages of the Balfour Declaration from the British point of view'.[21] Also, he joined the Syria Welfare Committee Sykes had set up in Cairo as a joint body of Arabs, Zionists and Armenians and co-ordinated this phase of his work with his work as a member of the Zionist Commission. Following the promulgation of the Balfour Declaration the British had set up the Zionist Commission to assess the condition of the Jewish community in Palestine and the prospects for future development of a Jewish national home, and to allay Arab fears of Zionism.[22]

Weizmann took this dual assignment very seriously. He later wrote 'during my stay in Palestine I tried my best to co-operate with the authorities and used all my endeavours to bring about an Entente between the Jews and the Arabs . . . my correspondence and reports have always been shown to the Authorities and no line was written by me without the consent of the Chief Political Officer.'[23] Israel Sieff, Secretary of the Zionist Commission, thought Weizmann had gone too far when he was interviewed upon his arrival in Egypt:

> There is no intention of setting up a Jewish government in Palestine in the near future. The Jews want Palestine to be a British Colony or Protectorate. He thought that the opinion of the Jews, thrown into the scales in favour of a British Palestine (which for us meant a Jewish Palestine) would have some weight at the Paris Peace Conference. There was complete accord between British and Jewish interests in regard to Palestine and it should be realized that those who are working against the Jews are also working against Great Britain.[24]

Weizmann went beyond even that: 'No matter what the British Government thought of the establishment of a British Palestine, the Zionists wished to see this outcome as a result of the war.'[25]

Weizmann's concept of an historical alliance with Great Britain stemmed from his general political outlook. For him, Britain was the model of justice, fairness and democracy.[26] Weizmann was absorbed with only one problem — the creation of a Jewish state in Palestine. He was aloof to the point of indifference towards the social and political ferment of his time. In his private letters and public pronouncements he scarcely mentioned the turmoil that rocked Europe as an aftermath of World War I and the Russian Revolution. The social conflicts and political struggles in Great Britain, the changing attitudes towards colonialism and the rise of the Labour Party interested him only to the extent that they affected the prospects of support for the Jewish national home.[27] His identification with the plight of the Jewish masses in Europe led him to espouse Zionism as their only solution, even though millions of Jews had to deal with the economic and social problems of Jewish life in the Diaspora. In this he differed sharply from leaders such as Dr Nahum Goldmann and Itzhak Gruenbaum, who did not neglect the day-to-day problems of the Diaspora, and took an active part in the struggle (with other minorities) for cultural autonomy and civil equality based on principles of human rights and democracy.

Weizmann's outlook was eclectic and embraced many contradictory elements. He envisioned a Jewish state as a progressive society to be built on the principles of social justice and democracy which would provide unlimited scope for innovative forms of economic and social organisation. He put national interests above those of free enterprise, and undertook the defence of the labour movement and its co-operatives and kibbutzim against capitalist elements in the Zionist movement who regarded them as unwarranted experiments. While trying to attract major Jewish investment, he defended the rights of the settlers to choose their own form of social life and economic organisation and revealed a deep sympathy for the socialist-oriented collectives — the kibbutzim. At the same time, he conceived of a Jewish state as an integral part of the British Empire, dedicated to the defence of British strategic interests in the Middle East. As early as 1915, Weizmann suggested that Jews would finance a fleet for Great Britain to be based in Palestine in return for her support of Zionism.[28] He also held that 'a strong Jewish community on the Egyptian flank would serve as an effective barrier against any danger likely to come from the north'.[29] With the weakening of the British position in other Middle Eastern countries, especially in Egypt, Weizmann saw the strategic importance of Palestine to the British Empire. Weizmann believed that the Suez Canal could be defended from Palestine and that it was of paramount interest to Britain to have 'a friendly Jewish people in Palestine which should remain friendly when the time comes for the withdrawal of the British Mandate and its setting-up as an independent state'.[30]

Weizmann could indulge in these contradictions because he was insensitive to the nature of imperialism and the struggle of colonial peoples for national liberation.[31] On these major issues Weizmann betrayed a nineteenth-century mentality — a faith in Europe's civilising mission among backward peoples. He firmly believed that the Zionist cause was a fight of civilisation against the desert, the struggle of progress, efficiency, health and education against stagnation.[32]

In 1830, Weizmann argued that the colonial peoples of the British Empire were not ready for independence: 'It is quite clear that the setting up of fake democracies in backward countries, utterly different in their tradition and standards of civilization from European countries, is mere eyewash, and these institutions are breaking down throughout the British Empire.'[33] As late as 1939, Weizmann spoke disdainfully of Arab nationalism at the Round Table Conference, when he asked:

> . . . what the Arabs have made out of the extraordinary opportunities offered to them . . . the Arabs are trying to run before they can walk . . . barren and destructive nationalism appears to hold sway . . . they are blinded by the mirage of brute force. They have all got their problems . . . but their one principle is a purely negative one, opposition to us.[34]

Weizmann either failed to see or would not see that the same imperial interests which prompted the British to sponsor Zionism as part of the post-World War I settlement, led also to British reluctance to implement a full Zionist programme later, when they concluded that it was damaging their position in the Moslem world. Having implicit faith in the integrity of the British government, he attributed at first to the Military Administration in Palestine (1918-20) the difficulties the Zionist movement was encountering and the obstacles placed in the way of the Zionist enterprise. He was convinced that the Military Administration, motivated by anti-Zionist and sometimes anti-Semitic sentiments, tacitly encouraged Arab opposition to the Balfour Declaration. Shaken by the riots of the spring of 1920, he wrote to his wife:

> The behaviour of the English towards us is shocking and all the promises they gave us at home, sound bitterly ironic here [in Jerusalem]. And in proportion as the English treat us badly, so the boldness and arrogance of the Arabs increase; they are already raising their heads in which the English no doubt are encouraging them. Among all the officials here there are perhaps 5-6 who treat Zionism more or less decently; all the rest are our secret or overt enemies.[35]

Bitter recriminations followed between Weizmann and the heads of the Military Government (Generals Allenby and Bols). 'I told them categorically that I consider their conduct dishonest . . . that they are ruining our cause and gravely harming that of the British . . . and that in fact behaviour like this is a public lie.'[36] Weizmann cabled London asking for a replacement of the Military Administration which he held responsible for the riots by fostering anti-Jewish attitudes.[37]

However, he was careful not to go too far. 'Although the riots [made] the situation very precarious, I still maintained and caused others to maintain the best possible relations with the authorities.'[38] The proceedings of the secret Court of Inquiry,[39] held after the riots, confirmed Weizmann's appraisal of the attitude of the military. However, the 'troubles' were not over when, in the spring of 1920, the Balfour Declaration was incorporated in the newly-born Mandate for Palestine and the British replaced the Military Administration with a civilian High Commissioner.

The Commissioner, Herbert Samuel, was a prominent Liberal and British Jew who was committed to a policy of moderation, even-handedness, and economic development.[40] Weizmann was convinced that a new era was dawning, and that with the troublesome military administration removed there would be no serious trouble from the Arabs and 'the construction of New Palestine would begin'.[41] But again, his expectations were to be disappointed. It was precisely under a civilian administration, scrupulously loyal to government policy and carefully avoiding a bias toward either side, that the full weight of Palestinian opposition to the Balfour Declaration made itself felt.

It fell upon Samuel, a Zionist who shared with Weizmann the ideal of a Jewish Palestine in the British Commonwealth, to disabuse Weizmann of the view that the Military Administration was the main source of the difficulty. In August 1921 he told Weizmann:

It is quite true that almost all the British officers in Palestine are not sympathetic to a Zionist policy which would be detrimental to the Arabs, and are not prepared to carry out with good will a policy which is likely to result in a regime of coercion. But if the whole of the present staff were replaced by others chosen by yourself, in six months the newcomers would hold precisely the same view.[42]

In an attempt to reconcile Zionism with the exigencies of British policy in the Middle East, Herbert Samuel was compelled to give a new interpretation to the Balfour Declaration. After a new series of riots in 1921, he stated (3 June 1921):

> . . . the Jews . . . should be enabled to found [in Palestine] their home, and that some among them, within the limits which are fixed by the numbers and interests of the present population should come to Palestine to help by their resources and efforts to develop the country to the advantage of all its inhabitants.[43]

Weizmann tried to overcome the reduced British commitment to the Balfour Declaration by emphasising the anti-British tendencies in the Arab world and the advantage of Zionism as a more reliable, stable and powerful ally of Great Britain in the Middle East. He argued to Balfour that: 'The somewhat shifty and doubtful sympathies of the Arabs represent infinitely less than the careful and considered policy of the Jewish people which sees in a British Palestine the realization of an age-old aspiration.'[44] He added later: 'When the Arabs finish with us the turn of the British will come with much more eclat, with much more violence and with the great difference that the sole friends of the British will have disappeared.'[45]

In 1939 Weizmann, Ben-Gurion and Sharett made a desperate attempt to avert a complete British retreat from their commitment to a Jewish national home by pointing out the superior military and economic potential of the Jewish settlement which could be more fully mobilised than the economy or society of the Arab states in event of war. Weizmann added that 'for us loyalty to Britain is almost an unconditional thing'.[46] Weizmann's perspective assumed the continuation, unchanged, of classical European imperialism based on the direct physical control of colonial countries, at a time when such ideas were under attack all over the world.[47] Indeed, the whole mandate system was evidence of this. The architects of Britain's Middle East policy understood far better than he did the inevitability of the decline of the imperial system and the rise of national liberation movements. Typical is the speech delivered by Sykes in 1916, in which he said: 'In 1950, Baghdad, Damascus and Aleppo will each be as big as Manchester. I warn the Jews to look through Arab glasses.'[48]

Prophetically, one of Weizmann's chief advisers among the British military wrote in 1924:

> In general, a year in Palestine has made me regard the whole adventure with apprehension. We have become an alien and detested

element into the very core of Islam, and the day may well come when we shall be faced with the alternative of holding it there by the sword or abandoning it to its fate: The Arabs are under-dogs for the moment but they will bide their time and wait. I feel sometimes that the time will come — perhaps soon — when England may have to go for a 'White' Empire policy, and leave all ideas of dominating 'brown' peoples.[49]

Weizmann and his colleagues failed to understand that it was precisely the growth of anti-imperialist forces in the Arab world that compelled Britain to abandon its commitment to a movement which was unable to reach an accommodation with Arab nationalism and which could be implemented only by means of military force. Weizmann also did not realise that the development of the Yishuv in Palestine based on a modern highly developed economy and a powerful labour movement was incompatible with a colonialist regime which derived its strength from keeping subject peoples in a condition of backwardness and dependence. The Jewish society Weizmann envisioned was inconsistent with colonialism and added to the difficulties of the colonial administration in neighbouring Arab countries. Yet, Weizmann clung to his belief in a Zionist-British identity of interests despite the repeated disappointments he received over the years from the Colonial Office and Palestine Administration.

While the British supported a Jewish state when they formulated the Balfour Declaration, once the Mandate was approved (in 1920), British policy was to reduce progressively its commitment to Zionism.[50] The 1922 White Paper drafted by Herbert Samuel limited Jewish immigration to 'the economic capacity of the country at the time to absorb new arrivals', repudiated Weizmann's formula of a Palestine 'as Jewish as England is English' and was specific in stating that the British government 'does not contemplate that Palestine as a whole should be converted into a Jewish National Home, but that such a Home shall be founded *in Palestine*'.[51]

The 1922 White Paper also involved the unilateral separation of Transjordan from the area embraced by the Balfour Declaration. From this point on, successive restrictions on land purchase and immigration followed each serious outbreak of Arab disturbances. In 1930, the sale of land to Jews was restricted and, in 1936, a 'political high ceiling' for Jewish immigration was suggested. This step by step erosion of the commitment to Zionism finally culminated in the White Paper of 1939, which prohibited land transfers to Jews in most of Palestine and restricted immigration to 15,000 a year for 5 years, with immigration beyond that point dependent on Arab consent.

The qualifying clause in the Balfour Declaration stating that 'nothing shall be done which may prejudice the civil and religious rights of the existing non-Jewish communities' in Palestine, became of equal weight —'a dual obligation' — in 1937, in the Royal Commission report. This report stated that the two obligations were incompatible. This was a personal tragedy for Weizmann, who made a dramatic plea at the Zionist Congress:

> This is a breach of a promise made to us in a solemn hour . . . I say this, I who for twenty years have made my lifework to explain the Jewish people to the British and the British people to the Jews . . . I say to the Mandatory Power: you shall not play fast and loose with the Jewish people. Say to us frankly that the National Home is closed and we will know where we stand.[52]

Weizmann's decision to link Zionist policy with the British Empire had its justifications at the time, given the military situation in the Middle East during and after World War I. But the complete subordination of Zionist activity to the tactics of British policy was not necessary. At that period Britain needed Zionism as much as the Zionists needed Britain. By becoming *totally* dependent on British policy, it was divested of leverage.

The part played by Weizmann in the British struggle against the Sykes-Picot agreement did not pay off in the end. In spite of all Sykes's stratagems, the agreement remained the basis of the Middle East settlement, and Zionism lost its battle for frontiers which would have allowed faster economic development and an enlarged area of colonisation. At the same time, it antagonised the French to the point that they encouraged anti-Zionist propaganda. Certain features of the present-day Zionist identification with the tactical and strategic needs of the USA in its struggle to dominate the Middle East over the Soviet Union bear a resemblance to the old Zionist support for the British against the French in the 1920s.

The result of Weizmann's 'British connection' was that the opportunity to formulate an independent Zionist policy towards the Arabs taking into account the enormous potential of the Arab world for economic and political development, was lost. Instead, the Zionist movement took recourse to stratagems and improvised positions, mainly aimed at neutralising Arab influence on British policy and, as

such, tending to increase rather than allay, Arab fears and suspicion.
'Many intelligent Arabs hate us because they genuinely believe that we
are the tool of the English; if not for the English . . . we could compara-
tively easily make friends with the Arabs . . .'[53]

A common cause with the Arabs against the British was excluded by
Weizmann from the beginning. His Arab policy was formed in the
crucible of British policy as she tried to resolve her contradictory
pledges to her Allies. Weizmann thus came to view the Arab problem
as secondary, to be dealt with only when Britain's tactical or strategic
requirements demand it, or when Arab opposition to Zionist immigration and settlement threatened to weaken British commitment to a
Jewish national home in Palestine. This is the clue to understanding
Weizmann's attitude towards Arab nationalism in general and the
Palestinians in particular.

The 'Hashemite Connection'

> The Arab has an immense talent for expressing views diametrically
> opposed to yours with such exquisite and roundabout politeness
> that you believe him to be in complete agreement with you and
> ready to join hands with you at once. Conversations and negotia-
> tions with Arabs are not unlike chasing a mirage in the desert: full of
> promise and good to look at, but likely to lead you to death by
> thirst.
>
> (*Trial and Error*, p. 271)

Weizmann's strategy of alliance with a Great Power (Great Britain),
which relegated the Arab problem to a position of secondary importance, was analogous to the policy of King Hussein, the Sheriff of Mecca
who initiated the Arab Revolt in 1916.

The Arab national movement also threw in its lot with the British
and regarded the Zionist factor as of secondary importance; however,
over-estimating the political influence and financial power of the
Zionists, the Arabs were ready to enlist their support to further Arab
national aims. While Zionism strove for an agreement with the Arabs to
facilitate its co-operation with Great Britain, the Arabs were interested
in an agreement only to the extent that would further their struggle for
independence. It is this divergence of aims which lies at the heart of
the failure of all the negotiations between Jews and Arabs (among the
most important, the Weizmann-Faisal meetings, 1917-20; Weizmann's
meeting with Palestinians, 1920-1; Saphir's negotiations with Syrian,
Palestinian and Egyptian leaders, 1922; Sharett and Ben-Gurion's

contacts with Palestinian, Lebanese, Syrian and Iraqi leaders, 1934-9; and numerous negotiations and contacts, 1944-6).

Another related aspect of Zionist attitudes towards the Arab problem was that the Zionists looked at it 'de haut en bas'. This was a reflection of an objective asymmetry at the time, though later it developed into a psychological complex of superiority, and was one reason why the Zionists considered an alliance with a Western power more important than one with the Arabs. At this time (1918), the Jewish people were equal in population to the Arab world (10 million to 11 million Jews as against 10 million to 11 million Arabs in the Turkish Empire) and in terms of economic development, industrial, financial and professional resources and international political influence, the Jews occupied a far greater position. Weizmann believed that a Jewish national home in Palestine would help the Arabs build up their economy and modernise their social and political structure. None of the Zionist leadership (except Dr Goldmann and the small group of intellectuals around Magnes) foresaw the potency and importance of national liberation movements in general, and in particular in the Arab world. Weizmann was persuaded that an agreement with the Arabs based on Jewish financial and technical assistance would speed up the economic development of the Arab world and did not understand why his offers of such assistance were not enthusiastically received by the Arabs.

He wished the Arabs well and sympathised with their aspirations for cultural renaissance, unity and independence, but viewed the anti-colonialist aspects of their struggle as an expression of a destructive, reactionary spirit. What is worse, he saw in the growth of anti-British tendencies in Arab nationalism, a better chance for the success of Zionism, as the faithful guardian of British interests in the Middle East.

Weizmann had an earnest desire for peace with the Arabs. The Weizmann-Faisal agreement of January 1919, in particular, is viewed as proof of his foresight, vision and tireless efforts to achieve a reconciliation between Zionism and the Arab national movement.

The record does not substantiate this impression. Having made the 'British connection' the basis of his entire policy, and under-estimating the force of Arab nationalism, Weizmann 'had no discernible Arab policy'.[1] He conceived Jewish-Arab relations only within the framework of close co-operation with Great Britain. Weizmann had no independent views on Arab nationalism and its various components. He accepted British assessments and policies; sometimes, even to the point of literally repeating British opinions. As a result, Weizmann's choice of allies in the Arab world was dictated more by British views and needs than by Zionist long-term interests.[2] Weizmann's meetings with Syrians, Palestinians, Emir Faisal, the son of the Sheriff of Mecca and his followers, as well as his famous agreement with Faisal in January 1919, must be seen in this context. In 1930, he wrote that the vision of Jewish-Arab co-operation in 1919 'remains a landmark of lost ground, not for us only'.[3] The enthusiasm he felt at the time of the negotiations with Faisal left a mark on Weizmann's views of a Jewish-Arab agreement and became a model which influenced his successors. Weizmann inherited from the British the concept of pan-Arab nationalism, based on the rejection of a distinct Palestinian national entity, and the reliance on a connection with the Hashemites. Both ideas have persisted. The Weizmann-Faisal negotiations set the pattern for all further Zionist contacts with the Arabs up to today's stubborn insistence by the Israeli Government on an agreement with the last Hashemite — King Hussein of Jordan — rather than with the Palestinian leadership.

It is, therefore, of interest to submit the Weizmann-Faisal episode to closer scrutiny, to see whether its failure was due exclusively to forces beyond the control of the Zionist movement, as the official Zionist literature claims, or whether the basic assumptions were wrong.

The idea of a Zionist-Arab entente originated as a British plan to arrange the territorial settlement and conflicting pledges in the Middle East to their advantage. With the successful British offensive in Palestine, including the occupation of Jerusalem in December 1917, and with preparations for the post-war peace conference based on the principle of self-determination already underway, the British, and in particular, the British diplomats and military officers within the Arab Bureau,[4] were determined that Britain should enjoy the full fruits of victory. In their view Britain had earned this by reason of its military effort and its political sagacity in backing the Arab Revolt of 1916. This meant the abrogation of the Sykes-Picot agreement, the exclusion of the French from the region by means of a British-sponsored pan-Arab kingdom, and by a British protectorate over Palestine.

Ormsby-Gore, then a member of Lloyd George's advisory team, argued that the Russian Revolution and the entry of America into the war had rendered anachronistic the Sykes-Picot agreement of 1916, and made it irreconcilable with British war aims.[5] 'Why should we who have shed dozens of lives in an effort to free the Arab speaking people from Turkish rule be content to give France exclusive rights in Syria?' He complained that the French representative (Picot himself) was posing as 'French High Commissioner in Palestine' in order to promote

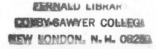

French political claims there, based on pretensions to be protectors of the Holy Land. Finally, he maintained that Britain could not afford to break its pledges to the Jews and Arabs.

Ormsby-Gore mentioned the advantage of Zionism for the British in their struggle with France, in that Zionism was working for a British protectorate over Palestine. Weizmann, in fact, echoed Ormsby-Gore when he wrote that the 'French pose as conquerors returning to the Holy Land'. He nevertheless conceded that it was necessary to retard Zionist land acquisition in order not to 'provoke the jealousy of France that . . . Great Britain had designs to annex Palestine, using the Jews as a blind'.[6]

The British were also concerned about Arab reaction to Zionist claims and, in particular, about the attitude of King Hussein, the Sheriff (guardian) of Mecca, the holiest city of Islam, whom the British had encouraged to revolt against the Turks in 1916 in return for which the British would support the creation of an independent Arab kingdom after the war.[7]

The conquest of Jerusalem by Allenby and the establishment of a British military government in Palestine in December 1917, brought to the forefront the question of contradictory pledges. The British Government decided in January 1918 to send a Zionist Commission, headed by Weizmann, to Palestine both to assess the prospects of Zionist development and to allay Arab fears of Zionism. The Arab Bureau was convinced of the necessity of reconciling the two British clients in the Middle East.

The Arabs interpreted the Balfour Declaration as promising a Jewish government in Palestine, a belief corroborated by some articles in the Jewish press. According to the Arab Bureau, the Balfour Declaration had 'made a profound impression' on the Arabs who 'viewed with dismay prospects of Palestine and even eventually Syria, in hands of Jews, whose superior intelligence and commercial abilities are feared'. The Arab Bureau felt the Declaration had made the Arabs even consider ending their revolt against Turkey, if the Turks would give them local autonomy.[8]

The British had been cautious even about publishing the Balfour Declaration in the Arab world: the Foreign Office had advised 'careful control over press comment in order that Arab susceptibilities should not be offended'.[9] Britain's chief political officer in Palestine, General Clayton, was sceptical about the wisdom of British policy of working for an Arab-Zionist common front against French designs in the Middle East. In a letter to Sykes, written shortly after the pronouncement of the Balfour Declaration, Clayton warned against excessive optimism. 'I quite see the advantages . . . but it must be done very cautiously and honestly, if it is to have a real chance of any great success . . . we have to consider whether the situation demands out-and-out support of Zionism at the expense of alienating the Arabs at this crucial moment.'[10]

Nevertheless, Clayton set out to implement the policy. He told Syrian nationalists in Cairo that if the Zionists who were very powerful in the world and controlled its finances did not succeed in securing rights in Palestine from the British, they would get them from the Turks and keep Palestine Turkish. On the other hand, he assured them the British would not allow the Jews to establish a state and that they would let the Syrians compete on equal terms with the Jews of Palestine. The Syrians replied that they could organise against the selling of land to Jews, and mobilise the financial resources to develop the country themselves and prevent the Jewish hegemony in the country.[11]

Clayton warned that the Sheriffians were likely to be more difficult to convince,[12] but thought that they might be won over by the argument that 'the Jews are an element of great strength if they are incorporated into a State, but bad enemies if a hostile attitude is taken up'.[13] In January 1918, Commander Hogarth of the Arab Bureau visited King Ibn Ali Hussein, to explain British policy to him. In reporting this meeting, Hogarth stated that 'the King would not accept an independent Jewish State in Palestine, nor was I instructed to warn him that such a State was contemplated by Great Britain'.[14] Hogarth's estimate was that King Hussein appreciated the financial advantages that would accrue from Arab co-operation with the Jews.

Throughout the winter of 1917-18, the British continued to pressure the Sheriffians and the Syrian nationalists, to acquiesce to Zionism. In March 1918, Sykes addressed a passionate appeal to Faisal, the military leader of the Sheriffians, enlisting his support of Zionism. Aside from its main thrust, the communication is instructive on the British perception of Arab feelings towards the Jews:

I know that the Arabs despise, condemn and hate the Jews, but passion is the ruin of princes and peoples . . . this race despised and weak, is universal, is all powerful and cannot be put down . . . In the councils of every state, in every bank, in every business, in every enterprise there are members of this race . . .

. . . And remember these people do not seek to conquer you, do not seek to drive out the Arabs of Palestine; all they ask for is to be able to do what they have not done elsewhere, to return to the land of their forefathers, to cultivate it, to work with their hands, to become peasants once more. This is a noble thought in the soul of the Jews . . . they do not desire to go there in millions, what they desire is to be able to feel in Palestine a Jew may live his life and speak his tongue as he did in ancient times . . . If you spurn the impulse then you will have against you a force which cannot be seen but which is felt everywhere.

. . . I entreat you . . . look on the Jewish movement as the great key to Arab success . . . Stand up for Arab rights; uphold the rights of the Palestinian people; make good arrangements, but always as between friend and friend, equal and equal, . . . recognize them as a powerful ally.[15]

The Sheriffian response, published in their newspaper in Mecca, was positive though vague:

The Jews knew that that country was for its original sons, sacred and beloved homeland . . . The return of the exiles to that homeland will provide, both materially and spiritually an experimental school for their brethren whose life is bound up with theirs in agriculture, trade, manufacture, and all aspects of labour and employment.[16]

The British had a far less difficult task in persuading Weizmann to arrive at a *modus vivendi* with the Arab national movement. Weizmann was eager to negotiate directly with the Arabs so that Zionism would not become just 'an appendix of a larger Arab scheme'.[17] In the course of negotiations with Sir Mark Sykes, regarding the Balfour Declaration in 1917, he had learned that 'the only people who are really interesting and with whom an entente is desirable are the Hedjaz people'.[18] When Weizmann arrived in the Middle East, as head of the Zionist Commission in March 1918, he faced a complex situation. Major Ormsby-Gore, who was the Commission's liaison officer, and Brigadier-General Clayton, who was Chief Political Officer, implored Weizmann to moderate Zionist demands; not to press for too much too soon, and in particular, not to mention that Zionism implied a Jewish state. On the other hand, 'the Jewish settlements and towns were full of hopes and expectations', as regards the immediate fulfilment of Zionist aspirations. The British Administration, worried about Arab hostility towards the Balfour Declaration and Arab suspicion of British aims, insisted on the application of the Law of War in captured enemy territory; that is, a policy of status quo. Weizmann was afraid that such a policy would cause disillusionment within the impatient Jewish community and undermine co-operation with Britain.[19] Clayton suggested that in Palestine the laws of war should be observed 'only so far as they do not preclude gradual and reasonable development of the ideas which lie behind Mr. Balfour's Zionist Declaration'.[20] He warned that otherwise, the British would lose 'any hope of securing Zionist influence at the Peace Conference in favour of a British Palestine', and that the Zionists might be thrown into the arms of America or even Germany.

The First Weizmann-Faisal Meeting

Clayton was also interested in strengthening the Sheriffian position in the Arab nationalist movement. He hoped that Weizmann's moderation would allay the Sheriffians' fears of Zionism, and that help from the Zionists would confirm them as leaders of the Arab world. At Clayton's suggestion, Weizmann journeyed to Aqaba early in June 1918, to meet Emir Faisal, the military commander of the Sheriffian forces.[21,22] The 45-minute conference with Faisal convinced Weizmann that an agreement with British-sponsored pan-Arab nationalism was possible and would provide a solution to all the troubles with the Arabs in Palestine.[23] The political situation at the time seemed to justify Weizmann's conviction, though the Weizmann-Faisal interview was rather inconclusive in character.

> Dr Weizmann pointed out that he had been sent by the British Government [to get] in touch with Arab leaders and co-operate with them [and he] pointed out that the formation and existence of a Jewish Palestine would be helpful to the development of an Arab Kingdom which would receive Jewish support . . . The Jews do not propose to set up a Jewish Government but would like to work under British protection with a view to colonizing and developing the country without in any way encroaching on anybody's legitimate interests.
>
> . . . Weizmann explained that he was proceeding shortly to America and would see Dr Wilson and that the influence of Jews in that country and elsewhere would be used in favour of the Arab movement and the establishment of an Arab Kingdom. This statement of Dr Weizmann afforded Sheriff Faisal great satisfaction.
>
> . . . Sheriff Faisal was unwilling to express an opinion, pointing out that in this question of politics he was acting only as his father's agent. As regards the future he considered the interests of both Jews

and Arabs must be closely allied together.

. . . Sheriff Faisal claimed that as an Arab he could not discuss the future of Palestine either as a Jewish colony or as a country under British protection . . . Later on when the Arab affair was more consolidated these questions could be brought up. Sheriff Faisal personally accepted the possibility of future Jewish claims to territory in Palestine.[24]

Weizmann firmly believed that this interview formed 'the basis of a life-long friendship' with Faisal[25] and was ecstatic that he had at last found an Arab ally for Zionism. Faisal attached great importance to Jewish financial support and political backing in America.

To Faisal, struggling to be leader of Arab nationalism, Clayton now stressed the benefits of the financial and political support of independent, international influence as represented by the Jews, arguing that dependence on Great Britain exclusively would so 'destroy the outward semblance of independence' as to end his hopes for 'universal [Arab] adherence'. On the other hand, Zionism was gaining the condition vital to its existence – the close sympathy of its Arab neighbours. Clayton hoped that though at first King Hussein would show 'dislike of the full Zionist programme, if made to understand fully its influence on Arab aspirations in Syria' would take a neutral or favourable attitude.[26]

Another prominent member of the Arab Bureau, General Reginald Wingate, also thought that they could convince the 'greater Arabs' that their interests lay not in Palestine but in Damascus.[27] Weizmann echoes these sentiments.[28]

I am sincerely convinced that the more the Arab Movement as represented by Faisal develops, the less conflict there will be between this movement and Zionism. I foresee – and Faisal and his counsellors fully agree on this point – the possibility of a sincere cooperation between the two nations which will lead to mutual benefit and to a consolidation of the British in the Near East . . . the real Arab movement is developing in Damascus and Mecca . . . the so-called Arab question in Palestine would therefore assume only a purely local character, and in fact is not considered a serious factor by all those who know the local position fully . . . I cannot help but feel in the way of Zionist and Arab aspirations stands the Sykes-Picot agreement . . .

Weizmann believed that the Jews and Faisal could form a common anti-

French, pro-British bloc in the Middle East.[29] A few days after the Faisal interview, Weizmann

> . . . stigmatized the Palestinians as a demoralized race with whom it was impossible to treat [*sic*] . . . [and] . . . contrasted the Palestinian . . . type with Faisal — a true prince and a man 'whom one would be proud to have as an enemy and would welcome as a friend'. He was delighted with his conversation with Faisal whom he found sympathetic and sufficiently well-disposed to Zionist aims in Palestine.[30]

Weizmann believed that Faisal was interested mainly in Syria.

> Faisal is the first real Arab Nationalist I have met. He is a leader! He is quite intelligent and a very honest man, handsome as a picture. He is not interested in Palestine but on the other hand he wants Damascus and the whole of northern Syria. He talked with great animosity against the French. He expects a great deal from collaboration with the Jews. He is contemptuous of the Palestinian Arabs whom he doesn't even regard as Arab.[31]

Weizmann's high esteem of Faisal, 'the greatest of all Arabs' (as he later wrote in his autobiography), contrasts sharply with his opinion of the Arab leadership. His image of the Arabs was that of a primitive and backward people who were easily swayed by power, money and success. They were treacherous and shifty, lacked moral values, could not be relied upon to take a principled stand, and did not appreciate European ideals.[32]

The Syrians, Palestinians and the Sheriffians

The obstacle to Jewish-Arab co-operation lay in the contradictory tendencies of the two components which made up the Arab national movement: the Sheriffians, who provided the military force but represented a corrupt and unpopular dynasty without the political, administrative and professional cadres for a modern state; and the Syrian nationalists, including Palestinians, who had no military power but who represented the ideological and political backbone of Arab nationalism. The latter viewed with suspicion the autocratic methods and theocratic character of the Sheriffians, and their dependence on the British.

The Arab Bureau was well aware of the difficulties involved in establishing an Arab kingdom ruled by the Sheriffians. As early as April 1917 Clayton wrote that while the people of Iraq were indifferent to rule by the Sheriffians, 'those in Syria will not welcome a government which they regard as reactionary and non-progressive'.[33] Clayton even hinted at the possibility of a 'free choice' when he pointed out that the McMahon-Hussein correspondence had committed the British to an Arab kingdom but not necessarily under the Sheriffians: 'Great Britain has always treated the Sheriff as the champion or spokesman of the Arab race rather than as their rightful and future ruler.'[34]

In November 1919, Clayton warned that 'there is a real fear amongst the Syrians of finding themselves under a government in which the patriarchalism of Mecca is predominant'.[35] Clayton understood the weakness of the Sheriffians in the Arab movement as a whole but hoped that Faisal's military success as Commander-in-Chief of the 1916 Arab revolt might give him the prestige that would enable him to control the Syrian nationalists. '. . . if not — the fate of Syria can only depend on our military operations, and in that case I doubt whether Faisal or any other Meccan will loom very large in the Syrian picture.'[36] Clayton knew that the Syrian nationalists were 'united in distaste for any solution separating Palestine from Syria' but argued they were emigrés (in Cairo) who were not representative of Syrians living in the country,[37] and later added that they were interested in Arab unity only as an excuse to speculate in another country (Palestine).[38] At Clayton's suggestion Weizmann met members of the Syrian community in Cairo (Dr Faris Nimer, Said Pasha Shuqayr, Soliman Bey Nasif, Dr Shahbandar), some of whom owned large estates in Palestine.

Weizmann and the Arab National Movement

These meetings with Syrian leaders in Cairo are wrongly interpreted as steps towards a Jewish-Arab understanding.[39] Weizmann thought that their interest was wholly financial, that they viewed Zionism as a movement bent on exploiting and dispossessing the fellahin, but nevertheless were prepared to trade with the Jews provided they could make a good profit. Weizmann was sceptical about their offer to help and discounted them as a moral force. To the extent that they found support among the British authorities they represented a danger to Zionist aspirations.[40]

The Syrian nationalists, for their part, were not convinced by Weizmann's denial of the ambition for Jewish statehood. Dr Faris Nimer, one of the Syrians Weizmann met, later told Commander Hogarth of the Arab Bureau:

he desired an integral Syria, as a federated state of an Arab union, but entirely self-governed and independent under Prince or King of its own . . . who on no account should be the King of Hedjaz; for if so, Moslem theocracy would prevail . . . he stipulated with heat and emphasis that a British Palestine must not be a step to a Jewish Palestine. He does not believe for the moment that the Zionists contemplate anything short of political control.[41]

Symes of the Arab Bureau evaluated the situation in June 1918, as follows:

It is suggested that unless and until we can find a common basis of agreement between them [Zionist, Sheriffian and Syrian policies], there is a serious danger of their disagreements being exploited at the peace conference . . .

Of the three, at the present moment, the Zionists, with their great financial resources and international political influence, seem the most likely to realize their aims. These clash with the Syrians over the question of the political separation of Palestine from Syria, and with the Sheriffians over the treatment of Arab elements in Palestine who realize that equal rights and facilities for Jews and Arabs in Palestine must tend, in the long run, to the disadvantage of the latter.

The Zionists, according to Dr. W., are ready and anxious to offer compensation − in cash to the Sheriffians, in the form of political support in Europe and America of their political aims to the Syrians. The chief point of difference between the Syrians and Sheriffians may be resolved by the offer by the former of their Emirate to Faisal. Both are opposed to French predominance in Syria and would welcome Zionist support of their opposition . . . From the foregoing it would seem that a mutually advantageous and politically efficient agreement might be reached between the three parties *if our obligation to France under the Sykes-Picot agreement were finally repudiated and all idea of conserving the privileges of the Palestine Arabs abandoned.*[42]

The British were doing everything to make the Sheriffians the much more important part of the Arab national movement. Weizmann believed that they had succeeded. Events were soon to disabuse the British, but not him, of this illusion.

In the fall of 1918, the British plans in the Middle East seemed to be coming to fruition. A final British offensive had shattered the Turkish Army, and the British advanced through Syria and Lebanon. Faisal's Arab Army, with British connivance, triumphantly entered Damascus and were received as 'liberators'.[43]

The British military appeared determined to ignore the Sykes-Picot agreement. With over 200,000 of their troops in Syria, the British set up their own administration (OETA) in the area. While the French were given nominal sovereignty in the Syrian littoral (OETA West), which they occupied with 6,000 troops, the British refused to permit the French franc or French language instruction even in what was supposed to become the French zone, and virtually ignored the French High Commissioner.[44] Weizmann believed now that it was certain an Arab kingdom in Syria was going to be created, and that if the Sykes-Picot agreement were definitely abrogated, the dream of a Jewish-Arab alliance could be realised.[45] What Weizmann did not understand was that with the occupation of Damascus by Faisal, and the British firmly in control of Palestine (OETA South), Zionism was becoming increasingly redundant and useless for the design to oust the French from Syria. The problem now was how to ensure Faisal's leadership and, in view of his violent opposition to the separation of Syria and Palestine, Faisal's contacts with Zionists were becoming a liability rather than an asset. Sykes reported that in Damascus the feeling was that 'there was too little Syria and too much Hedjaz'.[46]

The change in British attitude became apparent in the issue of financial support to Faisal which Weizmann undertook to provide after meeting him in June 1918. He mentioned then the figure of £40,000,000 (!) in addition to political support in Europe and the USA for Syrian autonomy under Sheriffians.[47,48] The issue became acute when Faisal became dependent on French subsidy, since Damascus was in the French zone of influence, according to the Sykes-Picot agreement. He and the British were looking now for an alternative solution.

In October, Eder wired Weizmann that there was a concrete request from Faisal — now installed in Damascus — for funds: 'Opinion is that Faisal . . . needs at present a loan and financial adviser. His engagements are 200,000 monthly without expectation of income until next harvest. Faisal would prefer loan from sources you mentioned rather than elsewhere.' The Foreign Office was at first in favour of this, though sceptical: 'The idea was due to Faisal's reluctance to become indebted to the French, and in order to establish good relations between Arab and Zionists. I think Dr. Weizmann should be asked what he can do.' It was then proposed to delay trying to arrange a loan for Faisal from the

French, and temporarily to continue the British subsidy.[49]

The British, however, soon changed their mind as evidenced by Weizmann's reply to Eder that 'it is not at present desirable to advance any money to Faisal'.

> We are very anxious to help Faisal with advisers both financial and technical . . . but we would *only like to do it with the consent of His Majesty's Government and after we have arrived at a clear and frank arrangement with Faisal, an arrangement which must be approved of by General Allenby, yourself, and the Government here . . .*
>
> On no account must an impression get abroad that the Jews are trying to hunt for concessions in Damascus and are making use of Faisal's financial embarrassment in order to lay their hands on the newly created Arab commonwealth.[50]

The penultimate sentence already contains a hint of the basic problem of the Weizmann-Faisal agreement: Weizmann was ready and able to support the Arabs to the degree that it was consistent with British policy, but British policy was moving away from the concept of Zionist-Arab alliance. This became evident only later, because the impending Peace Conference in Paris necessitated a co-ordination between Arab and Zionist demands. This was the background for the ambiguities of the Weizmann-Faisal agreement in January 1919.

Weizmann met Faisal in London on 11 December 1918. With Lawrence interpreting, they agreed that the 'Sykes-Picot agreement was equally bad for all concerned'.[51] But they apparently avoided discussion of political sovereignty for Palestine (Weizmann wanted the exclusion of these areas from the Arab state, while Faisal was willing to give special status to Zionism *within* an Arab state). Arnold Toynbee of the Foreign Office, Lawrence and Israel Sieff, agreed to draft a treaty to embody their agreements. When the document was submitted to Faisal, he substituted 'Palestine' for 'Jewish state'.[52] The parties signed the agreement on 5 January 1919. Faisal reportedly preferred to postpone the signing and wait until after the Peace Conference, but he yielded to intense British pressure,[53] and attached a unilateral codicil in Arabic, declaring that the agreement would be null and void if the Arabs did not receive their independence.[54]

The Weizmann-Faisal agreement contained the following provisions: (1) Arab and Jewish representatives would be established in their respective territories; (2) the Zionist Organisation would provide the

Arab State with economic experts and 'use its best efforts to assist in providing the means for developing natural resources'; (3) Jewish immigration to Palestine was to be encouraged on the basis of the Balfour Declaration, with religious rights and Moslem holy places guarded; (4) 'the parties were to act in complete accord and harmony . . . before the Peace Conference'; and (5) 'Any matters of dispute . . . shall be referred to the British Government.'[55] Essentially, this agreement was for collaboration before the Peace Conference — there was no agreement on the political future of Palestine. But carried away by his enthusiasm, Weizmann thought he could now press for a maximalist programme. He wired Eder in Palestine:

> W. most successful interview with Faisal who is in complete agreement with our proposals. He was sure that he would be able to explain to Arabs, advantages of Jewish Palestine. He assured Weizmann that he would not spare any effort to support Jewish demands at Peace Conference and would declare Zionism and Arab movement fellow movements and complete harmony obtained between them. The new proposals now ready stipulate that the whole administration of Palestine to be formed so as to make Palestine a Jewish Commonwealth under British Trusteeship.[56]

The Zionist Organisation therefore drew up its territorial demands in such a way as to maximise British interests (and their own) at the expense of the French. This meant a northern border north of the Litani River including Mount Hermon and the catchment of Jordan waters and an eastern boundary east of the Jordan river near the Hedjaz railway. In view of the prospects for co-operation with Faisal, the Arabs were offered a free zone in Haifa and a joint Arab-Jewish port at Aqaba.[57]

The Weizmann-Faisal agreement reflected the ambitious aims of the British Middle East Command to oust the French from Syria. The Command, however, did not consider the limits beyond which the British Government would not go in the conflict with the French over the Middle East. The Eastern Committee of the Foreign Office, meeting in December 1918, decided to support the Sheriffian movement only up to the point at which it would not prejudice good relations with the French 'who will never give up the whole of Syria without the most enormous convulsion'.[58] The British Government was ready to accept French pressure in Syria provided the British could have Mosul with its oilfields and Palestine 'from Dan to Beersheba'.[59]

Even the War Office was willing to cede Syria to France in return for Palestine as a 'buffer Jewish State if it can be created without disturbing Mohammedan sentiment'.[60]

Unaware of the discrepancy between the Arab Bureau and the Foreign Office, Weizmann and Faisal engaged in feverish efforts to enlist American support for the abrogation of the Sykes-Picot Agreement. In this, they followed a previous stratagem of Lloyd George and the Foreign Office 'to pretend to the French that we should give all Palestine and Syria to the Americans and then they [the French], in fear of losing Syria, would give us Palestine';[61] and 'to play the policy of self-determination for all it was worth'.[62]

On 14 January, Weizmann met President Wilson, who agreed that the French should not be in Palestine.[63] Faisal, aided by Rabbi Stephen Wise, met President Wilson on 23 January, and asked his support for an inter-allied Commission to ascertain the wishes of the Arabs as to their political future. Wilson favoured the idea of an enquiry and later pressed for its approval at the Supreme Allied Council.[64] The French opposed any attempt to oust them from Syria, and threatened a separate peace with Turkey and a deal with Faisal to support independence in Iraq and Palestine against the British.[65] The British Government was not prepared to jeopardise the Anglo-French entente,[66] and was alarmed no less than the French, at the prospect of an inter-allied Commission to determine the wishes of the population in the Middle East,[67] since it threatened to dismantle not only French claims in Syria, but also British claims in Iraq and Palestine. Though President Wilson forced through the proposed Commission at the threat of withdrawal from the Peace Conference,[68] the French refused to participate and the British, to avoid a complete break with the French, followed suit and, in addition, agreed to withdraw from Syria.[69] Therefore, the King-Crane Commission that set out in May 1919 to the Middle East, was wholly American in composition.

The British Government was alarmed at the prospect of a breakdown of Anglo-French hegemony in the Middle East in the wake of American intervention, and tried to restrain the ambitious designs of the Arab Bureau against France. Faisal was urged to come to terms with the French by agreeing to the French occupation of the coastal regions of Syria and Lebanon.[70] The Zionists were criticised for putting forward extreme demands likely to provoke Arab opposition. Curzon, the acting Foreign Secretary, wrote to Balfour of the reports from Palestine that a Jewish government would provoke an Arab uprising. Balfour protested that Weizmann had never asked for it.[71] Ormsby-Gore criticised the draft memorandum the Zionists submitted to the peace conference, stating that the British Government would never accept the obligations towards Zionism the document envisioned. He objected to the terms 'Jewish commonwealth' and 'Jewish government' as 'racialist' and 'religious'.[72] He believed that Weizmann was a moderate but was being pushed along by 'Jewish Jingoes' from the USA and Eastern Europe (though Curzon was convinced that Weizmann was striving for a Jewish state behind the screen of a British trusteeship).[73]

Faisal spoke before the peace conference on 6 February, and presented his case for Arab independence based on the right of self-determination. He demanded an Arab kingdom from Damascus to Arabia, 'reserving Palestine for the consideration of all parties concerned', and asked for an inter-allied Commission to investigate the genuine desires of the population.[74] It is worthwhile noting, however, that on 24 January he sent emissaries to the Zionist delegation to sound out the possibility of a Jewish-Arab alliance against the European powers in the Middle East.[75]

On 27 February, Weizmann stated his demands to the Peace Conference. He called for a British trusteeship in Palestine with enlarged boundaries, thus rejecting Faisal's idea of a Semitic entente directed against European involvement in the Middle East. He also added that Palestine would ultimately become 'as Jewish as England is English'.[76] The publication of this statement exploded in Palestine and Syria and convinced the Arab nationalists that Weizmann was a British agent who was trying to separate Palestine from Syria with the aim of making it a Jewish state. Faisal felt compelled to disavow support for a Jewish state: 'Let the unhappy Jews find refuge there . . . under a Moslem or a Christian government . . . But if the Jews desire to establish a state and obtain sovereign rights in the country, I foresee serious dangers and conflicts between them and other races.'[77]

The French were enraged because they believed that Faisal's demand for an inter-allied Commission and Weizmann's territorial and political programme were part of a British plot to oust them from their northern sphere of influence.[78] The British were upset for Arab independence endangered their position in oil-rich Iraq, while ill-concealed Zionist aspirations threatened both an open break with the French and the alienation of the Arabs.

Weizmann and Faisal had signed their agreement in the mistaken belief that Britain was interested in having the Zionists and Arab nationalists achieve their objectives. In fact, British objectives in the area were a mandate over Palestine and Iraq, control of oil supplies and Empire communication lines, including the Suez Canal and a land bridge from the Persian Gulf. The British decision to reach a settlement with the French deprived the Faisal-Weizmann agreement of whatever value it may have had at the beginning.

The Syrian National Movement, spurred by the intense debates at the Peace Conference on the principle of self-determination became a powerful factor, whose agitation for independence evoked a deep response and spread to many former officers of the Sheriffian Army, including Iraqis and Palestinians. The Arab Bureau began warning London that Zionism was jeopardising British hegemony in the Arab world, and that Faisal was becoming more dependent on the extremists. In May, Clayton wrote that 'fear of Zionism is the main issue preventing the Arab population in Palestine from favouring a British mandate; if His Majesty's Government desires a mandate, it should make it clear that the Zionist programme will not be implemented by force and in opposition to the wishes of the population'.[79] In August, Waters-Taylor wrote:

In my opinion, Dr. Weizmann's agreement with Emir Faisal is not worth the paper it is written on . . . if it becomes sufficiently known among the Arabs, it will be somewhat in the nature of a noose around Faisal's neck, for he will be regarded by the Arab population as a traitor.

He added an interesting remark about Weizmann:

It is difficult to gauge Weizmann's attitude, he must be either: (a) ignorant and misinformed as to the actual state of feeling in Palestine (b) convinced that the Moslems and Christians will tamely accept the fait accompli (c) desirous of trying the strength of the opposition, relying on British troops to subdue it if actively hostile . . . in my opinion he places undue reliance on Faisal . . . Faisal has been chosen as representative of United Syria and it is solely due to the feeling of nationalism that he holds that position.[80]

This correctly characterised Faisal's dilemma; let down by the British and threatened by the French, he had to rely increasingly on popular support. He still hoped for American assistance, and diplomatic and financial support from American Zionists, but he could not go against the nationalist tide.[81] In July 1919, the Syrian National Congress called for complete independence for all Syria including Palestine under American, or secondly, British tutelage; economic union with Iraq; and opposition to a Jewish commonwealth.[82] In his interview with the American Commissioners, Faisal declared that no separation of Palestine from Syria was acceptable.

> He stated that some months ago he was prepared to accept Zionism in its limited sense of a certain amount of immigration and exten-sion of existing Jewish colonies. The wider Zionist aspirations had, however, frightened the people and he now finds them determined not to have any part of it.[83]

The Weizmann-Faisal agreement was by now a dead issue. Weizmann complained that 'Faisal's behaviour before the [inter-allied] Commis-sion, was a flagrant violation of all his letters and other pronounce-ments'.[84] Yet he remained strangely optimistic that it would be possible to reconstruct the pro-British Arab-Jewish entente.

Weizmann's hope was based on Faisal's financial difficulties and growing political isolation. Faisal's American ploy had collapsed follow-ing an isolationist backlash in American public opinion. In September, the British, bent on reconfirming their alliance with France, committed themselves to withdraw their forces from the French zone of influence in Syria, and informed Faisal that he should look to the French for half his subsidy from now on.[85] Faisal bitterly complained 'he was being handed tied hand and foot to the French', and that 'this was a resurgence of the old imperialism'. Weizmann thought this was his chance; he met Faisal and reported to the British:

> I am under the impression he would accept the French on the Syrian coast if he would be assured of independence in the Damascus-Homs region . . . He is ready to take Jewish advisers and willing, even anxious, to have Zionist support in the development and even administration of the Damascus region. We, of course, would be willing to make a very great effort to help Faisal, as it would help us very much in establishing good relations with the Arabs both in Palestine and Syria. The agitation against us in Palestine is conducted from Syria.[86]

This shows how much Weizmann misjudged the situation. The British report on his negotiations states:

> Dr. Weizmann approached him [Faisal] and two long discussions

have already taken place. I understand that Dr. Weizmann in return for the Emir's help in Palestine towards the realization of Zionist aspirations, proposes to give money and advisers if required to the Arab government, and claims that the Zionists can persuade the French government to waive their claims to the interior. The Emir is strongly inclined to come to an agreement but matters at present are at a deadlock since he asks the Zionists to throw their lot definitely with the Arabs against the French, while Dr. Weizmann is in favour of allowing the French to occupy the coastal districts saying that they can be squeezed out later.[87]

The Foreign Office minuted: 'It would be better, if possible, that we should come to an agreement with Faisal and the French about Arab areas than that Faisal should ally himself with the Zionists to "squeeze out" the French.'

Actually, Weizmann was not ready to support Faisal's demand for ousting the French from the whole of Syria, while Faisal could not accept the Zionist demand for the separation of Palestine from Syria. During his visit to London (where he had returned in September to try and save Syrian independence, and had met Weizmann), Faisal gave an interview in which he stated frankly that Zionist aspirations for a Jewish state clashed with Arab ideas:

We Arabs cannot yield Palestine as part of our Kingdom. Indeed, we would fight to the last ditch against Palestine being other than part of the Kingdom and for the supremacy of Arabs in the land . . . But you Jews could do great work if you would co-operate with us in the formation of the Kingdom . . . Instead of our relying on any of the great powers for means of development, for material help, we should like to have the co-operation in these things of the Jewish people. You have the means and we have the numbers . . . it may be that there would be a concentration of your people in Palestine . . . when the Arab Kingdom is built up . . . and you would make of Palestine a Jewish sub-province . . .[88]

In November, Weizmann still apparently believed that Faisal was able to stop at will the anti-Zionist propaganda, as evidenced by his cable to the Zionist Bureau: 'Must impress Faisal solemn necessity immediately stopping anti-jewish propaganda over which he exercises absolute control.'[89] This assumption was unwarranted although Faisal was still interested in Zionist political and financial support.

Abandoned by his British allies, Faisal entered negotiations with the French in January 1920, in which the French agreed to:

1. a United Syria, including Palestine, with French assistance;
2. an autonomous Lebanon and Hauran;
3. acceptance of French political and expert advisers, and
4. the withdrawal of all French troops from Syria, provided the British evacuated Palestine and Mesopotamia.[90]

The Syrian Congress, an unofficial parliament whose legitimacy the French refused to recognise, withheld its confirmation from the agreement and pressed for full independence, by armed struggle if necessary. On 14 February, the Syrian Government declared a general mobilisation and on 7 March Faisal was proclaimed king of an independent Syria 'in its natural boundaries, Lebanon and Palestine included.'[91] There is strong evidence that the Arab Bureau tacitly supported and encouraged the Syrian extremists in their opposition to the agreement with France and to the separation of Palestine from Syria.

The dramatic events in Syria precipitated a groundswell of enthusiasm in Palestine. In Jerusalem, there was a mass demonstration, headed by Aref-el-Aref,[92] calling for unity between Syria and Palestine and a stop to Jewish immigration. The Deputy Military Governor of Jerusalem received a delegation, praised Moslem-Christian friendship, and assured them that the administration would defend Arab rights in Palestine.[93]

On 20 March, Faisal cabled Allenby (Commander-in-Chief of all British forces in the Middle East) asking him for recognition of an independent united Syria. He avoided mentioning Palestine and dissociated himself from the proclamation of Iraqi independence that had been issued by Iraqi officers in Damascus.[94] Allenby, who admitted that he knew that Faisal was going to be proclaimed king, in fact had already wired to the Foreign Office suggesting that it recognise Faisal as sovereign over an 'Arab Nation or Confederation embracing Syria, Palestine and Mesopotamia, the Administration of Syria being secured by French, and Palestine and Mesopotamia by British'.[95] Foreign Secretary Curzon immediately replied in the negative, asking whether 'the [treaty] machinery which has applied to every other mandate should be dispensed with here . . . and that we should accept the Mandate from Faisal? . . . How would recognition of Faisal be compatible with Zionist claims?'[96] Allenby continued to press for recognition of

Faisal and proposed to resolve the Zionist problem by reminding Faisal
of British commitment to a national home for the Jews without making
any reference to the separation of Palestine from Syria.[97] Allenby's
proposal was approved, but Faisal, now wholly dependent on the
Syrian Congress, refused to come to the Peace Conference unless it was
agreed in advance that Palestine formed an inseparable part of Syria.
He stated to Allenby:

> Being in need of calming people who are much agitated, I hope I can
> get from Great Britain some satisfactory declaration which I can also
> use in keeping in the hearts of Arabs the confidence which they have
> in a great ally, and to prove to them that any agreement between the
> British and the Zionists is in no way to be considered of more value
> than an agreement with King Husain or the President of the French
> Republic.[98]

There is little doubt that Faisal's hope to obtain British recognition of
his 'fait accompli' was encouraged by the British military in the Middle
East.

In April 1920, grave disturbances took place in Jerusalem when,
during the Nebi Mussa procession, Arab crowds (incited by rumours of
an attempt on the life of the Grand Mufti) attacked the Jewish quarter
while the security forces stood by. Political slogans supporting Faisal
and against the Balfour Declaration appeared. The Zionist Commission
accused the military administration of complicity in the demonstrations
and demanded a Court of Enquiry.[99] Under pressure, Allenby
nominated a Military Court of officers who investigated the political
background to the incidents. Their report, suppressed by the Foreign
Office,[100] throws an interesting light on the attitude of the Military
Administration.[101] It reveals how quickly the Arab Bureau had shifted
from a policy of an Arab-Jewish entente, and was increasingly conducting a Middle East policy of its own in opposition to Zionism, the
French and London at the same time. Their policy to legitimise the
Syrian *coup d'etat* clashed with the policy of the Foreign Office bent
on working out a compromise with the French. Thus the British
Government resolved to relieve Allenby of political responsibilities and
appoint a civilian High Commissioner for Palestine (Herbert Samuel)
in May 1920.

The report exonerated the military of the charges raised by the
Zionist Commission and counter-attacked the Zionist Commission for
attempting to set up a parallel administration to 'undermine their

authority, in order to create a Zionist "fait accompli" '. The report admits that the Syrian *coup* did not take the Administration by surprise and supports the Administration's claim that it was 'the culmination of a French intrigue', which Allenby tried to counter by recognising Faisal as King of a United Syria. The report conceded that the British political liaison officer in Damascus was well informed of the situation and that no warning had been given to Faisal between January and March. Curzon's last minute caution to Faisal (sent via Allenby) that 'an irresponsible action . . . would place the case of the Syrian people in opposition to the liberal intentions of the British and French Governments' arrived in Damascus too late or was ignored.[102]

The report shows the sharp anti-Zionist turn taken by the Arab Bureau. In 1918 they were encouraging a Weizmann-Faisal agreement and the promotion of Zionist colonisation. Now they were supporting an anti-Zionist pan-Arabism.[103]

> The proposition on extending British recognition of Faisal as ruler of an Arab State, including the English Provinces of Mesopotamia and Palestine was exceedingly tempting — it would probably put an end to French intrigue, satisfy the pride and national spirit of the Syrians by giving a nominal overlordship to Faisal, which would not interfere with the actual control of either ourselves or the French in our respective zones, and generally pacify the Arab States. The suggestion was viewed with favour by both Lord Allenby and Lord Milner . . . even though . . . it might tend temporarily to elate the Arabs and depress the Zionists . . .[104]

The Collapse of Faisal's Kingdom

The initiative of Allenby boomeranged. The proclamation of an independent Arab kingdom was in fact the spur which led England and France to settle their differences in the Middle East at San Remo (25 April 1920). The Anglo-French entente in Europe had to be preserved at all costs. Also the British were alarmed at the spread of popular anti-imperialist elements within the Arab national movement throughout the Middle East. This made Faisal's leadership more apparent than real. At the crunch, fearing she had lost control of Arab nationalism, Great Britain formally agreed to the territorial division of the Middle East.[105] The question of Mandates was settled and the Balfour Declaration incorporated in the Palestine Mandate, but the question of the border between Palestine and Syria was left open for future negotiations.

Faisal was put in an impossible situation by the decision. Deserted by the British, he tried to appease the French, but they were determined to drive him out of Syria (which they succeeded in doing in July 1920).[106] The desperate situation of the short-lived Syrian Kingdom was summarised by its diplomatic representative in London:

> ... the situation is growing worse ... the unrest among the Arabs today is due to their dissatisfaction at the peace settlement ... but it is also based on economic considerations ... In Syria today all trade and commerce are at a standstill. There is no outlet to the sea. The French occupy the ports; the French and British take what customs duties there are; and the population is in desperate straits ... the Syrian Government is left with insufficient resources to meet its expenditures ... The life of Syria depends on the freedom of communication with the sea and the Euphrates.[107]

In view of the deteriorating situation, Faisal was looking for help from any source, including the Zionists. Weizmann's representative in Damascus, Dr Fellman, cabled Faisal's desperate plea for aid:

> I forwarded to Faisal your letter. he seems to be very impatient about the loan. They are now 'dried up' and debilitated by financial difficulties ... the press conducts a violent anti-Jewish campaign, but the court and above all, Faisal, is for the time being in favour of the Jews ... I have started negotiations about a declaration in which he would express regrets about the riots in Palestine and appeal for collaboration between two brotherly peoples ... but the question was who to address the appeal; I proposed you but he was against this saying it would provoke the anger of the Arab population in Palestine ... For the moment the government is on our side ... hoping for financial aid from American Jewry. But I doubt this can last ... If we want to stop this trend detrimental to our interests it is indispensable to open without delay a fund here (a) to buy the most important papers in Damascus (b) to engage a few Arab agitators to make propaganda for us ...[108]

Faisal, indeed, wrote to Allenby stating that he regretted the anti-Jewish riots in Palestine, though still insisting that Palestine was part of Syria.[109] But Weizmann's interest in co-operation with Faisal had evaporated now that the Syrian Arab Kingdom had gone beyond British designs. 'Faisal in spite of his momentary success ... is in the

long run a broken reed.'[110] The Zionists lobbied the Foreign Office
to have Faisal excluded from Palestine and threatened trouble with
America if Britain did not take the Mandate for Palestine.[111] When the
San Remo Conference gave the Palestine Mandate to Britain, incorporating the Balfour Declaration, Weizmann abandoned Faisal to his
fate. On 28 April 1920, he wrote to his wife: 'Our trials have come to
an end: the Mandate has gone through, the Declaration has gone
through and in a few days the change in the administration will also
take place.' From San Remo (where he had journeyed) he added
significantly: 'A new era is settling in . . . Lloyd George and Balfour
behaved very well . . . But our French friends: what a trash! . . . the
Arabs walk about here with long faces . . .'[112]

On 24 July 1920, the French Army in Syria put an end to Faisal's
Kingdom, occupying Damascus, destroying the hastily mobilised Arab
forces, and ordering Faisal to quit Syria in disgrace and humiliation.
The Arabs viewed the Zionist failure to help the Syrian Kingdom in its
hour of need as the acid test of Zionist intentions towards Arab independence.

Dr Eder, head of the Zionist Commission, admitted frankly to
Faisal, who passed through Haifa on 20 August 1920 on his way to
exile in Europe:

> We favoured a united Arab nation, outside the limits of Palestine,
> with one representative with whom one could treat . . . If Faisal
> was the chosen representative and *could make himself acceptable to
> the Great Powers*, we should be in favour . . . but I had to point out
> to him that he had been too clever; he was a Zionist in Europe;
> he backed the anti-Zionists in Damascus. He was trying to play off
> the French against the British and vice versa . . .[113]

In summing up the Weizmann-Faisal episode, Moshe Pearlman[114]
writes that the Jews

> were not unsuccessful in their effort to press home to the many
> leaders of the Arabs a few general ideas which might serve as a broad
> basis for negotiations. These were the ideas of kinship of nations,
> of the benefits that would accrue to the Whole Arab East from a
> Jewish settlement in Palestine, of the non-imperialist character of
> that settlement, of Jewish support of Arab aspiration and of safe-
> guarding the Arabs in Palestine.

The factors that stood in the way of success were, in his view: lack of adequate propaganda; Jewish circles were morally unprepared; the British, if not actually hostile, were at least non-co-operative; the Jews were relegated to a position of unconditional dependence on Britain; and the equivocations of Faisal – the discrepancy between his public utterances against Zionist aspirations and his readiness to bargain with the Zionists behind the scenes.

The discrepancy in Faisal's public utterances and private talks also characterised Weizmann. In private talks he tried to allay Arab fears of Jewish domination by mass immigration and settlement, while in public he spoke of Palestine becoming Jewish. His identification with British aims and interests did little to make the Arabs believe in the non-imperialist character of Zionism. In the hours of need – when they opposed imperialist pressure – he disappointed them. Lastly, Zionism's total dependence on Great Britain and its faith in an historical alliance with Britain rather than with the Arabs were of its own choice.

Weizmann did not understand that Britain could not forever maintain its position in the Middle East by force. The setting in motion of the process of independence for Arab states – which began after the collapse of Faisal's Kingdom sparked off a series of anti-imperialist revolts (Iraq, Egypt, Syria) – also had its effect on the Palestinians. Deprived of an equal chance of statehood, they henceforth formed the core of Arab opposition to Zionism.

Weizmann and the Palestinians

Weizmann's under-estimation of the Palestinian leadership, like his pan-Arabism, was largely a product of British influence. Weizmann approached the Palestinian Arabs without the benefit of personal knowledge of them but with opinions formed by close associates of his. Among these were Aaron Aaronsohn, a Palestinian Jew who had been working for British intelligence and who became a member of the Zionist Commission,[1] and Brigadier Clayton.

Aaronsohn had a low opinion of the Palestinian Arabs which he freely expressed in the pages of the *Arab Bulletin*, the secret British intelligence weekly. In a report on the Jewish colonies, he explained why it was necessary for them to practise segregation from the Arabs:

Had we permitted the squalid, superstitious, ignorant fellahin . . . to live in close contact with the Jewish pioneers . . . the slender chances of their success . . . would have been impaired, since we had no power, under the cruel Turkish administration, to enforce

progressive methods . . . or even to ensure respect for private property
. . . so far as we know the Arabs, the man among them who will
withstand a bribe is yet to be found.[2]

Even before the Zionist Commission reached Palestine, Aaronsohn
outlined the basic line that Zionist policy towards the Palestinians was
to take. In reply to Ormsby-Gore, who had stressed the necessity of
allaying Arab fears of a Jewish government and land expropriation,
Aaronsohn maintained that it was not the fellahin who were virtually
landless, but the rich land-owning effendi who feared expropriation and
that the latter spread anti-Jewish propaganda in order to frighten Jews
into paying higher prices for land.[3] Weizmann subscribed to this view
and his initial contacts with Syrio-Palestinian leaders in Cairo only
confirmed his bias − that they could be bought off[4] or suppressed with
a little firmness, and that they did not represent a serious national
movement. He believed that as a negligible factor, they presented no
substantive obstacle to Zionist or British plans.[5]

The estimate of the Palestinians as unimportant was strengthened
by Weizmann's enthusiastic embrace of pan-Arabism (as represented by
Faisal). In a letter to his son, Weizmann compared the Arabs of Palestine to the rocks of Judea, as obstacles that had to be cleared on a
difficult path.[6] In another letter he stated that 'there is little chance of
our even finding a common language with the local element . . .'[7] Weizmann did not believe it was necessary or important to find a common
language with this local element because he was confident that the
British would force upon the Arabs a 'fait accompli'. Instead of engaging in an effort to allay Arab fears and dissipate their suspicions, he
kept entreating the Foreign Office to impress upon the Military
Administration and the Arabs that the Balfour Declaration was a *chose
jugée*.

Weizmann's estimate of the Palestinians was reinforced by the
British pan-Arabists who were his advisers, especially in the 'honey-
moon period' up to December 1918 when Faisal and the Sheriffians
seemed to be on ascent (culminating in Faisal's stage-managed entrance
into Damascus in October 1918).[8] The British Arabists, such as
Clayton, at first believed that there existed little national feeling among
the Palestinians, and that the local population had no aspirations for
independence.[9] Since the Palestinians had not been active in the Arab
Revolt they were discounted as a serious factor.

Weizmann echoed this view and repeatedly referred to the Palestinians as a minor problem, holding that politically speaking, the focus

of Arab interest is the Hedjaz, 'the triangle formed by Damascus, Mecca and Baghdad', that the Palestinians presented no political problem but an economic one which would in due time be solved.[10] He believed that if he reassured the Arabs of his moderation, it would be up to the British to take care of the Palestinian problem.

In a speech to Palestinian Arab notables prepared with the advice and assistance of Clayton,[11] Weizmann disavowed the intention of aiming at a Jewish state, stating he was only seeking to 'create conditions under which the material and moral development of those of our people who chose to come here can be rendered possible ... not to the detriment of any of the great communities, but to their advantage. There is land and room enough in Palestine.' He expressed 'the deepest sympathy and profound interest in the struggle for freedom the Arab race is now waging'; but for Palestine, as 'self-government is a complicated science which people cannot be educated to in one day', he supported a Mandate by a European Power. After his Jerusalem speech (27 April 1918) Weizmann wrote to his wife:

> I consider it unnecessary to bother with the Arabs any more for the present; we have done what was asked of us, we have explained our point of view; let them take it or leave it. If the Government would only take it upon itself to settle this thing with the Arabs that would be all that is necessary.[12]

Initially, the British were under the impression that Weizmann had succeeded in conciliating local Arab opinion. In April 1918, the director of the Arab Bureau wrote that the Palestinians had become convinced that Zionism had more modest aims than they had been led to believe and that they could substantially benefit from an accommodation with Zionism.[13] Soon, however, the British began to sense a growing Palestinian opposition to the Balfour Declaration, while Weizmann clung tenaciously to the illusion of the non-existence of a Palestinian nationality, 'the present state of affairs would tend towards the creation of an Arab Palestine if there were an Arab people in Palestine'.[14] This became part of his legacy to the Zionist movement.

The opposition of the Palestinians was sparked by the arrival of the Zionist Commission in the spring of 1918, and by what they viewed as its arrogance in demanding an equal share with the British military in administering the country, Hebrew as the official language, control over immigration and over land transfers. Nor did articles appearing in the Jewish press demanding emigration of Palestinian Arabs to the Arab state lessen their fears of displacement in their homeland.[15]

The British reported in December 1918 that 'Weizmann's disclaimers of political aims are not credited, partly because associates of his at home and in Palestine have not always endorsed them'. The British also disputed the Zionist contention that the opposition came solely from unrepresentative and corrupt leaders: 'Anti-Jew feeling is as strong as — perhaps stronger than ever among all classes of Arabs . . . if we openly and immediately promote a Zionist political state in Palestine, we shall be as unpopular as the French in Syria.'[16]

There were several Palestinian theories as to how to meet 'the Zionist danger'. Some were ready to fight the British for complete independence and ally with the Turks if necessary.[17] The majority welcomed the British as liberators, but were uneasy at the implications of British support for Zionism. The large-scale demonstrations organised by the Zionists on the first anniversary of the Balfour Declaration (2 November 1918) increased Palestinian apprehensions. The issuance of an Anglo-French declaration promising self-determination for the inhabitants of Syria and Mesopotamia only swelled the unrest. A Moslem-Christian delegation immediately went to the British Military Governor to ask whether Palestine was included in Syria and whether, therefore, the declaration applied to them.[18]

The British conquest of all of Syria and Palestine in October 1918 and the setting up of a separate military administration in Palestine (OETA South, under purely British auspices) and in Syria (OETA East under Faisal's Arab army) seemed to increase the appeal of the Syrian nationalist movement as protector of Palestinian interests against the Zionists. On the other hand, the idea of the separation of Palestine from Syria implied by the Balfour Declaration confirmed the Palestinians in their apprehension that their destiny would be different from the fate of other Arab peoples.

In this connection, the British intelligence reports on the effect of Faisal's entry into Damascus are instructive. After only a month of Faisal's rule in Syria, Clayton began to distinguish between the attitudes of the Syrians and Palestinians:

ARABS *In Syria.* Desire an independent Arab Government, but are apprehensive of reactionary Sheriffian influence.
ARABS *In Palestine.* Are strongly anti-Zionist and very apprehensive of Zionist aims. They were pro-British in the early days of the occupation, but are now showing a tendency to turn towards the King of the Hedjaz and the Arab Government of Damascus.[19]

The British became sceptical that the Weizmann-Faisal accord would help reduce Palestinian opposition. In a letter to Weizmann, written in December 1918, Clayton stated that even if it be assumed that Arab national aspirations could be completely fulfilled by the establishment of the Arab-Syrian state, these aspirations were of little interest to the Palestinians. The Palestinians were interested in maintaining a position in Palestine which they felt was threatened by Zionism.[20]

The Palestinian National Congress held in Jerusalem in January 1919, which drew up demands for the Paris Peace Conference, resolved that Palestine should be 'constitutional and independent', and also that it 'should be part of southern Syria, provided the latter is not under foreign control'. British intelligence explained that it was

> the fear of Zionism . . . that led the young pan-Arab element to favour its union with an independent Arab Syria, for with Palestine joined to an Arab Syria, the people of Palestine with the help of other Arabs would be able to successfully resist Jewish immigration and Zionist plans.

However, some delegates 'did not approve the change of name from Palestine to Southern Syria, saying that they wished only a sort of cultural union with Arab Syria'.[21]

Faisal's struggle at the Paris Peace Conference for an independent Arab Kingdom, and the Zionist campaign for a Palestine 'as Jewish as England is English', drove the Palestinians closer towards an apparently successful pan-Arabism. The Palestinians sent delegates to the all-Syrian General Congress in Damascus in June-July 1919, which called for an American mandate over all Syria and no Zionist state and no Jewish immigration or land purchase in 'southern Syria'. In September 1919, a newspaper, *Southern Syria*, was founded by Aref-el-Aref, reportedly with French financial assistance, and carried out violently anti-Zionist propaganda.[22]

Despite all signs to the contrary, Weizmann believed that Faisal would have absolute control over Palestinians.[23] In reality, the Palestinian nationalist leadership was becoming increasingly suspicious of Faisal because of his flirtations with the Zionists and his weakness towards the European powers. Articles appeared calling for the Palestinian Arabs to fight for their own cause rather than link it with that of the Syrians.[24]

Weizmann thought that British firmness could resolve the Arab troubles in Palestine.[25] He minimised the growing agitation as due to false rumours and ignorance of Zionism, to the economic interest of the inefficient 'effendis' who were afraid of losing their privileged position, and to foreign intrigues.

Less than two months after this analysis, grave political disturbances occurred in Palestine. The creation of an independent Arab kingdom in Syria in March 1920 led to mass demonstrations in Jerusalem demanding that Palestine be incorporated into Syria. There were also attacks on Jewish settlements on the border of the independent Arab Syrian state. Weizmann was shaken by the death of Trumpeldor defending the settlement of Tel-Hai and Metullah in Upper Galilee, and called the situation 'a great deterioration . . . the administration is frightened'.[26] This was followed by attacks in April on the Jewish quarter of Jerusalem led by the nationalists during the Nebi Musa religious procession, in which over 200 Jews were injured. Weizmann wrote of 'wild pogroms, looting, massacres . . . government protection inadequate'.[27] While he now understood that Faisal could not control the Arab Nationalists,[28] he did not believe that he was faced with a genuine national resistance in Palestine. He held British weakness responsible for what happened.[29]

The Syrian Kingdom in Damascus that Weizmann believed was the source of anti-Zionist emanations also disappeared in a few months. With the collapse of Faisal's rule in Damascus and the final partition of the Middle East, the Palestinians were left to face alone the British Mandate over Palestine incorporating the Balfour Declaration, with an administration headed by a High Commissioner who was both a Jew and a Zionist. The confusion that reigned among the Palestinians after the collapse of Faisal's kingdom in July 1920 did not last long. The agitation in 1919-20 for unity with Syria was motivated mainly by the idea that this was the best way to obstruct a special status for Palestine as implied by the Balfour Declaration. Already the Third Palestine Congress in Haifa in December 1920 dropped the demand for union with Syria and the definition of Palestine as Southern Syria, and concentrated on the demand for self-rule and opposition to Jewish immigration and to the idea of a Jewish national home.[30] The delegations in the Fourth Congress (May 1921) appointed to negotiate with the British Government were authorised to speak on behalf of the Palestinian people only. This did not mean a complete renunciation of the idea of Arab unity, but rather that the emphasis was on a national Palestinian government. In 1923, when the idea of an Arab Federation was revived in the negotiations between Britain and the King of Hedjaz, the Palestinians (in their Sixth Congress, June 1923) implored King

Hussein not to sign the treaty unless the Balfour Declaration was annulled. They were now opposed to a Sheriffian rule over Palestine and pressed for an elected legislative council and national government.

In March 1921, the new Colonial Secretary, Winston Churchill, arrived in Cairo to preside over the final consolidation of British interest in the Middle East after the collapse of Faisal's rule in Damascus (at this time responsibility for Palestine was transferred from the Foreign Office to the Colonial Office). The principal decision was to establish a Hashemite bloc by giving Transjordan to Faisal's brother, Abdullah; Faisal was due to be installed as king of Iraq. A Palestinian delegation from the Haifa Congress went to lobby for a halt to Jewish immigration and settlement. Churchill countered that the British were committed to the Balfour Declaration and flatly rejected Arab demands. This precipitated a new and even more serious wave of Arab riots. An attack on a workers' May Day procession through Jaffa in 1921 triggered numerous assaults on the Jewish community. Twenty Jews were killed and 80 wounded, and attacks on Petah Tikva were repulsed only with cavalry and airplanes. '[Churchill] treated the Arabs' demands like those of a negligible opposition to be put off by a few political phrases and treated like children . . . this put the final touch on the picture', wrote the British intelligence officer in Palestine.[31] An investigating commission reported that the main Arab grievances were the immigration of great numbers of 'low-class Jews, who were arrogant towards the Arabs and ill-behaved', the economic depression in agriculture, and the privileged position of the Zionists *vis-a-vis* the government.

When the Palestinians, following the Egyptian precedent, sent a delegation to London, paid for by popular subscription, Herbert Samuel urged Weizmann to arrive at an understanding with them. In a letter to Weizmann he wrote:

> After a year in Palestine I have come to the conclusion that the importance of the Arab factor had been underestimated by the Zionist movement; unless there is very careful steering it is upon the Arab rock that the Zionist ship may be wrecked.[32]

The Palestine Arab Delegation, headed by Musa Kazim el Husseini, a leading nationalist, offered the first independent Palestinian presentation of their case and was followed by successive lobbies. The Colonial Office treated the delegation with a great deal of ambiguity, demonstrated by the reluctance of the Colonial Secretary to meet the delegation or make a statement of policy.

> They started by asking for the immediate establishment of a respon-
> sible Government in Palestine on an elective basis . . . it did not take
> long to convince them of the absurdity of some of these proposals
> and the unlikelihood of the others being adopted. They then began
> to state their case more reasonably . . . I eventually got them to do
> what I had all along hoped they would do, which was to ask how we
> imagined that the Zionist policy could be carried out without
> prejudice . . . I said . . . that we were ready to put them in touch
> with the Zionist Organization so that they could get a concrete idea
> of the schemes being considered for the economic development of
> the country.[33]

On 29 November 1921 the delegation met Weizmann who agreed to
discuss limitation of Jewish immigration, and constitutional safeguards
against Jewish political ascendancy. The meeting was arranged at the
request of Shuckburgh of the Colonial Office. The delegation refused to
discuss the points with Weizmann before a clear interpretation of the
Balfour Declaration was given by His Majesty's Government. Following
is a comment on this meeting, given by a British official sympathetic
to Zionism:

> Dr Weizmann, while his speech was conciliatory, adopted an unfor-
> tunate manner in delivering it. His attitude was of the nature of a
> conqueror handing to beaten foes the terms of peace. Also I think he
> despises members of the delegation as not worthy protagonists —
> that it is a little derogatory to him to expect him to meet them on
> the same ground.[34]

Privately, Weizmann was even more scathing, calling them a 'fifth-rate
delegation' which 'cut a rather poor figure'.[35]
Faced with British refusal to abrogate the Balfour Declaration but
encouraged by hints of a 'new formula' as regards its meaning, the Arab
delegation put out tentative feelers towards reaching an accommodation with the Zionists.[36] Members of the Husseini family approached
David Eder of the Zionist Executive in Jerusalem in December 1921,
and

> stated that they were willing to accept the Balfour Declaration,
> government control of immigration, but demanded a legislative

assembly, that assembly to be entirely elected. The government would be appointed by the High Commissioner, not necessarily from members of the legislative assembly. They are thinking apparently of something like the Government which has been set up in Meso-potamia . . . I had only to explain that I considered the proposals of the Husseini meeting premature.[37]

The more moderate and realistic approach was beginning to have its impact. The Colonial Office was moving towards making concessions to the Arabs so long as it did not jeopardise their political control of Palestine, as shown by the 1922 White Paper. Besides formally separat-ing Transjordan from Palestine, this paper repudiated Weizmann's phrase of 'a Palestine as Jewish as England is English'.[38] The disavowal of the phrase, which became the most quoted phrase in Jewish-Arab policies, was painful to Weizmann, but he accepted it gracefully and suggested taking advantage of this concession to demonstrate Jewish readiness for co-operation against Arab intransigence. As another British concession, the 1922 Order-in-Council proposed the creation of a legislative council to give a semblance of self-government, the council to consist of twelve elected members (ten Arab and two Jewish) and eleven officials of the Palestine Administration, including the High Commissioner as Chairman.

Weizmann's support for the legislative council did not spring from a conviction that Palestine was entitled to self-government but from his realisation of its impact on international public opinion.

The Arabs of Palestine have one strong point in their favour of which they make ample use. They always point to the apparent contradiction between Article 23 of the Covenant of the League of Nations and the Mandate which runs against this principle of self-determination . . . to ordinary goyim not fully conversant with all the ins and outs of Zionism . . . the Arab argumentation makes a powerful appeal.[39]

As a matter of fact, the pressure of the Palestinians for self-government was viewed by Weizmann with grave anxiety. The British Government proclaimed the plan for a legislative council and forced the Zionist movement to accept it (Herbert Samuel, the High Commissioner, threatened to resign if the Zionist movement opposed it). Weizmann concluded that it was necessary to encourage the growth of the moderate Arab Party which would challenge the authority of the

Moslem-Christian Association and the Arab Executive Committee (a nine-man body elected by the Third Congress in Haifa, under the chairmanship of Musa Kazim el Husseini) and its delegations to London and Geneva. Already in May 1920, at the Zionist Executive he stressed the urgent need for the 'greatest possible activity among the Arabs' and recommended that Kalvarisky and Yellin, who were on intimate terms with them, be engaged for this purpose. In 1921, he explained that the Palestinian Delegation to London would lose its importance if the Zionists succeeded in organising another Arab party in the country.[40]

Weizmann believed that by exploiting family feuds, ambitions and personal rivalries between community leaders, frictions between Bedouins and farmers, tensions and conflicts between Moslems and Christians, and between rural and urban elements and by offering them grants and loans, an opposition to the Arab Executive and the Moslem-Christian associations could be fostered. For a while this attempt appeared promising. Personal and family feuds, competition between village and urban elites, and tension between Moslems and Christians all existed in abundance.

In the summer of 1921, Kalvarisky, head of the Arab Department of the Zionist Executive in Jerusalem, began to assist in organising 'National Moslem Associations' which would take a pro-British line in opposition to the Moslem-Christian associations. Playing on Moslem bitterness at Christian over-representation in government posts and the domination of the Palestinian leadership by a few Jerusalem families, he was successful in creating such associations, especially in a number of northern towns — Haifa, Acre, Nazareth and Tiberias. Zionist aid generally took the form of payments to the leaders to cover their expenses, the arranging of agricultural credit for them at bank rates rather than the usual usurious interest rates, and financial subsidies for newspapers which supported the associations.[41]

Weizmann attached great importance and considerable hopes to these activities.[42] He wrote to one supporter:

> It is essential to encourage the growth of a moderate party, of which we should have a very valuable nucleus . . . This action [should] . . . abstain from giving money to independent Arab without asking for a specific equivalent . . . we will maintain the Moslem Societies formed by Mr Kalvarisky . . . but we do not propose to pay out vast sums . . . and we have demanded from them public action in favour of cooperation between all sections of

the population on the basis on the Mandate . . .[43]

He added that the 'Moslem-Christian societies were losing ground'.

But the National Moslem Associations soon showed their political weakness when the question of elections to the legislative council came up in the winter of 1923. Though expressly organised by the Zionists for the purpose of taking part in these elections, they were afraid to break the declared Arab boycott. Afraid of being branded 'Zionist tools', and realising that they were not going to win any political spoils from the Palestine Government, the National Moslem Associations disintegrated. By the spring of 1923 the experiment had ended in decided failure.[44]

Under the impact of public criticism, and in order to save face, the leaders of the various opposition groups took refuge in outbidding the Arab Executive in extreme national demands and opposition to Zionism. This pattern was to be repeated in the stormy years of 1936-9, when the moderate leaders attempted to cover up their negotiations and agreements with the Zionists by taking an even more extreme position than the Mufti Haj Amin al Husseini.

A subsequent attempt by Kalvarisky to set up a 'National Farmer's Party' by similar methods also met with failure.[45] Although this approach was perhaps more serious, in that the party centred its main attention on concrete rural economic problems, it ended in failure because it represented the interests of the village landlords and not the small peasants.

The failure of elections to the legislative council due to the Arab boycott in the winter of 1923 — despite the fact that it signalled the demise of the 'National Moslem Association' — did not trouble Weizmann too much. After all, he had accepted the 1922 White Paper, with its promise of greater self-government in Palestine, only under duress. From Weizmann's point of view there was no real urgency in dealing with the problem of self-governing institutions. Weizmann persisted in the belief that the economic development of Palestine fostered by Zionist colonisation and the efficient administration of Herbert Samuel would benefit the Arabs, and they would lose interest in political opposition.[46] He was especially encouraged by the fact that for a substantial period after 1921, there were no more serious disturbances in Palestine and Jewish colonisation and settlement were progressing at an increasing tempo. Jewish immigration increased from 3,000 in 1923 to 31,000 in 1925.[47] In 1922, Herbert Samuel wrote that the tension that previously prevailed had decreased and that the size of the garrison could be reduced. He reported that economic activity was reviving, with the help of government investments in roads, railways, education and public health, and he believed that if a firm political line was observed there was 'some hope of a rapprochement between the opposing parties'.[48] Weizmann was also sanguine about the developments, describing the country as quiet and prospering and reporting that instead of the Arabs feeling that they are being exploited by the Jews, the Arabs of Akko and Gaza complained that the Jews do not come to them.[49]

The quiet years between 1922 and 1929 provided an opportunity to put into effect Weizmann's 'economic solution' to the Palestine problem. After all, he stated in 1918 that

the Arab peasant will fare better under a just administration than under a retrogressive feudal Arab regime. The capitalist and big landlord never flourished under Zionism . . . the principle of small holdings and nationalization of land is an unshakeable dogma with us . . . the small man whether Jew or Gentile will be amply protected.[50]

Yet, Weizmann never developed any concrete economic programme to aid the Palestine peasant. Even later, when the Zionist leaders promised economic assistance to neighbouring states, they never formulated a programme aimed at developing Arab agriculture *in Palestine*. In fact, they often opposed measures of the Palestine Government designed to protect the interests of the small cultivators.

Zionist land policy was directed at one aim — to secure the maximum amount of land for Zionist colonisation. From the moment the Zionist Commission arrived in March 1918, it insisted on freezing the land registers during the military administration in order to prevent speculation.[51] In 1919, the Military Administration proposed that they be allowed to give loans to small cultivators in order to tide them over until the next harvest, as the normal process of credit had been interrupted by the First World War. Weizmann opposed this measure on the ground that it would upset the status quo, for by getting a loan, small cultivators would be given *de facto* title to their land. In Palestine, where titles of ownership were not clear in many cases, this would make it more difficult for the Zionist organisation to acquire land.[52] Later, however, under heavy criticism in the British Parliament, he changed his mind.[53]

In 1920, Weizmann proposed opening the registers and the

compulsory breaking up of the large latifundia, with just compensation, and heavy taxation of unimproved value to force large tracts of land on the market for acquisition by Jewish colonies.[54] While pressing for assurances that adequate land would be available for Jewish colonisation, he never took the initiative to advocate legislation that would protect the interests of the small tenants, which would have demonstrated that Zionists had no intentions of dispossessing them.[55]

The Crisis of 1929: Transfer Proposals

This lacuna in Zionist policy had disastrous consequences when anti-Jewish riots broke out on an unprecedented scale in 1929. The old-established Jewish communities at Hebron and Safad were attacked with much loss of life, including women and children; six Jewish colonies were virtually destroyed; much property was damaged, 133 Jews were killed and 339 wounded.[56]

On the surface, the major cause of the riots was the dispute over Jewish rights to the Wailing Wall — to Jews, the symbol of their attachment to their religious and national tradition throughout 2,000 years of suffering in exile, and to Moslems, the site of the al-Haram al-Sharif, the third most holy place in Islam. The Jews made attempts to acquire the area of the Wall, often accompanied by expressions of hope and desire to rebuild the Temple. The Moslems interpreted this as a first step towards a Jewish takeover of the entire al-Haram al-Sharif area.[57] However, disputes concerning prayer procedure at the Wailing Wall had gone on since Ottoman rule in Jerusalem. The sudden flare-up of the dispute into bloody disturbances, coming after eight years of quiet in Palestine, cannot be explained simply by a few Jewish provocations.

Both the quiet between 1921 and 1929 and the sudden turn to bloodshed require a deeper analysis. The quiet was a result of a number of factors. In the years 1921 to 1929, Palestine was undergoing a process of rapid economic development, accompanied by a deep transformation of Arab economy and society. In the process, a variety of Arab political trends developed, expressed in the struggle between the older leadership of Moslem-Christian associations and Arab Executive and the rising Arab middle class (merchants, plantation-owners, contractors and industrialists). The struggle absorbed Arab political energy until 1928. In the meantime, the Zionist enterprise, after a few years of mass immigration and capital influx, suddenly experienced a severe economic setback, followed by a sharp decline in immigration and, in 1927, in net emigration.[58] In 1927-9, it seemed as though the whole Zionist enterprise was on the verge of collapse. In view of this prospect, the Arab leadership moderated their demands and entered into serious negotiations with the British on steps leading gradually to self-government. The Eighth Palestinian Congress which convened on 20 June 1928 in Jerusalem, and which embraced all political groups, including the Nashashibi opposition, refrained from adopting any explicit resolution against the Mandate, or the Balfour Declaration.[59] For the first time, the new executive, comprising members of the opposition, initiated negotiations with the new Colonial Secretary (the well-known socialist theoretician and writer, Sidney Webb, Lord Passfield) for the establishment of a legislative council.

The Arab negotiators, Musa Kazim el Husseini and Raguib al Nashashibi, no longer demanded the annulment of the Balfour Declaration and even agreed to a Council of 29 members composed of 14 officials, including the High Commissioner, and 15 representatives of the populace appointed by the government but in proportion to their respective numbers (10 Moslems, 3 Jews and 2 Christians).[60] Even the Mufti agreed, as reported by Judge Gad Frumkin, that the Council should not have jurisdiction over matters of immigration and land purchases.[61] The High Commissioner and Colonial Secretary now considered the time ripe for an agreement with the Arab leadership on the creation of a legislative council as a first step towards self-government.

The 1929 riots can be understood only against the background of the serious economic crisis in the country as a whole and in the Arab rural population in particular. The report of the Commission of Enquiry following the disturbances revealed for the first time the gravity of the problem of landlessness among Arab peasants. An enquiry conducted by two officials of the administration (Johnson and Crosbie) in 104 villages (about 10 per cent of the total number of villages) revealed that 29.8 per cent of rural families had no land at all and an additional 40 per cent of families possessed holdings smaller than the minimum required for subsistence, and that they depended on outside work. The Shaw Report pointed especially to congestion in the hilly areas and to the scarcity of arable lands, and placed in doubt the possibility of further Jewish settlement without further dispossession of masses of Arab farmers. It recommended large-scale development plans to resettle tens of thousands of farmers who were already dispossessed.[62]

The Shaw Commission had a devastating effect on public opinion in Britain, which until then was predominantly in favour of Zionism, and on a Labour government, committed to the principle of self-government and economic progress for colonial peoples. The Report of the Commission of Enquiry added weight to the disposition of the Colonial Office to impose new restrictions on Jewish immigration and settlement leading to acquisition of Arab land, and to initiate steps towards self-government.

Weizmann's reaction to these developments demonstrated his frustration as well as his inability to grapple with the problem. His insistence that the problem of Palestine Arabs was an economic one led him to the ill-conceived solution of transfer of Arabs to other countries. Weizmann now argued that the economic problem of the Palestinians need not be solved necessarily in Palestine. At first he insisted with the Commission of Enquiry that there would be no land problem if Transjordan had not been cut off from Palestine.[63] He leaped at the suggestion of a British official that a transfer of the Arab population was desirable.[64]

Some radical solution must be found, and [Dr Shiels] didn't see why one should not really make Palestine a national home for the Jews and tell it frankly to the Arabs, pointing out that in Transjordan and Mesopotamia they had vast territories where they could work without let or hindrance . . .

Weizmann replied that a solution like that was a courageous and statesmanlike attempt to grapple with a problem that had been tackled hitherto half-heartedly; that if the Jews were allowed to develop their National Home in Palestine unhindered the Arabs would certainly not suffer — as they hadn't hitherto. Some might flow off into neighbouring countries, and this quasi exchange of population could be fostered and encouraged. It had been done with signal success under the aegis of the League of Nations in the case of the Greeks and Turks . . .

Pinhas Rutenberg assumed the task of preparing detailed proposals and met Colonial Office officials to discuss them. The main point was a proposed loan of £1 million, to be raised by Jewish sources, to help move Arab farmers to Transjordan.[65] Sidney Webb, however, refused even to consider this scheme.[66]

The suggestion of transfer played an important role in the discussion with the British on the solution of the crisis. The White Paper of 1930 had included proposals for a development scheme to assist and resettle landless peasants. This had been resisted by the Treasury which was against undertaking any major financial commitments in a time of world economic crisis.[67] Weizmann hoped to seize on the British difficulty to suggest that the Zionists raise the loan (which would be guaranteed by the British) if Transjordan were to be included in the plan for Jewish colonisation and resettlement of Arabs from Palestine.[68] In private discussions with the Prime Minister MacDonald and the Foreign Secretary Henderson, Weizmann suggested that a round table conference be called with the Arabs to deal *inter alia* with the question of Transjordan. He urged that 'the problem of the congested area Cis-Jordan could be solved by the development of, and migration of Arabs to Transjordania'.[69] Though these suggestions were not implemented they were indicative of Weizmann's attitude towards the Palestinians which lay at the roots also of his subsequent proposals in the 1936-9 crisis.

Weizmann and Bi-Nationalism

No less significant was Weizmann's opposition to negotiations with the Palestinians themselves for a political solution. Precisely at the time when the Arabs, who boycotted the 1922 legislative council proposal, were adopting a more moderate and conciliatory posture, Weizmann came out vehemently against the attempts of Dr Judah L. Magnes, a well-known bi-nationalist, to mediate with the Arabs. Through St John Philby, acting as an intermediary, the Palestine Arab Executive proposed a draft agreement along the following lines: Palestine to become an independent state; a representative legislature to be established with proportional voting; the High Commissioner to have veto powers and control internal security; immigration to be governed by the country's economic absorptive capacity.[1] The British High Commissioner, John Chancellor, was personally in favour of these proposals, and advised the Colonial Office to 'withdraw from the Jews their specially privileged position . . . and grant a measure of self-government'.[2]

Weizmann and the Zionist organisation were militantly opposed to the setting up of representative institutions in Palestine which they regarded as inimical to hopes for a Zionist state. 'Full self-government for the Arabs would mean annulling the Palestine Mandate'.[3] Weizmann believed that Magnes's intervention was 'fatal', asserting that the 'present Arab leaders, murderers and thieves, want but one thing – to drive us into the Mediterranean'.[4] Arab self-government would lead to 'the peace of the graveyard . . . so long as we have not obtained satisfactory guarantees that the Mandate and Declaration are going to be carried out . . . there is no use our opening negotiations. These guarantees can only be given by the British government and the League of Nations, certainly not by the Arabs.'[5] His reaction to Magnes borders on hysteria:

> We do not want to bow down before anybody or be ruled by anybody — enough of that! Now come the Magnes's, the Bergmans and break our united front, presenting matters as if we do not want peace . . . that Tartuffe, that hypocrite Magnes lightly abandons the Balfour Declaration. He did not bleed for it, he only gained by it! Believe me, I know the Palestinian Arabs. If we give way now, we might as well pack-up . . .[6]

Weizmann opposed both a bi-national state[7] and self-government, explaining that democracy was not appropriate for backward peoples: 'Constitutional government is not a panacea . . . in a country like Palestine "democracy" cannot be introduced by decree. In most non-European countries Parliamentary government has proved a sheer farce.'[8] According to Weizmann, this has special relevance to Palestine where: 'whatever Assembly is created, its Arab side will merely be a gathering of feudal effendis . . . They are too primitive . . . and too much under the influence of Bolshevik, Catholic agitation . . . to understand what we are bringing them.'[9] He cautioned that although

> we wish to spare the Arabs as much as we can of the sufferings which every backward race has gone through on the coming of another, more advanced nation . . . we must not be driven into the position where any Arab complaint is considered sufficient ground for impeding our work . . . a Jew must be able to buy land from an Arab . . . and must not be made responsible for what may or may not happen to the willing seller, or possibly to his grandchildren.[10]

The idea that Weizmann was in intellectual sympathy with bi-nationalism, put forward by Susan Lee Hattis, is inaccurate and represents a confusion between bi-nationalism and the idea of political parity.[11] One item of evidence cited by Hattis, and repeated by Walter Laqueur,[12] concerning Weizmann's attitude towards bi-nationalism, is a letter he wrote to Robert Weltsch in January 1924, stating that 'as for the general policy regarding the Arabs, you know my views, they coincide with yours, but we both know that it will take a long period of education before the Zionists settle down to realities'. In the next sentence he explains what 'realities' Zionists ignore:

Only today I received the health statistics from Palestine. The natural increase in the Arab population amounts to about 15,000 a year. The Jews brought in last year 10,000. *How can people possibly speak of ever forming a majority, and striving to obtain all that would follow from being a majority*, if they don't throw every ounce of energy which they possess, and every spark of idealism which still exists in them, in order to do the apostolic work of getting the necessary funds and forces together to give us a proper position in Palestine? This will remain always the central axis of my policy and everything else will be subordinated to this one view and to this one fact, which haunts me like a nightmare . . .[13]

The reference in this letter to the agreement with Weltsch on his views regarding policy on the Arabs does not refer to bi-nationalism (which had not yet been proposed), but to another problem, that of the proposed legislative council and Arab Agency, as is made clear by the previous correspondence between them.

Weltsch had written to Weizmann on 1 January 1924 that it would be preferable for Weizmann to give effect to the Zionist Action Committee resolution of October 1923 opposing the creation of an Arab agency similar to the Palestine Zionist Executive. Weizmann at this time supported the idea of a legislative council and an Arab agency in order to encourage moderate trends among the Arabs; he was in favour of directly negotiating mutual concessions − Arab acceptance of the Balfour Declaration in return for Zionists enabling the Arabs to have a real constitution.[14] But Weltsch pointed out that though Weizmann might consider the resolutions of the Action Committee mistaken, by faithfully implementing their resolutions, he would gain the Zionist movement's trust in his leadership and succeed more easily in guiding its inner and foreign policy. There was a need for propaganda and education of Zionists in the spirit of a policy favourable to the Executive. In the matter of relations with the Arabs, most of the Zionist public opposed Weizmann's approval of the legislative council.[15] The other item cited by Hattis, that in July 1927 Weizmann authorised a payment of £100 to Brith Shalom[16] is not really important as a measure of Weizmann's sympathy with bi-nationalism, since he allotted far larger funds to various types of work with the Arabs (including bribes).

The real test of Weizmann's attitude towards bi-nationalism came with the crisis after the 1929 riots. Hattis submits that Weizmann tried to press for a bi-national programme − calling it parity − after the

1929 riots, being discouraged only by the lack of response in the Arab community.[17] Both Walter Laqueur and Susan Hattis argue that 'there is no doubt that they [the official Zionist movement] would have felt obliged to take account of the activities of Magnes and the bi-nationalists if they had held out any promise at all'.[18] A more accurate version can be gathered from following the emergence of the idea of parity in Weizmann's thinking in 1929-30. This will show that he was opposed to the initiatives of the bi-nationalists for a constitutional settlement with the Arabs, precisely because the Arabs were moderate enough to be likely to agree to it and thereby preclude forever the possibility of a Jewish state. He conceived parity *as an alternative* to a legislative council which would lead to independence and self-government, and as a temporary stage which would allow the Mandate to remain in force. Parity was not a final aim, but a means to postponement of formulation of the final aim until Zionism was stronger.

The main support for the view that parity was identical with bi-nationalism comes from a letter from Weizmann to Robert Weltsch on 15 November 1929: 'As to the principles of future policy in Palestine and cooperation with the Arabs on bi-national lines, I have never swerved from it.' He added, however, that the 'Arab mind is not ripe at all for any negotiations, they are not producing arguments, but tricks'. He therefore opposed Weltsch's call for action, for negotiations with the Arabs, and for declarations: 'such a step at present would be fatal'.[19] Even in this letter Weizmann made clear his opposition to Magnes and his initiatives; 'Magnes behaved like a child in having agreed to everything before the Arabs said a word in our favour.' Over the next few months his opposition to the bi-nationalists became even stronger. Soon after writing to Weltsch, Weizmann wrote 'with a heavy heart' to Albert Einstein, who had publically criticised the attitude of the Zionist movement towards the conciliatory proposals of Brith Shalom:

> The Arabs would laugh at us if we were to make overtures today . . . a conflict is fabricated between you and us, simply because we do not want to negotiate with the murderers at the still open graves of the Hebron and Safad victims.
>
> Naturally Bergmann and Magnes and even you (and this grieves my soul!) are now quoted against us . . . the thing that makes my life most bitter is the feeling that our faith in ourselves and justice of our cause has been shaken.[20]

In a letter to Felix Warburg, a non-Zionist in the newly constituted

Jewish Agency, Weizmann explained his beliefs regarding a Jewish state:

> You seem to accuse us Zionists of pressing for a Jewish state although we don't say so openly, that we ignore the White Paper [of 1922], in short, that we are political hypocrites. I would like to be explicit about that as well as about the other things. *If a Jewish state were possible I would be strongly for it.* I am not for it because I consider it unrealisable. If Palestine were an empty country, the Jewish state would have come about, whether we want it or not. Palestine, being what it is, the Jewish state will not come about — *unless some fundamental change takes place which I cannot envisage at present.* The propaganda which is carried out in certain Zionist circles, like the Revisionists, for a Jewish state, is foolish and harmful, but it cuts no ice, and you could just as well ask for a Jewish state in Manhattan Island. The Balfour Declaration speaks of a National Home. So does the Mandate. Opinions may be divided on the subject of how large this National Home can be, whether it will hold half a million, a million, or two million Jews, but whatever it will be, it won't be a Jewish state.[21]

This letter contains the genesis of Weizmann's proposals 'fundamentally to change' the situation in Palestine later in that same year — the transfer proposals referred to earlier. Weizmann also made clear that his final aim— his desired solution — was a Jewish state, not a bi-national state, but that what blocked it was the Arab population of Palestine ('not an empty country').

Weizmann explained his opposition to a bi-national state in a letter the next day to Louis Marshall, President of the American Jewish Committee. Part of this letter is again quoted out of context by Hattis to prove Weizmann's support for bi-nationalism: 'Now we should be content with a bi-national state, provided it was truly bi-national.'[22] This is not a positive commitment of support, as Hattis seems to indicate, but part of an historical survey of the deterioration of the scope permitted to the Zionist enterprise, and should be read 'Now [they say] we should be content with a bi-national state . . .' as the next sentence makes clear:

> But once the firm ground of the Jewish state was abandoned, the picture became blurred; the idea of a Jewish state could be easily understood, just as the meaning of the status quo — a cancelling of

the Balfour Declaration and Mandate — would require no interpretation. But equality in rights between partners as yet very
unequal in numbers required careful thought and constant watching;
one is there already in full strength while of the other so far a vanguard has reached it. The Arabs are the 'beati possidentes', while we
have to defend the rights of those 'qui ont toujours tort'. The forces
of inertia work in favor of the Arabs, and thoughts which run in
primary grooves cut across and undermine the foundations of that
thing to come, our National Home in Palestine. While we accept the
principle of equality between Jews and Arabs in the future Palestinian state, the Arabs press for having that State constituted
immediately, because circumstances would enable them to distort
it into an Arab dominion from which no path would lead back to
real equality [Weizmann to Marshall, 17 Jan. 1930].

It has been urged that Weizmann was in favour of bi-nationalism, but
that 'there was no political force in the Arab camp willing to co-operate
on the basis of the minimum conditions outlined by Magnes and his
friends'.[23] Hattis adds that the Zionist Executive rejected the Magnes-
Philby proposals when 'Kaplanski . . . received information from the
Labour Party in London that Philby had no authority and was regarded
in Labour circles as an adventurer journalist who was apparently trying
to initiate a certain Jewish-Arab understanding in order to impress the
Colonial Office. Dr Weizmann was informed by Sir John Shuckburgh
that Philby had no connection with the Colonial Office. The Zionist
Executive was not in that period inclined to act in opposition to the
Colonial Office, with which it was still on good terms, but had Philby
had real authority from any representative Arab to negotiate with the
Zionists, this attitude would have been inexcusable.'[24]

But the fact that Philby was no longer an employee of the British
Government had nothing to do with the question whether the Arab
overtures were genuine. Philby had drafted his final proposals after
'spending the whole morning at the offices of the Supreme Moslem
Council in conversation with Haj Amin al Husseini, the Grand Mufti
of Jerusalem, and a number of his chief lieutenants'.[25] The Philby-
Magnes proposals were similar to proposals for a legislative council
that were secretly put forward by the head of the Arab Executive,
Musa Kazim al Husseini, a few months before the riots.[26] The High
Commissioner personally supported the proposals for a legislative
council and representative self-government, both before and after the
1929 riots.[27] The Arab position did represent, as Magnes claimed[28]

(and as we pointed out before) a significant change from 1922: they did not demand the abrogation of the Balfour Declaration and the Mandate, and they accepted the veto power of the High Commissioner and immigration according to economic absorptive capacity.[29] Even Sharett later admitted that after 1929 the moderate trend gained the upper hand among the Palestinians.[30]

Weizmann, however, viewed this new and moderate trend in Palestinian nationalism, with grave suspicion:

> They wish a National Government, in order that they should become Ministers, who would run the show in Palestine, leaving to the British a shadowy position in the form of a veto, which might or might not be exercised by the High Commissioner. Such a Parliament, and such a government, would naturally pass legislation which would render our position untenable after the first few months. It is possible that if we would agree to it we might have peace for some time, but it would be the peace of the graveyard. Possibly the Arabs might give lip service and recognition of the Balfour Declaration and even of the Mandate, but if they control immigration, land, legislation in general, there is not the earthly chance for the realization of our desires.[31]

The claim that Dr Weizmann was intellectually inclined to bi-nationalism rests basically on his support for political parity between Jews and Arabs regardless of numbers from 1930 to 1936. But this confuses means with aims. The bi-nationalists saw as their *final aim* a bi-national state of Palestine, in opposition to those who wanted to formulate the final aim of Zionism as a Jewish state. Weizmann was opposed to the formulation of the final aim as a Jewish state, but for tactical reasons.

The Idea of Parity

In 1930 Weizmann began to sense that the odds were against him. The Labour Government and Lord Passfield (Sidney Webb) in particular, rejected Weizmann's proposals for transfer and resolved to conciliate the Arabs by proceeding with the plan for a legislative council and by slowing down drastically the development of the national home until the problem of landless Arabs was solved. The Zionist movement was then in the grip of a deep moral and financial crisis. The Jewish settlement suffered from unemployment and emigration. The Zionist movement was unable to recruit new elements for a revival of the pioneering effort and for a renewal of immigration. In these circumstances Weizmann decided to avert the worst by saving what could be saved.

It was at this point that Weizmann came to beat a tactical retreat and to endorse the idea of parity (equality in government between Jews and Arabs despite their actual numbers[32]), *as an alternative* to representative self-government with an Arab majority. In a letter in July 1930, to Magnes, he wrote: 'I agree some beginning on the road to self-government would have to be made, but it must be on the principle of parity between Jews and Arabs.'[33] Weizmann argued to the Zionist Inner Action Committee that 'it is not true that a Jewish state and Zionism are one and the same thing . . . perhaps we can have peace with the Arabs if our set aim were formulated. This set aim is however not a Jewish state nor a majority which will administer a minority in the land'.[34] He convinced Mapai (the Labour Party, the largest in Palestine) to support the idea of parity.[35]

Mapai adopted the formula of political parity but did not regard it as a programme for active policy and did not try to have it endorsed by the Zionist movement. (This was later to become an issue between Weizmann and the Palestinian Zionist Executive when the next crisis with the Arabs occurred.) Weizmann was desperately striving to devise means of opposition against the increasingly hostile attitude of the British Government expressed in the Passfield White Paper of October 1930,[36] which recommended the restriction of Jewish immigration and settlement in Palestine because of shortage of land for Arab peasants.[37] Weizmann resigned from the Jewish Agency as a protest, and intense international pressure to annul the White Paper was applied.[38]

Under the threat that the British would abandon support for Zionist immigration, Weizmann, with his tactical flexibility, sought a way out of the impasse that would prevent a direct confrontation between the Zionist movement (weakened and without prospects for mass immigration) and the British Government. It was under these circumstances that Weizmann persuaded the Basle Zionist Congress, meeting in Basle in July 1931, to reaffirm the principle of non-domination.[39] But in a press interview he went beyond this point and denounced the demand for a Jewish majority in Palestine.

> I have no sympathy for, and no understanding of, the demand for a Jewish majority in Palestine. Majority does not guarantee security, majority is not necessary for the development of Jewish civilization and culture. The world will construe this demand only in the sense that we want to achieve a majority in order to drive out the Arabs.[40]

This statement was repudiated by the Congress, which led to Weizmann's resignation from the Presidency of the World Zionist Organisation until 1935.

In retrospect it was precisely Weizmann's radical change of tactics at this period that saved the Zionist movement from collapse. The British Government, unsure of its ground, and fearing a total break with Weizmann, and the collapse of his leadership in the Zionist movement, annulled *de facto* the Passfield White Paper by publishing the MacDonald Letter of February 1931, in which the Prime Minister denied that the government was contemplating any prohibition of the 'acquisition of additional land by Jews' or 'of Jewish immigration in any of its categories'.[41] While this did not save Weizmann from defeat at the World Zionist Organisation, it did preserve the continuity of British co-operation with Zionism. This proved vital when in a few years, the rise of Nazism in Germany produced a massive wave of immigration to Palestine. In 1935 over 60,000 Jews came to Palestine, and Zionist leaders again became optimistic that no political concessions were necessary, as natural forces were working in their favour.[42]

It should be noted that the tactics of concessions proposed by Weizmann were aimed at stopping the erosion of British commitment to the Mandate rather than at an agreement with the Palestinians. To save British support for the Zionist enterprise, to prevent the growing opposition of British politicians and public opinion to the use of force in order to proceed with the implementation of the Mandate, it was necessary to achieve some degree of reconciliation with the Arabs. London, not Jerusalem, was the centre of political struggle, in the hope that the dream of a Jewish State as member of the British Commonwealth would one day become a reality.

Conclusions

Weizmann's attitude towards the Palestinians was the gravest error of his political leadership, more serious than any other because Weizmann did not deviate from his attitude for even a brief period. His disdain for the Palestinians originated not only in the fact that lacking previous contact with them, he was influenced by his British advisers. From the very beginning, he approached the Palestinians with a prejudice that blinded him to the most obvious facts.

He must have known of the existence of the Palestinian people and their opposition to Zionist colonisation, because as early as 1891, his spiritual mentor and close associate, Ahad Ha'am, had warned of major Arab resistance to Jewish immigration and settlement. Ahad

Ha'am had no solution to the problem, but urged that at least it be taken seriously. To lessen the conflict, he suggested prudent behaviour, just treatment and respect for Arab customs and culture. Weizmann followed Ahad Ha'am's guidance in his relations with all Arabs except the Palestinians; with regard to them, he listened to Aaron Aaronsohn, who viewed the Palestinians as backward, treacherous and corrupt.

It is safe to assume that Weizmann knew of the Palestinian opposition to Zionism during the Ottoman Empire, especially as this took on a pronounced political character upon the establishment of a Parliament, following the Young Turk Revolution of 1908, in which all national groups were represented. The Arab faction in the Turkish Parliament conducted a political campaign against Zionist plans to obtain a charter for a Jewish national home in Palestine.

Even then, two opposing Zionist orientations towards the Arab problem had emerged, which were to serve as prototypes for future positions. After the events of 1908, the Zionists were aware of the coming conflict between the Arabs and the Turks. On the one hand, in 1909 Jabotinsky proposed a Zionist alliance with Turkey to preserve the Ottoman Empire against dismemberment by Arab nationalism. At that time, the Arab population of the Ottoman Empire, at 10 to 11 million, was greater than the Turkish population of 7 to 8 million; and the Arabs were well represented in the highest echelons of the Turkish civil, religious and military administration. Jabotinsky suggested using the argument that massive Jewish colonisation in Palestine would dilute the homogeneity of the Arab sector. On the other hand, Victor Jacobson, the Zionist representative in Constantinople, conceived the idea of a Jewish-Arab detente against Turkish rule, based on mutual support of the national aspirations of the two groups.[1] Weizmann assimilated both trends in his political strategy, trying to come to terms with the Arab revolt against Turkey and at the same time offering Zionism to the British, as a means of 'breaking the Arab Belt from Morocco to Damascus'.[2]

It is possible that Weizmann was unaware of the important role the Palestinians played in Arab politics. The existence of a Palestinian national entity was obscured by the fact that the Palestinians had no ambition for an independent political future but saw themselves as eventually an integral part of a united Arab state. In this respect, they were like the Arabs in Syria, Iraq and the Arabian Peninsula. Their conception of Palestine as part of Syria (southern Syria) did not mean that they regarded themselves as Syrians. They identified with Syrian nationalism because in the Arab world, the Syrians were viewed as the carriers of Arab nationalism. In this context, it should be noted that in later years when Antun Sa'adih formulated a theory of Syrian nationalism based on the *non-Arab* historical heritage of Syria, he made a considerable impact in Syria and Lebanon but found few supporters in Palestine.

Together with Iraqis, Syrians and Meccans, the Palestinians strove for an Arab state extending from Turkey to the Persian Gulf. In the secret societies founded at the beginning of the twentieth century, which prepared the ideological and political ground for Arab nationalism, Palestinian Arabs played a prominent role. Jamal Husseini of Jerusalem was a member of 'al Muntada al Arabi', the literary club founded in Constantinople in 1909 by Arab officials and men of letters. Salim Abdul Hadi (Jenin), Hafez al Said (Jaffa) and Ali Nashashibi (Jerusalem) were members of the Ottoman Decentralisation Party, founded in 1912 and organised along modern political lines. Two of them were hanged by the Turks for treasonable nationalistic activities during the First World War. Auni Abdul Hadi (who accompanied Faisal to the Paris Peace Conference in 1919 and later founded the Palestinian 'Istiklal' Party) and Rafik Tamimi of Nablus were among the seven founders of 'Al Fatah' (the Young Arab Society), which was the most important secret society. It was instrumental in organising the Arab Revolt of 1916, and only in 1919 revealed its existence and transformed itself into a political party under the name of Hizb Al Arabi (the Party of Arab Independence).[3]

Another Palestinian, Najib Azouri, was one of the first to formulate a national and revolutionary programme. His views appeared in *Le Reveil de la Nation Arabe*, a book published in Paris in 1905. In this work he advocated a revolt against the Turks and the establishment of an Arab Empire stretching from the Tigris and Euphrates to the Mediterranean, Sinai and the Persian Gulf, but without Egypt 'whose inhabitants are not of the Arab race'. Azouri was the first to proclaim the inevitability of a Jewish-Arab confrontation on the outcome of which the destiny of the Middle East would depend. He saw Palestine as the centre of the struggle which would determine the fate of Arab nationalism. Later, Azouri changed his views and spoke favourably of the prospect of Jewish financial and technical help to the Arabs.

It was only when the plan for a consolidated Arab state collapsed and gave way to French and British Mandates over Syria, Lebanon, Iraq, Palestine and Transjordan, that the Palestinian Arabs began to develop a programme for an independent Arab Palestine and to foster an independent national movement.

The idea of Arab unity had a strong appeal for all Arabs since Arab unity coincided with the period in history of the highest achievement of the Arabs. However, the degree of identification and the motivation for adherence to the ideal differed in the various sections of the Arab national movement.

The Sheriffians, who did not represent a people but rather a distinguished family which, claiming its descent from the Prophet, was keeper of the most Holy Place of Islam, and had contacts throughout the Moslem world, were motivated by the desire to play a leading role in restoring the glorious Arab past. They were not attached to any particular territory. Faisal himself described Hedjaz as a 'barren, valueless land' and stated that only in Syria, 'the granary of the Middle East and hereditary seat of the Umayyid Caliphate', could his ambitions be fulfilled.[4] The propensity of the Palestinians for pan-Arabism was different. They represented a people with deep roots in the soil. Although Palestine was administratively divided in the Ottoman Empire, the people had a vague national consciousness, based on a feeling of collective destiny. This came to the surface at the same time as the beginning of Zionist colonisation. Ironically, Palestinian nationalism owes its birth to Zionism, for it was the impact of Zionist colonisation on the economic and social structure of the Palestinian people which brought Palestinian nationalism into being.

The pan-Arab (southern Syria) formula was a means of preserving Palestinian identity. Numbering only a half million, the Palestinians felt unable to confront alone the Jewish people, who outnumbered them 20 to 1 and commanded massive financial resources and international influence. This explains the shifts in the Palestinians' attitude toward the Sheriffians: their initial suspicion and opposition to Faisal's inclination to bargain wtih the Zionists at their expense; and then their enthusiastic support for his rule when he became the symbol of Arab unity, carried along by the nationalist ferment. At that time, Haj Amin al Husseini, who later became the most prominent leader of the Palestinians and an enemy of the Hashemite Dynasty (as represented by Faisal's brother Emir Abdullah of Transjordan), was a staunch supporter of the Sheriffians (until the collapse of the independent Arab Kingdom).[5]

Perhaps Weizmann might not have been aware of all this before he arrived in Palestine at the head of the Zionist Commission. But he was certainly able to witness the growth of Palestinian opposition to Zionism and the eruption of violent disturbances was clear proof of the intensity of Palestinian feeling, even after discounting the encouragement the Palestinians received from the anti-Zionist British Military Administration. Weizmann knew that the Palestinians were not a monolithic bloc hostile to Zionism. The very fact that he tried to set up Arab opposition parties, exploiting religious divisions and urban-rural conflicts proves that he believed that there existed a range of Palestinian political attitudes. But he elected to appeal solely to the elements out for personal gain — to the worst in Arab society. He complained that the Palestinians were a demoralised race, yet he was not averse to contributing to their demoralisation.[6]

Evidently, what was at the back of Weizmann's mind was the idea of the transfer of the Palestinian Arab population to neighbouring countries. He had the prudence not to make this stand public, but the transfer idea played a much greater role in Zionist thinking in the Mandatory Period than is usually admitted. It is true that on occasions Weizmann and other Zionist leaders reaffirmed their respect for the rights of the Palestinians, and expressed the opinion that the Palestinians would not be dispossessed, but would benefit from Zionist colonisation. 'In its nature it must benefit the whole country, otherwise we cannot be here.'[7] At the same time, schemes for transfer cropped up repeatedly in Zionist deliberations on Arab opposition in Palestine. These plans were suggested as feelers in negotiations with the British, though there was no mention of them in public announcements.

Weizmann and others rejected the argument that the idea of transfer of populations was immoral.[8] The example of the transfer of population between Greece and Turkey under the auspices of the League of Nations was offered as precedent for a rational and wise solution to the Arab-Jewish conflict.[9] It is not by accident that the idea of transfer was incorporated into the plan for the partition of Palestine in 1937. For reasons of political expediency, the Zionist leaders dissociated themselves from such plans when proposed by Zionist extremists, but the plans were nevertheless discussed within Zionist councils (see also the debate on transfer, in Chapter 7, Part Two).

The period from 1921 to 1935 offered many opportunities for the Zionist movement to try to come to terms with the Palestinians. Even the most anti-Zionist Palestinian leaders were at times considering realistic solutions, while the emergence of powerful opposition parties based on new development in Arab society, offered much room for manoeuvre. But an accommodation demanded that Palestine aspirations for national independence and self-government (similar to those in other Arab countries at the time) be met, at least gradually. Weizmann's attitude precluded this from the beginning. He accepted political parity as a tactical move during times of crisis to counteract the pressure on the British to grant representative self-government, but abandoned it as soon as the pressure was reduced. It was a temporary measure to overcome moments of the weakening of British support of Zionism and not a long-term basis for reconciliation with the Arabs.

Weizmann was sincere in his desire for a just solution to the conflict with the Palestinians. But his non-recognition of the Palestinians as a national entity could not but lead to a policy of injustice. When he stated that 'the conflict between us and the Arabs is not one of right against wrong, but a conflict between two rights', he did not have in mind the rights of the Palestinians but the rights of Arab nationalism in general. Consequently, when he said that 'Jewish right has precedence over Arab right because a Jewish homeland in Palestine is a question of life and death for the Jewish people, while the loss of less than 1 per cent of their territory is not decisive for the future of the Arabs', he ignored the fact that for those who lived in Palestine it *was* decisive.

Unfortunately, Weizmann's legacy in this most vital aspect of Jewish-Arab relations has had a more lasting impact than any other. The very definition applied by the Israeli Government to those Palestinians who returned after their flight in 1948 — 'present absentees' — is part of this legacy. The Palestinians were never regarded as an *integral* part of the country for whom long-term plans had to be made, either in the Mandatory period or since the establishment of the state. This explains why the Palestinian problem has remained at the heart of the Israeli-Arab conflict until the present day.

Notes

INTRODUCTION

1. Michael Brecher, *The Foreign Policy System of Israel* (London, 1972).
2. Abba Eban, 'Introduction', to *Trial and Error*, the autobiography of Chaim Weizmann (New York, 1966).
3. Weizmann to Sieff, 13 January 1919, Weizmann Archives, Rehovoth.
4. 'The backbone of our work is and must always be agricultural colonization. It is in the village that the real soul of the people — its language, its poetry, its literature, its traditions — springs up from the intimate contact between man and soil.' (Weizmann, *Trial and Error*, p. 346.) 'He watched with growing exultation the steady development of village life in Palestine and in particular of the collective settlements, which he thought the best form for training of newcomers to the land', and 'most able to establish and maintain itself in remote and unsettled parts of the country. The solitary settler or the small village of independent farmers could not have existed in the conditions prevailing [in Palestine]' (ibid., p. 370).

5.   Weizmann regretted 'the fierce struggle [which has] developed in Zionism between what [he] considered [a] premature emphasis on private enterprise and profit and the laying of national foundations' (ibid., p. 340).

6.   'It was my job to preach . . . the hard doctrine that the Balfour Declaration was no more than a framework which had to be filled by our own efforts. It would mean exactly what we would make it mean — neither more nor less. On what we would make it mean, through slow, costly and laborious work, would depend whether and when we should deserve or attain statehood' (ibid., p. 302).

7.   Moshe Sharett, *Political Diaries*, vol. II, 1937 (Tel Aviv, 1973).

8.   Chaim Weizmann, *Trial and Error* (London, 1949), p. 566.

THE 'BRITISH CONNECTION'

1.   Leonard Stein, *The Balfour Declaration* (London, 1961) is still the pre-eminent work, but see also Isaiah Friedman, *Question of Palestine 1914-1918* (New York, 1973); Frichswasser-Ra'anan, *The Frontiers of a Nation* (London, 1955); Mayir Verete, 'The Balfour Declaration and its Makers', *Middle Eastern Studies*, vol. 6, no. 1, Jan. 1970; D. Z. Gillon, 'The Antecedents of the Balfour Declaration', *Middle Eastern Studies* (Frank Cass reprint), May 1969.

2.   Weizmann to Levin, October 1914, quoted in Blanche Dugdale, *Arthur James Balfour 1906-1930* (London, 1930), p. 164.

3.   Weizmann to Zangwill, 10.10.1914 Letter No. 22, *The Collected Letters of Chaim Weizmann*, Vol. III, pp. 25-9.

4.   First interview with Balfour, quoted in Dugdale, *Arthur James Balfour*, p. 165.

5.   Weizmann to C.P. Scott, 16.2.1915, Letter 121, *Collected Letters*, pp. 154-5.

6.   Weizmann to Israel Rosoff, 21 Nov. 1917, unpublished correspondence, Weizmann Archives, Rehovoth, Israel; see also Weizmann to Rothschild, 12 Nov. 1922.

7.   Weizmann was unaware of Sykes' agreement with the French (Picot). 'Sir Mark . . . gave us his fullest support without even telling us of the existence [of the] agreement . . . it was not from him that we learned of [its] existence . . . and months passed — months during which we carried on our negotiations with the British and other authorities — before we understood what it was that blocked our progress' (Weizmann, *Trial and Error* (London, 1949), p. 238).

8.   The best account of Sykes-Picot is Jukka Nevakivi, *Britain, France and the Middle East 1914-1920* (London, 1969), ch. 2.

9.   Sykes to Hankey, 8 April 1917, Sykes Papers, Sledmere Collection, St Antony's College, Oxford. For the Cabinet decision to try to modify Sykes-Picot, see Imperial War Cabinet, Committee on Terms of Peace, April 1917: 'It is of great importance that Palestine be under British control.'

10.   FO 371/3053, 25 April 1917, interview with Ronald Campbell. This interview throws an interesting sidelight on Weizmann's gradualism: on being told the French would get Galilee, he replied that in any case it would take some time to colonise Judea, after that, 'they would have a strong case for overrunning Galilee'.

11.   Isaiah Friedman, *The Question of Palestine 1914-1918* (New York, 1973), pp. 211-17.

12.   FO 371/3052 F.O. to Sykes 28.4.17.

13.   'Communications of the Zionist Organization in 1917', MIIF (British Military Intelligence), 1 Feb. 1918.

14.   Ibid.

15.   Weizmann to Sokolow, 1 May 1917; Sokolow to Weizmann, 4 May 1917, FO 371/83053.

16.   David Ben-Gurion, 'Chaim Weizmann – Champion of the Jewish People' in *Chaim Weizmann: Statesman of the Jewish Renaissance* (Jerusalem, 1974), pp. 12-13.

17.   Dan Gillon, 'The Antecedents of the Balfour Declaration', *Middle Eastern Studies*, pp. 131-50 (May, 1969).

18.   Minutes of meeting of Prime Ministers of UK and Dominions, 13 Aug. 1918, CAB 23/43; Minutes of Imperial War Cabinet, 20 Dec. 1918, both quoted in Nevakivi, *Britain, France and the Middle East*, pp. 95-7. Lloyd George also favoured American involvement for a period. There were no lack of dissenting voices for playing 'the Zionist card'; for example Lord Hardinge of the Foreign Office:

> Every Zionist with whom I have discussed the question, Baron James de Rothschild, Dr. Weizmann, Mr. Sidebotham of the *Manchester Guardian* etc etc (and I believe Sir Mark Sykes and others who have had similar discussions have enjoyed the same experience) insist that the Zionist idea is based entirely on a British Palestine. They are unanimous in their opinion that the project would break down were Palestine to be internationalized . . .
>
> At the present moment we are encouraging Dr. Weizmann to leave his business here and to proceed to Egypt. Further, Baron James de Rothschild and Dr. Weizmann are telegraphing to Judge Brandeis, the well-known Jewish leader in America, suggesting to him to convene a representative meeting of American Jews to pass a resolution that Palestine should be handed over to Great Britain to administer. This may strengthen our position in the matter or it may provoke and solidify French opposition. But the point I desire to raise is whether we are justified in going so far in encouragement of the Zionist movement, based on a British Palestine, without giving the Zionists some intimation of the existing arrangements with the French . . . otherwise the odium of the failure of the Zionist project will fall entirely on us. [FO 371/3052, 21 April 1917.]

19.   Sykes to Graham, 8 May 1917 FO 371/83053.

20.   'Memorandum on Asia Minor Agreement' (by Sykes), 14 August 1917 FO 371/3059/159558; see also Sykes to Hankey, 14 Nov. 1917.

21.   'Communications of Zionist Organization', MIIF.

22.   Quoted in Ingrams, p. 22.

23.   Weizmann to Young, 2 July 1920, Letters, Weizmann Archive, Rehovoth, Israel.

24.   Minutes of the Third Session of the Zionist Commission, 22 March 1918, quoted in Jon Kimche, *Palestine or Israel* (London, 1973), p. 134. Sieff's reaction quoted from private interview, p. 135.

25.   Appendix 10 to the Minutes of the Fourth Session of the Zionist Commission, 27 March 1918. Conference at Shepard's Hotel, Cairo.

26.   Speech at the Round Table Talks, London, 8 Feb. 1939.

27.   Writing about Justice Felix Frankfurter (legal adviser to the Zionist delegation at the Peace Conference 1919), Weizmann admitted: 'he was quick, intelligent, scintillating, many-sided in contrast to myself, who have little interest in affairs outside Zionism and chemistry' (*Letters and Papers*, p. 309).

28.   Weizmann to C.P. Scott, 16.2.15, *The Letters and Papers of Chaim Weizmann*, vol. VII (Oxford University Press, 1968), pp. 154-5, no. 121.

29.   Weizmann to C.P. Scott 23.3.15, ibid., no. 147, p. 185.

30.   Weizmann to Kisch, 21.12.26. See also Weizmann to Rutenberg and Neumann, 9.11.24. Weizmann interview with Gilbert Clayton, 7 Nov. 1922; Weizmann to Marshall, 17.7.24: 'The British have to learn to protect the jugular vein of British Empire'.

31.   It is interesting to read Weizmann's impression from a visit to South Africa (op. cit., pp. 727-30). Not a single line is devoted to the problem of the black majority and apartheid. His interest is focused on the Jewish Community and the game reserve ('. . . animals in game reserve have . . . ideal conditions; they have no Arab problem').

32.   Weizmann, 'The position in Palestine', *Palestine Papers*, no. 2, pp. 24-5 (Jewish Agency for Palestine, London, 1929-30).

33.   Weizmann to Warburg, 16 Jan. 1930.

34.   8 Feb. 1939 quoted in Ben-Gurion, *My Talks with Arab Leaders* (Jerusalem, 1972), pp. 211-13.

35.   Weizmann to Vera Weizmann, 29.3.20.

36.   Ibid.

37.   Weizmann to FO, 13 April 1920. FO 371/5117 E.3180/85/44. The Military Administration would not allow this cable to be sent from Palestine and it had to be sent via Cairo.

38.   Weizmann to Young, 2 July 1920; see also Weizmann to Vera Weizmann, 21 March 1920.

39.   General Congreve to GOC Palestine, CO733/7; Report of the Court of Inquiry convened by Order of H.E. the High Commissioner and Commander-in-Chief, dated the 12th of April 1920, FO 371/5121, particularly pp. 20-30. See also Director of Military Intelligence, 'Some notes on the situation in Turkey', CAB24/108, 21 June 1920: 'There is general unwillingness of British troops to support Zionism.'

40.   Cf. his statement of policy on becoming High Commissioner, 3 June 1921, CAB 24/107.

41.   Weizmann to Vera Weizmann, 25 April 1920.

42.   Samuel to Weizmann, 10 Aug. 1921.

43.   FO 371/6376.

44.   Weizmann to Balfour, 30.5.18.

45.   Weizmann to Zionist Bureau, London, 25.3.20.

46.   Round Table Conference 8-17 Feb. 1939, quoted in Ben-Gurion, *My Talks with Arab Leaders*, p. 212.

47.   For example Curzon, who wrote in 1923 'Reliance on the Arabs is a policy fraught with considerable danger . . . I feel by no means confident that we could permanently count on Arab friendship; our difficulties in Iraq, which no one can attribute to Zionism should warn us.' Quoted in Elie Kedourie, *The Chatham House Version* (London, 1970), p. 79.

48.   Quoted in Blanche Dugdale, *Arthur James Balfour*, p. 168.

49.   Clayton to Walford, 3 March 1924, FO 800/156.

50.   The reason for the erosion of Britain's commitment was frankly stated in 1923:

It may be too much to hope that we can ever satisfy the Palestinian Arabs; but so long as the general body of Arab opinion is not against us, the dangers arising from local dissatisfaction ought not to be serious . . . the real alternative, therefore, seems to be between complete evacuation, on the one hand, and, on the other, the continuance of the policy as laid down in the [1922] White Paper.

Memo by the Secretary of State of the Colonies on Policy in Palestine, CAB 24/159 Jan. 1923 quoted in Ingrams, p. 174.

51.   Cmd. 1700, June 1922, quoted in Ingrams, 'Palestine Papers', Documents 1917-22 (London (1972)), pp. 164-7.

52.   Speech at the Zurich Congress, August 1937, quoted in *New Judea*. Aug.-Sept. 1937.

53.   Weizmann to Zionist Bureau, 25.3.20.

THE 'HASHEMITE CONNECTION'

1.   Isaiah Berlin, *Chaim Weizmann, Statesman of the Jewish Renaissance* (Confrontation Series), p. 74.

2.   'Sir Mark [Sykes] . . . believed that the Arabs would come to terms with us – particularly if they received Jewish support . . . Sir Mark anticipated the attitude of the greatest of the Arabs, the Emir Faisal', Weizmann, *Trial and Error*, p. 240.

3.   Weizmann to Louis Marshall, 17 January 1930.

4.   The Arab Bureau was a British military intelligence operation, based in Cairo, which had made for itself a role in policy-making by its sponsorship of the Arab Revolt. Headed by D.G. Hogarth, it included General Clayton, Col. Symes, Dawney, Storrs, T.E. Lawrence and Cornwallis; closely associated were Sir Reginald Wingate, British High Commissioner in Egypt and the Sudan, and Sir Mark Sykes, Foreign Office Near East representative. It was primarily a group of brilliant amateurs. See Storrs, *Orientations* (London: Nicholson & Watson, 1943), p. 154. It should be noted that British policy lines operated independently of each other, e.g. the India Office had responsibility for Iraq.

5.   FO 371/3399/35210 (30 Jan. 1918).

6.   Weizmann to Brandeis, 14 Jan. 1918.

7.   The McMahon-Hussein correspondence, a subject of controversy ever since. The British promised to 'uphold the independence of the Arabs' reserving the 'districts lying to the West of Damascus, Homs, Aleppo, and Hanna' for consideration with their other Allies. George Antonius, *The Arab Awakening* (London, 1938), pp. 413-27.

8.   Clayton to Sykes, DV 588/25 Nov. 28 1917, Sledmere Papers.

9.   FO to Wingate, 2 Nov. 1917, FO 371/3054.

10.   Clayton to Sykes, 15 Dec. 1917. Clayton Papers, Sudan Archive, Durham University, D147/1.

11.   Clayton to Wingate, 20 Dec. 1917, ibid.

12.   Clayton to Wilson, 17 Dec. 1917, FO 882/3.

13.   Quoted in M. Pearlman, 'Arab-Jewish Diplomacy 1918-1922', *Jewish Social Studies*, April 1944, p. 130.

14.   Reported by William Yale, American State Department agent in the Middle East (Intelligence Report No. 5, Dec. 1917, William Yale Papers, Yale University, New Haven, Connecticut).

15.   Sykes to Faisal, 3 March 1918, FO 882/3.

16.   Al-Qibla, 23 March 1918 (quoted in Pearlman, 'Jewish Diplomacy', p. 131).

17.   Weizmann to C.P. Scott, 20.3.1917 (*The Collected Letters of Chaim Weizmann*, vol. VII, pp. 344-5, letter 321).

18.   Weizmann to Frankfurter, 17.8.1917 (*Collected Letters*, p. 489).

19.   Weizmann to Balfour, 31.5.1918 FO 371/3395/4313.

20.   Clayton Memorandum, 18.5.1918, Clayton Papers.

21.   Clayton to Symes, 13.6.1918, Wingate Papers, 'Weizmann's recent visits instigated by me . . .'

22.   Dawney to Joyce, 27 May 1918 (Sledmere Papers DS 244/4): 'I saw Weizmann in Jerusalem very anxious to see Faisal and talk over Zionism.'

23.   Even 30 years later Weizmann held on to this view. 'The first meeting with Faisal in the desert laid the foundations of a life-long friendship . . . our negotations crystallized into an agreement drawn up by Colonel Lawrence and signed by the Emir and myself . . . Thus the leader of the Arab world who . . . initiated a new period of Arab revival came to a complete understanding with us and would have no doubt carried out this understanding . . . if his destiny

had shaped as we expected . . . it would' (Weizmann, *Trial and Error*, p. 244).

24.   'Interview between Dr. Weizmann and Sheriff Faisal on 4th June 1918 at Wahaida. Captain Ormsby-Gore unfortunately unable to attend due to illness.' Handwritten minutes by P. Joyce, FO 882/14.

25.   As he told the Palestine Royal Commission in 1936; quoted in Pearlman, p. 133.

26.   Clayton to Balfour, 1 July 1918 Clayton Papers.

27.   Wingate to Wigram, 17 June 1918 Clayton Papers.

28.   Weizmann to Balfour, 17 July 1918 FO 371/3398/138908.

29.   Interview between Dr Weizmann and Sheriff Faisal on 4 June 1918, ibid. Joyce's accompanying letter states 'my private opinion Faisal really welcomed Jewish co-operation and considered it essential to future Arab ambitions . . . one great point in common is outside Arabs and Jews no one has a territorial claim on Syria.'

30.   Note by Symes, Ramleh, 13 June 1918. Sudan Archive 148/10 Wingate Papers.

31.   Weizmann to Vera Weizmann, 17 June 1918. Cf. Clayton to Gertrude Bell, 17 June 1918.

32.   Weizmann to Zangwill, 15.2.1923; to Zion Executive 3.3.1920; to Balfour 30.5.1918.

33.   Clayton to Wilson, 18 April 1917 FO 882/12.

34.   Memo by Clayton, 3 April 1917 FO 882/16.

35.   Clayton to Sykes, 28 Nov. 1917 Sledmere Papers DV 558/25.

36.   Clayton to Sykes, 4 Feb. 1918 FO 371/3398/36757.

37.   Clayton to Balfour, 1 July 1918 FO 371/3398/123904.

38.   Clayton to Balfour, 21 Sept. 1918 FO 371/3384.

39.   Aharon Cohen, *Israel and the Arab World* (London, 1970), p. 135.

40.   First Report of Zionist Commission to Zionist Executive, 19 April 1918.

41.   FO 882/13, 18 June 1918.

42.   Symes Memorandum, 13 June 1918, Durham 148/10. (Italics added.)

43.   'The Capture of Damascus', Elie Kedourie, *The Chatham House Version* (London, 1970), pp. 33-47.

44.   Howard Sacher, *The Emergence of the Middle East 1914-24* (London, 1969), pp. 262-3.

45.   Weizmann to Brandeis, 29 Oct. 1918.

46.   Minutes of the Eastern Committee, 5 Dec. 1918, p. 8, CAB 27/24.

47.   This proposal seems incredible, considering the fact that the Zionist Annual Conference in London 1920 set the budget for £2 million a year. Louis Brandeis (Hon. President of the Zionist Organisation in America 1918-21) thought even this budget 'astronomical' and contended that the utmost American Jews could give was £500,000 a year (Weizmann, *Trial and Error*, p. 327).

48.   Symes Memorandum, 13 June 1918, Durham 148/10. It is clear that Weizmann, carried away with enthusiasm, was making promises far beyond the capacity of the Zionists to fulfill. Their income at that time was far below £1 million per annum. Just as with the British and the Balfour Declaration, Weizmann exaggerated the financial and political weight of American Zionists in trying to gain his objective.

49.   FO 371/3398/f.27647/178952 from Clayton 27.10.1918 (minuted 28.10.1918).

50.   Weizmann to Clayton, 5 Nov. 1918, Clayton Papers Durham 150/8. (Italics added.)

51.   Pearlman, 'Arab-Jewish Diplomacy', p. 134. Quoting Zionist Bureau London papers.

52.   FO 800/215, 16.1.1919; see also Jon Kimche, *Palestine or Israel*

(London, 1970), pp. 175-6.

53.   Antonius, who had access to Faisal's diaries, refers to this pressure, p. 287, *Arab Awakening*.

54.   It was characteristic that Lawrence mistranslated this proviso for Weizmann as 'If the Arabs are established as I have asked in my manifesto of Jan. 4 addressed to the British Secretary of State, I will carry out what is written. If changes are made, I cannot be answerable for failing to carry out this agreement.' Antonius gives the correct translation (p. 438): 'Provided that the Arabs obtain their independence as demanded in my memorandum . . . I shall concur in the above articles. But if the slightest departure of modification were to be made, I shall not be bound by a single word of the present agreement which shall be deemed null and void and of no account or validity . . .' This apparently had its effect on Weizmann, who later claimed (Round Table Talks, 8 February 1939, quoted in Ben-Gurion, p. 208) that the treaty incidentally had some caveat that had nothing to do with the substance of the agreement. He also stated at that time that 'frankly and honestly he explained to Faisal . . . our aims and intentions' (ibid).

55.   Antonius, *Arab Awakening*, pp. 438-9.

56.   FO 608/99/2401, 17 Dec. 1918. Weizmann appeared to think that he was Faisal's main support: 'Curiously we have got on well with Faisal . . . the French whom he loathes have got him by the throat. He can't make out what the British mean; and he looks upon us almost as his only friends'.Harry Sacher to Bentwich, 5 Jan. 1919, quoted in Nevakivi, *Britain, France and the Middle East*, p. 112. Weizmann's enthusiasm may have resulted from the fact that Faisal made several favourable references to Jewish-Arab co-operation publicly at this time (in an interview in *The Times*, 12 Dec. 1918, and at a dinner for Lord Rothschild on 31 Dec. 1918, in the presence of British officials). Quoted in Pearlman, p. 134: 'No true Arab can be afraid of Jewish nationalism. We are demanding Arab freedom . . . and we say . . . to the Jews – welcome back home.'

57.   Sacher, *The Emergence of the Middle East*, p. 386.

58.   CAB 27/24, pp. 9-15.

59.   Jukka Nevakivi, *Britain, France and the Middle East*.

60.   FO 371 3385/20912, 10 Dec. 1918, 'Strategic Importance of Syria'.

61.   Quoted by Lord Robert Cecil in a private letter to A.J. Balfour, 7 Oct. 1918, FO 800/201.

62.   Balfour at Eastern Committee, 5 Dec. 1918, pp. 10-11 CAB 27/24.

63.   Note by Louis Mallet, FO 608/98/157.

64.   Nevakivi, *Britain, France and the Middle East*, p. 134.

65.   Faisal-Picot negotiations, May 1919 (Nevakivi, ibid., p. 146).

66.   Vansittart, quoted in Nevakivi, ibid., p. 108.

67.   And possibly Egypt, which was also in the throes of popular agitation for independence. In the end Egypt was excluded and the Commission did not visit Iraq, which was the object of intense Arab Bureau propaganda.

68.   On the evidence of Robert Lansing, his Secretary of State (quoted by Nevakivi, ibid., p. 260).

69.   Nevakivi, p. 160.

70.   Balfour had been alarmed at Faisal's anti-French extremism ever since their first interview on 11 Dec. 1918. But he was not able effectively to control the operations of the Arab Bureau. Lawrence urged Faisal only to pretend to come to terms with the French in order to buy time to open up the possibility of an American mandate over Syria (Nevakivi, p. 143). The Foreign Office also was worried about the effect of pan-Arabism on their strategic prize, Iraq; Curzon cabled Clayton: 'The spread into Mesopotamia is causing considerable anxiety here . . . agitation may be deriving encouragement from British officers acting under mistaken belief that aspirations for immediate establishment uncontrolled

Arab government in Mesopotamia enjoy support of HMG' (24 June 1919),
Nevakivi, p. 178. The British military continued to operate independently in the
Middle East until the military administration was replaced by a civilian one in
the spring of 1920.

71.   Curzon to Balfour, 16.1.1919; Balfour to Curzon 20.1.1919, FO
800/215.

72.   Ormsby-Gore to Sokolow, 24.1.1919, FO 608/98/633.

73.   Curzon to Balfour, 26.1.1919, FO 800/215.

74.   Quoted in Antonius, *Arab Awakening*, p. 287.

75.   The two Arabs were Ahmed Kadry and Auni Abdul-Hadi, a Pales-
tinian who later founded the Istiqlal (Independence) party. London Bureau
Vol. 56, 25.1.1919, quoted in Frischwasser-Ra'anan, *The Frontiers of a Nation*
(London, 1955).

76.   His insensitivity towards Arab feelings was demonstrated when he said
that 'what the French could do in Tunisia – the Jews will be able to do in
Palestine with Jewish will, Jewish money, Jewish power and Jewish enthusiasm'
(Weizmann, *Trial and Error*, p. 305).

77.   *Le Matin*, 1 March 1919, quoted in Pearlman, 'Arab-Jewish Diplomacy',
p. 139.

78.   Nevakivi, *Britain, France and the Middle East*, p. 126. Clemenceau and
Lloyd George almost came to blows on 1 May.

79.   Clayton Memo 2.5.1919, FO 371/4160/f.2117/68848.

80.   30.8.1919 FO 371/4182.

81.   During June 1919, Faisal hoped to meet Brandeis, the American
Zionist leader who was visiting Palestine, but Weizmann blocked the visit (Kimche,
Palestine or Israel, pp. 186-8).

82.   Complete text in Antonius, *Arab Awakening*, pp. 440-2.

83.   FO 608/86/15548.

84.   Weizmann to Eder, 17.8.1919.

85.   Nevakivi, *Britain, France and the Middle East*, p. 199.

86.   Weizmann to Balfour, 25.8.1919.

87.   Cornwallis Memo., FO 371/4183/f.2117/13493, 25.9.1919. There is no
evidence that Weizmann's claim to influence on the French had any foundation;
the French were encouraging an anti-Zionist campaign against the separation of
Palestine from Syria and for the Sykes-Picot boundaries to apply to the northern
frontier. But it was not the first time that Weizmann tried to impress the Arabs
with Jewish political influence in the world.

88.   *Jewish Chronicle*, 3 Oct. 1919, quoted in Pearlman, 'Arab-Jewish
Diplomacy', p. 145.

89.   20 Nov. 1919.

90.   Report of the Court of Enquiry . . . convened on 20 April 1920; FO
371/5121.

91.   Nevakivi, *Britain, France and the Middle East*, p. 216.

92.   A militant opponent of Zionism, accused of instigating the riots and
sentenced together with the Mufti Haj Amin al-Husseini to prison; later he became
a historian and diarist of the Palestinian Arab Movement.

93.   Report of Zionist Commission, 10.3.1920.

94.   Faisal to Allenby, FO 371/5023, 20 March 1920.

95.   Allenby to Curzon, 18 March 1920, FO 371/5023 (Ingrams, p. 90).

96.   Curzon to Allenby, 19 March 1920, ibid.

97.   Allenby to FO, 27 April 1920, FO 371/5035.

98.   Faisal to Allenby, 13 May 1920, FO 371/5035/4658.

99.   Report of Zionist Commission, 16 April 1920.

100.   By Curzon in FO 371/5121.

101.   Court of Enquiry, FO 371/5121, p. 51.

102.   8 March 1920, quoted in Nevakivi, *Britain, France and the Middle East*, p. 217.

103.   Weizmann's agent in Damascus reported that the British told Faisal that the Jews were to blame for the riots in Palestine. Fellman to Weizmann, 25 April 1920; also Court of Enquiry, pp. 51-2.

104.   Court of Enquiry, pp. 51-2.

105.   Curzon put it bluntly later: 'reliance on the Arabs is a policy fraught with dangers . . . even if we abandoned Zionism I am not sure we could count on Arab friendship.' Quoted in Elie Kedourie, *The Chatham House Version*, p. 79.

106.   Zeine B. Zeine, *The Struggle for Arab Independence* (Beirut, 1960).

107.   Memo. from General Haddad, received by FO, July 1920, FO 371/ 5036.

108.   Dr Fellman to Weizmann, 23 April 1920.

109.   Faisal to Allenby, 14 April 1920, FO 371/5117.

110.   Weizmann to Zionist Bureau, 25 March 1920.

111.   Sokolow interview, FO minute, 15 April 1920, FO 371/5117.

112.   Weizmann to Vera Weizmann, 20 April 1920; it is significant that the discussion on the Arab Question at the Zionist Executive on 7 May included no reference to the threatened Arab Kingdom, but blamed the British for defeating attempts at co-operation (meeting of Pol. Com. XVLa).

113.   Eder to Weizmann, 14 and 21 August 1920, quoted in Kimche, italics added.

114.   'Arab-Jewish Diplomacy 1918-22', *Jewish Social Studies*, April 1944, p. 153.

WEIZMANN AND THE PALESTINIANS

1.   Aaronsohn was a brilliant agronomist who was convinced that Palestine would never prosper under the Turks. He organised a spy ring (Nili) for the British during the war, then escaped to England. His sister was captured and committed suicide, while he was killed in a plane crash during the Paris Peace Conference. He was considered a reliable substitute for Weizmann as head of the Zionist Commission by Sykes (cable to R. Graham, 9 May 1917, FO 371/83053).

2.   *Arab Bulletin*, no. 64, 7 October 1917, pp. 389-91, FO 882/26.

3.   Minutes of the Second Meeting of the Zionist Commission, aboard the SS. *Canberra*, Taranto, 14 March 1918. It is interesting to note that in the *Arab Bulletin*, Aaronsohn had claimed that it was necessary to 'forcibly remove' Arab tenant-farmers (who didn't own their land) when Jewish colonies purchased land. Leon Simon noted in his diary that Weizmann had fallen under Aaronsohn's influence 'a thoroughly bad beginning', quoted in Jon Kimche, *Palestine or Israel* (London, 1970), p. 141.

4.   See below for evidence of Weizmann's belief that gifts of money would 'buy' Arab leaders, held throughout his life. Cf. Eder to Weizmann, 21.5.1920 asking him to 'take care' of certain members of Palestine Arab delegation; also personal interview, Col. Yecheskel Sahar, 4 Dec. 1971, who recalled Weizmann's gift of £10,000 to an Iraqi politician in 1938 − 'that was typical of Weizmann's political work with the Arabs'.

5.   Weizmann to Sokolow, 20 April 1918. He wrote 'they are not a moral force, nor are they a material danger to us, only the British are unnecessarily sensitive to them . . .'

6.   19.8.1918.

7.   3.8.1918.

8.   As documented previously in Elie Kedourie, *The Chatham House Version* (London, 1970).

9.   Clayton to Sykes, 4 Feb. 1918, FO 371/3398/36757; Clayton to Gertrude Bell, 17 June 1918, Sudan Archive, also Ormsby-Gore speech to Zionist

Political Committee 16 August 1918, FO 371/3389/147225. He advised the Zionists not to pay too much attention to Syrian opponents in Palestine.

10.   Weizmann to Balfour, 30.6.1918; Weizmann to Balfour, 17.7.1918. Both these letters were composed with Clayton's help according to Kimche, *Palestine or Israel*.

11.   Minutes of the Eighth Meeting of Zionist Commission, 21 April 1918.

12.   Weizmann to Vera Weizmann, 27 April 1918.

13.   Memorandum by K. Cornwallis, 20 April 1918, FO 371/3394/85169.

14.   Weizmann to Balfour, 30 May 1918.

15.   Arab and British view of the Commission is revealed in the suppressed Report of the Court of Enquiry, 12 April 1920, main press articles were by Israel Zangwill in the *Jewish Chronicle*, London.

16.   FO 371/4198 Report by Hogarth, 18 Dec. 1918.

17.   See letter from Weizmann to Balfour, 30.5. 1918.

18.   Report by Ronald Storrs, Telegram 2611.A from OETA (in C.Z.A.), 7 Nov. 1918.

19.   Clayton to Balfour, 15 Nov. 1918, FO 371/3385/f.1747, cf. Clayton to Balfour, 21 Sept. 1918, FO 371/3384.

20.   Clayton to Balfour, 6 December 1918, FO 371/3386.

21.   J.N. Camp report, 2 Feb. 1919, FO 371/4153/41476.

22.   Kimche, *Palestine or Israel*, p. 188. The French were interested in embarrassing the English in Palestine in order to extract better boundaries between their zone and the English-ruled Palestine. For their role in fostering an anti-British Palestinian nationalism, see Yehoshua Porath, *The Emergence of the Palestinian-Arab National Movement* 1918-1929 (London, 1974).

23.   Weizmann to Zionist Bureau, Nov. 1919.

24.   Southern Syria, Jan. 1920, quoted in Kimche, *Palestine or Israel*, p. 198.

25.   Weizmann to Sieff, 12 Oct. 1919.

26.   Weizmann to Vera Weizmann, 21 March 1920.

27.   Weizmann to PM, 10 April 1920.

28.   Weizmann to Zionist Bureau (London), 22 March 1920.

29.   Weizmann to Vera Weizmann, 21 March 1920. He also added approving approvingly, 'in Egypt and Mesopotamia they use an iron hand'.

30.   Quoted in Sacher, *The Emergence of the Middle East*, p. 397.

31.   Memo. by Capt. Brunton, CAB 24/125, 9.6.1921.

32.   Samuel to Weizmann, 10 Aug. 1921.

33.   CO 733/14, note by H. Young.

34.   Notes by Shuckburgh and Mills, 2.12.1921, CO 537/855.

35.   Weizmann to Eder, 8 Dec. 1921.

36.   Note by Shuckburgh quoted in Ingrams, 'Palestine Papers', p. 139.

37.   Eder to Weizmann, 14 Dec. 1921.

38.   Cmd. 1700, pp. 10-11.

39.   'Herbert Samuel and the Government of Palestine', in Elie Kedourie, *The Chatham House Version*, pp. 73-6.

40.   Weizmann to Morris Rutenberg and Emmanuel Neumann, 9.11.1924.

41.   Weizmann to Eder, 8 Dec. 1921.

42.   Y. Porath, *The Emergence of the Palestinian-Arab National Movement 1918-1929* (London: Frank Cass, 1974), pp. 215-16.

43.   Weizmann to Wormser, February (no day) 1923.

44.   Porath, *Emergence of the Palestinian-Arab National Movement*, pp. 219-20.

45.   Porath, ibid., pp. 229-30. Weizmann refers to this in his previously cited letter to Wormser: 'We are going to advance small sums on definite security to the Sheiks of villages.' The failure of Zionist finances in 1927 led to the collapse of that party.

46. Weizmann to Wormser, Feb. 1923.

47. Memo. of Jewish Agency for Palestine (1936). Net immigration: 1923, 3,055; 1924, 10,819; 1925, 31,650.

48. The Situation in Palestine, report by High Commissioner, 8 Dec. 1922, c.p. 2379, CO 733/35.

49. Weizmann to Rappard, 15 Nov. 1924.

50. Weizmann to Clayton, 5 Nov. 1918.

51. Minute by D.G. Osborne, FO 371/4226.

52. Weizmann to Graham, 13.7.1919.

53. Weizmann to Young, 2.7.1920.

54. Weizmann to Curzon, 29 Jan. 1920.

55. Cf. Weizmann's remarks to Samuel on the Land Transfer Ordinance (October 1920), December 1920, FO 371/5140, quoted in Ingram, 'Palestine Papers', p. 110.

56. Shaw Report, Cmd. 3530, Jan. 1930, p. 64.

57. Porath, *Emergence of the Palestinian-Arab National Movement*, pp. 258-9.

58. Memo. of Jewish Agency for Palestine (1936). Net immigration: 1926, 5,716; 1927, 2,358; 1928, −10.

59. Porath, *Emergence of the Palestinian-Arab National Movement*, p. 253.

60. Porath, ibid., p. 256.

61. Gad Frumkin, *The Way of a Judge in Jerusalem* (Tel Aviv, 1954-5, p. 287 (Hebrew).

62. Cmd. 3530, Shaw Report, Jan. 1930.

63. Minutes of the 43rd Meeting of the Zionist Executive, London, 22 Jan. 1930.

64. Interview between Dr Weizmann and Dr D. Shiels, held in a private room of house of Commons, 4 March 1930. Notes by Dr Weizmann.

65. Colonial Office files on this are closed; see Weizmann to Warburg, 15 May 1930; Weizmann to Melchett, 26 May 1930; Weizmann to Felix Green, 23 June 1930 (he wired for immediate details of land available in Transjordan).

66. 'Neither the British nor the Palestine Government could possibly touch this Transjordan project', letter to PM, 23 July 1930, RRO Premier 1, 102.

67. See Sheffer, 'The Passfield White Paper – Intentions and Results of British Policy', *Middle Eastern Studies*, vol. 9, no. 1, Jan. 1973, pp. 52-3.

68. Minutes of the Joint Meeting of Zionist Executive with Special Political Committee, 1 Dec. 1930.

69. Private conversation in Mr Henderson's room at the House of Commons, 4 Dec. 1930. Present: Messrs Henderson, Weizmann, MacDonald and Namier.

WEIZMANN AND BI-NATIONALISM

1. CO 733/175/8821 Philby to Lord Passfield (Colonial Secretary), 21 Oct. 1929 (misdated 1919) and 1 Nov. 1929. Philby talked directly with the Mufti, Haj Amin Husseini. See also Magnes to Warburg, cable, 1 Nov. 1929.

2. Chancellor to Colonial Office, 17 Jan. 1930, CO 733/183, quoted in G. Sheffer, 'Intentions and Results of British Policy in Palestine: the Passfield White Paper', *Middle Eastern Studies*, vol. 9, Jan. 1973, p. 44.

3. Weizmann to Marshall, 17 Jan. 1930.

4. Weizmann to Einstein, 20 Nov. 1929.

5. Weizmann to Warburg, 16 Jan. 1930.

6. Weizmann to Einstein, 30 Nov. 1929.

7. Weizmann to Marshall, 17 Jan. 1930.

8. Weizmann to Marshall, 17 Jan. 1930.

9. Weizmann to Einstein, 30 Nov. 1929.

10. Weizmann to Marshall, 17 Jan. 1930.

11.   S.L. Hattis, *The Bi-National Idea in Palestine during Mandatory Times* (Tel Aviv, 1970), p. 82.

12.   W. Laqueur, *A History of Zionism* (London, 1972), p. 254.

13.   Weizmann to Weltsch, 13 Jan. 1924. Italics added.

14.   Minutes of Action Committee Conference, October 1923, Central Zionist Archives, Jerusalem, Z4/266/109.

15.   Weltsch to Weizmann, 1 Jan. 1924.

16.   Hattis, *Bi-National Idea*, p. 58.

17.   Hattis, ibid., p. 87.

18.   Laqueur, *History of Zionism*, p. 254; cf. Hattis, *Bi-National Idea*, p. 69.

19.   Quoted in Hattis, ibid., p. 57 and repeated in Laqueur, ibid., p. 255.

20.   Weizmann to Einstein, 30 Nov. 1929.

21.   Weizmann to Warburg, 16.1.1930. Italics added.

22.   Hattis, *Bi-national Idea*, p. 88.

23.   Laqueur, *History of Zionism*, p. 253.

24.   Hattis, *Bi-national Idea*, p. 69.

25.   Philby to Lord Passfield, 1 Nov. 1929, CO 733/175/8821.

26.   Y. Porath, *The Emergence of the Palestinian-Arab National Movement 1918-1929* (London, 1974), pp. 256-7.

27.   G. Sheffer, 'The Passfield White Paper: Intentions and Results of British Policy, *MES,* vol. 9, no. 1, Jan. 1973.

28.   Magnes, *Like All the Nations*, p. 34.

29.   Philby to Passfield, 'Pass field White Paper', CO 733/175/8821.

30.   Moshe Sharett, *Political Diary*, vol. I (1936), p. 134 (vol. II, 1937; vol. III, 1938; vol. IV, 1939) (Tel Aviv, 1968-74) (Hebrew).

31.   Weizmann to Warburg, 16 Jan. 1930.

32.   Weizmann to Magnes, 26 June 1930.

33.   Action Committee 27.8.1930, in Hattis, *Bi-national Idea*, p. 89.

34.   Minutes of Mapai Central Committee, 29.3.31, quoted in Hattis, ibid., pp. 90-1.

35.   Ibid.

36.   Cmd. 3692, Palestine, Statement of Policy.

37.   21 Oct. 1930, quoted in Sheffer, 'Passfield White Paper', p. 54.

38.   Quoted in Hattis, *Bi-national Idea*, p. 91.

39.   J. Hurewitz, *The Struggle for Palestine* (New York, 1956), p. 38.

40.   Jewish Telegraphic Agency interview, July 1931, quoted in Robert Weltsch, 'A Tragedy of Leadership', *Jewish Social Studies*, vol. XIII, no. 3, July 1951, p. 212.

41.   3 Feb. 1931, quoted in J.C. Hurewitz, *The Struggle for Palestine* (revised edition, 1976, New York), p. 23.

42.   The total immigration 1932-5 was 150,000 which represented almost a doubling of the existing community.

CONCLUSIONS

1.   See Ya'acov Roi, 'The Zionist Attitude Towards Arabs, 1908-1914', *Middle Eastern Studies*, vol. 4, no. 3, April 1958; Neville Mandel, 'Attempts at an Arab-Jewish Entente, 1913-1914, *Middle Eastern Studies*, vol. 1, no. 3, April 1965.

2.   Minutes of the Second Meeting of the Zionist Commission, aboard S.S. *Canberra*, Taranto, 8 March 1918.

3.   George Antonius, *The Arab Awakening* (London, 1938), pp. 108-11.

4.   Faisal India Office Interview, 1 January 1919, FO 371/4162/605f.

5.   See British Military Intelligence Reports, 1920.

6.   Conversation with Symes, 9 June 1918. R. Wingate Papers, Sudan Archive, University of Durham, 148/10.

7.   Minutes of Evidence to the Royal Commission, CO 134 (July 1937), para. 4530.

8.   Ben-Gurion speech, 1937 Zionist Congress, Zurich, Aug.-Sept. 1937, *New Judea*, p. 220.

9.   Memorandum of conversation with Dr Sheils, March 1930 (see also note 64, p. 63).

2 JABOTINSKY AND THE REVISIONIST MOVEMENT

Jabotinsky's Position in Zionism

[It is] a dangerous fallacy to seek a solution to the Arab-Jewish confrontation through a 'rapprochement' with the Arabs. Palestine was the meeting of two cultures which had no common spiritual aspiration and a genuine rapprochement between them was an organic and historic impossibility.

(Zev Jabotinsky, Speech in Tel Aviv, 1929)

The popular image of Weizmann as a statesman who spared no effort in exploiting every avenue towards a just settlement with the Arabs, was largely due to the fact that throughout his career he had to wage a courageous battle against an adversary who constantly defied and challenged his leadership: Wladimir (Zev) Jabotinsky, the father and founder of the Revisionist movement. It is extremely difficult to underestimate the impact of Jabotinsky and his followers on the action and thought of the Zionist movement. Most of the crucial decisions of the Zionist leadership were taken during heated and passionate debates with Jabotinsky, and bore the marks of this struggle whether the final decision made was to counteract his policies or whether it represented a victory for the pressure he brought to bear.[1]

Jabotinsky himself did not restrict his struggle to the inner councils of the Zionist movement. Except for two short periods of co-operation with the Zionist Executive (in 1908-9 and 1921-3) he fought his battles in the open appealing to the Jewish masses and to world public opinion, defying Zionist discipline, challenging the authority of the Zionist leadership to represent the Jewish people and even negotiating over their heads with foreign statesmen and governments. In his bid for power he knew no bounds and did not refrain from undertaking risky ventures that created for the whole Zionist movement and the Yishuv deeply embarrassing and frequently intolerable situations.

The role of the Revisionist movement in exacerbating Jewish-Arab relations in Palestine is on record: the demonstration it organised at the Wailing Wall (15 August 1929), which was a major provocation even in the eyes of Jewish public opinion, led to the bloody riots and disturbances of 1929; the violation of the Haganah line of self-restraint (*havlaga*), and indiscriminate attacks on the civilian Arab population in

96

1937 led to a vicious circle of terror and reprisals; the attack on Deir-Yassin in 1948, the ruthlessness of which shocked Jewish and world public opinion alike and drove fear and panic into the Arab population, precipitated the flight of Arab masses from their homes and villages; and so on.

But the doubtful exploits of the Revisionist movement and its off-shoots — the 'Irgun Zvai Leumi' and 'LEHI' — were not confined to the area of Jewish-Arab relations. Time and again they created a situation of near civil war in the Jewish Yishuv in Palestine: in 1933-5 when they tried to break the monopoly and strength of the Histadruth by organising strike-breakers[2] and by setting up a rival trade union federation; and in June 1948 when they brought into Tel-Aviv a ship with ammunition and combatants in defiance of the authority of the Provisional Government of Israel and of the truce signed by it in compliance with the UN Security Council Resolution.

Also in the sphere of external diplomatic relations the Revisionists tried to become an independent factor, claiming to represent the Jewish people. They broke away from the Zionist Organisation and founded a 'New Zionist Organisation' which evolved a diplomacy of its own in relations with the League of Nations, the Mandatory Power and other states. The assassination of Lord Moyne (November 1944) and of Count Bernadotte (September 1948) by members of the terrorist groups originating from the Revisionist youth movement (Betar) placed the Zionist movement in tight and dangerous corners. The Zionist leadership viewed all these deeds as irresponsible and misconceived adventures. The Revisionists still regard them with pride, as proof of Jabotinsky's historical foresight and sense of timing and as a decisive contribution to the realisation of the goal of a Jewish state in its historic boundaries.

The Arabs did not regard the internal struggle in Zionism as a reflection of genuinely contradictory trends in Zionism, but rather as a 'Jekyll and Hyde' phenomenon of the same movement. Worse, they believed that Jabotinsky's was the true face of Zionism, while Weizmann's and his colleague's condemnation of Revisionist outrages was no more than a hypocritical cover up.

In the eyes of his followers Jabotinsky was the greatest statesman in Zionism, who rebelled against the meekness and cowardice of the leadership, bogged down in opportunistic pragmatism. However, the power of Jabotinsky's attraction and magnetism was not confined to the Revisionist movement alone. His manifold talents — he was a talented poet and novelist, a brilliant journalist, versatile in many languages[3] and a powerful orator who could hypnotise, incite and hold in suspense huge audiences with his brilliant rhetoric which he punctuated with hammer blows and breath-taking crescendos — brought him popularity and fame among the masses of the Jewish people and in selective intellectual circles alike.

Weizmann started as an unknown Zionist militant who had to work his way up with diligence and perseverance until he reached the level of leadership. Jabotinsky, on the other hand, joined the Zionist movement as an already well-known speaker and writer and as a 'favourite child' of Russian Jewry. Even then he derived a 'mischievous joy from causing an uproar' and satisfaction from the popularity attached to being a controversial figure. Jabotinsky's appeal to the masses was not due only to his oratory skills or his personality, which was a blend of courtesy, chivalry, pugnacity and impetuosity. He aroused a response because his concepts appealed to the mentality, deep-seated instincts and yearnings of the Jewish masses suffering from economic adversity, anti-Semitism, discrimination, humiliation and feelings of powerlessness and frustration in the conditions prevailing in Eastern Europe before and after World War I.

Jabotinsky's biographers[4] attribute to him the resurrection of Herzl's 'political Zionism' which aimed at 'a Jewish State as a prerequisite of Jewish mass-settlement in Palestine' as opposed to 'practical Zionism' which concentrated on short-term practical work and 'relegated the political struggle to a subordinate tenth-rate position'.[5] This is only partly true. Jabotinsky's concept of Zionism resembled Herzl's doctrine in a number of respects. He negated totally Jewish existence in the Diaspora: 'liquidate the Exile (Galut) or the Exile will liquidate you'.[6] Zionism for him meant total negation and liquidation of the Exile.[7] He fought for equality of Jewish rights, cultural autonomy and the liquidation of anti-Semitism. Nevertheless, even a 'normal' Galut, without pogroms, was to him a life without significance, while the meaning of Zionism was the restoration of glory and heroism to the Jewish nation.[8] 'Zionism is the answer to the lie called Galut or else Zionism is itself a lie.'[9]

Herzl believed that the liquidation of the Galut could be effected by the simple means of transportation, once a charter for the colonisation of Palestine was achieved. The 'practical' Zionists understood that immigration and settlement could progress only as a part of a prolonged and complicated process of transformation: economic and social 'Umschichtung'. Jabotinsky shared with Herzl the concept of a mass exodus of Jews. He even developed this concept into a policy of 'evacuation' on the basis of an agreement with states which suffered from an 'overload of Jewish population'. 'The economic collapse of European Jewry, complicated ten-fold because of the impossibility to emigrate [to Palestine] is painful not only to us, but also to the states in which this process is developing. From this derives our tactic to link Zionism with the problem of evacuation. In other words to mobilise for Zionism a number of states for their own interest and then to launch a campaign [against British policy].'[10]

Jabotinsky embarked on political negotiations with ruling circles in Poland, Romania, Lithuania, Latvia, etc. – known for their anti-Jewish policies – to formulate a plan for the evacuation of one million Jews from Eastern Europe.[11] It is interesting to note that at his debut in Zionist affairs, at the Basle Congress, when Herzl was severely criticised for negotiating with the anti-Semitic Minister of the Interior in Russia, Von Plehve, Jabotinsky defended this move emphasising that 'one should not confuse ethics with tactics'.[12] The essence of his political philosophy was developed in his speech at the Seventh Zionist Congress in 1905: 'Politics is power . . . This power we do not possess. Zionism must endeavour to become a power . . . The moral appraisal of the means and methods used by a fighter must be governed *exclusively* by the measure of real public good and real public harm, they result in.'[13] Herzl's policy – first to obtain a political charter and then to proceed with large-scale colonisation – failed, and only practical work in Palestine remained the way to advance the Zionist cause.

With the attainment of the Balfour Declaration (by a 'practical Zionist', Weizmann), the whole debate between 'political' and 'practical' Zionism acquired a different meaning. The Zionist movement then faced the task of maximising the opportunities offered by the British Mandate in Palestine, through both political and practical work.

Jabotinsky's new contribution to the Zionist doctrine was the elaboration of a militarist concept of Zionist realisation – the idea of a 'Jewish Legion' to fight at the side of the Allies for the liberation of Palestine and for the establishment of a 'colonising regime' as a prerequisite of Jewish mass immigration and settlement. From the notion of a 'Jewish Legion' evolved all his ideological, political and educational activities. The idea of a Jewish Army, after 2,000 years in exile – though answering a deep-felt longing of the humiliated Jewish masses in the ghettos – had nothing to do with Herzl's conception of Zionism. Herzl never conceived a military confrontation with the Arabs and the conquest of Palestine by force. On the contrary, his vision of the future was that of a state *without* an army, free from all the paraphernalia of militarism.

Jabotinsky advanced the proposal for a 'Jewish Legion' in 1915, after Turkey's entry into the war. It had no connection with the actual state of Jewish-Arab relations in Palestine. Arab suspicion and hostility towards Zionist settlement was known, but Arab nationalism at this time was in its infancy and the Palestinians had no national leadership or programme that would warrant the organisation of a Jewish military force to deal with their opposition. The 'Jewish Legion' idea — like all other Zionist concepts including the doctrine of Socialist Zionism — originated in the mentality and conditions of the Jews in the Diaspora, their political and social outlook and their orientation towards the forces liable to shape their future. One part of the Jewish middle classes — which formed the overwhelming majority of the Jewish people, and which suffered from the development of a capitalist economy and national competition from the indigenous middle classes and artisans — conceived its future in terms of proletarianisation. Its orientation was directed either towards an alliance with the non-Jewish working class and the advent of a social revolution, or towards a socialist workers' society in Palestine (the doctrine of Socialist Zionism). Another part of the Jewish middle class cherished the dream of maintaining its social status and position by assimilation in the Diaspora or of achieving Jewish statehood in Palestine which would liberate them from foreign rule and discrimination, and provide them with the power to master and shape their own condition. Jabotinsky's political philosophy reflected this latter orientation. The 'Jewish Legion' concept was based on the assumption that at the end of the Allies' war with Germany, Turkey would be defeated and dismembered and thus the Zionist movement must *bank*[14] on an allied victory and set up a 'Jewish Legion' to fight on the side of the Allies and to assist in the liberation and occupation of Palestine 'in exchange for certain promises'.[15]

Jabotinsky was obsessed with this idea to the point of 'maniacal insistence' (as was later remarked by the chief of the Hagana, Eliahu Golomb).[16] Jabotinsky saw in 'the Legion Movement and the Legion [a] truly noble part of Jewish history'.[17] In his own *The Story of the Jewish Legion* he did not cease to exalt 'the historic mission [of the Legion] which shaped the destiny of Zionism'.[18] It was not for him a passing episode because he never ceased in his attempts to revive the idea and most of his policies revolved around it.

The Jewish Legion: Myth and Reality

The proposal to set up a Jewish military unit was made by Jabotinsky early in 1915, when he and Joseph Trumpeldor (a former officer in the Russian Army and the founder of Halutz (Pioneer) Movement in Russia) happened to meet Jewish refugees in Alexandria who had been expelled by Jamal Pasha from Palestine. Jabotinsky proposed to them the setting up of a military unit which would fight the Turks in conjunction with the British. Five hundred men enlisted but General Maxwell, whom Jabotinsky and Trumpeldor approached, replied that the British Army was not considering a military offensive in Palestine, and he could use the unit only for mule transport at the Turkish front in Gallipoli.

Joseph Trumpeldor — who thought that in war even transportation was an important function, and that in order to 'smash the Turks and ultimately reach Palestine' every battle front was important — formed the Zion Mule Corps with 562 men which was sent without delay to Gallipoli. This did not appeal to Jabotinsky's sense of honour and dignity and penchant for romantic adventure (he eulogised adventurism and 'square-jawed adventurists ready for hardships and failure'[1]): 'You may be right — but I personally will not join a unit of that sort', he told Trumpeldor.[2] Instead he went to London to propagate the Legion idea in Zionist and British circles.

Nearly the whole Zionist leadership rejected the idea. The Zionist Action Committee in Stockholm condemned it as a violation of the principle of Zionist neutrality in the war. Even Max Nordau, Herzl's associate and protagonist of the Jewish state concept, thought that Zionism should 'preserve unity and remain above battle' as Jews were fighting in both camps, and the Jewish Yishuv in Palestine, occupied by the Turkish Army, should not be jeopardised.[3] American Jews, many of whom were of Russian origin, and Ussishkin, the head of the Zionist movement in Russia, could not tolerate the idea of Zionism allied with Russia, a country notorious for its persecution of Jews. Ussishkin, who always viewed events through the prism of Jewish history, thought it ungrateful to fight Turkey which had opened its door and cordially received the Jews expelled from Spain.[4]

The only support for the Jewish Legion came from the Russian Minister of Foreign Affairs and, surprisingly, Weizmann, who promised to support it at the proper time. While most of the Zionists were concerned with the fate of the Jewish colonies in Palestine, Jabotinsky retorted 'we have never looked upon the Yishuv as "Selbstzweck" [aim in itself] . . . we saw in it one of the powerful tools of political Zionism . . . the best of our aces in the political game. But we shall not agree to this same Yishuv, all of a sudden, becoming an obstacle to a decisive political game.'[5]

Jabotinsky continued his efforts trying to persuade Russian Jews in London, who as foreign subjects were exempted from conscription, to join a Jewish Regiment as volunteers. The idea of fighting for the Tzar did not appeal to them and Jabotinsky was met with cries of 'Militarist, Murderer, Provocateur'.[6] No opposition, though, could influence Jabotinsky's unyielding temper. The situation, however, soon changed fortuitously in his favour. The February 1917 Revolution removed the main psychological obstacle to Jews volunteering for the war, namely the Tsar, and Joseph Trumpeldor returned from the front with a group from the disbanded Mule Corps to join in the propaganda for a Jewish Legion. Trumpeldor went to Russia to set up a Halutz Movement and a Jewish Army of 75,000 to 100,000 to fight its way through to Palestine. However, the collapse of the Russian front in 1917 prevented the realisation of this aim. Jabotinsky remained in London pressing for an agreement between the British and the Russian Provisional Government on the promulgation of a bill for the conscription of Russian subjects residing in England or their repatriation to Russia for military service there. The Bill was passed in August 1917 and Jabotinsky set in motion, with the help of 'tough guys' from the Zion Mule Corps, a vigorous recruitment campaign using the threat of repatriation to Russia. Even this did not reduce the opposition of Russian Jews, including Zionists, to enlisting in the Jewish Legion. The bulk of the Jews opted for repatriation (20,000) and only a few hundred volunteered to what was called the 38th Battalion of Royal Fusiliers (later the 'Judean Regiment'). The rest of the unit was formed of conscripts pressed into service. Jabotinsky 'won the battle for the Legion [but] remained for some time the best hated man in Jewish London'.[7]

While Jabotinsky was recruiting the 38th Battalion, the leaders of the labour movement in Palestine — Ben-Gurion, Ben-Zvi, Eliahu Golomb and others who were equally enthusiastic about the 'Great Dream' of a Jewish Army — were building up the 39th and 40th Battalions. These were composed entirely of Jewish volunteers from the USA, England and Palestine who viewed military service as a means of realising their main aim: settlement in Palestine as members of the labour movement.

The 'war record' of the 38th Battalion was not very impressive. It arrived in Palestine in April 1918, after training in Egypt, to face a lull in fighting until June. Not until 19 September, when it engaged in combat to capture a ford across the Jordan River, did it participate in any major war activities except for night patrols and guard duties. However, it had to face an enemy stronger than the Turks — malaria. In August 1918, the 38th Battalion consisted of 800 men and 30 officers. When it returned to Lydda after the signing of the armistice with Turkey (October 1918) there were 150 men and 15 officers. Twenty had been killed, wounded or captured, while the rest had been stricken by malaria (from which 30 eventually died).[8]

In December 1918 the 40th Battalion, comprised of Palestinian Jews, arrived from Egypt so that the three Jewish Battalions in Palestine at the beginning of 1919 comprised 5,000 men, or one-sixth of the British Army of Occupation.[9] Jabotinsky continued his recruitment efforts in the USA, England, Russia and Palestine in order to garrison Palestine after the war. The British Military Administration opposed the plan and accelerated the demobilisation of the Jewish Battalions. The volunteers themselves were in no mood 'to continue in just wearing Khaki' and pressed for their discharge. Many of them, especially the Americans and Palestinians, did so in order to settle down in the country. In vain, Jabotinsky used all kinds of arguments and pressure to prevent the demobilisation: lack of employment and housing, threat of Arab pogroms, moral obligations, etc. By the spring of 1919, of the original 5,000, only 300-400 remained as part of the force. The plan to keep the Jewish battalions to garrison Palestine — at least until the signing of a peace treaty with Turkey — collapsed.

Jabotinsky claimed that 'half the Balfour Declaration belongs to the Legion'.[10] This is not evidenced by the meticulous studies concerning the origin and history of the Balfour Declaration that have been undertaken and published by a number of distinguished scholars. On the contrary, the British attitude towards the Legion idea was a by-product of the general British attitude towards the Zionist movement. The British Government had neither need nor interest in a Jewish military contribution towards the liberation of Palestine from the Turks, but it had a vital interest in gaining the support of the Zionist movement in facilitating the entry of the USA into the war, intensifying the American war effort and keeping Russia, after the February Revolution, on the side of the Allies in the war. This was the origin of the Balfour Declaration as summarised most authoritatively by the Royal Commission of Enquiry (The Peel Commission) in 1936. The British gave in reluctantly to the demand for a Jewish Legion, only to disband it as soon as possible after the occupation of Palestine in 1918. The Legion was no more than an episode, a side effect which passed without leaving any trace on British policies, though it remained a subject of controversy inside the Zionist movement.

Jabotinsky's conception of the Yishuv as the 'ace in the political game' led to an estrangement between him and the partisans of the Legion idea inside the labour movement. The alienation soon developed into an animosity and open hostility. For the labour movement the Legion was a means to attract and absorb idealist and pioneering elements who would be channelled after the war into constructive work and settlement in Palestine. It regarded the creation of settlements and their defence as the decisive factor, not the deployment of an army for political purposes. The divergence of views became apparent when Joseph Trumpeldor, Jabotinsky's associate in the foundation of the Legion, decided to defend isolated settlements in Northern Galilee (Tel Hai, Metullah, Kfar Giladi) threatened by Bedouin tribes which were harassing the French in their occupation zone (OETA North). Jabotinsky saw no military significance in the defence of these settlements and called upon Trumpeldor and his comrades to withdraw before it was too late.[11] He opposed the Labour call for mobilisation to help the threatened settlements. In the event Trumpeldor and six comrades were killed, Tel-Hai was evacuated and the incident did not determine the frontiers. Nevertheless the heroic death of Trumpeldor acquired the dimension of a national legend of such immense appeal to the young Jewish generation that Jabotinsky thought it advisable to exploit it by naming the Revisionist youth movement after Trumpeldor.

The disbandment of the Legion posed a problem of self-defence in view of the danger of Arab riots. The labour movement started to build up, illegally, the defence force 'Haganah' which Jabotinsky opposed on the grounds that an illegal organisation could not be effective. He insisted on a legal Jewish Military force even if it were to be under British High Command and part of the British garrison in Palestine. He forced his view through in the Zionist Action Committee and in the Twelfth Zionist Congress (1921), although the prospects of obtaining a legal military defence sanctioned by the British Government grew dimmer and dimmer.

The 'Haganah' versus 'Legion' controversy continued to alienate Jabotinsky from the labour movement.[12] Sharett reported Jabotinsky as saying: 'I will break the Haganah even for the sake of a remotest hope for the establishment of the Legion.'[13] Jabotinsky even went as far as suggesting to a British official (Wyndham Deeds) that the government should sanction the organisation and training of the Haganah and appoint a British officer, trusted by the Zionists, as Chief Instructor, in return for which the Hagana would surrender its arms and place them in the custody of trustworthy persons.[14] The Haganah Chief's reaction was: 'we will not agree to sacrifice our real strength, if ever so small, on the altar of Jabotinsky's illusions.'[15]

This incident sounds paradoxical in view of Jabotinsky's vicious campaign against Weizmann's 'blind faith and confidence in British intentions'. It becomes more logical when Jabotinsky's attitude towards the British is properly analysed.

Jabotinsky and Britain

In spite of the bellicose posture and pungent language adopted by Jabotinsky towards Britain, and in particular towards the Palestine administration, he was far from pursuing an anti-British policy. He believed, more than did Weizmann, in the identity of Zionist and British interests and in the possibility of an alliance. In fact he accused Weizmann of being more responsible than the British for the erosion of Britain's commitment to the Balfour Declaration. If he pressed 'to have it out' with Britain and threatened, from time to time, non-co-operation, the boycott of British goods and that he would demand the withdrawal of the Mandate from Britain, it was from the conviction that such acts would put an end to British equivocation and vacillation in Palestine and would encourage Britain to fulfil her obligation towards the Zionist movement. His belief in this prospect was not shaken by the bitter experiences he had to undergo personally as a result of the hostility of the Palestine administration towards him, such as his discharge from the Judean Regiment against his own will; his sentence of 14 years in prison in Acre following the organisation of Jewish self-defence during the Jerusalem riots in spring 1920; his dis-honourable release from prison (together with Arab criminals); the order in 1929 banning him from entering Palestine, etc. These incidents incidentally played a decisive role in building up Jabotinsky's image as a national hero; a kind of 'Jewish Garibaldi'. He left prison with a statement that he remained 'a true and devoted friend of England and a staunch admirer of British justice'.[1]

The entire political programme of the Revisionist Party was based on the assumption that it was possible to get Britain to participate actively in bringing about a Jewish majority in Palestine which would transform the national home into a Jewish state. Hence the demand for a 'colonising regime' as a prerequisite for mass settlement — a regime in which the mandatory power would become a fully-fledged partner in the Jewish effort by carrying the burden of public services, by transferring uncultivated or inadequately cultivated land to a 'State

Land Reserve' for purposes of colonisation, and by assigning all the responsible government positions in Palestine, including the police and security forces, to persons who recognised the establishment of the Jewish national home as the basic aim of the British Administration (Resolutions of the Foundation Conference of the Revisionist World Union, Paris, April 1925).[2]

The demand for a 'colonising regime' became the trumpet-call of Jabotinsky's propaganda. He claimed that the Jewish Agency's policy of readiness to carry alone the burden of health, education services and settlement enabled the Palestine administration to shirk its duties. He thought the British Mandate was a 'contract' between Britain and the Jewish people. The Jews fulfilled their share by bringing in immigrants and establishing settlements and industries, but Britain failed to honour her side of the bargain.

Although Jabotinsky was scathing in his indictment of the British 'criminal administration',[3] following the riots of 1929, he laid the blame for the 'breach of contract' on Zionist policy: 'The Zionist leadership asserted that the Jewish people aspired to nothing more than to be allowed to do everything by themselves. That was a political blunder of the first magnitude. An Administration cannot remain inactive in a country [which is] in the process of colonization – it has either to identify itself with our work or identify itself with the antagonism of another section of the population. That was precisely what happened in Palestine.'[4]

As early as 1922, following the riots of 1920 and 1921, Jabotinsky demanded that Britain be 'forced' to clarify her position *vis-a-vis* her commitment. Rejecting the argument that this might invite a negative answer, he stated that he was convinced as firmly as ever that there is 'a real coincidence of interests between Zionism and the British position in the East Mediterranean' and that 'no British Government will break the Balfour pledge . . . therefore [a] straight question will bring a favourable reply'. He continued: 'If the Mandate has no foundation but bluff it is dangerous and immoral and of no use to keep up appearances.'[5] He maintained the same belief after the riots and the Passfield White Paper in 1929-30: 'Great Britain was in no way prepared to abandon either Egypt, Iraq or India. Piecemeal concessions granted to those countries were no indication that London was ready to abdicate the British imperial interests . . . The British Government could be induced to make a serious effort on behalf of the Zionist cause only by a truly great historical aim . . . the present Zionist leadership could not be entrusted with this task [of representing the statehood concept] . . . Instead of denouncing the treacherous British regime in Palestine [they] preferred to offer apologetic explanations . . . to argue that Jewish colonization was beneficial to the Arab population and to assure the Arabs and the Mandatory Power that the Jews did not aspire to govern the country, requesting only the right to exist.'[6]

In Jabotinsky's simplistic evaluation British policy was moving away from the Balfour Declaration only because the Zionist leadership, Weizmann in particular, was meek and cowardly, did not spell out in unmistakeable terms the aspiration for statehood in historical Palestine and did not adopt a defiant and adamant posture in dealing with the administration. A threat of non-co-operation and revision of the Mandate would have brought Britain back to full partnership with Zionism. 'Either Britain will go along with us or she will have to go from here . . . The Arab states will reach independence; one after the other they will eject British rule. Britain will be ejected from Palestine too if the country is not populated by a people which does not belong to the Arab race. The British will understand this and will be on our side regardless of whether they hate or love the Jews. They love Britain and are concerned with the future of the British Empire.'[7] The more the British were relinquishing their obligations to Zionism and restricting Jewish immigration and settlement, the more violent and unbridled became the Revisionists' attacks on the Zionist leadership which, in their eyes, was responsible for the failure and thus had to be removed.

Jabotinsky's concept of Zionist-British relations gave rise, after the 1929 riots, to two contradictory trends in the Revisionist movement. On the one hand there was growing pressure to engage in anti-British actions such as non-co-operation in Palestine, protest demonstrations in European and American capitals, litigation at the League of Nations, Jewish boycott of British goods, etc. Indeed Jabotinsky himself had to restrain these pressures and he called for 'calm', arguing that the divorce from Britain was premature and that Britain had to be given a 'last chance' to better her ways. On the other hand, some Revisionist leaders (Grossman, Schechtman) proposed a 'pause' in Zionist activities in order 'to make it clear to the Mandatory Power and to world public opinion that the Zionists were not prepared to continue investing effort and money in Palestine under all circumstances and that British sabotage might compel them to suspend or curtail this investment'.[8] This idea was rejected by the World Revisionist Conference in Prague (August 1930) (though an allusion to it was made in the resolutions and Jabotinsky did not exclude it altogether). Both trends reflected the unrealism of Revisionist concepts, their misreading of the nature of

Zionist-British relations and the cause of their deterioration.[9]

Jabotinsky over-estimated the British commitment to the Balfour Declaration and the importance of the Zionist movement and the Jewish people to British imperial interests. Weizmann, on the other hand, recognised the fragility and weakness of both. Consequently he did not believe in the 'maximalist' rhetoric and in threatening gestures, and based his hopes instead on the development of a dynamic Jewish Yishuv as the decisive factor in the triangle of Jewish-British-Arab interests. He believed there was no point in making radical demands and threatening speeches at a time when the Zionist movement itself suffered from internal weakness and was not able to produce the men and the capital necessary for a rapid advance of the Zionist enterprise in Palestine. He was also well aware of Britain's vital interests in India and the Middle East and gradually came to recognise the weight of Arab nationalism in the context of British imperial interests. He thus adopted the strategy, reminiscent of Lenin's formula, of taking one step backwards in the spheres of political declaration and geographical area in order to take two steps forward in building up the economic and military strength of the Yishuv.

Jabotinsky's concept of a mass exodus (evacuation), his obsession with a 'Jewish Legion' and his penchant for adventure blinded him to these realities. He thought the gradual building up of the Yishuv was a waste of time and opportunity. The pursuit and promotion of 'Legionarism' pervaded all his writings and political and educational activities. The youth movement 'Betar', which he founded and cherished as his most important creation, was conceived and imbued with the spirit of military education and preparedness, and with the aim of providing the nucleus of a Jewish army in Palestine. Its members were enjoined upon arrival in Palestine not to be immersed in 'small-scale colonisation' so as not to become 'prisoners' of economic interests which would erode their Zionist faith and limit their freedom of action. Indeed of all the Zionist formations in Palestine the Revisionists were the only ones who possessed no kibbutzim, moshavim or economic institutions of their own.[10] They ridiculed the policy of slow and gradual growth ('dunam to dunam, goat to goat') followed by the Zionist institutions. Jabotinsky attributed the failure of the Zionist movement to mobilise the Jewish masses and large-scale resources to the fear of spelling out loudly the historical aim of Zionism: a Jewish state in the whole of Palestine, including Transjordan. This was in his opinion also the cause of the growth of pro-Arab tendencies in British policy.

At one time Jabotinsky went through a short period of loyal co-operation with Weizmann, who was one of the few leaders to view with sympathy the idea of a 'Jewish legion' though he did not attach to it the cardinal importance Jabotinsky did. After his release from prison in February 1921, Jabotinsky, who was then at the peak of his popularity, was enticed by Weizmann into joining the Zionist Executive. He became head of its political department as well as the Director of Propaganda on behalf of the Zionist Foundation Fund (Keren Hayesod). The two years of co-operation with Weizmann (during which time he consented to the Executive's decision to accept the White Paper of 1922 which excluded Transjordan from the area of the Balfour pledge) ended in abysmal failure. Totally isolated in his opposition to the British plan of 1922 for a legislative assembly in Palestine, he was forced to resign from the Executive in an atmosphere of hostility, abuse and indignation owing to a misadventure that was to follow him for the rest of his life. This was his 'pact with the devil' — an agreement with the 'Government in Exile' of the Ukrainian Ataman Petliura who planned in 1922 a new invasion into Ukraine to fight the Soviet regime there.

Petliura made himself notorious as a rabid anti-Semite in 1917-20, when his armies roamed through the Ukraine organising hundreds of pogroms against the Jewish population. Jabotinsky promised to raise money and men to form a Jewish gendarmerie to follow Petliura's armies, without engaging in fighting, in order to garrison and defend the Jewish population in the towns which would be occupied. In the event, the planned invasion did not take place because the West, tired of financing interventionist plans, dropped Petliura and his 'government'. Nevertheless, a flood of indignant protests demanding Jabotinsky's resignation came from every direction from people concerned about the violation of Zionist neutrality and the danger of disastrous repercussions for Zionists in the USSR.

Perhaps it was the disreputable outcome of Jabotinsky's earlier attempt to conquer the Zionist Executive 'from within' that explains the vehemence with which he set out a few years later to 'overthrow' Weizmann's leadership in the Zionist organisation by founding the Revisionist World Union in 1925. When even this challenge proved unsuccessful he seceded from the Zionist organisation to create the 'New Zionist Organisation' in 1935.

The 'New Zionist Organisation'

In founding the New Zionist Organisation (NZO) in 1935 — to challenge the Weizmann-Ben-Gurion dominated Zionist movement — Jabotinsky claimed to be liberating Zionism from 'minimalism' and socialism and restoring the Zionist vision to monistic purity: 'when a generation or generations are facing the all absorbing mission of creating a state — we call upon them: renounce all other dreams, serve only one idea.'[1]

Among the aims and principles of the NZO were: 'the redemption of Israel and its land, the revival of its sovereignty and language';[2] 'implanting in Jewish life the sacred treasures of Jewish tradition';[3] 'a Jewish state on both sides of Jordan'; and 'social justice without class struggle in Palestine'.[4] These formulations indicate the direction in which the NZO envisaged the rallying behind it of social and political forces capable of confronting the Weizmann labour coalition. The slogan of 'social justice without class struggle' was clearly aimed at challenging the hegemony of the labour movement in Palestine and in the Zionist movement. Jabotinsky made no secret about his total opposition to a class struggle and the permeation of the Zionist idea with socialist concepts.

In his early years Jabotinsky selected Jewish socialists, Zionist and non-Zionist, as targets for his violent polemics: 'it would be utterly naive to think that the role of the bourgeoisie has already been played to the very end . . . I even dare to believe that not only in 1923 [the deadline foreseen by Herzl for the creation of the Jewish state], but in 1950 as well, a good fifty per cent of the civilised world . . . will still be only dreaming and longing for the fulfilment of a genuine bourgeois liberalism'.[5,6] Jabotinsky acquired the reputation of being a 'reactionary', an 'anarchist', a 'bourgeois' and it cannot be said that these labels were attached to him unjustly. He did everything to make himself the spokesman and advocate of the middle classes and their economic interests: 'our true field is the "Mittelstand" [middle class]. We will never come to terms with people who possess in addition to Zionism another ideal.'[7] The Revisionists consistently demanded the endorsement of the principle of private land ownership, the revision of the Zionist budget in favour of industry and commerce, the encouragement of private initiative in agricultural colonisation, subsidies and loans to artisans,[8] the prohibition of strikes and lock-outs and national arbitration in labour disputes.

In the early 1930s Jabotinsky headed a vigorous campaign against the inclusion of non-Zionists, as equal partners of the Jewish Agency. In this he was supported by many radical Zionist leaders like Goldmann, Gruenbaum, etc. who fought for an 'undiluted' Zionist programme and for a genuinely democratic structure of the Zionism, as a popular movement, not subject to pressure of economic interest. W. Laqueur viewed Jabotinsky's struggle against the enlargement of the Jewish Agency as proof of his opposition to the Jewish big capitalists. In fact, Jabotinsky opposed the inclusion of non-Zionists not because they were representatives of 'big capital' but because they were unlikely to support his political programme of a Jewish state on both sides of the Jordan.

Jabotinsky claimed that 'we have been taught almost to despise that strong and important element the Jewish merchant, who now comes into his own in Zionism, and we were influenced a little too much by the ringing rhetoric of what our friends in Germany call "Umschichtung" — a dream of creating a nation — of farmers and labourers without a single merchant among them . . . trade is the basis of all economic progress . . . and of national commercial and social development . . .'[9] However, the Revisionist campaign was not limited to the rehabilitation of the artisan, merchant and industrialist. In spite of Jabotinsky's claim that Revisionism would and should unite all social trends in Zionism, the daily he edited (*Doar Hayom*) undertook a ferocious campaign against the socialist parties in the Zionist movement. It contained a column (edited by Aba Ahimeir and entitled Anti-Ma) denouncing Marxists and Socialism in terms similar to the Nazi anti-socialist propaganda in Germany.[10] 'Jabotinsky's own articles reflected the complaints of the private sector of the Palestine economy', wrote his biographer and friend Joseph B. Schechtman. Jabotinsky declared defiantly 'if there is a class in whose hands the future lies it is we — the bourgeoisie, the enemies of the supreme police-state, the ideologists of individualism . . . the establishment of a socialist order is neither desirable nor inevitable nor even feasible . . . humanity is not moving towards socialism, it is going in the reverse direction.'[11] Thus, 'by identifying with the bourgeoisie as a class, Jabotinsky had, in fact, embraced the very same class philosophy he had so vigorously denounced'.[12]

The violent anti-labour campaign, accompanied as it was by venomous propaganda, brawls and physical violence on both sides, created in the 1930s a tension resembling a state of civil war. The attempt to challenge the labour hegemony failed and boomeranged against the Revisionists themselves. They earned for themselves a reputation as fascists due to the viciousness of their anti-socialist propaganda, their unbridled hatred of kibbutzim, their 'character assassinations', the unconcealed sympathy of some members towards the authoritarian regimes (Hitler, for example, was described as the saviour of Germany, Mussolini as the political genius of the century), and their military parades, drills, training and brown shirts resemblant of the fascist movements in Europe. Furthermore, they did not hesitate to recourse to street violence, and they glorified 'terror' against 'traitors'.[13]

Jabotinsky's identification with anti-labour forces alienated the most dynamic Zionist camp precisely at a time when the activist leaders of labour (led by Ben-Gurion) were moving closer towards the idea that the time was ripe for the establishment of a Jewish state. By accentuating class conflict, contrary to his own philosophy, Jabotinsky condemned the NZO, if not to total failure at least to playing a secondary role, just at a time when conditions were ripening in Palestine and for world Jewry for a final decision on the fate of the national home.

Jabotinsky's appeal was more successful in the religious camp, though neither he nor the other founders of the Revisionist movement had a religious background, or outlook. They were all agnostics, brought up in secular environments, and their commitment to a Jewish state on both sides of the Jordan was not conceived through religious conviction. On the other hand, for the National Religious Party (Mafdal) Transjordan was part of the Land of Israel (Eretz Israel) by virtue of divine promise. Mafdal could not conceive of a state without Jerusalem, Hebron, the whole of Judea, Jericho, Shehem (Nablus) and the other territories assigned in the Covenant to the tribes of Israel. The religious 'Misrahi' accordingly opposed the partition plan of 1937, since it excluded places of vital historic significance from the proposed Jewish state. However, the Religious Party concentrated mainly on striving for more influence and better positions from which they could press for the application of religious law in the Yishuv, rather than interfering in matters of foreign policy. It maintained a coalition with the labour movement based on a 'give and take' arrangement whereby the Misrahi left the field of foreign policy in the hands of labour in return for a larger share in the budget and more influence on legislation for religious education and status. In fact not all the religious group supported the demand for historic borders. Indeed, in 1937 a minority of the Misrahi favoured the Peel Partition Plan (Moshe Unna, Pinchas Rosenbluth) although they did not obtain approval to vote accordingly. However, Rabbi Meir Bar-Ilan, head of the Misrahi, refused to proclaim such a vote to be a religious sin.[14]

The NZO platform had a considerable appeal to the religious camp in Zionism. While the older generation of the leadership continued the pragmatic policy of alliance with labour, the sympathy of the younger generation lay with the NZO, and not an insignificant number of religious groups joined the organisation and participated in its activities.

In the late 1930s, the Revisionists and the NZO succeeded in mobilising considerable support among the Jewish masses who were suffering from a grave economic crisis and yearned for immigration. The doors of Palestine — which was experiencing a period of trouble and turbulence — were, however, closed. The spectacular methods of the NZO to have them opened, such as mass demonstrations in Warsaw and New York, negotiations with Poland and Romania on 'evacuation', appeals and protests to the League of Nations, were all in vain. Moreover, the introduction of the 1939 White Paper and the imposition of a British naval blockade along the coast of Palestine, ensured that illegal immigration made hardly any progress.

With the advent of World War II and the Nazi holocaust, an entirely new situation was created. The Revisionists rejoined the Zionist Congress in Basle in 1946 and the NZO disappeared from the scene. Although the NZO had little impact on developments in Palestine, the Irgun Zvai Leumi left its mark on Jewish-Arab relations in the stormy years of the Arab Revolt in 1936-8 and again in 1948. By this time the Irgun had become the main carrier of Revisionist ideas.

Jabotinsky and the Arabs

While Weizmann ignored the Palestinians, he did not under-estimate the growing potentialities of the Arab world. Jabotinsky, on the other hand, ignored both and did not share the attitude of the Zionist leaders that an agreement with Arab nationalism was desirable or necessary. He thought the Arabs were completely irrelevant to the question of Zionism except as enemies. He viewed the conflict with the Arabs as natural and inevitable, but did not regard them as an independent force capable, on their own, of shaping the future of Palestine. As he saw it, there was no solution to the conflict until the Arabs were faced with an 'iron wall', the reality of a Jewish majority and a Jewish power in control of the country.

As regards the creation of a Jewish majority and a Jewish power, he considered the decisive factor to be the British not the Arabs. Once the Arabs were faced with this 'iron wall' and renounced further opposition, he would be ready to give them a fair deal to include full equality of rights, cultural autonomy, recognition of Arabic as an official language, an Arab vice-president, government ministers and participation in economic management — in short, everything the Jews demanded for themselves in the Diaspora. The Arabs would not be required to emigrate from the state, although he would not feel overly distressed if they did.

Towards the Arab national movement at large, Jabotinsky felt what he described as a 'polite indifference'. Of all the Zionist formations, the Revisionists were the least interested in the Arab question. The Arabs concerned them only as enemies, and as enemies they had to be treated without pity. In other words to be smashed as there was no room for compromise. This Revisionist attitude had a strong impact on Jewish public opinion, particularly during times of open conflict and riots.

Jabotinsky's first encounter with the Arab world took place in 1908-9 when he was commissioned to organise and conduct Zionist propaganda in Constantinople. He was able then to observe that Turkish-Arab relations were 'bound to develop into a competition between two equally strong adversaries'.[1] Unlike Victor Jacobson, who was the representative of the Zionist Executive and who toyed with the idea of a Zionist-Arab alliance against the Turks, Jabotinsky warned against over-estimating Arab strength and of attempting to accommodate Arab political aspirations or supporting their anti-Turkish or particularist trends 'because it would do us more harm in Constantinople than it would help us in Palestine'.[2] As a result of his experience in Turkey, Jabotinsky retained a violent dislike of the Orient in general and of Constantinople in particular. This feeling was reflected in one of his stories: 'The East: It is entirely foreign to me . . . mine is a Westerner's mentality . . . And the mob! a sort of permanent row of a yelling rabble, dressed up in savage-painted rugs.'[3]

The 'Jewish Legion' experience brought Jabotinsky to Palestine, where he soon became a member of the Zionist Commission and head of its political department (January 1919). Already then he became critical of Weizmann's methods. He warned Weizmann of the 'growing Arab impudence' and of the anti-Zionist attitude of the British Military Administration. He criticised Weizmann for 'giving a certificate of faith' to British intentions and he threatened to resign 'so that the cry of Palestine shall be heard in Europe'.[4] Reporting on Arab anti-Jewish propaganda and preparations for a pogrom, he demanded 'to make the Arabs realise, once and for all, the firm attitude of the government'.[5]

Typical of Jabotinsky's attitude to the Arabs was his refusal, at his trial for organising self-defence during the Jerusalem riots, to answer questions posed by an Arab court secretary. 'I shall not answer a court secretary who belongs to the tribe of murderers, whose attacks upon innocent people, coupled with pillage and raping, are still going on beyond these walls.'[6]

Jabotinsky violently opposed any plan to give the Palestinian Arabs a voice in the administration. The issue of the Legislative Council in 1922 caused his resignation from the Zionist Executive which had accepted the plan. The Revisionists opposed everything that would 'legalise' co-operation with the Arabs in any field, be it country-wide municipal elections[7] or a sports event.[8] (This referred to an invitation of the Tel Aviv municipality to the Arab Legion for a charity sports event to help destitute Arab families following an earthquake in Northern Galilee.) The Arabs were a 'primitive', 'arrogant' race of murderers and rapists and any attempt at negotiation, conciliation or rapprochement was 'contemptible and repellent'. The Revisionists spearheaded a campaign against the Brith Shalom movement branding the group's call for Jewish-Arab rapprochement as 'political treachery and defeatism'.[9] The role of the 'March to the Wailing Wall' – which was organised by the 'school for Betar instructors' to counter 'Arab arrogance' – in precipitating the riots in 1929 was referred to above. Jabotinsky fully endorsed this 'march' and declared: 'The argument that the Arabs should not have been stirred up is a heritage of the ghetto . . . in Palestine we are not just tolerated guests; and in order to show it the demonstration was necessary.'[10]

In a speech following the 1929 riots (December 1929) Jabotinsky denounced 'the dangerous fallacy of seeking a solution to the Arab-Jewish confrontation through a "rapprochement" with the Arabs. Palestine was the meeting of two cultures which had no common spiritual aspiration, and a genuine rapprochement between them was an organic and historic impossibility.'[11] The Revisionists campaigned against the inclusion of Dr Judah L. Magnes in the Yishuv delegation to a League of Nations Committee which was to investigate Jewish and Arab claims to the Wailing Wall, and they forced the withdrawal of his candidature.[12]

The anti-Arab attitude of the Revisionists reached its peak in the years of turbulence 1936-9, when they broke the line of self-restraint ('havlaga') which had been decided upon by the Jewish Agency, the Va'ad Leumi (National Council – the representative body of Palestine Jewry under the British Mandate) and by the Haganah. 'Self-restraint' (the policy of no retaliation against the innocent civilian population) was motivated by the fear that an escalation of riots and bloodshed would bring about the immediate cessation of immigration: 'If we argue that immigration itself is the means to overcome the disorders and prevent streams of blood, then we cannot commit acts of vengeance . . .'[13] In spite of this, members of the Irgun launched terrorist attacks on civilians causing an escalation of violence on an unprecedented scale. It can be said that the Irgun established the pattern of terrorism adopted 30 years later by Al-Fatah. Among its actions were the wheeling of a vegetable barrow containing a bomb into an Arab market in Jerusalem, firing at a bus and throwing bombs into market places (Jerusalem, Haifa).[14] The perpetrators of these acts were declared national heroes and martyrs. Jabotinsky endorsed this terrorism without hesitation: 'The worst of all horrors known to history is galut, dispersion. The blackest of all characteristics of galut is the tradition of cheapness of Jewish blood "hadam hamutar", the permitted blood, the spilling of which is not prohibited and for which you do not pay. To this an end has been made in Palestine, Amen.'[15]

From the 1936-9 period the Irgun Zvai Leumi was the main carrier of Revisionist policy influencing actual events in Palestine. Jabotinsky himself was Commander-in-Chief of the Irgun but this had more of a symbolic than real significance. The 'Haganah' had to reckon with the existence of the Irgun and was compelled sometimes to combat it and sometimes to collaborate with it as the evolving political situation required. The Irgun made full use of this situation to strengthen itself and to pursue its own plans. In 1947 the Irgun did not reject, as in 1937, the partition decided upon by the UN, but it did not give up its struggle for the whole of Palestine either. It declared its readiness to accept the authority of the Haganah and the Jewish Agency in the areas assigned by the UN to the Jewish state or in the areas controlled by a Jewish government — but it reserved the right to continue its activities in the areas excluded from it (Jerusalem, Jaffa, etc.). The Ben-Gurion provisional government was uneasy, though not entirely, about this arrangement which allowed the official Israeli policy during the war to move in conformity with the UN resolution and at the same time to make use of the Irgun's continued irredentism in other areas whenever it seemed opportune. However, the existence of the Irgun as an independent military formation was not compatible with the principle of state sovereignty, and Ben-Gurion seized upon the first opportunity that offered itself[16] to force the dissolution of the Irgun and the integration of its members and its arsenal into the Israeli Defence Army. From then on the Revisionists had to assume the guise of a political party.

Conclusions

Jabotinsky failed to rally behind him the majority of the Yishuv and the Jewish people and to 'take over' the leadership of Zionist affairs — but he did not lose the ideological battle entirely. The Yishuv and the Jewish masses in the Diaspora rejected most of his concepts, but he left an indelible mark on the Zionist attitude towards the Arab question. He implanted in Jewish psychology the image of the Arab as the mortal enemy, the idea of the inevitability of the conflict and of the impossibility of a solution except by sheer force. He propagated the 'either-or' notion by which all and every means was justified including terror and ruthless retaliation in the struggle for survival.

Attitudes of this kind could not be maintained without an appeal to the most primitive instincts of fear and self-defence, without unleashing emotions of hate and vengeance, without painting the Arab as a primitive, evil and cruel creature scheming diabolical plans, and without inflating feelings of self-righteousness to the point where the whole, absolute truth and justice were on one side only. Once such a psychological structure was erected it served as a partition concealing reality and as a blind obscuring the vision.

The Jewish people rejected Jabotinsky's concept of 'evacuation', 'mass exodus' and purely 'political Zionism'. They opted instead for the Weizmann and labour method of dynamic construction and 'revolutionary practice'. They refused to gamble everything on the adventure of a 'Jewish Legion', and resented the military spirit and style which Jabotinsky was trying to introduce into the young generation. They chose the path of 'self-defence' harnessed to pioneering work.

Above all, the anti-labour and anti-socialist campaign — conducted in a style and manner reminiscent of the Nazi anti-communist propaganda — had a devastating effect on Jabotinsky's image and earned him the reputation of a 'fascist'. Added to this were the many rituals, symbols and ceremonies of the Betar movement which were imitative of fascist movements, the undisguised sympathies for fascism of the neo-Revisionist groups of Aba Ahimeir (from which Jabotinsky never dissociated himself clearly) and, not least, Jabotinsky's own autocratic methods resembling the 'Führer' cult in the Nazi movement. (In 1933, in Kattovitz, Jabotinsky suspended the elected bodies of the Revisionist Conference, nominated a new provisional executive and assumed the role of the 'Leader' with an unlimited mandate.)

The paradox was that it was in the labour movement that the greatest number of 'activists' resided who shared Jabotinsky's idea of a Jewish state in the whole of Palestine as was revealed in the post-1948 period and in particular after the Six-day War in 1967. It was the strategy of these labour activists — who instead of seeking a peace settlement with the Arabs pursued a policy of re-establishing the unity of the country through annexation of Arab territories — which saved Jabotinsky's legacy and paved the way for the ascent to power of his successor Menahem Begin.

Note

This chapter was written and added to the book at the request of the publisher who thought, rightly, that the inclusion of this subject is necessary in order to cover the whole range of Zionist attitudes towards the Arab question — especially in view of recent developments in Israel. Shortage of time did not allow me to look for and peruse primary sources. Rather, I had to rely mainly on personal recollections of events I have lived through and experienced as a member of the Zionist-Socialist Movement, Hashomer Hatzair. However, I have checked these recollections against the official literature of the Revisionist Party. I was rather pleasantly surprised to find that these sources, even though they were written in the spirit of identification with Jabotinsky's view and admiration for his personality, contained enough objective information for a factual appraisal.

Notes

JABOTINSKY'S POSITION IN ZIONISM

1.   Joseph B. Schechtman and Yehuda Benari, *History of the Revisionist Movement*, vol. I (Tel Aviv, 1970), p. ix.
2.   Walter Laqueur, *History of Zionism* (London, 1972), pp. 350-1.
3.   Jabotinsky left behind 18 volumes of fiction, poetry, translations (of Omar Khayyam, Edgar Allan Poe, Dante, Conan Doyle, etc.), articles, feuilletons and speeches: *The World of Jabotinsky*, edited by Moshe Bella (Tel Aviv, 1975), p. 12.
4.   Joseph B. Schechtman, *Rebel and Statesman* (New York, 1956); and Schechtman-Benari, *History of the Revisionist Movement*.
5.   Schechtman-Benari, ibid., p. 1.
6.   Bella, *World of Jabotinsky*, p. 28.
7.   Bella, ibid., p. 141.
8.   Schechtman-Benari, *History of the Revisionist Movement*, p. 67.
9.   Schechtman, *Rebel*, p. 303.
10.   Bella, *World of Jabotinsky*, p. 25.
11.   Laqueur, *History of Zionism*, p. 372.
12.   Schechtman, *Rebel*, pp. 85-6.
13.   Ibid., pp. 89-90.
14.   Schechtman-Benari, *History of the Revisionist Movement*, p. 2.
15.   Schechtman, *Rebel*, p. 202.
16.   Ibid., p. 306.
17.   Ibid., p. 285.
18.   Bella, *World of Jabotinsky*, p. 136.

THE JEWISH LEGION: MYTH AND REALITY

1.   Bella, *World of Jabotinsky*, pp. 19, 24.
2.   Schechtman, *Rebel*, p. 204.
3.   Ibid., pp. 209-10.
4.   Ibid., p. 213.
5.   Ibid., p. 229.
6.   Ibid., pp. 231-2.
7.   Ibid., pp. 240-8.
8.   Ibid., pp. 268-71.
9.   Ibid., pp. 271-3.
10.   Ibid., pp. 252-3.
11.   Ibid., pp. 314-15.
12.   Ibid., pp. 282-3.
13.   Ibid.
14.   Ibid.
15.   Ibid., p. 384.

JABOTINSKY AND BRITAIN

1.   Schechtman, *Rebel*, p. 369.
2.   Schechtman-Benari, *History of the Revisionist Movement*, pp. 35-6.
3.   Jabotinsky mockingly called the British administration in Palestine the 'Hebron government', following the anti-Jewish riots in Hebron in 1929.
4.   Schechtman-Benari, *History*, pp. 296-7.
5.   Schechtman, *Rebel*, p. 425. Jabotinsky's belief in Zionist-British co-operation was evident from his acceptance of the 'Seventh Dominion' project proposed in 1928 by Colonel Joseph Wedgwood. The idea of a Jewish state as the Seventh Dominion of the British Empire was not included officially in the Revisionist programme but Jabotinsky accepted the Chairmanship of the Jerusalem branch of 'League for the Seventh Dominion' built up with the help of the Revisionist movement (Schechtman-Benari, *History of the Revisionist Movement*, pp. 164-5).
6.   Schechtman-Benari, ibid., p. 266.
7.   Bella, *World of Jabotinsky*, pp. 54-5.
8.   Schechtman-Benari, *History of the Revisionist Movement*, pp. 303-4.
9.   The 'pause' idea was proof of how detached had become the Revisionists' 'political Zionism' from the real source of political power, namely the dynamic construction in Palestine. The anti-British trend prevailing in the main among the Revisionists in Palestine was rooted in the reality of the conflict with Britain. It led ten years later to what Jabotinsky, in spite of his anti-British rhetoric, was trying to prevent, i.e. an attempt to divorce Zionism from Britain. But the proposal to separate from Britain arose at a time when both Britain and the Jewish people were facing the same enemy in Hitler. With the outbreak of World War II the offshoots of the Revisionist movement – the Irgun Zvai Leumi (Etzel) and 'Lohamei Heruth' Israel ('Lehi' or Stern group) clashed with their parent movement over the attitude towards Britain. The Irgun fought the White Paper of 1939, but stopped its activities against the British between November 1940 and spring 1944 to give priority to the war with Germany. Lehi maintained that the future of the Jewish people would be determined by the achievement of independence, to which the obstacle was not Hitler but Britain. The leader of the group, Yair Stern considered a deal with Hitler whereby a large German fleet with tens of thousands of Jews would enter the Mediterranean in order to break through the British blockade against Jewish illegal immigration. He even sent a delegate (Naftali Lubentschik) to Vichy-controlled Syria to seek contacts with German and Italian agents. Lubentschik was arrested. In the autumn of 1941 Stern discussed the plan with Nathan Friedman (Yellin-Mor) and proposed to

him that he should make his way to the Balkans and establish the necessary contacts there. Friedman got as far as Syria, where he too was arrested and sent back to imprisonment in Palestine. Although Stern was killed in 1942, Lehi continued the fight against the British throughout the war and was responsible for the assassination of Lord Moyne in November 1944 (S. Katz, *Days of Fire* (London, 1968), pp. 55-6; Laqueur, *History of Zionism*, pp. 377-8).

THE 'NEW ZIONIST ORGANISATION'

1. Bella, *World of Jabotinsky*, p. 21.
2. Ibid., p. 167.
3. Schechtman-Benari, *History of the Revisionist Movement*, p. 238.
4. R. Isaac, 'The Land of Israel Movement', doctoral dissertation, University Microfilms, p. 93.
5. Schechtman, *Rebel*, p. 100.
6. Jabotinsky conceived social progress as the 'liberation of the individual from the chains of the collective', and he defined collectivism as 'mechanical equalisation, subordination of human personality to uniform rules' (see Schechtman, p. 72).
7. Schechtman-Benari, *History of the Revisionist Movement*, p. 223.
8. Ibid., pp. 143-5.
9. Ibid., p. 185.
10. Ibid., p. 187.
11. Ibid., p. 224.
12. Ibid., p. 235.
13. Aba Ahimeir's neo-Revisionist group called itself symbolically 'Brit Habiryonim', which meant 'ruffians' or 'thugs', and it eulogised the 'Sikrikin', a group of assassins in besieged Jerusalem (73 A.D.) which engaged in killing leaders whose inclination was to negotiate surrender to the Romans.
14. R. Isaac, 'Land of Israel', p. 267.

JABOTINSKY AND THE ARABS

1. Schechtman, *Rebel*, pp. 151-2.
2. Ibid.
3. Ibid., p. 160.
4. Ibid., pp. 296-7.
5. Ibid.
6. Ibid., p. 331.
7. Schechtman-Benari, *History of the Revisionist Movement*, p. 105.
8. Ibid., p. 120.
9. Ibid., p. 255.
10. Ibid., pp. 257-8.
11. Ibid., p. 265.
12. Ibid., p. 325.
13. Moshe Sharett, *Diary*, vol. 1 (Tel Aviv, 1968), p. 163.
14. S. Katz, *Days of Fire*, pp. 31-7.
15. Ibid., p. 41.
16. The attempt to bring into Tel Aviv a ship (the *Altalena*) with arms and combatants for the Irgun in violation of the truce agreement imposed by the Security Council Resolution, June 1948. The final dissolution of the Irgun took place on 21 September 1948 after the assassination of Count Bernadotte, and following an ultimatum issued by the IDF.

3   DR NAHUM GOLDMANN

Dr Nahum Goldmann rose to the decision-making level of the Zionist movement only a few years before the State of Israel was established. Since 1935, he had been serving as the Jewish Agency representative to the Mandates Committee of the League of Nations. However, already while acting in that capacity there was evidence of his forceful personality, rich intellectual background, independent thinking and natural qualities of leadership which elevated him to the top echelon of the Zionist movement.

From the very outset of his political career Dr Goldmann understood the vital importance of the Arab problem. He at no time supported the idea of a bi-national state, and he was always unequivocally in favour of the establishment of a Jewish state though not as an aim in itself but rather as an instrument for the creation of a territorial centre in which the Jews would become a sovereign people and thus, in co-operation with Diaspora Jewry, would ensure the continuity of Jewish history. At the same time, however, he maintained that a Jewish state, in order to survive, must achieve peace with its Arab neighbours and become an integral part of the life of the Middle East. Peace between Jews and Arabs was for him — and remains — an over-riding priority. To achieve this goal he has formulated time and time again imaginative proposals and undertaken bold and, at times, risky initiatives. His activities in this field have led to many clashes and stormy debates with the Zionist establishment. In 1937 he was in favour of partition and it was he who revived the idea in 1946 forcing the issue in the Zionist movement against violent opposition from a number of quarters. Yet when he saw that there was some hope, however slim, of agreement with the Arabs he proposed that the proclamation of the state should be postponed in order to see whether there was any way in which a war could be avoided.

In the early 1920s, Goldmann belonged to the Radical Zionists, a group which conceived of Zionism as a popular revolutionary movement whose ideological outlook and militant programme were calculated to make Zionism the dominant force in shaping the cultural, social and political future of the Jewish people. The group took sharp issue with those who assumed that after the incorporation of the Balfour Declaration in the peace treaty with Turkey, signed at San Remo in 1920,

121

Zionism had completed its political task, and that all that remained to be done was to organise practical support for the economic develop-ment of Palestine with the aid of Zionists and non-Zionists alike.

Goldmann was critical of this view. In an incisive article entitled 'Zionist Politics Before and After San Remo',[1] he urged that the Zionist movement must be concerned not only with the economic development of the land but with the means used to secure it. 'Every act we perform, every step we take in our effort to obtain Palestine as our homeland will place its stamp on the character of the Jewish society that arises in Eretz Yisrael.'[2] The form of life that would develop in the Jewish homeland was of primary concern to him.

This attitude brought the Radicals into conflict with Dr Weizmann, who was determined to secure American support and financial aid for Palestine by the creation of a Jewish agency composed of both Zionists and non-Zionists. The Radicals maintained that such a step would lead to the weakening of the Zionist idea in contending the primacy in the Diaspora, and to the renunciation of the special character and pioneer-ing spirit of Jewish settlement in Palestine. Though on this issue the Radicals were allied with the Revisionists, there were great differences in their respective approaches to the major social and political problems of Palestine.

The Revisionists favoured full freedom for private capital and viewed the socialist labour movements and the collective settlements in Palestine as a deviation from the principles of nationalism, and of sound economic practice. The Radicals regarded the kibbutzim and the labour movement as the pioneers of a new type of society based on productive work, social justice, and the primacy of national over private interests.

An enormous gap divided the Radicals led by Goldmann and the Revisionists on their attitudes towards the Arab question and relations with the Mandatory Power. Goldmann rejected the militarist and chauvinist concepts of Jabotinsky. In the platform submitted by Dr Goldmann to the Twelfth Zionist Congress — which took place after violent Arab riots in Palestine — he took issue with Jabotinsky's idea to create a Jewish Legion to 'deal with the Arabs'. He opposed such an idea as immoral and politically disastrous, as it would discredit the idea of Zionism as a progressive movement, and would intensify Arab opposi-tion to the point of nullifying all political achievements.

The talk about a Jewish state identifying itself with the diplomatic-imperialist system (i.e. the British Empire) has discredited us morally and damaged us politically. With all this we have gained neither a State nor a really 'imperial' diplomacy. We have become the Don Quixote of politics, alas on the wrong and morally dangerous side. The 'Legion' idea will suffer the same fate. We shall find ourselves in the sway of a militarist policy, we shall betray our ideals, and we shall arouse and intensify Arab hatred — but we shall not get a Jewish Army. The demand for a Legion will remain a demand. But the danger is in the 'legionairist' mentality that would be created, and that must be rejected.[3]

Dr Goldmann called upon all of the radical elements in the Zionist movement to oppose this idea and 'save the movement from the danger of falling under the hypnosis of military heroism and a military mentality'.

Even at the earliest stage, when the Zionist movement was reacting in a mood of enthusiasm and euphoria to the Balfour Declaration, Dr Goldmann had doubts about the hopes with which the Zionist leadership viewed British promises of support. Therefore it came as no surprise to him that the Zionist Commission, headed by Weizmann, discovered — to its shock, upon its arrival in Palestine — the hostile attitude of the British Military Administration and the violent opposition of the Arabs.

Dr Weizmann ascribed this attitude solely to the anti-Zionist and even anti-Jewish prejudice of the military. Dr Goldmann was the only Zionist leader at that time who took a different view of the situation. He believed that the Arab attitude towards Zionism would prove the decisive factor in British policy. As he put it at the time, he would have found an Arab Balfour Declaration ten times more valuable than a British Balfour Declaration. He did not doubt the sincere wish of the British Government to implement the policy of a Jewish national home, nor did he attribute the 'sabotage' of the Palestine Military Administration to anti-Semitic feelings or lack of loyalty to London. The 'heart of the matter' was Arab opposition: 'Let us not delude ourselves, and let us be honest. We did not have success in the Arab Question. The Arabs were and have remained our enemies.'[4]

Goldmann used the term an 'Arab Balfour Declaration' to draw attention to the importance of the Arab problem for Zionism. But there may have been more to this than he himself realised. The Arabs had an interest in Jewish financial, technical and political help, and were not opposed to Jewish immigration as the basis for a cultural and spiritual renaissance so long as it did not lead to a separate, politically sovereign unit. At various times in the Mandatory Period, leaders of Transjordan, Lebanon, Syria and even Iraq indicated their willingness to see Jewish settlement in their territories. Some of them expressed preference for Jewish aid, even colonisation, to dependence on imperialist powers. But the *conditio sine qua non* was the renunciation of the aim of a Jewish state. The Zionist leadership could accept a British protectorate but psychologically could not entertain the thought of an Arab protectorate, even if this substantially enlarged the prospects for settlement.

Goldmann warned of exaggerating the importance of the Weizmann-Faisal agreement in which Faisal had pledged support for a Jewish home in Palestine, emphasising that Faisal had qualified his suppport, and had also issued anti-Zionist declarations; in any case, Faisal's power and influence proved to be very limited. In Goldmann's view, Britain would not and could not ignore Arab opposition to Jewish settlement, and this opposition would inevitably hamper the full application of a pro-Zionist policy. He did not believe that Britain would suppress Arab opposition by force:

> Perhaps there are Zionist politicians who believe it – they will be disappointed. It is impossible nowadays in the long run to oppress an overwhelming majority of a country. Britain can do it today less than before. Think of Egypt and India. Does one really believe Britain came out of the war stronger and more powerful? True, Britain is a world power, but such power is ultimately ephemeral, based on authority, numbers, fear and respect. The time for such power is up – nations awaken, classes awaken, people awaken . . . [5]

Dr Goldmann sharply criticised Zionist policy on the attitude of Weizmann and the Zionist Executive towards the Palestinian Arabs:

> Our policy is to a large extent only diplomacy. It disregards reality . . . We have until now bypassed the Arab Question. We did so already before the war. We negotiated in Constantinople; we besieged all foreign embassies; we passed time in the waiting rooms of Ministers and dignitaries. But who concerned themselves with the Arab population in Palestine, the most real, firmly rooted, and in spite of its relative international unimportance, in reality the most powerful element? None of our leaders appreciated this; even our settlers in Palestine did not appreciate it; more than that, even the workers in Palestine, who because of their outlook should have shown the most understanding, were dominated by the slogan of

'Jewish labour' and faced this problem without comprehension. Then came the war. We conducted negotiations in all of the chancelleries, we tried to talk with the Turkish Government, we made contact with various political parties and the press . . . there was no factor we did not take into account. But we overlooked the most real and important: the Arabs. Even in the last stage of our Palestine policy, the Balfour Declaration, we by-passed the Arab Problem; because the intermezzo of our negotiations with Emir Faisal cannot be considered seriously as dealing with the Arab Problem, certainly not today. On the contrary, this intermezzo shows how much our leaders are affected by diplomatic mentality; instead of grappling with realities they dealt with an accidental sympathizer on the assumption that his attitude would have a permanent influence on Arab behaviour towards us.

The Arab problem can only be solved non-diplomatically, *by entering into direct contact with the population* . . . as long as we do not initiate such a policy . . . a bold effort to talk directly to the Arabs, to discuss the principles of neighbourly friendly relations and co-existence, to thresh out these problems directly, people to people, Jewish colony to Arab village, group to group, over the heads of Agents, Clubs, cliques, journalists, Emirs, and emissaries — the Arab question will remain a dark spot in the Palestine Problem and the problem will remain unsolved. It should be clear that Lord Balfour and Curzon and Milner cannot 'give' us the sympathy of the Arab population, which is more important than diplomatic guarantees and festive declarations. So long as the population continues to fight us, every British administration will find it difficult to meet our demands.[6]

Dr Goldmann shared with the bi-nationalists the conception of Zionism as a movement aspiring not only for the territorial ingathering of the Jews to their ancient homeland, but also for the creation of a new society which would realise the essential values of Judaism. But he did not subscribe to the idea of a bi-national state.[7] He regarded the attainment of Jewish sovereignty as a necessary part of Zionist realisation.[8] But he accorded the highest priority to the achievement of peace with the Arabs. Goldmann was the only Zionist leader to grasp the dynamics of Arab nationalism, which he regarded as the primary factor to be reckoned with, with the British Empire as only a transitory phenomenon. At a time when the exponents of the Arab cause were Bedouin princes, sheiks and emirs, this indeed demonstrated a unique prophetic vision.

Reviewing this period in retrospect, Goldmann wrote in his autobiography:

> One of the great oversights in the history of Zionism is that when the Jewish homeland in Palestine was founded, sufficient attention was not paid to relations with the Arabs. Of course, there were always a few Zionist speakers and thinkers who stressed them . . . And the ideological and political leaders of the Zionist movement always emphasized — sincerely and earnestly, it seems to me — that the Jewish national home must be established in peace and harmony with the Arabs. Unfortunately these convictions remained in the realm of theory and were not carried over, to any great extent, into actual Zionist practice. Even Theodor Herzl's brilliantly simple formulation of the Jewish question as basically a transportation problem of 'moving people without a home into a land without a people' is tinged with disquieting blindness to the Arab claim to Palestine. Palestine was not a land without people even in Herzl's time; it was inhabited by hundreds of thousands of Arabs who, in the course of events, would sooner or later have achieved independent statehood, either alone or as a unit with a larger Arab context.[9]

Goldmann possessed a sense of political timing and realism which prevented him from falling into the trap of phraseology and maximalist slogans. Therefore he rejected the extreme proposals of Jabotinsky; though instrumental in forcing the resignation of Weizmann in 1931, he allied himself not with the Revisionists but with the Labour Party, which continued Weizmann's policy of co-operation with Great Britain and of constructive development in Palestine.

Given his lack of faith in the possibility of a bi-national state, and his scepticism of the official Zionist belief in the possibility of unhampered immigration under the British Mandate, Goldmann became the leading advocate of Partition. If Weizmann was the symbol of collaboration with Great Britain, Goldmann was the symbol of Partition. Goldmann played a dominant role in effecting partition, a role which accelerated his rise in the Zionist hierarchy.

Two other features distinguished Goldmann's outlook on the future of Zionism from the earliest moments and made him the spokesman for an ideological and political position critical of the official Zionist leadership: his view of the Diaspora and his awareness of the international situation which determined the limits of Zionist endeavour.

In the first instance, Goldmann maintained that a dynamic and two-sided relationship existed, and would continue to exist, between the Jewish enterprise in Palestine and world Jewry. He disagreed with the commonly-held Zionist view that the Diaspora would be 'liquidated' by the immigration of all Jews to Palestine, as the only salvation from an impending catastrophe. As early as 1919, in an essay entitled 'The Three Demands of the Jewish People', he put forward the demands for national autonomy for Jews in countries of the Diaspora and for full civil equality there, as equal to the demand for a national home in Palestine.[10] He denied that there was any contradiction between these demands, insisting that both demands expressed the reality of Jewish life:

> Palestine and the Diaspora do not negate and eliminate each other; they form a unity. Palestine and the Diaspora are two forms of Jewish existence, Palestine the higher, the purer, the more harmonious; the Diaspora the more difficult, the more problematic and specific; but the Jewish people form a unity existing in two spheres.[11]

Similarly he argued that the demand for equal rights was both a realisation of the national existence of the Jews in the Diaspora, and an expression of the fact that Jews were an integral part of the states in which they lived.

This conception of Zionism differed from the mood prevailing in the Zionist movement as a whole, which viewed the demand for national autonomy and civil equality as a dangerous illusion which diverted attention from the real struggle. Millions of Jews were affected by the social, economic and political upheavals in Eastern Europe in the wake of the First World War, accompanied by the new pogroms and anti-Semitic policies which were a threat to the physical existence of Eastern European Jewry. Emigration seemed the only solution, and hundreds of thousands were on the move from East to West.

The Balfour Declaration and the British Mandate gave rise to high hopes in the Zionist movement that Palestine would give salvation to the millions of Jews in Eastern Europe. As it was, these hopes did not materialise. The Russian Revolution (which cut off the largest section of Eastern European Jewry), the sabotage of the British Military Administration, and the violent Arab opposition ended the prospects of immediate large-scale Jewish settlement in a national home. Hence, the Diaspora politics of Dr Goldmann, far from being an illusion and a distraction, became a dire necessity.

Dr Goldmann's preoccupation with Diaspora problems led him to take the initiative in the creation of the World Jewish Congress in the 1930s, as a body uniting the diverse strands of world Jewry. This sprang out of his belief in the importance of the Diaspora in Jewish existence, and its continued importance even after the creation of a Jewish state.

Dr Goldmann always maintained that 'nothing can be falser than the belief that Zion can be built on the ruins of the Galut'. In debates with the distinguished scholar Jacob Kaltzkin, Goldmann opposed the view that the assimilation would destroy Jewish life in the Diaspora:

> . . . the Diaspora fulfills some deep need of the Jewish spirit or collective Jewish soul. We went into the Diaspora of our own free will, just as we voluntarily created the ghetto in order to survive in the Diaspora. Somehow we have at one and the same time a roving and adventurous spirit of a world people and a yearning for the homeland, a longing to be left alone with God and our culture. Jewish history has always shifted between these two poles and this led me to the conclusion that our situation cannot really be normalized by assembling a small portion of the people in Palestine and writing off the rest. I cannot accept the desirability of our becoming just a nation like all the rest, relinquishing the openness to the world and the global breadth of outlook that characterize us today. If the Diaspora could survive along with the Jewish centre, this would make our little country, which is destined to forever remain small, unique and distinctive.[12]

Dr Goldmann did not reject the idea of a Jewish state. He believed the bi-national solution desirable but impractical; but he maintained that the state could not be aim in itself: 'Nothing is more absurd than to regard any state as an end in itself.' In retrospect, he said:

> Even in those bygone years when I, with many other Zionist leaders, fought on the diplomatic front for the acceptance of the Jewish claim for a state in Palestine, I wondered whether we should not ask for a state of a specific character, more in conformity with the special nature of the Jewish people and Jewish history.[13]

More than any other Zionist, Dr Goldmann took the position that it was necessary to move with history, to formulate solutions which corresponded to the long-term trends in international politics. Every

Jewish problem — equality of rights, national autonomy in the Diaspora, anti-Semitism, emigration, the Zionist enterprise in Palestine — were conceived by Goldmann as involving expressions of universal human aspirations as well as specific Jewish needs. It is this international orientation of Goldmann — who understood that Israel must make a moral *as well as* a Realpolitik claim in the world — that makes him unique among Zionist leaders. Most Zionist thinkers have tended to view the international arena within which the realisation of the Zionist ambition was to take place, as *static*. Theodor Herzl's vision of the world was that of an enlightened bourgeois society carrying the message of civilisation and progress to 'uncivilised peoples' who hungered for progress. His ideology sprang from and became inextricably bound with the thinking of nineteenth-century European colonialism. To Dr Weizmann, Arlozoroff and Sharett, the British Commonwealth — or Empire as it then was — was the embodiment of morality, democracy, social justice and political maturity. It was an image that Ben-Gurion was later to transfer to the United States. Despite the bitterness of the relationship between Great Britain and the Zionist movement as it developed during the years of Mandatory Government, a Middle East that lacked a British presence was an unthinkable idea to most Zionist leaders. Reinforced by his experience in guiding the World Jewish Congress, and representing the Zionist cause at international forums, Goldmann was able to oppose the exclusive British orientation of Weizmann and the policy of military strength of Ben-Gurion and his successors.

Goldmann put the highest value on political realism and what he called 'timing'. He argued that only by appreciating the social and political trends in the world could one be a successful statesman. And Goldmann's main perception was that the rise of new nationalistic movements and the decline of the imperialistic system was inevitable. He saw that the rise in power of the Arab states surrounding Israel was therefore inevitable, and that Israel's protection by a great power likely to be transitory and destabilising. Envisioning that Israel would emerge as a unique, neutral state, he saw the necessity for reaching a realistic and immediate political compromise with the Arabs. This is why he was the most faithful advocate of the one solution which offered such an immediate possibility, partition.

Notes

1.   In *Freie Zionistische Blätter*, no. 1, Heidelberg 1921.
2.   Platform of the Radical Zionists submitted to the Twelfth Zionist Congress, published in *Der Jude*, no. 4, Berlin 1919/20.
3.   Ibid.
4.   Ibid.
5.   Zionist Politics Before and After San Remo'', *Freie Zionistische Blätter*.
6.   'While I would not be opposed in principle to a bi-national state in Palestine one would have to consider what is better for us: a bi-national state in the whole of Palestine or a Jewish state in part of the country ... But there is no need today to go into the many complex aspects of the question for the simple reason that the Arabs ... are not psychologically ready for it ... If we were living between 1917-1919 when the League of Nations was created and when the spirit of tolerance was more widely accepted than it is today, the situation might have been different. But we are no longer living in that era. In the meantime the Arabs have learned from Europe the ways of extremist and aggressive nationalism. As a result, the prospect of an agreement between Jews and Arabs is just a utopian dream today and this alternative has been removed from our choice.' (Speech of the Zionist Congress, August 1937.)
7.   'The second aim of Zionism to secure the continuity of Jewish culture and history – would be impossible; would be made impossible in a multi-national state.' (Interview in *New Outlook*.)
8.   N. Goldmann, 'Chronik', in *Der Jude*, New York, 1919-20. Italics added.
9.   N. Goldmann, *Memories: The Autobiography of Nahum Goldmann* (London, 1970), p. 284.
10.   In *Judische Rundschau*, 1919.
11.   Ibid.
12.   Goldmann, *Memories*, pp. 75-80.
13.   'The Future of Israel', *Foreign Affairs*, New York, April 1970.

4 BEN-GURION AND SHARETT

There is no conflict between Jewish and Palestinian nationalism because the Jewish Nation is not in Palestine and the Palestinians are not a nation.

> (Ben-Gurion speech to Inner Action Committee,
> Jerusalem, 12 October 1936.)

David Ben-Gurion

It is impossible to imagine two more contrasting personalities than David Ben-Gurion and Chaim Weizmann. In his bid for the leadership of the Zionist movement in 1946, Ben-Gurion ousted Weizmann from any effective role in decision-making. Though Weizmann's historical role in Zionism was acknowledged in the choice of him as the First President of the state, he was not even invited to sign Israel's Declaration of Independence. Yet, despite their differences, Ben-Gurion agreed with Weizmann's basic strategic concepts. Ben-Gurion, like Weizmann, believed that an alliance between the Zionist movement and a great power was the *sine qua non* for its success. Ben-Gurion foresaw the decline of Great Britain as the decisive factor in the Middle East, and the emergence of the United States as a global superpower, and eventually switched the alignment of the Zionist movement from Great Britain to the United States. Weizmann, on the other hand, retained his faith in an alliance with England up to the moment when she placed the Jewish-Arab problem before the United Nations. Still, until 1939, when the British abandoned their commitment to the Balfour Declaration, Ben-Gurion basically agreed with Weizmann on all major issues. Their disagreements related only to tactics.

Ben-Gurion shared Weizmann's views on the constructive work of the Zionist movement. Like Weizmann, Ben-Gurion was in favour of a Jewish state, but believed it could come about only through steady, practical, constructive work in Palestine which would create an economic, political and military force powerful enough to determine the fate of the country. When the Balfour Declaration was announced, he wrote:

> England is not capable of returning the land to us . . . a people acquires a land only by the pains of labour and creation, by the efforts of building and settlement . . . the Jewish people must itself

131

convert this right into an established fact.[1]

In private discussion, Ben-Gurion was emphatic that his ultimate goal was a Jewish state. 'The independence of the Jewish people was inconceivable without Palestine as an independent political unit, that is, a Jewish state.'[2] He claimed that his party — Ahdut Avoda — was the first to formulate a demand for a Jewish state.[3] Even when he accepted parity and the principle of non-domination ('it is not our aim to dominate anybody'[4]) he made it clear that this was a temporary formula which should not preclude large-scale immigration and a Jewish state:

> The question of parity is one of public opinion . . . we are not dis-
> cussing the final aim . . . we wish to introduce in the area of the
> Mandate, the question of parity, and only as long as the British
> Mandate lasts . . . I do not want a formula which could be inter-
> preted as numerical parity . . . I want a clear, limited formula.[5]

However, like other Zionist leaders, he was sensitive to British opinion and publicly renounced statehood as the aim of Zionism. Thus, in 1936, he told the Peel Royal Commission: 'We did not say it at that time and we do not say it now.'[6] His denial of ambitions for statehood recognised the vital necessity of preserving British support in order to allow the practical work of immigration and settlement to go forward. When asked in 1921 why he, a leader of the workers, followed Weizmann and insisted on co-operation with the British, he explained: 'that so long as we were few and weak, co-operation with the Mandatory Government was thus of vital importance for increasing our numbers and strength in the country.'[7] Like Weizmann, Ben-Gurion regarded co-operation with the British as far more important than co-operation with the Arabs. He too looked down on the Arabs 'de haut en bas':

> From the point of view of mentality, social outlook, public spirited-
> ness and many other aspects, there is a marked difference and
> inequality between the two peoples. There is a difference between a
> nation living in the 20th Century, and people living in the 15th
> Century, some of them in the 7th Century.[8]

The Arab leaders whom Ben-Gurion met in the 1930s reported that his attitude was one of 'arrogant superiority' that showed contempt for the opinions of the Arabs.[9]

Ben-Gurion stressed that the Zionist movement had to look to Europe for its primary orientation.

> Although we were an Oriental people, we had been Europeanized and we wished to return to Palestine in the geographical sense only. We intended to establish a European culture here, and we were linked to the greatest cultural force in the world.[10]

He also emphasised that the aim of Zionism was to become attached 'to a greater unit; that is, the British Commonwealth of Nations'.[11]

Ben-Gurion echoed Weizmann's 1939 round table assessment of the 'unconstructive' and 'negative' Arab national movement:

> There was a basic difference between the Jewish National movement and the Arab National movement. The Arab movement was political only and almost entirely negative in nature. It had done nothing for the development of the country, and Arab leaders were not even contemplating such an activity. The essence of Zionism was that it was a creative movement. We were creating national cultural values in agriculture and industry. We were developing the country and only thus could we make immigration possible.[12]

Ben-Gurion made it clear that Zionism would not join the Arabs in their struggle against colonial powers:

> I did not say that I would mobilize Jewish forces to help the Arabs in Syria, on the contrary, I criticized the Arab National Movement for being based on negation alone, concerned solely with the fight against foreign domination. Our movement was based on positive goals – economic and cultural activity.[13]

He too hoped that the Hashemites could and should control the Palestinian Arabs: 'I would suggest that Abdullah be given supreme religious authority over all Moslems in Eretz Israel, in return for opening up Transjordan to us.'[14] He also thought the Palestinians could be appeased by the promise of the economic benefits from Zionist development. Ben-Gurion assured the Palestinian leaders:

> On the basis of our settlement experience and detailed scientific research, we are convinced that there was room in the country for both Arabs and large-scale Jewish settlement. They would benefit

from the tremendous economic development. We would teach the Arabs modern work methods . . . we would improve sanitary conditions, we would open schools in every village . . . we would ensure an adequate area of land for tenant farmers and we would help improve the Arab economy.[15]

Undoubtedly, Ben-Gurion and other Zionist leaders sincerely believed in the validity of this argument. Why should the Palestinians oppose economic and social benefits in Palestine? Only religious fanatics and feudal landlords defending their narrow corrupt interests would reject such a prospect.

Ben-Gurion believed that the Jews represented the progressive and modern force in the Middle East,[16] and was puzzled that the Arabs did not respond to his generous offer to put Jewish financial and scientific superiority at their service. He stated frankly that the support of Great Britain was primary and that anti-imperialist alliance was out of the question:

Auni Abdul Hadi asked whether we would help the Arabs to get rid of France and England, I answered frankly . . . we would not fight against the English. We too had grievances against the Mandatory government, perhaps no less than those held by the Arabs. But the English had helped us and we wanted them to continue to do so. And we were faithful to our friends.[17]

Besides viewing the Arabs as a secondary factor, weaker and far less important than the great power in the area, Ben-Gurion also shared Weizmann's views about the support for pan-Arabism as substitute for the recognition of the Palestinians as a national entity: Ben-Gurion followed Weizmann's line when he stated that: 'there is no conflict between Jewish and Palestinian nationalism because the Jewish Nation is not in Palestine and the Palestinians are not a nation.'[18] Like Weizmann, he saw the solution to the Arab problem not in terms of an agreement with the Arabs in Palestine, but in the context of a general agreement with an Arab Federation built up with the financial and technical help of the Jews, and eventually including a Jewish Palestine within it. 'If the Arabs agree to our return to our land, we would help them with our political, financial and moral support to bring about the rebirth and unity of the Arab people.'[19] Like Weizmann, Ben-Gurion refused to recognise the Palestinian Arabs as a major party to the Arab-Jewish conflict. He viewed the problem as a confrontation between the

Jewish nation, of which the Yishuv was only a part, and the Arab nation stretching over a vast territory from the Atlantic to the Indian Ocean. The two national aspirations were, in his view, not incompatible; the ingathering of the Jewish nation into a small patch of Arab territory would not impede the realisation of Arab unity in a sovereign state of their own.

> Jewish immigration . . . could not endanger the social, political or national status of the Arabs, who in Eretz Israel constituted only a small part of a large and decisive Arab community in this part of the world. Looking at the issues of the Palestinian Arabs from an overall Arab viewpoint, this was merely a question of a land less than 2% of the total area occupied by the Arabs in the East, and containing 3% of the total number of Arabs in the world . . . there was no comparing the value of Eretz Israel for the Arabs with the importance it held for the Jewish people.[20]

> Our wishes are opposed by the Arabs of Eretz Israel, but they are only a small part of the Arab people as a whole. Today, the Arab people are weak, suppressed, and disunited. The same was true in the past of a number of European nations, such as Italy and Germany, who succeeded in freeing themselves from a foreign yoke. The unification and liberation of the Arab peoples will not be interfered with by a Jewish Eretz Israel. On the contrary, if there is an alliance between us and the Arabs, we can help liberate and then develop the Arab peoples.[21]

> The characteristic difference between the interests of the Jews and non-Jews of Palestine [is] the non-Jewish rights consist of existing assets . . . the Jewish interests consist mainly of the age-old opportunity to develop the natural resources . . . which the Jewish people is destined to uncover and exploit . . . the non-Jewish interests are conservative; the Jewish interests are revolutionary.[22]

To Musa Alami, a Palestinian leader, he said:

> If we formed an alliance and invested manpower, organization, technology, and money in the development of the Arab economy, the entire economic and cultural situation of the Arabs might change . . . we would assist not only in the development of Palestine and Transjordan, but also in that of Iraq. That country offered tremendous possibilities. It had an abundance of fertile land and water. We

were interested in its maximum development both politically and economically.[23]

Ben-Gurion's faith in this approach was so deep that he repeated the proposal to Shakib Arslan, the representative of the Syrian-Palestinian delegation to the League of Nations, promising political support for Syria and capital investment in Iraq, Saudi Arabia and Yemen. Ben-Gurion never understood why this patronising approach angered and offended the Arabs.

There were a number of differences between Ben-Gurion and Weizmann, representing only variations in emphasis but not in strategy. These were partly due to objective circumstances and partly to psychological differences in temperament.

Ben-Gurion entered the arena of international Zionist politics in 1933, when he was elected to the Jewish Agency and the Zionist Executive. This was a time when the Yishuv was well-entrenched, and indeed, during the most dynamic period of its development. While Weizmann formulated his basic strategy during a period when Zionism was very weak (only 27,000 immigrants had entered Palestine in the first four years after the Balfour Declaration), from 1933 to 1935 immigration was at such a rate as to raise the prospect of achieving numerical equality with the Arab population in a relatively short time. The prospect for the maintenance of the Zionist enterprise through Jewish power in Palestine was far more real for Ben-Gurion, who did not see the development of the Yishuv in such a long-term perspective as Weizmann. For Ben-Gurion, the rapid build-up of the Jewish community in Palestine took precedence over everything. He often stated that while England was the decisive *external* factor, the decisive factor 'under all conditions and circumstances is the Jewish people'.[24] He triumphantly recorded: 'We are now living in 1936, and the scale of immigration of the preceding 15 years is devoid of any real value for the Jewish people.'[25]

At the height of Weizmann's activity, the small and weak Jewish settlement in Palestine was entirely dependent on the moral, financial and political support of the Zionist movement and its leadership in London. By the time Ben-Gurion entered upon the stage of Zionist politics, the Yishuv, well-developed politically and economically, had become the most dynamic factor in the World Zionist movement, which had been demoralised by successive crises in the late 1920s and 1930s. The centre of gravity had moved from London to Jerusalem.

Weizmann lived and operated in the circle of the British political elite. Prime ministers, cabinet members, members of Parliament and prominent journalists were among his personal friends and often discussed policy with him over dinner at his spacious house in London. By contrast, Ben-Gurion was a militant trade unionist and labour politician who rose to prominence through sharp conflicts both with Jewish bourgeois parties and a colonial administration hostile to the modern and democratic structure of Zionism, and even more so to its socialist-inspired labour movement.

Weizmann used to say 'The Palestine Administration and England are not identical . . . There is another England. Let us thank God for that.'[26] Ben-Gurion's concept of Britain was formed by bitter experience of an ambivalent relationship with the Palestine Administration, which, deprived of the trimmings of liberalism, free debate and democratic procedure, was a truer expression of British imperial policy than Westminster.

The difference in the emphasis Ben-Gurion and Weizmann placed on the importance of developing the Yishuv through immigration versus that of preserving the relationship with Great Britain was illustrated by Weizmann's readiness for a voluntary cessation of immigration in order to end the Arab Revolt of 1936. This was in response to the suggestion by Nuri Said, the Iraqi leader, who thought that a suspension of immigration temporarily would lead to negotiations resulting, eventually, in a Jewish Palestine incorporated in an Arab Federation.[27] Weizmann later negotiated with the Mufti through an intermediary, a Quaker missionary, despite the fact that the Zionist leadership had rejected the idea of such a concession.[28] The Mufti was unwilling to accept a concession from the Jewish Agency (Weizmann had offered not to take up the immigration certificates that the British Government had issued to the Agency). The Mufti wanted the British themselves to refuse to issue immigration certificates.[29] Ben-Gurion made it clear that Weizmann faced the twin dangers of civil war in Palestine (only the determination to avoid suspending immigration had prevented Jews from retaliating against Arab attacks) and a split in the Zionist movement if he persisted in his course of action.[30]

There was another profound difference between them. Weizmann was a statesman without a party, the spokesman for World Jewry whose unique position was due to his intellect, political insight, charm and diplomacy. Ben-Gurion was a power-oriented politician. As the leader of the Labour Party, he aimed for the leadership of the working classes; as the General Secretary of the Histadruth, he strove to achieve the hegemony of the labour movement in the Yishuv; and as Chairman of the Jewish Agency in Palestine, he prepared the Yishuv to become the decisive factor in the Zionist movement.

Ben-Gurion's adoption of Weizmann's idea of an alliance with Great Britain did not occur immediately. In the late 1920s the labour movement was not represented in the Zionist Executive and opposed unconditional co-operation with the Mandatory Administration (influenced by their hostile attitude towards labour and suspicion concerning their intentions towards the Jewish national home). Ben-Gurion's party, Ahdut Avoda, had, at that time, a Socialist-Marxist platform which included opposition to imperialism as one of its central planks. After the Passfield White Paper (1930), voices were raised in the Labour Party for a campaign in the League of Nations against the British Mandate. Tabenkin (one of the founders of the Achdut Ha'avodah Kibbutz Federation) suggested that international supervision should replace one-sided dependence on Britain. Ben-Gurion threatened all-out Jewish struggle against the British Empire in the wake of the White Paper restriction on immigration and settlement, and some suggested non-payment of taxes or a boycott of English goods. Berl Katznelson expressed deep suspicion of British imperial interests, and questioned Weizmann's optimism concerning British intentions.[31]

But these feelings did not lead to the formulation of an anti-British policy; there was no alternative power to Britain which could take over the Mandate, nor would the League of Nations. Ben-Gurion undertook the task of transforming the attitude of reservation and criticism of the British connection to one of active support for Weizmann, as Mapai rejoined the Zionist Executive. He justified and defended Zionist co-operation with Great Britain at a meeting of the Socialist International in Berlin:[32]

Not because I don't know what the Colonial Office and the British Empire mean, but because we have the right to exist, to work, and to live even in this corrupt world and this corrupt regime; we don't have to wait until a new world emerges before we can breathe. We have the right to come to this country today, and we are not responsible for the existing world order, neither the evil in Russia nor British or French Imperialism. Our aim is to live and work, and we have the right to work under all conditions. We have to make use of all the forces in the world in order to settle a maximum number of Jews in Palestine and build our life there. If we can make use of the devil, we will ally with him. As long as Russia – Tsarist or Communist – and a Labour Britain or the Britain of Balfour, make it possible for us to work here in the task of creation, to strike roots as a nation in this country, we have to make use of all our opportunities and we are not responsible for anything that occurs outside our sphere of work. All the phrases about improving the world are lies and hypocrisy if we cannot transform our nation of weak and suffering shopkeepers into a working and productive people.

The differences between Ben-Gurion and Weizmann were reinforced by psychological factors. Ben-Gurion was blunt, pugnacious and single-minded. He was a realist in politics; but he would follow one line to its very end, to retreat sharply and dramatically only when faced with an insurmountable obstacle. While Weizmann was an incurable optimist and leaned towards smoothing out obstacles and allaying fears, Ben-Gurion was a pessimist, full of distrust and suspicion. He was obsessed by the fear of a British sell-out. Up to 1939, he supported Weizmann's gradualist and pragmatic strategy with respect to a British protectorate. However, he did not share Weizmann's complete identification of Jewish and British interests nor his implicit faith in the 'decency' and morality of British diplomacy. Ben-Gurion distrusted the British and feared the possibility of conflict with them, and criticised Weizmann's exaggerated submission to their wishes. As a Palestinian, his dealing had been mainly with the hostile, pro-Arab and sometimes openly anti-Semitic British Mandatory Administration, not with the parliamentary and press friends of Zionism whom Weizmann had cultivated. As early as 1936, he was sceptical of the value of the Balfour Declaration, holding that:

We are staking everything on the Balfour Declaration. The declaration is a broken reed. Since the issuance of the Balfour Declaration, the Versailles Treaty has been torn to shreds, the Covenant of the League of Nations, signed by 34 nations, had been rendered valueless . . . the Assyrians and Armenians have been deceived, and the Locarno Pact nullified – a pact guaranteed by England, Italy and France, three powerful nations. Italy has violated the law (in Ethiopia) in the face of the entire world. This piece of paper is not in itself enough. England has violated an agreement signed by Baldwin and the President of the United States.[33]

In his analysis of international politics he was more realistic than Weizmann, who was blinded by his enchantment with Britain. Ben-Gurion's support for the British tie was motivated, instead, by his greater perception of the temporary Jewish weakness *vis-a-vis* the Arabs:

> At the moment there is a quarrel between us and the Arabs. For the Arabs it has probably come too late. They are a bit late because we already constitute a force in this country which it will not be easy to liquidate. For us it is too soon, because we are not yet strong enough to face this struggle alone. To a large extent the continuation of our efforts depends on England.[34]

Ben-Gurion's attitude towards the Arabs was apocalyptic, expecting and preparing for the worst. It was not the result of historical foresight, though in many cases he proved to be right. He formed his image of the Arab as an implacable and hostile enemy after only a few years in Palestine. At Sejera in 1900, 'I saw for the first time the acuteness and danger of the Arab problem . . . Jews being murdered simply because they were Jews.'[35] The 1921 Arab riots moved him to say that 'what we had suffered at Arab hands was child's play compared with what we might expect in the future'.[36] In the early 1930s he was already privately counting the manpower potential of the Arab states in the event of war with them.[37]

It was then impossible to predict the course of development of Jewish-Arab relations in Palestine, much less the rise of Arab nationalism in the Middle East. This admonition to plan for the worst, which had all the elements of a self-fulfilling prophecy, was not the result of a careful and rational analysis of trends and developments; rather it grew out of his temperament and his penchant for viewing reality through the prism of the traumatic experiences in Jewish history.

Ben-Gurion's pessimism allowed him to take seriously the Arab Revolt of 1936-9. By 1938 open guerrilla warfare against the British, aimed at preventing partition, was rampant and a massive pacification campaign by the British Army against Arab guerrillas was underway. On the Jewish side 'self-restraint' was breaking down and dissident military groups began attacking Arab civilians in retaliation. Criticism against passive self-defence tactics had spread even within the Haganah itself, the military organisation under the control of the official Zionist movement. Anti-Arab feeling quickly developed into anti-British feelings when one of the Jewish terrorists was caught and hanged by the British, provoking frenzied demonstrations against both the Jewish Agency and the British. Ben-Gurion's intervention was designed to reduce the agitation, restore the authority of the Agency, and stem the deterioration of Jewish-British relations. His ability to see things clearly and not to be governed by passion is illustrated by his appraisal of Arab terrorism in 1938:

I want to destroy first of all the illusion among our comrades that the [Arab] terror is a matter of a few gangs, financed from abroad . . . We are facing not terror but a war. It is a national war declared upon us by the Arabs. Terror is one of the means of war . . . This is an active resistance by the Palestinians to what they regard as a usurpation of their homeland by the Jews — that's why they fight. Behind the terrorists is a movement, which though primitive is not devoid of idealism and self-sacrifice. From the time of Sheikh Izz al din al Qassam it was clear to me that we were facing a new pheno-menon among the Arabs. This is not Nashashibi, not the Mufti, not a matter of a political career or money. Sheikh Al Qassam was a zealot ready to sacrifice his life for an ideal. Today we have not one, but hundreds perhaps thousands [like him]. Behind them is the Arab people. In our political argument abroad, we minimize Arab opposition to us. But let us not ignore the truth among ourselves. I insist on the truth, not out of respect for scientific but political realities. The acknowledgement of this truth leads to inevitable and serious conclusions regarding our work in Palestine . . . let us not build on the hope the terrorist gangs will get tired. If some get tired, others will replace them. A people which fights against the usurpation of its land will not tire so easily . . . it is easier for them to continue the war and not get tired than it is for us . . . The Palestinian Arabs are not alone. The Syrians are coming to help. From our point of view, they are strangers; in the point of law they are foreigners; but to the Arabs, they are not foreigners at all . . . The centre of the war is in Palestine but its dimensions are much wider. When we say that the Arabs are the aggressors and we defend ourselves — this is only half the truth. As regards our security and life we defend our-selves and our moral and physical position is not bad. We can face the gangs . . . and were we allowed to mobilize all our forces we would have no doubts about the outcome . . . But the fighting is only one aspect of the conflict which is in its essence a political one. And politically we are the aggressors and they defend themselves. Militarily, it is we who are on the defensive who have the upper hand . . . but in the political sphere they are superior. The land, the villages, the mountains, the roads are in their hands. The country is theirs, because they inhabit it, whereas we want to come here and settle down, and in their view we want to take away from them their country, while we are still outside. They defend bases which are theirs, which is easier than conquering new bases . . . let us not think that the terror is a result of Hitler's or Mussolini's propaganda — this helps but the source of opposition is there among the Arabs.[38]

But his accurate assessment of the deep-rooted character of the Arab Revolt did not lead him to serious negotiations with the Palestinian Arabs. It led him to an even more militant line on the need to build up Jewish military strength in order to coerce the Arabs. His warning about the seriousness of Arab opposition was designed to make the Jewish community realise that it had no choice but to reaffirm its ties to Great Britain until it was ready for a full-scale confrontation with the Arabs.

Ben-Gurion's Talks with Arab Leaders

Unlike Weizmann, Ben-Gurion did not try to conciliate the Arabs and allay their fears. He preferred to state Zionist aims bluntly. He believed that Arab fears were an essential stimulant for an admittedly *temporary* and tactical agreement with the Arabs.

The legend of the domination of the world by the Jews is for them a fact . . . This is the source of the fear that grips all the Arab leaders. And although this fear causes us a lot of trouble, it may also serve as a stimulus and an incentive for an agreement. For if we can mitigate their fear by means of certain arrangements, it is not out of the question that they will accept a temporary agreement . . . which contains a blessing for us and at the same time reduces the danger to them, as they picture it in their minds, even though this danger does not really exist or is much smaller than they envisage it.[39]

Ben-Gurion took the initiative in the early 1930s (after his ascendancy to the Zionist leadership) in meeting a number of Arab leaders. At this time a spirit of self-confidence and belief in the speedy realisation of Zionist aims predominated Zionist policies. Arab political life was marked by a resurgence of the pan-Arab idea, in Palestine as well as in Syria and Iraq, which were on their way to independence. Ben-Gurion approached Arab leaders known for their pan-Arab views, in the hope that they would recognise Zionist aims in return for political, financial and technical support for Arab unity.

Ben-Gurion demanded more from the Arabs than he got from the

British — renunciation of their political and national rights in Palestine. The Mandate had promised a national home for the Jews, while Ben-Gurion demanded a sovereign state. He demanded from the Arabs freedom of Jewish immigration and settlement; he rejected all proposals for agreed quotas on immigration or even a ceiling for a limited period. He offered aid to the Arabs, but made it clear that Zionism would proceed with the establishment of a Jewish state in all Palestine, including Transjordan, despite their opposition. 'We had come here and would continue to come with or without Jewish-Arab understanding.' In response to Antonius' question whether the Jews would be prepared to modify their goal if it should become evident that the aspirations of the two sides were irreconcilable, Ben-Gurion declined to answer. Ben-Gurion had no illusions that the Arabs would be eager to come to agreement. He recognised their fears of massive Jewish immigration in an inevitable struggle for Palestine, but he rejected Dr Magnes' idea to dispel Arab fears by fixing a maximum figure for Jewish immigration for a specified period: 'Were I an Arab I would not accept this proposal.'[40]

In response to the peace proposals of 'The Five' in 1936, for Arab-Jewish reconciliation, Ben-Gurion wrote out the following statement:

They will mislead the Arabs into thinking that the Jewish people will abandon Erez Israel and thus intensify Arab intransigence. It is not in order to establish peace in the country that we need an agreement . . . peace for us is a means. The end is the complete establishment of Zionism. Only for that do we need an agreement. The Jewish people will never agree to, and dare not agree to, any agreement not designed for that purpose . . . a comprehensive agreement is undoubtedly out of the question now. For only after total despair on the part of the Arabs, despair that will come not only from the failure of the disturbances and attempt at rebellion, but as a consequence of our growth in the country, may the Arabs finally acquiesce in a Jewish Erez Israel.[41]

Ben-Gurion emphasised the necessity of Jewish power in the attainment of Zionist aims:

I say: there is no example in history that a nation opens the gates of its country, not because of necessity . . . but because the nation which wants to come in has explained its desire to it. My prognosis is that agreement will be reached because I believe in our power, in our power which will grow, and if it will grow agreement will come . . .[42]

Ben-Gurion's territorial aims were large. He never tired of reminding his Arab listeners of the historical boundaries of Erez Israel. He had advocated these historic boundaries since 1918,[43] quoting the Bible to prove that the Hebrews had settled on both sides of the Jordan. In his talks with Musa Alami he demanded unhampered Jewish settlement in Transjordan as the price of a peace settlement with the Arabs though this was excluded by the White Paper of 1922, which the Zionist Organisation opposed but accepted.[44]

These talks with Arab leaders in 1934-6 (Auni Abdel Hadi, Musa Alami, George Antonius, Shakib Arslan and others) amazed, frightened and angered the Arabs. Their suspicions that the moderate declarations of Zionist leaders were public relations were confirmed when Ben-Gurion demanded that they accept a Jewish state in all of Palestine including Transjordan, and Jewish settlement in Syria and Iraq, in return for Zionist support for the establishment of an Arab federation including Palestine. The difference between Weizmann's conciliatory tone and Ben-Gurion's bellicose approach, as well as the striking contrast between Ben-Gurion's private pronouncements and public statements, provoked angry reactions in all centres of Arab political activity and destroyed the last vestiges of trust in the sincerity of Zionist declarations. He was later criticised within the Zionist movement by Werner Senator, a member of the Jewish Agency Executive:

> He made declarations about maximalist aims of Zionism. Ben Gurion thought it was a great achievement leading to negotiations. But the result will be Arab distrust of our public declarations which will be quite different. If we now declare we support parity, Arabs will not believe it and for a long time we will not be able to regain their trust. The Arabs will say Ben Gurion is an honest man and in his talks revealed what the Jews really want . . . It's time to stop double-faced politics.[45]

Ben-Gurion on Parity

The clearest illustration of Ben-Gurion's basically tactical approach to relations with the Arabs — dealing with them only when they affected the British connection — is his position on parity — the proposal for equality between Jews and Arabs in government whatever their ratio in the population.

For some time before 1930, Ben-Gurion believed in a cantonal system as a stage to the political realisation of Zionism (Jewish and Arab independent territorial units joined in a legislative framework to deal with foreign affairs, as in Switzerland).[46] He actually drafted such a programme as the first constitution of Mapai, the Labour Party that was created in 1930 by the merger of Ahdut Avoda and Hapoel Hatzair. In 1931, Weizmann persuaded Mapai to adopt the parity formula as the concrete political expression of the principle of non-domination. Ben-Gurion accepted this as a 'transitional programme' only.

> Jews and Arabs would participate in the executive branch on a parity basis. The ultimate result would be an independent state linked to the Arab Federation and with British interests protected . . . the status of Transjordan still required clarification — whether it would be an integral part of Eretz Israel or would have some intermediate status between Eretz Israel and Iraq but Jewish settlement without any political restrictions would be assured too.[47]

But Ben-Gurion when he became Chairman of the Jewish Agency in Palestine (1935) made no attempt to have parity adopted as an official position of the Zionist Organisation. When the crisis of the Zionist movement in the early 1930s was over, giving way to growing immigration of Jews fleeing European persecution in the mid-1930s, overt support for parity fell by the wayside. The British Government began to move slowly towards a more formal acceptance of parity, but Shertok (Sharett) told the British High Commissioner in 1935 that: 'Parity was never put forward formally but as a tentative suggestion assuming that if accepted by Government, might be endorsed by Zionist Organization.'[48] Sir Arthur Wauchope reported his reaction as one of great surprise: 'This astonished me greatly for I had thought both Arlozoroff and Ben Gurion and he himself had repeatedly and strongly urged this claim . . . no hint was ever given to me that they represented only themselves and not the Agency.'[49]

The reason for the change in attitude on the Legislative Council and parity was expressed by Ben-Gurion in a cable to the Zionist Executive: 'Ben-Gurion stated we fundamentally categorically opposed whole scheme [Legislative Council] even if based on parity. Explained opposition now particularly strong in view of present position diaspora and possibility rapid development Palestine.'[50]

However, the Arab Revolt of 1936 made the issue of parity important again — because of its influence on the now hesitant British attitude towards free Jewish immigration into Palestine. As Ben-Gurion outlined the situation:

> England is not wholly in accord with our enterprise . . . she is hesitant, apprehensive. She wants the friendship not only of the Jewish people, but the Moslem and Arab world . . . If we succeeded in removing the growing obstacle of Arab opposition we will immensely strengthen our political position with England . . . the great, decisive struggle over the scope of immigration is still before. An agreement with the Arabs will give us a tremendous advantage.[51]

> We will strive for a Jewish-English agreement. In order to increase the possibility we must be prepared for a Jewish-Arab agreement . . . it is not enough to say No. I am for parity that gives something real both to the Arabs and to us.[52]

With the advent of the Royal Commission, Weizmann and Namier in London proposed an immediate declaration in favour of parity. They argued that this was the reply to all the professed fears of the Arabs of Jewish immigration leading to a Jewish majority, and at the same time an advantage to the Jews, being a minority. Further, it would impress British public opinion.[53]

But Ben-Gurion opposed any declaration for parity. This tactical division was the first serious difference he had with Weizmann, and the first time his view prevailed. Ben-Gurion did not want to concede too much in advance by agreeing to parity, because the British would take this as the starting point for further concessions limiting the Jews to permanent minority status.[54] He also felt that the Arabs would interpret a Zionist proposal for parity as an Arab victory or a trick against them.[55] It would not allay their fears.[56]

Later Ben-Gurion explained the reasons for his position. First, British public opinion, unfamiliar with the complications of Palestine, would not see the declaration as a concession; secondly, such a declaration would arouse hostility in the Arab world; and thirdly, it would make it difficult for the Peel Commission to propose parity itself.[57]

But it was not only these tactical considerations that prompted Ben-Gurion to oppose a declaration on parity, which he favoured in principle. Ben-Gurion claimed that his decision was due to the paramount importance of maintaining the unity of the Zionist movement — as leaders of the right-wing and religious faction (Ussishkin, Fishman,

Gruenbaum) had threatened a split if parity was made official policy.[58] There can be little doubt, however, that unity was not Ben-Gurion's over-riding consideration in opposing Weizmann. Less than a year later Ben-Gurion was willing to fight for partition against much more serious opposition within the movement. The appeal to support from the right wing was a manoeuvre in the struggle for leadership that Ben-Gurion was to repeat in subsequent years until he was able to defeat Weizmann at Basle in 1946.

Ben-Gurion succeeded in delaying the meeting of the Zionist Action Committee until he was sure of a majority to prevent a declaration on parity.[59] He argued that if the British Commission were to propose parity, the Zionists should accept it, but they should not propose it themselves and should speak only of 'non-domination'. A number of Mapai leaders (Kaplan, Sprinzak) were inclined to support Weizmann, but Ben-Gurion received the support of its most authoritative leaders. Ben-Zvi added that 'today parity is an advantage to us, tomorrow it will be a concession. For the Arabs it is the opposite.'[60] They revealed their growing mistrust of Weizmann when Berl Katznelson stated: 'After all, we are more for parity than he is. For us it is a principle, for him a manoeuvre.' Sharett was among those who could not 'understand the difference between accepting the principle of parity and public declaration in favour of it', but Ben-Gurion sharply reminded him that 'Zionism did not declare its final aim — this does not mean it doesn't have one.' Sharett was also worried by Weizmann's threat not to testify before the Royal Commission if he was not allowed to declare for parity.[61]

When Weizmann arrived in Palestine for the meeting of the Jewish Agency Executive, he expressed surprise that the principle of parity was being debated.

Had I known that the principle itself was in dispute I would not have pronounced parity in Basle [in 1931] . . . 'non-domination' was a new political platform not a vague propaganda formula. There are Englishmen who regard the Balfour Declaration not as a commitment but as a propaganda manoeuvre motivated by war needs. We reject this interpretation. The same should apply to our statements . . . Otherwise Zionism will lose its credibility after it has pronounced the principle of non-domination . . . it would be a disaster in our relations with Great Britain and the world.[62]

After a heated debate, the meeting approved only the reiteration of the 'non-domination' formula to the British, and an agreement to discuss parity if it were to be proposed. Weizmann's suggestion, to accept such a proposal immediately, was not voted upon.

The debate on parity only demonstrated that Ben-Gurion was able successfully to contest Weizmann's heretofore monopolistic hold over the Zionist movement and present himself as a factor of equal weight. From this time on, Ben-Gurion was able to strengthen his position as the representative of the Yishuv and ultimately the undisputed leader of the whole movement. Within a year, both Ben-Gurion and Weizmann accepted the creation of a Jewish state in part of Palestine (partition) as the only solution which would assure the future of Zionism. Their tactical differences did not diminish, but increased over the years leading to statehood in 1948; the issue in dispute, however, concerned the standpoint *vis-à-vis* the British, not the Arabs. Weizmann always considered persuasion and diplomacy as the only way to achieve full co-operation from Great Britain. Unlike Weizmann, Ben-Gurion, drawing upon the effectiveness of the Arab Revolt on British policy, believed that confrontation with Britain was in certain circumstances an inevitable and more efficient means of pressure. His complex tactical campaigns to achieve similar goals in 1937 and later, both within and without the Zionist movement, will be analysed in subsequent chapters.

Moshe Sharett

An important Jew told me that we must obtain an agreement with the Arabs because without it the danger will grow. I answered him that I know the danger is great and will grow, but this is not enough to make an agreement [possible] because there are problems without a solution. He answered that there are no problems without a solution. I said: the problems without a solution are those that only time will resolve.

Moshe Sharett (speech in Jerusalem, 22 May 1936.)

Of all the Zionist leaders in the pre-state period, Sharett was the only one who showed a deep understanding of the Arab problem. Having lived for many years in an Arab neighbourhood, he acquired a thorough knowledge of the Arab language as well as of Arab culture and psychology. The close friendship between his family and Arab neighbours led Sharett to respect and to view with affection aspects of Arab social life and human relations. His private diary does not lack expression of admiration for the politeness and cultured behaviour of a group of Arab pupils or for the beauty of a religious sermon delivered by the

Mufti Haj Amin al Husseini.[1] More than any other Zionist, he understood the nature and problems of Arab nationalism and of Palestinian
opposition to the Zionist venture.

The commonly-held Jewish view of the Arab Revolt of 1936 was
that it was an expression of mob violence and terrorism instigated by
criminal elements at the behest of the Arab Higher Committee, and
encouraged by the Mandatory Government in order to cover up its
intention of limiting Jewish immigration and settlement. Sharett claims
that the Arab fears of Jewish domination were real and deep, irrespec-
tive of whether they were objectively warranted. He believed that these
fears motivated the opposition of the Palestinians to the development
of the Jewish national home.[2]

Sharett rejected the superficial view that the Arab protests were
orchestrated by the Mandatory Administration and that it deliberately
tolerated the spread of violence and terrorism. He viewed the Arab
rebellion as part of the world-wide revolt against colonial rule. Sharett
pointed to the riots in India, Iraq and Egypt, where no Zionist problem
existed and in which the British possessed military forces far more
numerous than in Palestine.

In a speech to the Mapai Political Committee on 9 July 1936, he
stated:

> I spoke about a revolt and 'masses'. There was a time when we said
> that there is no Arab movement. There are only Effendis defending
> their personal interests. I was already against this view in the Karls-
> bad Congress. I said there that the Arabs have genuine national
> interests which prompt them to oppose us. Some comrades say that
> the present Arab leadership is not the legal representative [of the
> Palestinians]. I warn you of this illusion. There is no Arab in Pales-
> tine who is not harmed by Jewish immigration; there is no Arab who
> does not feel himself part of the Great Arab Nation which includes
> Iraq, the Hedjaz, and Yemen. For him Palestine is an independent
> unit that had an Arab face. That face is now changing. In his eyes
> Haifa was an Arab town, and now it is Jewish. His reaction cannot
> be but resistance. Even if this resistance contradicts his personal
> economic interests, it continues to be deeply rooted in his heart —
> and in stormy times, when free rein is given to the people who have
> been jostled out of their daily routine, who can strike and revolt
> without restraint, while the government looks on as if nothing is
> happening — that something in the heart makes the movement a
> popular one and this is not artificial . . . No doubt opposition to us

embraces today masses of Palestinian Arabs. Even if one day the masses will revenge themselves on their leaders for their suffering and losses, their suffering today does not reduce their opposition but intensifies it. The masses know that all this is because of the Jews, and they believe that because they suffer they must gain something. The present leadership consists of people brought to the top by this mood, and we cannot say that because the leadership was not elected it is not a leadership. We can't say that we are ready to negotiate and at the same time discredit the leadership. The Arab public recognizes them as such, the Government recognizes them as such . . . If one claims that we cannot negotiate with this leadership because it does not represent the Arab people, one should give up altogether contacts with the Arabs.[3]

In another speech to his party, on 28 September 1936, Sharett was even more emphatic about the seriousness and popular character of the Arab revolt.

I am convinced that the Arabs genuinely fear Jewish growth and domination. If this is not true, then all the years I studied Arabic and have met with Arabs were in vain. And if I am wrong on this fundamental question I am not fit to be here. There are diverse elements in this revolt — anti-British and anti-Jewish, as was not the case in Syria. But if this is not a revolt then the uprisings in Egypt and Syria were not revolts. The revolt would have erupted anyway and I am not sure the Government could have prevented it.[4]

His conclusion that Arab opposition to Zionism took the form of a genuine mass movement stemmed from the appearance of new elements that had not been present in previous Arab protests: the active participation of the Christian Arabs and even Christian women in support of the guerrillas operating in the country; the sympathy and even enthusiasm of the urban intelligentsia for the resistance; and the fact that a desire to 'save' the Arab character of the country, and not opposition to Jews as such, seemed to be the fundamental motivation for the revolt.[5] In fact the revolt of 1936 differed fundamentally from the riots of 1929, which were characterised by pogroms against Jews in Arab towns. There were no attacks for many weeks in 1936 on Jewish settlements (except for the destruction of orchards and crops), and most of the Jewish victims were killed during demonstrations or in roadside ambushes.

Sharett's evaluation of Arab nationalism differed radically from Weizmann's and Ben-Gurion's 'pan-Arab' approach which completely ignored the Palestinian aspect of the problem. Sharett was too honest intellectually to believe the Arab problem could be solved by offering Zionist support for the realisation of Arab unity. As head of the political department of the Jewish Agency, he and his lieutenants were in continual contact with Arab leaders. Sharett himself met and talked with Emir Abdullah of Transjordan, Nuri Said of Iraq, Riad al Sulh of Lebanon and other Egyptians, Saudis, Lebanese and Palestinians in one year alone (1936). He thought pan-Arabism was only an ideal and that many conflicts blocked its fulfilment.

The East is not a monolithic bloc, but a mixture of nationalities torn by religious and national conflicts. In this pattern we claim our place.[6]

A Jewish state economically and militarily strong will gradually integrate in a Middle East federation. But this is a dream, the realization of which does not depend on us. We shall not build an Arab Federation, for the time being it's a dream and nothing points to the fact that the Arabs are going to realize it. Syria and Iraq are first interested in strengthening their national economies and independence. It's not a solution for today.[7]

Sharett closely followed developments in Iraq and Syria, which seemed to confirm his scepticism about pan-Arabism. He wrote about Iraq: 'The new Government of Iraq is more Iraqi than Arab and relies more on elements opposed to pan-Arabism and is aiming at an alliance with Turkey and Persia.' He added that in a talk with a Kurdish politician very close to the government, aid was sought to help strengthen Iraqi-British relations, while he (Sharett) was trying to obtain proofs for British public opinion to counter the argument that the whole Arab East has been stirred to opposition to Britain by her policy in Palestine.[8]

Sharett analysed Syrian motivations similarly:

The new National Bloc government of Syria [established by the Treaty of Independence of 9 Sept. 1936] must provide bread and services. Palestine is first in Syrian exports; Syrian labourers in Palestine return money to the country and the Government is interested in Jewish financial and technical aid. The leaders of the

National Bloc told the Palestinians even before independence that they want quiet in Palestine.[9]

Sharett's concern was that pan-Arab propaganda would be taken too seriously by Great Britain, not that it was useful in appeasing the Palestinians:

> One of our difficulties is that we don't know if our efforts corre-spond to British policy in the Middle East. As an example . . . the conflict between the rigid nationalistic concept based on Arab racial consciousness and the constructive concept of practical policies based on the specific needs of every Arab state . . . we are worried, not knowing which of these trends is supported by Great Britain. We are inclined to think that the traditional policy of supporting pan-Arabism has the upper hand.[10]

> It will be important to prove to the British that the argument that there is a hostile pan-Arab world united and ready to help the Palestinians is devoid of truth, that the devil is not terrible and Britain will not lose its positions in the Middle East if it implements the Mandate in full.[11]

He opposed the plan to involve the Arab states in the Palestine conflict through an appeal to the Palestinians to call off the general strike. 'Nuri Said's intervention is contradictory to the Mandate. Palestine is not an Arab country . . . the Arabs in Iraq don't need another home because they have their own.'[12]

The dilemma of Sharett was that while he posed deep questions he provided no answers.[13] In the debate on the line to be taken before the Royal Commission sent to investigate the 1936 disturbances he had painstaking queries for his Labour Party colleagues:

> We'll be told that the Arabs don't want us — what will be our answer? that they have no rights and we claim Palestine for us? We will be told that the Arabs are worried about their future. What will we say: 'pay no attention to this'? We can't say that we are not obliged to disperse Arab fears, that they don't suffer as individuals and that their suffering as a nation does not concern us because we are here as a nation and they have other countries . . . I doubt if we can adopt such a position . . . We çannot refrain from proposing a solution. We have to be ready to give guarantees for non-domination

and against their dispossession from the land. What is the answer: cantonization? legislative council? parity? Are there other ways to prove our readiness not to dominate the Arabs?[14]

It was characteristic of Sharett that he confided his doubts and uneasiness of conscience to his diary, only rarely sharing them with his comrades in the leadership of the Labour Party. Outwardly, in his negotiations with the British or in the debates in the Jewish Agency Executive he was a staunch supporter of the 'official' line. Thus on the same issue, when discussed by the Jewish Agency, Sharett spoke of the necessity of realising Zionist aspirations regardless of Arab attitudes and by force if necessary. While understanding that there was a Palestinian people, he felt it was their fate to suffer at the expense of Zionist goals:

> Their suffering as a nation does not concern us because we are to have the nation and they have other countries.[15]

> We aim at statehood though we don't have to use the word state. For us Palestine is the only country . . . When we demand Palestine for us it is not at the expense of the Arab Nation as a whole, only at the expense of the demand of Palestinian Arabs to be recognized as an Arab people of Palestine, the only owner of the country . . .[16]

In his contacts with the British High Commissioner, Arthur Wauchope, he proved himself a harsh and uncompromising negotiator, objecting forcefully to any restriction of Zionist purpose or programme regardless of opposition. He demanded a 'strong hand' towards the Arab leaders who encouraged strikes and riots; the arrest, deportation, and dismissal from office of all those who advocated civil disobedience and strikes, or refused to pay taxes. He was not against the imposition of martial law and emergency regulations which would make any activity conducive to the continuance of the protests illegal,[17] although he had doubts about the efficacy of such stringent measures and believed they might prove counter-productive, and a potential instrument of oppression against the Jewish community (as indeed later proved the case).

As a matter of fact, Sharett shared with Ben-Gurion the same order of priorities in Zionist policy. In his view, immigration and settlement, and the creation of Jewish economic and military power, must precede all other objectives, including peace. Anything endangering these priorities must be vigorously opposed. Sharett told the High Commissioner:

> The problem of peace between Jews and Arabs cannot be resolved
> by persuasion . . . it can be resolved only by faits accomplis — the
> establishment of a Jewish community large enough to give the Arabs
> a permanent feeling of respect and dissuade them from any thought
> or intention of destroying it or preventing its growth through acts
> of violence.[18]

For Sharett, immigration took precedence over everything else. He was
for an agreement with the Arabs on parity, not because he believed in
it, but because he hoped it would prevent the limitation of immigration.

> The parity formula deprives the Arabs of their weapon — fear of
> Jewish domination — and will make it difficult for the Peel Commis-
> sion to lean to the Arab side and to propose limiting immigration.
> Our fate in Palestine will be determined not by political formulas
> but by the number of Jews.[19]

In the crucial Inner Action Committee meeting of the Zionist Executive he argued:

> If there is opposition to parity, that it is against our interests, that
> we shall debate; but if it is because it is unlikely to be accepted by
> the Arabs, such an argument is weak . . . The connection between
> parity and immigration is that parity is at the moment one of our
> strongest weapons in the war for immigration . . . The question of
> parity is not a matter for our decision, it is a verdict, fate.[20]

In this period Sharett was a Ben-Gurionist, not a Weizmannist. In the
end he supported Ben-Gurion's position on parity. He joined Ben-
Gurion in his fight against Weizmann's initiative in trying to end the
Arab Revolt by offering a temporary concession on immigration. He
told the Central Committee of Mapai (9 July 1936): 'As for Weizmann,
we know his weaknesses. That is why it is essential for our people to be
next to him in London. That is why it was essential for Ben-Gurion to
return there immediately.'

Weizmann had discussed the proposal for a temporary suspension of
immigration with Nuri Said, the Iraqi Foreign Minister, in London.
Sharett subsequently met Nuri Said in Jerusalem and made it clear to
him that the Palestinian Zionist leadership opposed Weizmann's line,
in the following dramatic interview.[21]

Nuri Said: I discussed with Weizmann how to restore the great idea contained in the Weizmann-Faisal agreement. A psychological bridge is necessary to restore the trust of the Arabs, who are not convinced of Jewish sincerity. Voluntary suspension of immigration would serve this purpose.

Sharett: The Jewish Agency is united in opposing this.

Nuri Said: In the First World War the lines of Jewish-Arab co-operation were laid out: if one great Arab State was established, even a million Jews in the Jewish National Home wouldn't matter. But this state did not come about; instead, a number of small and unstable states, including Palestine, were created. The Arabs are afraid of superior Jewish intelligence [*Sharett:* We are of the same race; *Nuri:* but you are more developed] and Jews must take the first step.

Sharett: The Arabs have started killing Jews. The Jews aren't killing the Arabs. The cessation of immigration would mean that the Jews have lost because they didn't retaliate. The Arabs are the stronger party as they are the majority. They must be made to understand that violence doesn't pay; otherwise they'll always use it. If we agree the Arabs will think that the Jews have panicked and asked for pity.

Nuri Said: Why do you consider only the reaction of the mob? Why don't you consider the effect on public opinion in the other Arab States? They will be impressed by such a step.

Sharett: You assume that after such a step, an agreement will be reached. But what if there is no agreement?

Nuri Said: If you do this there will be negotiations and we'll help you. We will declare you have taken this step at the request of the Government of Iraq. Why don't you look towards the future? A great deal of hostility is developing towards you in Arab countries. If you don't make this gesture to show that you genuinely want peace and are willing to sacrifice something to get it, I am very worried about the future. [He showed a letter from a Moslem leader in India threatening a boycott of the British if they did not reach a settlement in Palestine.] Where is your good will to end this conflict in peace?

Sharett: Our good will is expressed by the fact that we are willing to sit and talk with Arabs even in the present circumstances.

Nuri Said: Weizmann was prepared to go farther than you! He spoke in numbers and restrictions of land reserves. How can we advance? There is suspicion against you and you have to show your good will.

Sharett: What you want is an admission that immigration is only possible with Arab consent. That you won't get. We are ready to explore the possibilities of peace. But if we don't reach an agreement we are not going to renounce our right to immigration. That right does not depend on Arab consent.

Like Ben-Gurion, Sharett believed that only Jewish strength could solve the Arab problem:

I don't believe we'll reach agreement with the Arabs for our force to grow. But I believe that the moment will come, when we'll be stronger and will achieve a stable alliance with Great Britain, as a force with force, and we'll achieve agreement with the Arabs, as a force with force. The precondition is that the Arabs don't regard us as potentially but actually powerful.[22]

It was clear to him that peace must be relegated to a more distant future. In a speech to the Executive of the Jewish Agency in Jerusalem on 22 May 1936, he stated:

An important Jew told me that we must obtain agreement with the Arabs because without it the danger will grow. I answered him that I know the danger is great and will grow, but this is not enough to make an agreement because there are problems without a solution. He answered that there are no problems without a solution. I said: the problems without a solution are those that only time will resolve.

Like Ben-Gurion and Weizmann, Sharett regarded London and not Palestine as the battlefront where the vital decisions about the future of Palestine would be taken. It was only there that Zionism mobilised its full resources to counter Arab pressure against British support for a Jewish national home: 'There is the Arab factor, that is to say its influence on Great Britain, its effect on British policy as a result of the conclusions the British draw from it.'[23] Like other Zionist leaders, he suggested that Zionism would be a better ally of the British in the Middle East. At the Round Table conference (1939) he 'stressed the unreliable nature of the Arabs in contrast with the unquestioned loyalty in the Jews . . . the Jews in Palestine could do as much as Egypt or Iraq to help Great Britain'.[24] He, too, emphasised the strategic value of Palestine:

The development of air traffic has made Palestine indispensable for the British Empire; no connection with India, the Persian Gulf and Iraq is possible without it. Haifa, built with Jewish money, has become more important to them, and if they'll need Aqaba we'll build it up . . . Therefore I don't think the British will abandon the Balfour Declaration or stop immigration.[25]

Like Weizmann and Ben-Gurion, Sharett excluded the possibility of an anti-British or anti-French alliance with the Arabs.

As long as the troubles in Palestine continue, we will not support Syrian independence in Paris; on the contrary, the riots in Palestine prove the Arabs are not ready for independence. We will negotiate with the Palestinians only with the knowledge and approval of the British, not behind their back. Our support for the Syrians is within the framework of their agreement with France.[26]

Given these attitudes, it becomes clear why Sharett was unable to create an ideological and political alternative to Zionist policy towards the Palestinians, despite his deep sympathy and understanding. Personally he felt closer to Weizmann, with whom he shared the character traits of sensitivity, wide intellectual horizons, and an open-minded, liberal approach. Like Weizmann, he was an accomplished diplomat with charming manners, fluency in many languages, and a skillful debating style. But in his approach to Zionist strategy he followed Ben-Gurion, with whom he shared the conviction that rapid creation of demographic, economic and military *faits accomplis* should be the central and inviolable aim of strategy.

Sharett enjoyed great popularity within the Labour Party's rank and file, had many friends and supporters in important positions, and yet he never attempted to contest Ben-Gurion's leadership.[27] Like all other leading members of the party, he accepted Ben-Gurion's authority though not without question, and believed in his unique sense of direction and courage to take important decisions. Perhaps this was a result of Sharett's own indecision; his sophistication and sceptical nature led him to see many aspects of the political problems and to consider a variety of solutions. Ben-Gurion's single-minded resolution was able to mobilise all resources and energies for a chosen course, regardless of the losses and risks involved, and proved irresistible in times of great crisis.

Typical of Sharett's voluntary submission to Ben-Gurion's authority and suppression of his own doubts was the letter Sharett sent him on the eve of publication of the Royal Commission Report on Palestine:

> Your appreciation [of evidence to the Royal Commission] is for me
> a moral backbone . . . For years I have measured myself, my achieve-
> ments and deficiencies on the basis of your opinion . . . I did not
> have in the last few years a guide to direct me and to stimulate me,
> only your appreciation and criticism . . . You are for me not only a
> senior comrade, not only a leader of the movement, which is my
> home and my life. You are for me a man whose moral authority I
> have accepted since the days of my youth.[28]

But perhaps the deeper reason for the willing submission to Ben-
Gurion's authority was Sharett's loyalty to the party. He regarded the
Labour Party (MAPAI) as the only reliable guarantor of the success of
the Zionist-Socialist ideal to which he was devoted. The interests of
the party, its unity and hegemony in Palestine and in the Zionist
movement, stood paramount in all his considerations. It was not the
petty politician's interest in the continued welfare of the party bureau-
cracy. Sharett regarded the work of the labour movement − the
pioneering enterprises, the Kibbutz movement and co-operatives, the
educational network, the youth movement and the Haganah − as the
essence of the realisation of Zionism; and for him only MAPAI could
serve as the organisational basis and guiding force in this process. While
he professed a belief in democratic socialism and individual freedom,
his attitude towards the party was typically 'Bolshevik': 'The party
[the movement as it was called] is always right.'

This was demonstrated during the passionate debates in the Labour
Party and the Zionist movement on Partition in 1936-8. Sharett had the
gravest misgivings about the feasibility of partition and believed neither
in the readiness of the British to implement it nor in the possibility of
a compulsory transfer of Arabs from areas which formed the only
reserve for future Jewish colonisation. From time to time he voiced
his doubts in deliberations of the Labour Party leadership, only to be
chided by Ben-Gurion for encouraging a pessimistic view of the plan.
In spite of this, Sharett volunteered his extraordinary talents of
persuasion to have the partition plan approved by the Zionist movement. Together with Weizmann and Ben-Gurion, he participated wholeheartedly in the diplomatic efforts to overcome the reluctance and
opposition to this solution on the part of Zionism's friends in Britain.
Even more, he became (at the behest of Ben-Gurion) the chief planner
and executor of a colonisation scheme in the Beisan Valley designed

to create a geographical *fait accompli* which would influence the configuration of the future Jewish state before the Peel Commission report was announced.

> He was the prime mover in the formulation of a policy and a strategy of settlement designed to concentrate men and materials and to control the timing and direction of all settlement efforts in order to gain the maximum political, strategic and economic gains from them.[29]

This complicated political make-up is responsible for the fact that Sharett, who of all the Zionist leaders had the deepest understanding of the Arabs and the most sympathy for a peaceful reconciliation, came most into conflict with the bi-nationalists, who like him were sensitive to the problem. They continuously sought contacts with Arab leaders to encourage peace and an end to bloodshed. Weizmann encouraged them in private. Ben-Gurion, though unsympathetic, was willing enough to use them for tactical purposes at times. It was Sharett who was most uncompromising, and viewed the efforts and contacts of the bi-nationalists with distrust and disapproval, trying either to prevent them or to discredit them in the eyes of the Arabs. In his talks with Musa Alami, Antonius, Nuri Said and others, he repeatedly stressed that Dr Magnes and his friends in 'Brith Shalom' were totally unrepresentative of Jewish public opinion and Zionist policy.[30] It was Sharett who engaged in the most bitter polemics and reciprocal accusations and recriminations with the group that was closest to his understanding of the vital importance of the Arab problem, accusing Magnes of 'wilful deceit, lying and misrepresentation'.[31] Sharett wrote in his diary: 'Violently opposed to Magnes initiation . . if a private group arrives at an agreement with the Arabs and then the Jewish Agency repudiates, we have lost prestige and the chances of another agreement are remote.'[32]

The element of 'professional envy' was not an insignificant part of this encounter. Sharett was the head of the Political Department of the Jewish Agency and of its Arab section. As such he felt that contacts with Arab leaders were his prerogative and viewed with suspicion the meddling of 'well-wishers' into this most explosive area of Zionist diplomacy. This was made worse when such 'meddlers' happened to be intellectuals and public figures whose standing made them resistant to pressure from the Jewish Agency. Sharett regarded the cultivation of contacts with top-level Arab leaders as a monopoly of the political department of the Jewish Agency and its Arab section which he headed, and the intrusion of others as damaging to the prestige of the policy-making bodies of the Zionist organisation. He felt particularly hurt when on one occasion the Executive of the Jewish Agency authorised a group of personalities called 'The Five' to continue their talks with the Arabs.

The difference between Sharett and Ben-Gurion was, however, in their long-range views. Sharett did not share Ben-Gurion's fatalistic views of the necessity of conflict with an implacable Arab foe who would only relent from trying to destroy a Jewish state out of utter despair at complete military defeat. Sharett was aware of Arab hostility but he did not ignore the existence of factors and interests working for an accommodation. He regarded the existence of a Jewish military force as a precondition for a settlement, but not necessarily the *use* of that force. He devoted himself wholeheartedly to the difficult task of building up Jewish economic and military potential but he never lost sight of the final aim of reconciliation, which he thought could come about only by a political process and not through an inevitable military confrontation. But these differences in perspective emerged only after the creation of the state. After this was assured, Sharett believed that one should go on to the next priority — peace with the Arabs — while Ben-Gurion considered that immigration, settlement and military power remained the over-riding priority also in the post-1948 era.

Notes

DAVID BEN-GURION

1.   14 November 1917. Ben-Gurion, *My Talks with Arab Leaders* (Jerusalem, 1972), p. 6.
2.   27 August 1934 (to Musa Alami), *My Talks*, p. 30.
3.   David Ben-Gurion, *My Talks*, p. 3.
4.   Minutes of Evidence given before the Royal Commission on Palestine, Colonial Office 134 (London, 1937), p. 289, para. 4540.
5.   Inner Actions Committee, Zionist Executive, 14 October 1936.
6.   Minutes of Evidence, para. 4539.
7.   *My Talks*, p. 12.
8.   Testimony to United Nations Special Commission on Palestine, 10.7.1947.
9.   Shakib Arslan, Musa Alami, and George Antonius, *My Talks*, pp. 38, 52, 96.
10.   To George Antonius, 17 April 1936. *My Talks*, p. 50.
11.   Minutes of Evidence to the Royal Commission, para. 4542.

12.   To Antonius, 17 April 1936, *My Talks*, p. 60.
13.   Comment on Shakib Arslan's version of his meeting with Ben-Gurion in 1934, *My Talks*, p. 39.
14.   Letter to Sharett, 9 June 1936, *My Talks*, p. 82.
15.   To Musa Alami, 13 August 1934, *My Talks*, p. 25.
16.   *My Talks*, p. 11.
17.   18 July 1934, *My Talks*, p. 20.
18.   Speech to Inner Actions Committee, 12 October 1936.
19.   18 July 1934, *My Talks*.
20.   Conversation with Fuad Bey Hamzah, April 1937, *My Talks*, p. 124.
21.   Speech to the Jewish Agency Executive, 19 May 1936; *My Talks*, p. 68.
22.   'Der Yiddischer Kempfer', 29 January 1918, *My Talks*, p. 8.
23.   *My Talks*, p. 31.
24.   Ibid., p. 68 (19 May 1936).
25.   Letter to Sharett, 9 June 1936, ibid., p. 81.
26.   Speech to Zionist Congress, August 1937.
27.   Meeting 9 June 1936, Moshe Sharett, *Diary*, vol. I (Tel Aviv, 1971), p. 394.
28.   For initial Zionist response, see Dugdale Diary, 10 June 1936; for Weizmann's continued negotiations, see Jewish Agency Report, 20 July 1936, S25/3234 C.Z.A.
29.   Ibid., 'Haj Amin deems it a shame on the Arabs and on himself to accept any compromise coming from a Jew.'
30.   Meeting of the Political Advisory Committee, 15 June 1936.
31.   A National Council of MAPAI, October 1930. Quoted in J. Goldstein, 'Anti-British Tendencies in MAPAI in the 1930s', *M'ASEF* , Tel Aviv, May 1976, pp. 122 ff.
32.   Ibid.
33.   Speech at Jewish Agency Executive, 19 May 1936, *My Talks*, p. 68.
34.   *My Talks*.
35.   *My Talks*, p. 5.
36.   Ibid., pp. 6, 12-13.
37.   Michael Bar-Zohar, *Ben-Gurion* (Tel Aviv), p. 309.
38.   Speech at the Mapai Political Committee, 6.7.1938.
39.   Ben-Gurion to Jewish Agency Executive, 2 June 1936, *My Talks*, p. 81.
40.   17 April 1936, ibid., pp. 43-4.
41.   Letter to the Jewish Agency Executive, 9 June 1936 (quoted in ibid., p. 80).
42.   Speech to the Jewish Agency Executive, 25 October 1939 (Zionist Archives S25/3104, quoted in S.L. Hattis, *The Bi-national Idea in Palestine during Mandatory Times* (Tel Aviv, 1970), pp. 223-4.
43.   *My Talks*, pp. 8-10.
44.   Ibid., pp. 30-1 (discussion of 27 August 1934).
45.   Senator in Jewish Agency Executive, 29.10.1936.
46.   *My Talks*, p. 23.
47.   Ibid., p. 34.
48.   18 June 1935, cable to Zionist Executive (Hattis, *The Bi-national Idea*, p. 112).
49.   Wauchope to MacDonald, 17 July 1935 (ibid., p. 113).
50.   19 June 1935, cable to Zionist Executive (ibid., p. 112).
51.   Letter to Executive, 9 June 1936, *My Talks*, p. 81.
52.   Jewish Agency Executive, 19 May 1936, ibid., p. 69.
53.   Namier to Ben-Gurion, 29 September 1936, S25/6327 Central Zionist Archives, Jerusalem.
54.   Ben-Gurion to Blanche Dugdale, 16 October 1936, S25/12 C.Z.A.

55.   Jewish Agency Executive, 4 October 1936.
56.   Mapai Political Committee, 12 October 1936.
57.   Ben-Gurion to Brodetsky, 7 December 1936.
58.   Mapai Political Committee, 9 November 1936.
59.   Ben-Gurion to Dugdale, 16 October 1936, S25/ 12 C.Z.A.
60.   Jewish Agency Executive, 1 November 1936.
61.   Mapai Political Committee, 9 November 1936.
62.   Jewish Agency Executive, 22 November 1936.

MOSHE SHARETT

1.   Moshe Sharett, *Diary*, vol. I (Hebrew) (Tel Aviv, 1970), entry 8.2.36,
p. 51; also p. 236, vol. II, p. 140 (May 22 1937).
2.   Speech to Mapai Political Committee, 21.5.1936.
3.   Speech to Mapai Political Committee, 9.6.1936, *Diary*, vol. I, pp. 164-5.
4.   Speech to Mapai Political Committee, 28.7.1936, ibid., pp. 248-9.
5.   *Diary*, I, p. 212.
6.   Testimony to Anglo-American Commission of Enquiry, 26.3.1946.
7.   Speech to Jewish Agency Executive, 22.5.1936 (*Diary*, I, p. 134).
8.   *Diary*, vol. II, p. 10 (31 January 1937).
9.   Ibid., p. 20.
10.   Conversation with John H. Hall, Chief Secretary of Palestine Government, 13.5.1937 (*Diary*, II, p. 24).
11.   Speech to Zionist Actions Committee, 11.2.1937, *Diary*, II, p. 21.
12.   Meeting with High Commissioner, 2.9.1936, *Diary*, I, pp. 291-8.
13.   As Katznelson complained at the Mapai political committee meeting, 30.7.1936, *Diary*, I, p. 251.
14.   Speech to Mapai political committee, 28.7.1936, ibid., I, p. 247.
15.   26.7.1936, ibid., I, p. 248.
16.   Speech to Jewish Agency Executive, 22.5.1936, ibid., I, pp. 132-4.
17.   Ibid., p. 113, see also pp. 313-16 (27.9.1936).
18.   Ibid., p. 112.
19.   To Jewish Agency Executive, 22.11.1936.
20.   To Action Committee, Zionist Executive, 14.10.1936.
21.   Meeting with Nuri Said, Jerusalem 22.8.1936, *Diary*, I, pp. 271-4.
22.   Jewish Agency Executive, 22.5.1936, ibid., I, p. 127.
23.   29.1.1936, ibid., I, p. 39.
24.   Quoted in Ben-Gurion, *My Talks*, pp. 235-7 (14 February 1939).
25.   To Jewish Agency Executive, 22.5.1936, *Diary*, I, p. 129.
26.   23.7.1936, ibid., I, p. 239.
27.   Noah Lucas, *The Modern History of Israel* (London, 1974), p. 377.
28.   Moshe Sharett, *Diary*, II, p. 236.
29.   Elchanan Oren, 'Tel Amal: Pioneer of Stockade and Watchtower Settlement' in *Zionism: Studies in the History of the Zionist Movement and of the Jewish Community*, vol. LV (1975), p. 450 (in Hebrew).
30.   In *My Talks*, pp. 93-7, meeting with Musa Alami, 24 January 1936.
31.   Ibid., pp. 162, 171, letter to Magnes.
32.   *Diary*, I, 2 June 1936, p. 147.

5 THE BI-NATIONALISTS

Brith Shalom

The Arab Revolt in 1936 signalled the end of the hope of co-operation between the two communities. A number of groups in the Zionist camp opposed the policy of the leadership in the crucial years before the revolt and suggested a bi-national solution. None of these elements, however, could mobilise public opinion against the fixed policy.

The first group to promote the idea of bi-nationalism was Brith Shalom (Covenant of Peace) founded in 1925 by Dr Arthur Ruppin, a member of the Zionist Executive and the Director of the Palestine Land Development Company. The group included a number of prominent intellectuals from the Hebrew University of Jerusalem.[1]

Some are inclined to attribute the emergence of the bi-national idea to Central European Jewish intellectuals, liberals and pacifists who stressed the humanistic and moral aspects of Zionism. In this view, bi-nationalism was created by idealists and 'dreamers' ignorant of the cruel realities of the Jewish-Arab conflict in the Middle East. This is echoed by Professor Laqueur in his *History of Zionism*, in which he speaks disparagingly, it appears, of the origin of the bi-nationalists as German – 'All these Arthurs, Hugos and Hans' '[2] – and claims that among them there were no oriental, and few Eastern European, Jews.

Central European intellectuals were prominent in Brith Shalom but the originators of the bi-national idea were the Zionist activists who shouldered the responsibility for the practical work of building up the Jewish settlement in Palestine long before the Balfour Declaration. It is no accident that Brith Shalom was founded by those responsible for Zionist colonisation from the earliest days. Those included Dr Ruppin, head of the Palestine Office; Dr Thon, his assistant and successor as Director of the Palestine Land Development Company; H.M. Kalvarisky, at the time Director of the Palestine Jewish Colonisation Association in the Galilee; Dr Joseph Lurie, Director of the Education Department and leader of the Teachers' Union.

Among the supporters of bi-nationalism were some of the earliest East European settlers of Palestine, including Itzhak Epstein, born in Russia, immigrated in 1886, who in 1907 published his famous article 'The Hidden Question', criticising the attitude of immigrants who were antagonising the Arab population; Eliahu Saphir, born in Jerusalem;

163

Moshe Smilansky, Russian born and head of the Farmers' Federation; David Yellin, born in Jerusalem and Chairman of the Va'ad Leumi, 1920-9; and Aahron Ginzberg (pen-name, A. Hermoni), born in Lithuania, who immigrated in 1898. These were Palestinian-based Jews, who were acquainted with the Arab language and culture whose work brought them in contact with Arabs and who advocated the integration of Zionism into the Arab East.

Among the oriental Jews who were adherents of bi-nationalism, were Dr Nissim Malul, born in Safad in 1892, son of a Tunisian Jewish family, who studied and taught at Cairo University and wrote for the Arabic press before returning to Palestine in 1911 to work for Dr Ruppin. Malul was an advocate of the renaissance of a 'symbiosis' of Arabic and Hebrew in opposition to Western culture, and was a member of a group of oriental Jews in Jaffa who promoted the idea of Jewish-Arab understanding. The group's chairman, Dr Shmuel Moyal, contributed many articles on that theme to the Hebrew daily *Hacherut*.[3] These people appreciated the full weight of Arab opposition to Zionism as well as the trends towards moderation and agreement and were the first to conceive both the possibility and necessity of a constructive policy towards the Arabs in order to promote the Zionist enterprise. Significantly, even the Zionist representative in Constantinople before the First World War, who was inclined to the Revisionist views, conceded this possibility.[4]

Although not all these people became formal members of Brith Shalom, they preceded the group of Central European intellectuals in suggesting the accommodation between Zionism and Arab national aspirations.

The first Zionist thinker to formulate the essence of bi-nationalism was Ahad Ha'am. In 1921 he wrote:

[The historical right of the Jewish people] does not invalidate the right of the land's inhabitants, who have a genuine right to the land due to generations of residence and work upon it. For them too this country is a national home and they have the right to develop their national potentialities to the utmost. This, therefore, makes Palestine into a common possession of different peoples, each endeavouring to establish here a national home, and under such circumstances it is impossible that either of them should be complete and contain everything included in this conception.[5]

He was followed by a group of prominent intellectuals, scholars and writers in Germany and Czechoslovakia who became alarmed by the growing influence in the early 1920s of the Revisionists and their militaristic anti-Arab attitudes in the Zionist movement. In their effort to combat the spread of chauvinistic and militarist ideas in Zionism, they stressed a distinct concept of Zionism, the essential elements of which were: the realisation of the general human endeavour in a search for new social values; pacifism; and return and integration with the peoples of the East in the process of spiritual, cultural and national awakening.

The humanistic component is described by Hans Kohn, one of the prominent bi-nationalists as follows:

> I and a group of friends saw in Zionism a moral-spiritual movement, within which we could realize our general human convictions, our pacifism, liberalism, and humanitarianism. It had often stood against us that within the European nations we were not able to act for pacifism . . . Zion was to be the place for the realization of our human endeavour.[6]

The pacifist approach that characterised this group was both a reflection of pacifist trends in Europe after World War I and a reaction to events in Palestine. The Arab riots of 1920 and 1921, in which 95 persons were killed and 219 seriously hurt, put an end to the illusion that the Zionist enterprise would proceed with the blessing, or at least the passive acquiescence, of the Palestinian Arabs. In reaction to these events, the idea of suppressing Arab opposition by force acquired considerable support in the Jewish community. Jabotinsky, the founder of the Revisionist movement, was an advocate of an armed force to deal with Arab 'disturbances'. The Revisionist solution had a strong appeal to the masses of Eastern European Jews whose psychological reaction to persecution in Europe made them receptive to the idea of revenge in Palestine. A stormy debate developed at the Twelfth Zionist Congress at Karlsbad (1921), where Jabotinsky and his followers spoke of the Arabs as 'mortal enemies' with whom a violent confrontation was inevitable. It was against this trend that the bi-nationalist Robert Weltsch posed the cardinal question of whether the Zionist movement was heading for war or peace in Palestine. His draft resolution to the Congress on Jewish-Arab relations stated that any thought of conquering Palestine by Jewish arms and the creation of a Jewish army for this purpose was incompatible with the real aim of Zionism. Martin Buber, who was later to become one of the leading bi-nationalists in Palestine, warned at the same Congress that the Zionist movement was facing a fateful choice. Upon Zionist policy would depend whether the Arabs, whose sensitivity to social and political discrimination would grow, would become allies or enemies.

The bi-nationalists saw the problem of Jewish-Arab relations in the larger context of relations between Europe and Asia, between imperialism and the underdeveloped countries. They often connected their belief in Arab-Jewish reconciliation with the philosophical view that the Jewish people should become spiritually part of the East and reject Western domination and materialism. Buber, for example, wrote of the Jews as an 'Eastern type' who were destined to bridge the gap between the two worlds.

> We shall strive towards this destiny not as servants of a great Europe, doomed to destruction, but as allies of a Young Europe, still weak but consecrated to the future, not as a middle man of a degenerating civilization, but as champions of a new civilization whose creation we are party to . . . we have no connection with its [the League of Nations] methods, which are imperialism decorated with the flags of humanism. We must hereby emphasize that we will refrain from any foreign policy — except for the paths and activities necessary for instituting a permanent and friendly accord in all areas of life, to achieve a comprehensive formal creation.[7]

Hugo Bergmann, another bi-nationalist strongly influenced by Buber, observed:

> One of the most important causes of the suspicion between Jews and Arabs is the Western mentality — the overwhelming of religion and spirit by politics, which has taken possession of both people. The only basis, I think, on which we could come to an agreement would be the withdrawal of both peoples from the influence of the West and their return again to the original spirit of the East.[8]

As we have seen, these ideas were not new and were suggested before the British Mandate by Zionist activists during the Ottoman regime (Epstein, Malul, Hermoni, Kalvarisky) but Brith Shalom provided the first organisational framework for promoting these ideas, and for cultivating a specific attitude within the Jewish community.

Brith Shalom had no popular base nor a political organisation and had neither the intent nor ambition to create them. Its members were not agreed on whether their task should be confined to propagating their ideas, study and research, whether they should undertake to initiate political contacts and negotiations, or whether they should co-operate with the official Zionist leadership or work independently or even in opposition. This indecision explains, in part, the inability of Brith Shalom to play a more important role in Jewish-Arab relations.

Arthur Ruppin

Dr Arthur Ruppin was the founder of Brith Shalom and a major Zionist figure whose practical impact on the socio-economic development of the Yishuv was recognised in the prominent position he occupied in the Zionist movement as member of the Executive and Director of the Palestine Land Development Company.

Dr Ruppin, an economist and a sociologist, not only had professional expertise with an outstanding talent for planning, organisation and administration, but was a scientist with a profound knowledge of the economic problems of the Middle East: he was a man of the utmost integrity, honesty and devotion. These qualities brought him both the respect of Jewish businessmen and the confidence of the labour movement. Ruppin was deeply interested in social problems and regarded Zionism as an instrument for creating new social conditions in Jewish society. He wrote in his diary that were he not 'a captive of Zionism, I could not imagine a higher aim than to be working in Russia now [in 1921] on the peaceful reorganization of that country . . . I very much respect the magnificent ideas inherent in Bolshevism'.[1] He was hopeful that in Palestine the same ends could be obtained without the destructive violence of Russia: 'European capitalism has not yet arrived in Palestine; therefore, nothing will have to be destroyed before anything can be built [the Soviet system], and positive construction can begin at once. A new and more just social order will issue from Palestine.'[2] He was able to win the support of American Jewish businessmen, whom he impressed with his efficiency and concrete plans;[3] yet he advocated strengthening the labour movement as a counterweight to the greater influence of capitalist elements in the Jewish Agency.[4]

Ruppin's approach to the Arab problem was dominated by his belief that Zionism cannot succeed without integration into a Near East Federation and an agreement with Arab Nationalism.[5] As early as 1922, he demanded enlarged cultural contacts with the Arab world and praised the Cairo talks with pan-Arab leaders that Weizmann eventually blocked.[6] He criticised Kalvarisky's methods: 'we will pay heavily in the future for the temporary advances he is striving for . . . it is not possible to pursue Arab policy in Palestine; it must be pursued in the real centres of Arab politics, that is, Baghdad, Cairo, and Damascus'.[7] He was not even disturbed by the proposed Britain-Hedjaz Treaty of 1923, which promised help to create an Arab confederation including Palestine, a proposal which had aroused Weizmann's ire.[8]

Ruppin did not have much faith in diplomatic promises, such as the Balfour Declaration, as opposed to an agreement with the Arabs.

> I think that I shall not be able to continue working for the Zionist movement if Zionism does not acquire a new theoretical foundation. Herzl's conception of the Jewish state was possible only because he ignored the existence of the Arabs and believed that he could manipulate world history by means of the diplomatic methods of the Quai D'Orsay. Zionism has never been able to free itself entirely of this 'diplomatic' imperialistic connection. The rejoicing over the Balfour Declaration, as if the Jewish state had actually been established, is only the latest manifestation of this erroneous conception.[9]

Precisely during the quiet years of the 1920s, when Weizmann was convinced that everything with the Arabs was going well, Ruppin raised some searching doubts: 'What continually worries me is the relationship between the Jews and Arabs in Palestine. Superficially, it has improved, inasmuch as there is no danger of pogroms, but the two peoples have become more estranged in their thinking. Neither has any understanding of the other, and yet I have no doubt that Zionism will end in a catastrophe if we do not succeed in finding a common platform.'[10]

These reflections led him in 1925 to initiate discussions with like-minded colleagues on the bi-national state as a solution to the conflict with the Arabs, and to create Brith Shalom as a framework for Jewish-Arab understanding. Among its founders were Robert Weltsch (editor of *Judische Rundschau*), Felix Rosenbluth (later Pinhas Rozen, a Cabinet Minister), Jacob Thon (a colleague in the Settlement Department), Sprinzak (one of the central figures of Hapoel Hatzair, later speaker of the Knesseth), Kalvarisky (then Director of the Arab Department of the Palestine Zionist Executive), as well as a number of intellectuals from the Hebrew University (Hugo Bergmann, Ernst Simon, Gershom Sholem and Hans Kohn). Ruppin outlined their perspective:

In the foundation of Brith Shalom one of the determining factors was that the Zionist aim has no equal example in history. The aim is to bring the Jews as second nation into a country which already is settled as a nation – and fulfill this through peaceful means. History has seen such penetration by one nation into a strange land only by conquest, but it has never occurred that a nation will freely agree that another nation should come and demand full equality of rights and national autonomy at its side. The uniqueness of this case prevents its being, in my opinion, dealt with in conventional political-legal terms. It requires special contemplation and study. Brith Shalom should be the forum in which the problem is discussed and investigated.[11]

Brith Shalom promoted private discussions, published a magazine, *Our Aspirations*, and offered classes in Arabic.

Ruppin conceived Brith Shalom mainly as a framework for study and research and for propagating the idea of bi-nationalism, without formulating a programme for political action. This caused a dispute among the members of Brith Shalom which came to the fore over the question of a legislative council in 1928-30. The Arabs had been pressing for constitutional and representative self-government on the road to independence. But Ruppin was sure that 'all the Palestine Arabs are opposed to the Zionist movement, and until we can offer a satisfactory solution to the clash of interests, they will continue to be our enemies. If in the present conditions a constitution is given, logic states that the Arabs will use the rights promised them by the constitution in order to prevent, as a majority, any economic development of the Jewish minority.'

Not unlike Weizmann he doubted whether 'one can immediately apply to Palestine the principles of democracy . . . as long as the majority of the Arabs remain illiterate the crowds will blindly follow a few leaders'. Further, he did not see such proposals as the role of Brith Shalom: 'I wonder whether it would be breaking faith with the Yishuv to address a statement above their heads directly to the Arabs. If we enter the political arena, it will lose its good name forever.'[12]

Ruppin was sharply criticised for his stand on the legislative council by Dr Judah L. Magnes, the Chancellor of the Hebrew University and subsequently the central figure among the bi-nationalists, who most probably did not join Brith Shalom because of the divergence of views. Magnes pointed out that 'the way to train a people in self-government is to place responsibility on it, not to withhold self-government from it'. He argued that 'It is not possible, even if it were desirable, to maintain the present status quo — an absolutist colonialist regime. It is not possible, because the British Government is making or has made political concessions in Egypt, Iraq, and India, even in wild Transjordan, and the French Government has been doing the same in Syria. Why not then in Palestine? Because the Jews are here? The Jewish conscience will not bear this for long. It must recognize, sooner rather than later and from goodwill rather than through compulsion, that the inhabitants of this country, both Arab and Jews, have not only the right but the duty to participate, in equitable and practical ways, in the government of their common homeland.'[13] In answer to the question, should we reward the 'butchers of Hebron and Safad', he replied that we should ask 'Are my own hands clean of blood . . . let at least Israel not be hypocritical and self-righteous . . . We are told that when we become the majority we shall show them how just and generous a people in power can be . . . if as a minority we insist on keeping the other man from achieving just aims, and if we keep him from this with the aid of bayonets, we must not be surprised if we are attacked and what is worse a moral degradation sets in amongst us.'[14]

Ruppin was not in principle against a legislative council. In a memorandum to the Zionist Executive in April 1929 he formulated a constitutional programme for a bi-national Palestine with an upper chamber consisting of equal numbers of Jews and Arabs.[15] But he did not think the situation ripe for a practical policy in this direction, and the Arab anti-Jewish riots of August 1929 strengthened his opposition to any formalisation of his constitutional proposals. In the climate of high passion created by the riots, 'Brith Shalom has become the scapegoat on which the Jews vent their displeasure at the present circumstances'. Ruppin believed that some members of Brith Shalom had gone too far: 'the Arabs interpret our conciliatory tone as weakness'.[16] As he explained later, the premature publicity by Brith Shalom members, before the Jewish public had been properly prepared, obliged him to resign from public activities.[17]

Ruppin did not abandon his belief in bi-nationalism. In 1932 he worked with Magnes on a draft plan for a gradual development towards a bi-national constitution for Palestine. However, he was pessimistic about the very future of Zionism in these years of little immigration. About his bi-national plan he wrote: 'But what good does it do that a small circle has reached agreement when there is no prospect of making the draft acceptable either to the Jews or the Arabs?'[18] In a letter to Victor Jacobson he explained the reasons for his pessimism:

Undoubtedly the Arabs have greatly strengthened their political position during the past few years and are much less ready to make concessions than they were ten years ago. The situation is paradoxical; what we can get [from the Arabs] is of no use to us, and what we need we cannot get from them. At most the Arabs would agree to grant national rights to the Jews in an Arab state, on the pattern of national rights in Eastern Europe. But we know only too well from conditions in Eastern Europe how little a majority with executive power can be moved to grant real or complete equality to a minority. The fate of the Jewish minority in Palestine will always be dependent upon the goodwill of the Arab majority, which would steer the state. To Jews of Eastern Europe, who form the overwhelming majority of all the Zionists, such a settlement would be completely unsatisfactory, and it would kill their enthusiasm for the Zionist cause and for Palestine. A movement that would agree to such a compromise with the Arabs would not be supported by Eastern European Jews and would very soon become a Zionism without Zionists.[19]

Ruppin's opposition to a legislative council grew with the resumption of large-scale immigration to Palestine by German Jews (1933-5), made possible by an agreement with the German Government which he himself had helped to bring about. He advised the British High Commissioner not to proceed with the proposed legislative council and suggested as an alternative a number of palliative measures to ease the situation. In these years he finally moved away from Brith Shalom. In a letter to Robert Weltsch he explained that he did not believe that there was a good chance of coming to an agreement with the Arabs based on the economic advantages from Jewish colonisation – 'the political attitude of people is governed not by rational arguments, but by instincts'. Therefore 'not negotiations, but the development of Palestine towards a larger percentage of Jews in the population and a strengthening of our economic position can and will bring about an easing of tension . . . When coming to an understanding with us will no longer mean that the Arabs will have to make concessions to us, but only a question of coming to terms with realities, the weight of facts will bring about an easing of tensions.' In the wake of the 1936 riots he argued: 'That we are living in a latent state of war with the Arabs which makes loss of life inevitable . . . is a fact; if we want to continue our work in Palestine, we will have to accept such losses.'[20]

At the time of the Arab Revolt of 1936, he explained to Weizmann that with modern irrigation assured by new discoveries of water resources, two million dunams would be sufficient for large-scale Jewish settlement without displacing any Arabs.[21] He suggested telling the Peel Royal Commission that the Zionist movement would in the next ten years buy only 500,000 dunams (4 to 5 per cent of arable land) and would subtract from that total land which was allotted to it by government land development projects. In addition, an independent commission would oversee each purchase to assure that the present cultivators would not be dispossessed.[22]

This approach led Ruppin to a unique position on partition in 1937. He proposed that instead of a Jewish state with a majority or a large minority of Arabs, the request should be for an autonomous Jewish district mainly on the coastal plain, of 2 million dunams with 400,000 Jews and only 100,000 Arabs.[23] This proposal led to Ruppin's gradual estrangement from decision-making circles in the movement.[24] His idea of close Jewish settlement was diametrically opposed to Sharett's strategic frontier settlement ideas. Eventually, he was replaced in the Settlement Department of the Jewish Agency, though he still carried prestige in public dealings in the movement.

The curious point about Ruppin was the contradiction between his understanding as an economist and sociologist of the impact of Zionist policies on Arab economy and his loyalty to these policies, which he himself helped to formulate. On moral grounds, he was opposed to dispossession of the fellahin — he even suggested paying an additional fee to the owners of land for the resettlement of the tenants — and told the Shaw Commission that enough land for Jewish settlement would automatically become available as the fellahin changed over to intense methods of cultivation, with the money they would receive from the sale of part of their land.[25] Yet, he was aware of the fact that such money might not reach the fellahin, who were mainly tenants, or that it might not be used for agricultural development works, due to the general indebtedness of the farmers as well as lack of government plans and capital for development.

Land is the most vital condition for our settlement in Palestine. But since there is hardly any land which is worth cultivating that is not already being cultivated, it is found that wherever we purchase land and settle it, by necessity its present cultivators are turned away. The problem is intensified because of the fact that the buying price rarely reaches the actual cultivator, but runs into the pockets of the land owners or money lenders. What we pay the real cultivators only raises the price of land, and certainly the price should not be raised infinitely; in any case the land is already expensive and additional cost will make it economically not worthwhile. In future it will be much more difficult to purchase land, as sparsely populated land hardly exists. What remains is densely populated land. The advice we tend to give to the Arabs — to work their land more intensively, in order to manage with a smaller allotment of land — may appear to the Arabs a joke at the expense of the poor. For intensification of farming a fairly large amount of capital is needed, as well as much agricultural knowledge — both of which the fellahin lack.[26]

In fact, it was Ruppin who had first initiated the policy of economic segregation in Palestine, in his desire to create a new Jewish social order in a 'closed economic circuit' in which the Jews were producers, consumers and middlemen. He was morally affected by the contradiction to which he himself had contributed. This was one of the major reasons for his pessimism which ultimately led him to despair of a Jewish-Arab agreement and fatalistically to accept the continuation of the conflict with its inevitable loss of life.[27]

The ideological differences within Brith Shalom between the group of Zionist activists who insisted on loyalty to official Zionist policy and the radicals who demanded independent political action contributed to the disintegration of the group by the early 1930s. The first differences appeared in 1928 when Professor Hugo Bergmann suggested that it was desirable to have a constitution in Palestine. He advanced this idea in an article in *Our Aspirations* under a Brith Shalom imprint, supported by an open letter from Kalvarisky. This caused the first open public attacks on Brith Shalom, coming as it did immediately after the first incident at the Wailing Wall in October 1928, when the British authorities forcibly removed the prayer partitions during Yom Kippur.[28]

In 1929, Ruppin resigned the chairmanship of Brith Shalom in favour of Joseph Lurie. The majority of the group came out in favour of a legislative council and some of its members, including Ernst Simon, demanded a declaration that Jews would be willing to remain a permanent minority in a bi-national state in order to pave the way to an agreement. This Zionist 'minimalism' provoked sharp reactions inside Brith Shalom by those who did not see a contradiction between binationalism and large-scale Jewish immigration.[29] Other steps by the organisation hastened its disintegration; for example, the demand for amnesty for the Arabs sentenced to hang for murdering Jews during the 1929 riots.

'Kedma Mizraha' ('Towards the East'), the successor to Brith Shalom, was no more successful and left even less visible traces of its activities. The group was founded in April 1936, by some of the former members of Brith Shalom. Its aim was to foster Jewish-Arab understanding, based on the recognition of Palestine as the location of the Jewish national home, the beneficial influence of Jewish colonisation on the Arabs, and the ties between two ancient branches of the Semitic race. Its principles were: (1) Political understanding and economic development as preconditions for the development of both people in Palestine; (2) opposition to chauvinistic propaganda on both sides; (3) opposition to political or economic separation which obstructs constructive development and mutual understanding; (4) true peace to be based on a democratic-national basis regardless of numbers; (5) friendly relations with all peoples; (6) the association to be non-political; and (7) readiness for co-operation with Jewish Agency and National Executive. Because of its less pronounced political line, Kedma Mizraha had much broader public support. Among its active members were Dr J. Thon, H.M. Kalvarisky, J. Mejuhas, Radler-Feldman, Dr Sally Hirsch, Dr E. Simon, and David Yellin. Kedma tried to avoid the problems which caused the disintegration of Brith Shalom and sought to co-ordinate its activities with those of the Zionist authorities, thus reducing its role to that of a propaganda agency in the Arab world for the Zionist organisation. This did not prevent individual members like Kalvarisky from pursuing contacts with Arab leaders in Syria, Iraq and Egypt, with a view to promoting the plans for an Arab Federation and bi-national Palestine. As such, it was condemned to ineffectiveness in the stormy years of the Arab Revolt. If Brith Shalom failed because of its tendency towards becoming an opposition to official Zionist policy, Kedma Mizraha disintegrated for the opposite reason: it identified itself too closely with official Zionist policy, which provided no basis for a Jewish-Arab agreement.

Judah L. Magnes

The most courageous and consistent advocate of a bi-national solution was Dr Judah L. Magnes, Chancellor and first President of the Hebrew University of Jerusalem. Dr Magnes was the central figure in initiating contacts and serious negotiations with Palestinian Arab leaders in 1929 and 1936. He also arranged for the Zionist Executive to meet Arab and Palestinian leaders. His independent initiatives earned him the enmity of the Zionist leadership and the resentment of the community at large; despite these, he never wavered in his commitment to bi-nationalism.

Dr Judah Magnes was essentially a militant Ahad Ha'amist. He shared with Ahad Ha'am the vision of Zionism as meaning the creation of a cultural centre rather than a state. He sought to put into practice Ahad Ha'am's often-expressed injunctions in favour of Jewish-Arab co-operation. As early as 1915 he wrote:

> Zionism must mean now, as it has in the past for most of us, the building up of a Jewish cultural centre in Palestine through the inner cultural strength of the Jewish people in Palestine, an Ottoman province . . . in the Zionist sense, then, the war cannot give Palestine to the Jews; the Turkish government cannot give Palestine to the Jews. All that the war, all that the Turkish government can give to the Jews, is free ingress into Palestine and equal rights.[1]

In 1930 when the Yishuv was still shaken by the pogroms by Arab mobs against defenceless Jewish communities in the predominantly Arab towns of Tiberias, Safed and Hebron, he published his views in a pamphlet entitled 'Like Unto All the Nations'. He wrote:

> What is Zionism? What does Palestine mean for us? . . . I can answer for myself in almost the same terms that I have been in the habit of using for many years:
>
> Immigration.
> Settlement on the land.
> Hebrew life and culture.
>
> If you can guarantee these for me, I should be willing to yield the Jewish state and the Jewish majority; and on the other hand, I would agree to a legislative assembly, together with a democratic political regime so carefully planned and worked out that the above three fundamentals could not be infringed. Indeed, I should be willing to pay almost any price for these three, especially since this price would in my opinion also secure tranquillity and mutual understanding.
>
> What I am driving at is to distinguish between two policies. The one maintains that we can establish a Jewish home here through the suppression of the political aspirations of the Arabs, and therefore a home necessarily established on bayonets over a long period . . . The other policy holds that we can establish a home here only if we are true to ourselves as democrats and internationalists, thus being just and helpful to others . . . and intelligently and sincerely at

work to find a modus vivendi et operandi with our neighbours.[2]

Dr Magnes maintained that the living Jewish people of the Diaspora were the heart and core of Judaism and would not be 'liquidated' by a Zionist solution but would remain in creative tension with the Jewish community in Palestine.

Magnes shared the uneasiness among radicals about the implications of Zionist collaboration with imperialist diplomacy, as expressed by the Balfour Declaration. In a speech in 1923 he said:

According to my concept Zionism does not mean to uproot the Jewish nation from its place in the struggling world . . . what will the character of [Jewish nationalism] be? In their effort to create a national organism here, will the Jews prostrate themselves before the idol of economic imperialism and militarism? . . . Is it possible that one of these days it will be regarded as political treason if some one repeats seriously in Jerusalem the doctrine of Isaiah — 'and they shall beat their swords into plowshares and shall learn war no more'?[3]

The riots of 1929 did not weaken his faith in compromise with the Arabs as the only solution to the Arab-Jewish conflict. This he demonstrated in a dramatic clash with Weizmann which started with a conversation Magnes had with a Joseph Levy, New York Times correspondent, and led to an initiative by Magnes in promoting a compromise, the Arabs had offered before the 1929 riots and which they apparently had not abandoned.

The source of the information Magnes received from Levy was St John Philby, the British agent and Arabist who had become a Moslem and adviser to Ibn Saud and was close to Arab leaders both within and without Palestine. On 25 October 1929, Philby met the Mufti who confirmed to him what Philby had heard from certain leaders of the Nationalist Party in Damascus regarding proposals suggesting a basis for a settlement.[4] These proposals, which involved acceptance of a legislative council and immigration in line with the capacity to absorb it, had, in fact, been privately submitted by Musa Kazim al-Husseini, to the British Government before the 1929 riots. They reflected the moderate wing in the Arab leadership which desired to co-operate with the British rather than enter into conflict with them. The proposal had support also of the extremists in the Arab leadership who believed that Zionism 'confronted with a serious crisis of emigration, had ceased to be an economically viable movement'.[5]

Philby confided to Levy the substance of these talks and when it became known to Magnes, he promptly began a campaign to convince the Zionist leadership and the Jewish public to accept the Arab proposals as a basis for negotiations and settlement. Following negotiations at the end of October between the Mufti and Magnes, with Philby acting as intermediary, Magnes wrote to Felix Warburg in New York, enlisting his support for negotiations based on the proposals,[6] which Magnes described as follows:

1. Balfour and Mandate remain
2. Free immigration depending on economic capacity
3. Legislature elected Arabs Palestine Jews according numbers population
4. High Commissioner responsible public security and British military forces under his control; also absolute veto any Executive or Legislative Act inconsistent international obligations or detrimental minorities foreigners or injurious peace prosperity
5. Above arrangement subject revision League of Nations every five years and no basic constitution alterations without consent Council League of Nations.[7]

In the climate created by the anti-Jewish riots, the Zionist establishment was in no mood for negotiations with the Palestinian Arabs. In addition, the Zionist leadership regarded Magnes as breaking Zionist discipline, threatening their hegemony by appealing to the non-Zionists on the Jewish Agency. Their main concern, however, was the effect of Magnes's activities in London — by suggesting that the Jews did not want to negotiate peace, he was turning public opinion against them and also inviting further concessions to the Arabs by creating the impression that the Jews could be split and that some would accept a more moderate solution.[8] Magnes nevertheless continued publicly to demand that Jews, though the wronged party, should make concessions.

Magnes was not formally a member of the Brith Shalom group. At this time he was in favour of continuation of the Mandate and of the proposals for a legislative council. It was only at a later stage that he came to formulate a programme for a gradual transition from the British Mandate to a bi-national, independent state.[9]

Magnes pursued his beliefs despite attacks. As he wrote to Warburg: 'You do not expect that once having felt it my duty, after such hesitation, to enter the political fray, I can, because of possible misunderstanding, refrain from continuing to say and do what I think necessary.'[10]

In the 1930s Magnes was responsible for a number of meetings between Arab leaders and Ben-Gurion, Sharett and others. In 1937, following another serious outbreak of Arab violence, he was again the intermediary in important negotiations, on the so-called Hyamson-Newcombe proposals, which again led him to bitter polemics with the Zionist Executive (see the chapter on partition in Part Two).

In the 1940s, Magnes became active in a new group, Ihud, along with Martin Buber and other leading bi-nationalists. He vigorously put forward the case of Jewish-Arab understanding and a bi-national state against growing Jewish demands for statehood (as formulated in the Biltmore Programme), and testified before the Anglo-American Committee of Enquiry in 1946 and the UN Special Committee on Palestine in 1947 in favour of the bi-national solution.

Magnes understood well the importance of the economic problems of the Arab peasants as central to the prospects of peace. In 1930 he wrote:

> The situation of the fellahin is one of the cardinal problems of the country. Here is a field for a great constructive programme in which both Jews and Arabs should combine. The country can never be prosperous and happy with the Arab peasants half serfs. I know there are some who think that if the Arab peasant rises in the scale, the Jews will have no more chance . . . is it not the case everywhere that with the rise in the economic and cultural scale of oppressed elements in the population, the general welfare is served?[11]

Poalei Zion Left

Another group which zealously devoted itself to the idea of reaching an agreement with the Arabs was Poalei Zion Left, which split from the World Poalei Zion (Worker's Zionist Federation) in 1920. Poalei Zion was a Socialist-Zionist party in the tradition of Borochov, which formulated the Zionist solution to the Jewish national problem in Marxist terms.

Borochov was close to Stalin's definition of a nation as a community created in the process of historical development and possessing a common territory, economy, language and cultural-psychological traits. Stalin argued against the claim that the Jews represent a nation inasmuch as they lacked all these elements. They possess in common neither territory nor an economy nor a language and national culture. Borochov, on the other hand, thought that a people lacking some of these features should develop a national movement aimed at acquiring the missing attributes. For him, the Jewish problem stemmed from the absence of the basic condition of production — a national territory. The Jewish masses in the Diaspora, driven to proletarianisation by the development of capitalism, are the victims of a national competition and unable to create a working class rooted in the basic spheres of production — agriculture, mining, heavy industry. As a result, a socio-economic anomaly developed — the so-called 'reverse pyramid'. Contrary to normal patterns, the majority of the Jewish people were concentrated in trade, services, liberal professions and secondary and tertiary spheres of production. National competition resulted in the eviction of the Jews from basic industries, causing mass emigration of the Jews to less developed countries, where, however, the same process was sooner or later repeated.

The Marxist doctrine enabled Poalei Zion to mobilise the Jewish working class for Zionism and, at the same time, remain part of the International Labour Movement (The Second International). Borochov envisaged the realisation of Zionism through a mechanistic division between the functions of various classes. He saw Jewish capitalists building up the economy in Palestine, while the Zionist labour movement confined itself to organising the proletariat for immigration and the class struggle. This concept turned out to be unrealistic in Palestine, since few Jewish capitalists were attracted by the unprofitable returns and limited natural resources. Even those who were preferred cheap Arab labour to the organised and class-conscious Jewish workers. The Jewish labour movement in Palestine found it necessary to take over the function of developing the national economy itself, through the organisation of co-operative enterprises. Borochovist doctrine became gradually a matter of terminology and ideological faith rather than a guide for action.

A gap developed between those in Palestine engaged in pioneering activities, and members of Poalei Zion in Europe, who still adhered to the idea that the party should not affiliate to the Zionist Congress (which was a framework for co-operation between classes) nor engage in the creation of economic enterprises. The precipitating cause of the break, however, was the Russian Revolution of 1918 and the formation of the Third International (Comintern), in 1920. With the Red Army near Warsaw and a revolutionary ferment passing through Eastern Europe, there seemed to be the possibility that the majority of Jews would soon find themselves within the orbit of Communist Revolution. The left wing of Poalei Zion thought it necessary to join the new

International and support the revolution wholeheartedly, in order to be able to defend the interests of the Jewish masses during the coming social transformation, and in order to leave the option open for free immigration to Palestine with Soviet support. This proposal was approved by a vote at the Poalei Zion World Congress in Vienna, 1920, which split the party in two, the Palestine branch leading the opposition.

The Poalei Zion Left remained Zionist and Borochovist, committed to the principle of the territorial concentration of the Jewish people in Palestine as the only solution to the Jewish problem. In Palestine a normal socio-economic structure could be built up and the Jewish working class would have a strategic base for a normal and victorious class struggle. The Poalei Zion Left was left with a dilemma with respect to the order of priorities — between, on the one hand, the immediate and urgent task of integrating Jewish masses into the new social order in the USSR and of assisting the spread of social revolution in Europe and, on the other hand, the organisation of the Jewish masses for immigration and settlement in Palestine ('Palestino-centrism'). The Poalei Zion members in Palestine also had to resolve the contradiction between its anti-imperialist and revolutionary outlook and the fact that the Zionist movement which gave direction to Zionist enterprises acquiesced and collaborated with British imperialism. The solution was found in a Marxist-Leninist stance: no co-operation with British or the Zionist Congress, but the establishment of a Jewish-Arab working-class alliance against Arab feudalism, Jewish bourgeoisie and British imperialism alike. In the eyes of Poalei Zion, such an alliance was the only way to a Jewish-Arab agreement.

Initially, Poalei Zion did not accept bi-nationalism. Its formulation of the final aim of Zionism went through many changes, at times calling for a Jewish socialist state (1942), then for a 'socialist state in Palestine with a revolutionary government of workers and peasants' with 'political equality between the two peoples in their common homeland, in which the territorial concentration of the Jewish people will be realized, without one dominating the other' (1943), and later again for a 'Jewish socialist state', integrated in a 'socialist federation of Arab states'.

Poalei Zion did not believe in an agreement with a reactionary Arab nationalist movement led by feudal land-owners. They fought for the concentration of the Jewish people in Palestine through unlimited immigration, which, they believed, would precipitate the collapse of all reactionary structures and lead to a Soviet-type republic of Jewish and Arab workers and peasants. They criticised the *petty*-bourgeois intellectuals for ignoring the class struggle in both nations and for basing peace on collaboration with British imperialism, and were indefatigable in their efforts to establish joint Arab-Jewish workers' clubs and trade unions. However, they were not able to bridge the chasm between the two working classes, in conditions of a widening gap and growing tensions between Jews and Arabs.

Brith Shalom, in turn, did not believe that it was possible to apply the doctrine of revolutionary class struggle to the Jewish-Arab conflict. Professor Hugo Bergmann wrote that

> Jewish immigration, in spite of all the benefits that it conveys upon the Arab worker, weakens politically one people while it strengthens another, at a time when the two peoples are engaged in a struggle which no class ideology can eliminate as long as a Jewish-Arab agreement is not achieved . . . no Arab nationalist and no nationally conscious Arab worker would agree to a common [workers'] organization whose aim is the removal of all obstacles to Jewish immigration . . . the Jewish worker is 100% nationally minded and maintains a common front with the Jewish bourgeoisie, and consequently the same right belongs to the Arab worker.[1]

Poalei Zion Left found itself in growing isolation and decline because it was impossible to apply the Marxist-Leninist concepts (revolutionary class struggle and anti-imperialism) to the realities of the Jewish-Arab conflict. While insisting on territorial concentration and free immigration to Palestine as the solution to the Jewish problem, it adopted a negative attitude both to Arab nationalism, which it regarded as serving the interests of feudal landlords, and the Zionist movement, which was based on the collaboration between Jewish labour and capitalism. For the same reason, it criticised the involvement of the Histadruth (Trade Union Federation) in the creation of economic enterprises and collective agricultural settlements (kibbutzim) which it regarded as both utopian and a diversion from the class struggle. It also opposed co-operation with Great Britain and called for the abolition of colonial rule in Palestine. By 1937, the lack of popular support and the menacing international situation led to a split and a change in its ideological position and to its joining the Zionist Congress and recognising the predominance of the national question for the Jewish and Arab working class. The group gradually disintegrated, with most of the members joining one of the two other left-wing opposition parties (Hashomer Hatzair and Ahdut Avoda which left Mapai in 1941), which eventually united to form the United Workers Party (Mapam) in 1947.

The force of events, especially the Arab Revolt of 1936-9, considerably weakened the idea that the doctrine of revolutionary class struggle was the road to Jewish-Arab agreement. The problem of reconciliation between the two national movements became a *precondition* for Arab-Jewish working-class solidarity. In spite of their abstract and unrealistic theoretical framework, Poalei Zion Left took the initiative in setting up the League for Jewish-Arab Rapprochement (August 1939). By relegating the political programme to the future and concentrating on the practical task of promoting the idea of Jewish-Arab co-operation in everyday life, in economic and municipal affairs, commerce, education, culture, etc., it created a broadly-based coalition embracing personalities from many walks of life and political affiliations.

> The League is not a political organization . . . [its members] are united by one idea: the necessity for Jewish-Arab understanding . . . everyone of us will promote it in accordance with his political orientation, each class on both sides will develop contacts with its corresponding class . . . a common political programme requires as a precondition real cooperation in life; in the present circumstances, to promote the idea of cooperation it suffices to have the slogan 'not to dominate − not to be dominated'.[2]

The pace of events, however, pressed for the formulation of policy. The XXIst Zionist Congress in 1939 decided to set up a committee to investigate the possibilities of Jewish-Arab co-operation in various fields.[3] The League established an independent committee to submit proposals under the chairmanship of Mordechai Bentov of Hashomer Hatzair and including Peretz Nafthali (Mapai, later a Cabinet Minister), M. Bilski, P. Rozenblitt (Liberal Party, first Minister of Justice) and Dr Nir Rafalkes (later the member of Knesseth for Mapam).

The report submitted by this committee in June 1941, known as the 'Bentov Book', marked a new phase in the League's activities. For the first time it formulated a constitutional proposal for a bi-national state in Palestine as part of an Arab Federation, to be established after a transitional period in which 'the fundamental rights and vital interests of the Jewish people returning to its homeland and of the Arab people living in Palestine will be secured'. The bi-national programme became the official policy of the League and served as an alternative to the so-called Biltmore Programme formulated by Weizmann and Ben-Gurion in May 1942 in New York and calling for the establishment of a Jewish Commonwealth in Palestine.

Hashomer Hatzair

The disintegration of Brith Shalom was not the result only of its advocacy of the bi-national idea, as was demonstrated by the fate of Hashomer Hatzair, another grouping in the Zionist camp that advocated bi-nationalism. It was rather the 'Zionist minimalism' of some members of Brith Shalom that engendered the fiercest opposition. This was seen as a typical manifestation of a ghetto mentality based on compliant response to anti-Semitic outbreaks – a complex which Zionism was duty bound to eliminate. In addition, while possessing a deep sense of history, the members of Brith Shalom had no sense of politics and political timing. By choosing the moment that was correct morally, but disastrous politically (following the 1929 riots) to launch their programme, they condemned themselves to isolation and precluded the creation of a large membership.[1] There were, however, outside Brith Shalom elements in the Zionist camp with a larger mass following who inclined to the bi-national idea. One of the central figures in Mapai, Shlomo Kaplansky (later head of the Technion, Haifa), leaned sympathetically towards the idea and supported it in the great debates of the 1940s on the future of Zionism.

Bi-nationalism gained its most significant support from Hashomer Hatzair, the largest Zionist youth movement, which created its own kibbutz federation (1927) and later a political party (1946). In the later years of the Mandatory Period, Hashomer Hatzair became the main political force in favour of the bi-national programme. Hashomer Hatzair refused to co-operate with Brith Shalom in 1931, because of the latter's Zionist minimalism, but remained loyal to the bi-national idea in the most adverse circumstances, and fought for its adoption in the Zionist movement and the Labour Federation (Histadrut).

Far from being ostracised, Hashomer Hatzair had considerable success in mobilising public support for its programme. In the 1941 elections to the Histadruth, it received nearly 20 per cent of the total vote. This was due to the fact that Hashomer Hatzair was recognised as one of the main pioneering forces of Zionist colonisation, being the leading element behind the creation of the new agricultural collective settlements in outlying areas, and prominent in the formation of the Jewish defence forces.

Hashomer Hatzair professed 'maximalist Zionism': the ingathering of the majority of the Jewish people to their homeland and the creation of a Jewish majority in Palestine. What distinguished it from the Revisionists was that it combined this belief with the vision of a 'bi-national socialist society in Palestine and its environs'. It formulated its bi-national programme in 1927, and at the same time it established the Kibbutz Artzi (federation of Hashomer Hatzair Kibbutzim),[2] as one of the essential components of the synthesis between revolutionary socialism and Zionist pioneering. The roots of its ideological position may be found in the conditions of Jewish middle-class youth in Central and Eastern Europe during and immediately after the First World War, where the social basis of Hashomer Hatzair lay.

The existing ideological, political and socio-economic structures of the Jewish people in Eastern Europe were destroyed by the explosive social and national conflicts that followed in the wake of the First World War. The collapse of the multi-national Empires (Austro-Hungary and Tsarist Russia), the struggles for national independence, the economic crisis following the devastation caused by the war and later the Civil War in Russia, demobilisation – all this wreaked havoc on Jewish communities and led to massive dislocations, unemployment, hunger, anti-Semitism and pogroms.

Two events served as a powerful attraction for idealist Jewish youth who had grown up into a world of chaos and crisis: the Soviet Revolution and the Balfour Declaration. The first promised social redemption and the abolition of class and national discrimination – the creation of a new social order which would reshape the future of humanity. The second awakened the age-old dream of national revival, and provided an opportunity for a Jewish national renaissance in the ancient homeland through constructive work and a return to the soil. A messianic era seemed to be at hand. The opportunity to create from scratch a new society and culture with new forms of social life caught the imagination of the Jewish youth.

These forces shaped the ideological position of Hashomer Hatzair: a synthesis between militant socialism and pioneering Zionism based on the determination to translate theory into practice. The working out of this synthesis was not achieved by a rational intellectual effort; rather, it was the product of trial and error in the process of self-realisation. This was accompanied by setbacks and ideological confusion. It would be a mistake, however, to concentrate too much on the contradictory tendencies in the early stages of the 'youth culture' of Hashomer Hatzair, as if this negated its subsequent ideological evolution.[3]

The ideological attitude of Hashomer Hatzair was a response to an objective situation both in the Diaspora and in Palestine. Hashomer

Hatzair channelled the revolutionary potentialities of middle-class youth into the movement for national renaissance, providing an outlet for pent-up energies in the creation of a new social and economic organisation, the Kibbutzim, which laid the foundations for the development of the Zionist enterprise.

The Hashomer Hatzair kibbutzim inspired by the ideas of socialism not less than the task of Zionist pioneering, were distinguished by preoccupation with the Jewish-Arab problem. As early as 1926, Hashomer Hatzair demanded the joint organisation of Jewish and Arab workers during its electoral campaign to the Histadrut (General Federation of Jewish Workers). A year later, when the Federation of Kibbutzim of Hashomer Hatzair was founded, its platform stated as its aim the concentration of most of the Jewish people in Palestine and adjacent countries, and the creation of 'a bi-national socialist society in Palestine and its environs'. Hashomer Hatzair envisaged two stages in the campaign for implementation of these aims. In the first stage, defined as the 'pioneering' phase, the objective would be the advancement of the Zionist enterprise until a Jewish majority was formed and an economic base for independence was created in Palestine. In this stage, an alliance of classes within the Zionist movement was required, as well as co-operation with the British Mandatory power.

Hashomer Hatzair maintained that along with the pioneering efforts to build up the country, the working class in the Yishuv would strive to establish its hegemony. A Federation of Jewish and Arab Workers would be created to prepare for the second stage, when the national alliance within the Zionist movement and collaboration with the British would give way to a struggle for political independence and socialist revolution.

The synthesis between Zionism and revolutionary socialism crystallised in the sphere of ideas but it faced a much harder test in its practical application to the conditions of Palestine. The task of national pioneering was facilitated by the Zionist Organisation which supported and financed the establishment of kibbutzim in their initial stages. The active participation in the struggles of the working class was more difficult as it was limited in time to the period in which the Hashomer Hatzair kibbutzim spent in the colonies as hired labourers (mainly in plantations). After a number of years the kibbutzim were cut off from day-to-day contacts with workers, when they were leaving to create settlements in distant areas (though they were able to maintain some influence through the Kibbutz Federation's representation in the Histadrut, which they had helped found). Most difficult of all was the task of putting into practice the ideas for Arab-Jewish brotherhood. In the years of wage labour, members of Hashomer Hatzair kibbutzim were the chief carriers of the attempt to set up joint Arab-Jewish trade unions and supported and encouraged the few Arab strikes. But once in the collective farms, facing a hostile environment and harassed by problems of security and self-defence, the actual possibilities of creating contacts with Arab villagers were very limited. Hashomer Hatzair tried to solve this dilemma by an intense ideological indoctrination of its members and a courageous struggle for the defence of the bi-national idea, in the realm of politics, but was unable to match this ideological struggle in the Jewish community with efforts in the field of contacts with the Arab population.

Also, the Hashomer Hatzair Kibbutz Federation and its sympathisers proved ineffectual despite their commitment to Jewish-Arab co-operation and their courageous battle for bi-nationalism within the Zionist Federation and the Histadruth. The reason lay in the specific character of this movement, which was concerned primarily with the creation of a collectivist structure within a capitalist society. The practical and theoretical problems of the kibbutzim — the prototypes of the socialist society of the future — took up most of the energies of the movement. Hashomer Hatzair was not originally a political party, and for many years this was regarded as contrary to the principle of 'self-realisation' on which kibbutz life was built. It was only after ten years of passionate debates that the kibbutzim agreed to organise and co-operate with groups in towns and villages politically close to them (1936), and another ten years before the two sections merged to form a political party.

In these conditions the idea of Jewish-Arab solidarity was more a strongly-held belief than a guide for action. At conferences within the Zionist movement, Hashomer Hatzair staunchly defended its bi-national ideals, but its actual contacts with Arabs were extremely limited. In 1935, a plan for such activity was drawn up including the study of Arabic, aid to Arab farmers in modern agricultural methods, organisation of Arab workers into trade unions, social and cultural contacts (including information on Zionist aims), etc. But this effort, in the words of Aharon Cohen, 'was hampered by the lack of suitably trained personnel . . . and by the Arab riots of 1936-9'. It was only in the 1940s that Arab activities received a new boost with the creation of the political party and participation in the activity of the League for Jewish-Arab Rapprochement. A cadre of six members (including Aharon Cohen) were sent from their kibbutzim for six months to live in Arab villages and study the language and customs. All this came too late to reverse the course of events.

The principles of bi-nationalism served as the basis for the development of Hashomer Hatzair as an independent political force, but they were not adhered to dogmatically, without regard to the actual development of Jewish-Arab relations. The Arab Revolt of 1936-9 revealed that the situation of the Arab working class also had a national dimension, and that without an agreement between the two national movements the way to working-class solidarity and socialist revolution remained blocked. Thus in April 1942, the Hashomer Hatzair Kibbutz Federation adopted a resolution urging the Zionist Organisation to declare its readiness for a 'bi-national regime in Palestine based on the unhampered advancement of the Zionist endeavor and on parity in government without regard to the numerical strength of the two peoples; the Zionist Organization should also favour the federal association of Palestine with neighbouring countries'. This new position led directly to the entry of Hashomer Hatzair into the League for Jewish-Arab Rapprochement in June 1942, although individual members had been prominent in the League since its foundation.[4] This brought the bi-nationalist cause for the first time in association with a political organisation which was deeply interested in the Arab question and had considerable popular support.

The League was then able to conduct intensive propaganda both in the Jewish and Arab communities, and to engage independently in negotiations with Arabs with a view towards gaining support for a bi-national solution within the Arab National Movement.

By the time the League for Jewish-Arab Rapprochement had reached this point, it was too late. The crucial period in which attitudes were formed and policies crystallised — on both sides — was over. Between 1917 and 1936, Jewish-Arab relations steadily deteriorated, climaxing in the Arab Revolt of 1936. This event was the turning point during which irreversible choices had been made both by the Zionist and Arab leadership.

Notes

BRITH SHALOM

1. The first major study was Susan Lee Hattis, *The Bi-national Idea in Palestine during Mandatory Times* (Tel Aviv, 1970). Recent contributions include Yosef Gorni, 'The Roots of Awareness of the Jewish-Arab Confrontation 1900-1918', *Zionism: Studies in the History of the Zionist Movement and the Jewish*

Community in Palestine, vol. IV (1975); Neville Mandel, 'Attempts at an Arab-Jewish Entente', *Middle Eastern Studies*, vol. I, no. 3, April 1965; and Yaacov Roi, 'The Zionist Attitude to the Arabs 1908-14', *Middle Eastern Studies*, vol. 4, no. 3, April 1968, pp. 198-242.

2.   Walter Laqueur, *A History of Zionism* (London, 1972), pp. 251-2. He repeats Hattis (ibid., pp. 46-7). While it is true that no Oriental Jews were in the *leadership* of Brith Shalom, the full membership is not listed in either Hattis (who claims 200 members, p. 38) or Laqueur, who reduces it to 100 members (p. 251).

3.   Gorni, 'Roots of Awareness'.

4.   Neville Mandel, 'Attempts at an Arab-Jewish Entente', *Middle Eastern Studies*, vol. I, no. 3, April 1965, pp. 238-67.

5.   Aham Ha'am, preface to the Berlin edition of *At the Crossroads* (1921) quoted by Judah Magnes, 'Like All the Nations?' (Jerusalem, 1930), pp. 72-3.

6.   Letter to Feiwel, 21 Nov. 1929, Buber Archive (quoted in Hattis, *Bi-national Idea*, p. 42).

7.   Buber article, March 1919, quoted in A. Cohen, *Israel and the Arab World* (London, 1970), p. 241.

8.   Letter to R. Tagore, 26 June 1921, quoted in Hattis, *Bi-national Idea*, p. 72.

ARTHUR RUPPIN

1.   Tel Aviv, 31 December 1921, *Arthur Ruppin: Memoirs, Diaries, Letters*, edited Alex Bein (Jerusalem: Weidenfeld and Nicolson, 1971), p. 195.

2.   Ibid., 29 April 1923, p. 208.

3.   Ibid., 10 December 1922, p. 202: 'they regard me as a strange animal because of speed with which I develop my plans'.

4.   Ibid., 31 December 1928, p. 243.

5.   Ibid., 13 April 1923: 'I think that Zionism is tenable only if provided with a completely different scientific foundation . . . we will once more have to take our place among oriental peoples and create a new cultural community in the Near East . . . Zionism is less justifiable now than ever except by the fact that racially the Jews belong to the peoples of the Middle East.'

6.   Minutes of the Palestine Executive, 29 March 1922; Diary entry, 29 March 1922, p. 197: 'these discussions have been a light in the darkness . . . it is the only solution to the otherwise insoluble Arab-Jewish conflict.'

7.   *Diary*, 22 February 1922, p. 196.

8.   Ibid., 11 June 1923, pp. 208-9.

9.   Ibid., 30 October 1923, p. 211.

10.   Ibid., 31 December 1924, pp. 215-16.

11.   Ruppin to Hans Kohn, 29 May 1930, quoted in Susan Lee Hattis, *The Bi-national Idea*, p. 48.

12.   Ruppin to Hans Kohn, 30 May 1928, ibid., pp. 237-8.

13.   Judah L. Magnes, 'Like All the Nations?' (Jerusalem, 1930), p. 16.

14.   Ibid., pp. 15-16, 28, 34.

15.   Jerusalem, 20 April 1929, *Ruppin Diaries*, p. 244.

16.   Ibid., Jerusalem, 24 November 1929.

17.   Ibid., Ruppin to Weltsch, 18 March 1936.

18.   Ibid., Jerusalem, 4 February 1932, p. 259; see also 23 April 1932: 'Things are looking black for Zionism.'

19.   Ibid., Ruppin to Victor Jacobson, 31 December 1931, p. 258.

20.   Ibid., Ruppin to Weltsch, 18 March 1936.

21.   Ibid., 25 April 1936, pp. 207-8.

22.   Ibid., 24 August 1936, p. 280.

23.   Ruppin to Weizmann, 14 May 1937, pp. 283-4; *Diary*, 7 August 1937,

p. 285. This proposal was later taken up by the Woodhead (Partition) Commission.

24. *Ruppin Diary*, Zurich, 1 August 1937. 'Every simple Jew replies: "Why less? Take what you are given" '; 23 August 1937, 21 September 1937 for the cooling of his relations with Weizmann.

25. Ibid., 31 December 1929, p. 249.

26. Ibid., Ruppin to Hans Kohn, 30 May 1930.

27. Ibid., Ruppin to Robert Weltsch, 18 March 1936.

28. Ibid., 26 May 1928; 21 October 1928; 28 November 1928.

29. Hattis, *Bi-national Idea*, pp. 51-4.

JUDAH L. MAGNES

1. Norman Bentwich, *For Zion's Sake* (Philadelphia, 1954), p. 71.

2. Magnes, 'Like All the Nations' (Jerusalem, 1930).

3. Speech to Hapoel Hatzair, 8 June 1923, quoted in Hattis, *Bi-national Idea*, p. 65.

4. Philby to Passfield, 21 October 1929, and 1 November 1929, CO 733/175/8821.

5. In Y. Porath, *The Emergence of the Palestinian-Arab National Movement* (London, 1974), pp. 256-8.

6. In a speech at the opening of the Hebrew University on 18 November, and in a pamphlet on 5 December entitled 'Like All the Nations?'.

7. Magnes to Loeb, 1 November 1929, CO 733/175/8821. See also Philby to Passfield, 21 October 1929; 1 November 1929; Chancellor to Shuckburgh, 8 November 1929.

8. See Weizmann's attitude in previous section 'now come the Magnes's to break our united front . . . I am the Hugenburg and he the Stresemann'. For evidence that Magnes's intervention did affect the High Commissioner's attitude, see G. Sheffer, 'The Passfield White Paper — Intentions and Results of British Policy', *Middle Eastern Studies*, vol. 9, Jan. 1973.

9. *Ruppin Diary*, 4 February 1932.

10. Magnes to Warburg, 7 August 1930.

11. 'Like All the Nations'.

POALEI ZION LEFT

1. Quoted in E. Margalit, *The Anatomy of the Left: Poalei Zion Left* (Tel Aviv, 1975), pp. 225-6.

2. Nir Rafalkes, 22.9.1939, quoted by Margalit, ibid., p. 230.

3. The Jewish Agency Committee consisted of the following members: S. Kaplanski (Dean of the Haifa Technion), Chairman; Dr Judah L. Magnes, Dr J. Thon, David Auster, H.M. Kalvarisky, Michael Assaf and Rabbi Uziel.

HASHOMER HATZAIR

1. Hattis estimates the number of Brith Shalom members to be 200. Laqueur speaks of 100.

2. Susan Lee Hattis incorrectly states that bi-nationalism did not become the official position of Hashomer Hatzair until 1930.

3. This seems to be the position taken by Walter Laqueur, whose *History of Zionism* discusses Hashomer Hatzair primarily as subject to adolescent idiosyncrasies, characteristic of a youth movement.

4. A detailed account of the activities of the League for Jewish-Arab Rapprochement is given in Aharon Cohen's book, *Israel and the Arab World*. Aharon Cohen was the Secretary General of the League until its dissolution in 1948; a member of Kibbutz Shaar Haamakim, he was one of the founders of the Arab Department of Hashomer Hatzair and later Mapam.

PART TWO: CRUCIAL DECISIONS

FOREWORD

The following pages deal with the question of how attitudes towards the Palestinian Arabs influenced decisions of the Zionist leadership in crucial stages in the evolution of the conflict in Palestine. These crucial stages can be regarded as turning points because both sides were faced with decisive choices as regards their objectives and strategy. The general view of most studies of Zionism in relation to its conflict with the Arabs is that the decisions taken were determined by external conditions: there were no alternative strategies possible. This view is best formulated by Professor Ben Halpern in *The Idea of the Jewish State* (Cambridge, Massachusetts, Harvard University Press, 1961), p. 247:

> Neither Zionist principles nor other ideological factors, neither long-range geo-political calculations nor a clever grasp of short-range tactical opportunities were truly decisive. The external pressures on Israel were so severe and the country was forced into so tight a corner, that the basic principle of its foreign policy became hardly an exercise of sovereignty at all, but rather an acceptance of necessities to which there was no alternative.

Professor Ben Halpern refers to the state of Israel and its foreign policy but the 'no-choice' (*ein breira*) concept is used by most official historians of Zionism also to explain its policy in the pre-state period. The following is an attempt to disprove this assumption. Contrary to current myths, the Zionist leadership was facing real choices and *was aware of it* as shown by the passionate debates on strategy, which often led to serious splits and crises in the Zionist movement. The decisions taken were a product not only of external pressures and absence of alternatives but also of a conscious choice influenced by rigid adherence to certain strategic and political concepts. The attitude towards the Palestinian Arabs — the non-recognition of a Palestinian national entity — played a major role in the elaboration of social and economic policies of the Zionist movement and in two crucial stages in Jewish-Arab conflict: in the years of the Arab Revolt 1936-8, which determined the relations between Zionism and Palestinian Arabs; and in the war of 1948 which set the course for a generalised conflict between the Jewish state and its Arab neighbours.

The analysis of Zionist policies in these turning points in the escalation of the conflict is the theme of the following pages.

193

THE POLICY OF ECONOMIC AND SOCIAL SEPARATION

Introduction

The Jewish-Arab relations in Mandatory Palestine had their socio-economic roots which, in turn, had an important bearing on the political conflict between the two peoples. Two equally distorted versions of socio-economic development in this period have been put forward: one Arab and one Jewish. According to the Arab version, there was a colonial dispossession of a native people by a white settler class bent on expansion at their expense. In the Zionist version, Jewish immigration to Palestine brought the benefits of development to all the inhabitants of the country, but met with the resistance of the feudal landlord class whose vested interests were jeopardised by the modernisation of the country, and it was the intransigence of this class that brought calamity to the Palestinian people.

Neither of these views gives an accurate account of what happened in Palestine in this period. The 'colonial settler state' thesis has been widely adopted by the European left, and has become axiomatic in Third World countries which have by and large accepted the equation between Zionism, racism and colonialism. The transformation of the Palestinians to refugee status after 1948 and the continued occupation by Israel of vast Arab territories since 1967, have contributed to this image.

No doubt certain features of Israeli Arab relations since the establishment of the state in 1948 have resembled a colonialist pattern. Israel expropriated without compensation the property of those Arabs who had fled during the fighting in 1948, and since 1967 has been exploiting cheap Arab labour and mineral resources from the occupied territories. An historical analysis, however, is crucial to determining whether the colonialist pattern was inherent in Zionist policy during the Mandatory period.

The thesis that Zionist colonisation in Palestine was a product of the surge of European imperialism at the end of the nineteenth century, and that Israel therefore originated as a colonial settler state,[1] is inaccurate. Jewish settlement in Palestine before 1948 was not the result of a military conquest of the native population by the white settler population. All the colonial states in Africa and Latin America were based on an identity between the settlers and a European power which conquered and expropriated the land and resources of the native population. In Palestine the Jewish settlers were not identical to the colonial power which, given her important interests in other Arab countries, was ambiguous about encouraging a Jewish national home. Thus, Jews purchased land from the Arabs on the open market, subject to increasing restrictions by the colonial administration. In 1948, Jews owned less than 12 per cent of the cultivated land.

The relations between Jews and Arabs in Palestine were not those of colonisers and natives. This is borne out by comparing Palestine to the North African countries which were subjected to French colonisation. The structure of employment and land ownership was such as to reduce the native population to dependence and prevent its autonomous development. By contrast, in Palestine, the Arab sector of the economy developed at a quickened pace between 1917-48; what emerged was not the exploitation of one sector by another, but the competition between two separate national economies, each growing rapidly, accompanied by a crisis of modernisation in the Arab sector.

In 1917, Arab industry in Palestine was primitive and the area served as a hinterland for Beirut and Damascus. But by 1936, 23 per cent of the Arab population of Palestine was engaged in manufacture, construction, transport and commerce, while the number in agriculture and other branches of primary production was 62 per cent. (The remainder were in the services sector.) Due to the impact of the Second World War, by 1945 the number in primary production had dropped to 50 per cent, and the percentage in the above sectors increased from 23 per cent to 30 per cent. Likewise, output per person increased substantially.

In the area of land ownership there is a marked disparity between the patterns in the Maghreb and in Palestine:[2]

Table 6.1: Land Ownership in North Africa and Palestine

Country		Population (per cent European)	Cultivated land (per cent European)
Algeria	(1955)	10.3	40
Morocco	(1955)	6.7	18
Tunisia	(1955)	7.7	12
Palestine	(1946)	34	12

Thus, in contrast to European ownership in the Maghreb, Jews in Palestine owned less land than their percentage in the population would warrant. This reflects the overwhelmingly urban concentration of the Jewish population and the lack of absentee Jewish land ownership. A more detailed breakdown shows that European colonialists in Algeria engaged in agriculture owned 147 hectares per head, while the Jewish agricultural population had an average of 3.0 hectares per head.[3]

A comparison related to an extended period shows the difference between a colonial pattern of development in agriculture and the course of Jewish settlement in Palestine. While the increase in the total agricultural revenue in Algeria between 1880 and 1955 barely kept pace with population growth, the European sector managed to increase its dominance of the sector. By contrast, in Palestine both Jewish and Arab agricultural income increased rapidly over a much shorter period, spurred by the rapid population growth due to Jewish immigration and a high rate of natural increase by the Arab population.[4]

Table 6.2: Agricultural Revenue in North Africa and Palestine

Country	Agricultural population	Revenue	Per capita
		1880 (milliard F)	
Algeria:			
Arab	2,000,000	48	24,000F
European	145,000	30	204,000F
		1955 (milliard F)	
Algeria:			
Arab	5,300,000	117	25,000F
European	145,000	93	641,700F
		1936 (million £)	
Palestine:			
Arab	600,000	4.2	7.0
Jew	58,000	1.6	25.7
		1945 (million £)	
Palestine:			
Arab	850,000	25.5	30.0
Jew	200,000	10.0	50.0

A similar pattern applies to the industrial and commercial sectors. For the whole of North Africa in 1955, two-thirds of the income in the non-agricultural sector went to the European population which made up less than one quarter of the non-agricultural population. Per capita, the colonialists received nine times the income of the natives. In Palestine the difference in income per head was about 2.75:1. Actually, the difference was even less because the age structure of the two populations was radically different: the Jewish population was predominantly of working age, while the Arab population had a large number of children. Thus, in 1936 the output per employee was in the ratio of only about 2:1. By 1946, the gap narrowed to 1.5:1.[5] In Algeria the European sector took 70 per cent of non-agricultural income in 1880, and 75 per cent of a vastly increased total in 1955.[6] It is significant that the gap did not increase in Palestine during a period of rapid industrialisation. The non-agricultural sector in Palestine also experienced fast development, spurred on in part by the Second World War. The output per worker in the Arab sector grew four times between 1936 and 1945. Admittedly, this was partially offset by an increase in the number of dependents per worker and inflation.[7]

The non-employment of Arab labour in the Jewish sector had its impact on the pattern of economic development. In Algeria, over 70 per cent of native agricultural income was received for work on European-owned plantations;[8] overall the European income per capita was seven and a half times the native income (it was nine times in Morocco and seven times in Tunisia).[9] In Palestine, the difference in the per capita income never exceeded three times between Jews and Arabs, and the total income of each national sector was roughly in balance.[10] The campaign for Jewish labour in the Jewish sector prevented the integration of the Arab peasantry into a colonial system of exploitation; it did not, however, prevent the growing crisis of the Arab agricultural sector — due to the impact of the rapid development of capitalism in Palestine.

The Zionist version of the benefits brought to the mass of the Arab population as a result of Jewish settlement in Palestine is just as misleading as the Arab version of Zionism as a colonial phenomenon. No doubt the economic level of the Arab community in Palestine was higher than that of the Arab population in neighbouring countries. Annual per capita income for an Arab was £27 (sterling) in Palestine, as compared to £12 in Egypt and £16 in Syria and Lebanon. The wages of the Palestine Arab worker were four to five times higher than those in Egypt. Annual government expenditures per capita were £4.4 for an

Arab in Palestine as opposed to £2.3 per person in Egypt and £1.8 in Lebanon.[11] Public services, especially education and health services, expanded, as reflected in the dramatic drop in the infant mortality rate, which gave Palestine the highest rate of population growth in the world at that time. The urban areas affected by Jewish development — Haifa, Jerusalem amd Jaffa — were growing faster than the purely Arab towns. The expansion of Arab industry and citriculture was largely financed by capital obtained from Jewish land purchase.[12]

The process of rapid capitalist development of the country cannot be attributed only to Zionist colonisation, for it also resulted from infrastructure investments by the Mandatory Government (as well as military expenditures), and from a high rate of population growth in the Arab sector. The socio-economic transformation of Palestine was faster than that of any other Middle Eastern country, but it brought in its wake problems that were not fundamentally different from those of other developing countries — landlessness among the peasants and under-employment among the fast-growing urban masses. It also led to a rapid social transformation of Arab society, resulting in the creation of new classes and a new structure which might have served as the basis for an agreement with Zionism, were it not for the fact that the political conflict developed in conditions of economic segregation. As the United Nations Special Commission on Palestine summarised in 1947:

> The economic life presents the complex phenomenon of two distinctive economies — one Jewish and one Arab, closely involved with one another and yet in essential features separate . . . this economic separateness . . . finds its expression in certain facts which may be briefly summarised as follows:
>
> 1. Apart from a small number of experts, no Jewish workers are employed in Arab undertakings and apart from citrus groves, very few Arabs are employed in Jewish enterprises . . . Government service, the Potash Company and the oil refinery are almost the only places where Arabs and Jews meet as co-workers in the same organizations.
>
> 2. There are considerable differences between the rates of wage for Arab and Jewish workers in similar occupations, differences in the size of investments and differences in productivity and labour costs which can only be explained by the lack of direct competition between the two groups.

3. Arab agriculture is based to a considerable extent on cereal production and tends to be of a subsistence kind. Only about 20%-25% of Arab agricultural produce (excluding citrus) is marketed — Jewish agriculture is largely intensive and cash crop farming. About 75% of Jewish agricultural produce is sold on the market.

4. The occupational structure of the Jewish population is similar to that of some homogenous industrial countries, while that of the Arabs corresponds more nearly to a subsistence type of agricultural society. [Report of the United Nations Special Commission on Palestine (UN SCOP) 1947.]

The economic separation of the two communities, which had a profound impact on the possibilities of political co-operation, was essentially the result of two factors: (1) the policy of the Zionist leadership aimed at the establishment of a fully autonomous and independent Jewish economic sector in order to create a new type of Jewish society, which would reverse the 'economic pyramid' of the Jewish people in the Diaspora, with its preponderance of middlemen and lack of productive workers. By establishing Jewish basic branches of industry, agriculture and mining, Jewish life would be normalised. It should be stressed that this basic tenet of Zionism was motivated solely by a reaction to conditions in the Diaspora, in a desire to create a new society rooted in the land and productive labour. (2) The use of economic boycott of Jewish goods and services as a political weapon by the Palestinian Arab movement in an attempt to restrain the development of Zionist enterprise and the counter-boycott organised by the Yishuv. Two economic problems played a major role in the estrangement between the two communities: land and labour.

Jewish and Arab Labour

The struggle for '100 per cent of Jewish labour' in the Jewish sector of the Palestine economy occupied the energies of the labour movement for most of the Mandatory years and contributed more than any other factor to the crystallisation of the concept of territorial, economic and social separation between Jews and Arabs. The principle itself of the exclusive right of the Jewish worker to the Jewish economy implied the complete separation between the two economic sectors. The struggle for the application of this principle, though conducted consistently and with all the powers of persuasion and pressure, did not achieve its objective: the elimination of Arab labour from the Jewish sector, in particular from the citrus groves, where most of the Arab workers were employed. In times of riots and disturbances, Arab labour was reduced or disappeared, but emerged again after the tension receded. But it was precisely the *failure* of the struggle to achieve '100 per cent of Jewish labour' which enhanced the tendency for separation, and created the psychological and political condition for the acceptance of partition as the only solution to the Jewish-Arab conflict.

However, the concept of 'Jewish labour' did not originate in racial or national prejudices. The idea of the 'productivisation' of the Jewish people was one of the fundamental tenets of Zionism, shared by a spectrum far broader than the labour movement itself. 'Return to the soil' and 'manual labour' were the standard ideals of Zionist education and ideology. Most of the immigrants, until the mass immigration of the middle classes in 1924-5, came from circles influenced by socialist doctrines, and many of them were members of political parties and youth movements committed to principles of international working-class solidarity.

The 'Jewish labour' concept arose from the shock of confrontation between their Zionist and Socialist vision and the reality of the Yishuv in Palestine. They saw before them pioneers of the First Aliya, who went to Palestine as idealists and became a class of settlers abandoning Zionist ideals for higher profits. They saw Zionist settlements in a process of moral decay, based on the exploitation of cheap native labour. The call for 'Jewish labour' was a reaction to this demoralisation. The attempt to revive the Zionist ideal of a new society, rooted in the soil and living by its own labour, was first made through an appeal to the national sentiments of the settlers. The new immigrants tried also to replace Arab labour by agreeing to work at lower wages, but unaccustomed to the climate and hard work in plantations and to the humiliating conditions of exploitation they could not compete with Arab labourers, ready to work long hours for extremely low wages.

It was against this background of these bitter experiences and the failure to change the character of the first Zionist settlements that new concepts of colonisation took shape: the concept of the Jewish economy as a closed circuit, in which Jews would fulfil all the functions and which would become independent of Arab labour and food supplies; the concept of national funds and nationalised land as the basis for colonisation and a guarantee against land speculation and exploitation of Arab labour; the concept of co-operative settlements based on self-labour and motivated by Zionist ideals unlike the individual settler who sought higher profits. Along with these concepts developed also the strategy of settlement in contiguous areas where the danger of interaction with Arab population would be minimised and where the Jews would rapidly become a majority and set up their autonomous institutions until they became a majority in the whole of the country and able to establish a Jewish state.

All these ideas, which were developed in the period of 1905-14, in an abortive attempt to eliminate Arab labour from the old Jewish colonies, were taken up with great enthusiasm by the immigrants of the Third Aliyah 1917-23, who were in the main young people of Socialist-Zionist youth movements imbued with the spirit of militant socialism and revolution.

The concept of 'Jewish labour' did not seem to be inconsistent with their socialist outlook. They were familiar with the problem of national competition in the labour market as it also existed in their home countries and was a point of departure for Borochov's analysis of the Jewish question. In Palestine they faced the reverse of the situation in Europe — the 'foreign' (Jewish) labour was the better organised and class-conscious — while the 'Jewish capitalists' preferred cheap unorganised native labour. As class-conscious socialists and as Zionists, the Third Aliyah immigrants believed it was their duty to eliminate the exploitation of cheap unorganised Arab labour by Jewish settlers; otherwise Zionism would become a colonialist phenomenon. The exploitation of cheap Arab labour was incompatible with their vision of a socialist society. They thought that by forcing Arab workers to seek employment in the Arab sector, they would stimulate the class conflict in Arab society and prevent the Jewish-Arab national conflict from attaining as well a class dimension.

A socialist society seemed, at the time, realisable to the majority of the labour movement. This mood was a result of both the revolutionary atmosphere after World War I and Bolshevik Revolution in Russia, and the character and composition of the Third Aliyah itself. Private capital and capitalists played a very insignificant role in it; the national funds were the main instrument of Zionist colonisation while collective and co-operative settlement seemed to be its most suitable form.

Contrary to some interpretations, Zionism, in this period, was not a movement propelled by big Jewish capitalists and financiers.[1] Even the few philanthropists (like Rothschild and Montefiore) upon whom Jewish settlement was heavily dependent in the early years, were opposed to Zionism's political aims of statehood and supported Jewish colonisation efforts not only in Palestine, but throughout the world, in order to relieve the pressure on their countries of the Jewish masses spilling out of Eastern Europe. The image of Zionism as having enormous financial resources at its disposal was, in part, created by the Zionist leaders themselves, eager to impress foreign powers who were deciding the fate of Palestine (we have mentioned Weizmann's proposal to Faisal in 1918, of a loan of £40 million at a time when the total Zionist budget of £2 million was regarded as 'astronomical' even by the 'rich' American Zionists).[2] In fact the entire investment of Zionist institutions in Palestine, during the whole Mandatory period (1922-48) scarcely totalled this sum.[3] Dr Ruppin, for many years the Director of Zionist colonisation efforts, repeatedly threatened to resign because of the lack of means to develop the country. Private capital, in this period, was not interested in investment in Palestine, poor in natural resources and possessing limited markets.[4]

No wonder that in these conditions in which pioneering work, national funds and co-operative settlements were the chief, if not the only, instruments of Zionist colonisation, the belief grew strong that it would be possible to develop a socialist economy, a network of Kibbutzim and co-operative settlements without passing through the stage of capitalism and private enterprise. In particular Itzhak Tabenkin, one of the founders of the 'Gdud Avoda' (The Legion of Labour) and, later, of its successor Hakibutz Hameuhad, at the time the largest Kibbutz-federation, entertained the utopian vision of a full and immediate realisation of Zionism as a socialist society. Even in this socialist concept of the future the principle of separation remained intact. Tabenkin saw as the major obstacles to the realisation of this vision 'Foreign capital, private enterprise and cheap Arab labour'.[5] The task of the Arab workers was, according to Tabenkin, to instigate a social change and become the vanguard of revolution in the Arab world. This was also the view of Ben-Gurion in the early twenties, when it was thought that the Balfour Declaration ushered in an era of full and speedy realisation of Zionist aims. Ben-Gurion rejected at the 1924 convention of his party, Ahdut Avoda, the proposals for a constitutional development in Palestine,[6] which would provide the framework for an unhampered development and integration of the Jewish and Arab sector. Ben-Gurion favoured the development of contiguous Jewish areas and thought that the expansion of these areas, within an autonomous Jewish constitutional system would ultimately lead to a territorial autonomy and a Jewish state.[7] Ben-Gurion's idea of autonomous Jewish areas crystallised later in a plan for cantonisation of Palestine: but the Jewish cantons were to be based exclusively on

Jewish labour and to form a closed economic circuit.[8]

The concept of separation was not easily absorbed by those in the labour movement which professed to be loyal to the principles of socialism and working-class solidarity — and which was still accustomed to use Marxist terminology in its analysis of social and economic developments. There were some moral qualms, especially with regard to forceful eviction of Arab workers, and a debate about the future relationship between the Jewish and Arab worker became inevitable. The more so as the growing sector of government services, public works and international companies (Iraq Petroleum Company, Shell, etc.) posed the problem of status of the Jewish worker in this mixed sector of economy.

The two left-wing parties, Poalei Zion Left and Hashomer Hatzair pressed, in different ways, for a joint trade union movement. For the Poalei Zion Left, Jewish-Arab workers' solidarity was an overriding priority and the key to the solution of the problem. They believed Arab opposition to Zionism to be motivated solely by class interests of Arab feudal landowners and clergy — while the interests of the Arab worker lay in the economic and social development, the driving force of which was free Jewish immigration and settlement. In their eyes the whole question was that of educating the Arab worker towards class-consciousness and workers' solidarity — by opening the Histadruth to Arab membership and organising joint trade union activities and struggles against the Jewish employer, Arab effendis and British imperialism. Members of Poalei Zion, employed in the mixed sector, devoted years of painstaking efforts to educate Arab cadres for this common struggle. It was due to their efforts that the International Union of Railway Workers[9] was founded and maintained for a number of years.

The position of Hashomer Hatzair members was more qualified. While recognising the necessity of a joint trade union movement as the only instrument for social change and the key to the solution of the national conflict, they proposed to develop it gradually on the basis of national sections. Like Poalei Zion, they opposed the slogan of '100 per cent Jewish labour' but did not ignore the problem of absorption of Jewish immigration, in particular in the colonies employing Arab labour. Hashomer Hatzair demanded the cultivation of contacts with the Arab workers and the organisation of those permanently employed in a joint trade union, composed of two national sections and run by a joint committee. Members of Hashomer Hatzair took an interest, during their stay in the colonies, in the conditions of Arab labour, encouraged their demands for higher wages and organised acts of solidarity with their strikes (in Ness-Ziona, Benyamina, Hadera in 1930 and 1931). These activities, though very much limited in scope and time, provoked stormy debates in the Histadruth. The political resonance of these debates in the Jewish community exceeded by far the impact of the actual activities in the colonies. Hashomer Hatzair members were only temporary residents and with their departure nothing was left of their efforts, the more so as many of the Arabs too were temporary workers commuting from place to place and from job to job. In the course of time Hashomer Hatzair specified the term 'permanently employed' meaning two years of employment in towns and one year in the colonies.

Within the Histadruth, prior to the creation of Mapai, the controversy raged between Arlozoroff of Hapoel Hatzair who saw no purpose in creating joint trade unions and Ben-Gurion who still considered the possibility of a joint national trade union structure with two autonomous national sections and a Central Committee formed on the basis of proportional representation of the national unions. Arlozoroff dismissed the argument that the organisation of the Arab worker and joint trade union would facilitate the struggle against unorganised cheap Arab labour in the colonies, because — as he claimed — the unlimited supply of Arab labourers from the villages would undercut and undermine any labour conditions achieved by a trade union.

With the creation of Mapai (through the unification of Hapoel Hatzair and Ahdut Avoda, 27 May 1929), the last remainders of the concept of joint trade unions disappeared. The resolution spoke only of comradely relations and promoting peace and understanding between the two peoples 'while the struggle for 100 per cent Jewish labour'[10] was renewed with more vigour, especially after the riots in August 1929.

The policy of separation, though not officially proclaimed, seems to have won the upper hand. The Zionist movement did not try to re-establish the Jewish Quarters in Nablus, Hebron and Gaza — evacuated during the riots.[11] The Mapai leadership was determined to exploit the tension in the colonies, created by the riots, to replace the Arab workers who departed, by Jewish labour and to prevent the return of the former. An ideological assault was staged against the demand of Poalei Zion Left and Hashomer Hatzair to reconsider relations with Arab workers. 'Yes, we *do* have to exploit this moment [after the riots of 1929] for the consolidation of the Hagana for speeding up of our enterprise, and for the imposition of Jewish labour' (Ben-Gurion at the Histadruth National Council, 2 October 1929).[12]

By this time the problem of '100 per cent Jewish labour' ceased to be an internal, moral problem of the Jewish labour movement and became a political issue *par excellence*. The Shaw Commission sent to investigate the causes of the 1929 riots attacked the principle of 100 per cent Jewish labour and challenged the control of the Histadruth over labour certificates. In 1930 John Hope Simpson blamed the policy of 'Jewish labour' for the grave unemployment in the Arab sector.[13]

The problem of separation versus integration became a matter of controversy between the Zionist movement and the Mandatory power. Lord Passfield, the Colonial Secretary, came out against the consideration of the absorptive capacity of the Jewish sector alone as the criterion for new immigration, as this sanctified the separation of the Jewish and Arab economy.[14] The British Prime Minister, in his letter to Dr Weizmann, reaffirmed the commitment to regard the Jewish absorptive capacity as the criterion for immigration. The High Commissioner Arthur Wauchope opposed the principle of Jewish labour and rejected Ruppin's proposal to regard existing Arab labour in the Jewish sector as an absorptive capacity.[15]

The issue of Jewish labour became thus part of the larger problem of the scale and pace of Jewish immigration. This would explain the strange fact that the campaign for '100 per cent Jewish labour' reached its climax precisely in the years of prosperity and large-scale Jewish immigration in 1933-5. The paradox of the situation was in the fact that Arab labour in the Jewish colonies increased not in the wake of competition between Jewish and Arab workers and not due to the employers' search for higher profits, but due to the *shortage* of Jewish labour, in the rural sector in particular. The economic boom in towns, the higher wages in construction drew thousands of Jewish workers away from agriculture and no moral appeal to Zionist ideals and national interest could persuade the workers in the colonies and the new immigrants to renounce a higher standard of living and lucrative employment offered by the economic boom in the cities. No more successful were the appeals to students and urban workers to rescue Jewish agriculture by volunteering to help the farmers and citrus growers for a few weeks. A vast campaign of propaganda in schools and in the media and the pressure of the powerful labour federations, labour council and labour economic enterprises, produced no more than a few hundred workers and a similar number of students.[16]

The shortage of Jewish labour and the economic boom threatened to wreck the policy of economic and social segregation: Arab workers were drawn in increasing numbers into construction sites in the cities and to the new colonies in the Sharon in which, up till now, the principle of 100 per cent of Jewish labour was preserved. To oppose this drift the labour leadership (now well entrenched in the Jewish Agency with Ben-Gurion and Sharett heading its Jerusalem section) took recourse to drastic measures which had far-reaching conseqences on the relations between Jews and Arabs. In 1933 the Histadruth launched, for the first time, a campaign to remove Arab workers from the cities. Specially formed mobile units moved from place to place to identify and evict by force, if necessary, Arab workers from construction sites and other Jewish enterprises, This campaign in the cities especially in Haifa and Jerusalem, which had a mixed population, assumed dramatic dimensions and had a devastating effect on public opinion. Every single case of removal of Arab workers — and in many cases the operation took the form of ugly scenes of violence — was reported in the Jewish press and reverberated in the Arab media creating an atmosphere of unprecedented tension.

The other drastic measure was the organisation of a nationwide campaign of picketing citrus groves in the Sharon (Kfar Saba) employing Arab labour. As a matter of fact the citrus growers in the Sharon were ready to employ Jewish workers but these were not available. The campaign took on the character of a crusade. Teachers, writers, journalists, artists, professors, were called upon to demonstrate their opposition to Arab labour by joining the picketing for a few hours, although the real reason for the breach in Jewish labour was simply the fact that the labour exchange was not able to provide Jewish workers.[17] The campaign was explained by the argument that the continuation of Arab labour in the Jewish sector would provide the Mandatory Government with a pretext to restrict Jewish immigration, as the shortage of labour could be compensated for by the employment of Arab workers and did not necessitate Jewish immigration.

As it was, the Zionist leadership in 1933-6 believed in the possibility to achieve within a short time a Jewish majority in Palestine which would resolve the problem of confrontation with the Palestinian Arabs, and pave the way for a sovereign Jewish state free to absorb the masses of European Jewry threatened by the rising power of Hitler's Germany. In view of the events that took place later — the above consideration might appear today valid and vindicated. However, the leadership of the Palestinian Arabs was aware too of the fact that a few more years of Jewish immigration on the scale of 1934 and 1935 would make their cause a lost one. They were eager to precipitate a crisis that would foreclose this development. The campaign for Jewish labour in the years of prosperity played into their hands: the atmosphere of tension and hostility created by the forceful eviction of Arab workers in the cities and by the acrimonious propaganda which accompanied this operation amplified the natural Arab fear of a Jewish majority, and transformed it into a state of panic thus precipitating the outbreak of the Arab rebellion in 1936 which put an end to Zionist expectation of a majority and statehood. At this crucial moment in Jewish-Arab relations, the absence of contacts and co-operation between the Jewish and Arab workers — which was not a result of negligence but of a deliberate policy — proved to be of disastrous consequences.

The Histadruth decided time and again to organise the Arab workers in the government services and public works in federative union with the Jews, and assigned to this task qualified cadres and a budget. Opportunities for joint trade union activities existed all throughout the years. Many Jewish workers were ready to devote their time to this task. Arab workers in conflict with their employers — Jewish and Arab — were turning to the Histadruth for aid and advice. On some occasions joint activities emerged spontaneously (the strike of Jewish and Arab drivers in November 1931 demanding to reduce the costs of driving licences, fuel and tyres). However, the Histadruth's approach to this problem was half-hearted, hesitant and sometimes reluctant. The Histadruth was faced with a dilemma. On the one hand it felt compelled to strive for the improvement in wages and working conditions of *all* employees in the mixed sector of economy; otherwise few Jews would remain in their jobs. On the other hand it was reluctant to encourage joint trade unions with a large Arab membership which would contribute to the consolidation of the Arab workers' position at a time when Jews fought for a larger share in employment in government services. Ben-Gurion refused to allow the IURW (Union of Railway, Postal and Telegraph Workers) to transform itself into a joint trade union, but instead insisted on maintaining its separate national sections, with the Jewish section *only* affiliated to the Histadruth. This solution proved to be harmful to the idea of solidarity between Jewish and Arab workers. Out of more than 1,000 Arab workers on the railways and postal and telegraph services, only 18 joined the IURW. Although the Jewish militants supported wholeheartedly the Arab workers' struggle for higher wages and against victimisation the Arabs viewed with suspicion and distrust the Histadruth which pursued a policy of '100 per cent Jewish labour' in the Jewish economy, and of pressing for an increased share of Jewish workers in government services. The result was that the Arab members of the IURW soon became the nucleus of a separate Arab trade union movement (Palestine Arab Workers Society) under the control of the Arab national parties. Later, when the political tension between the two communities deepened the gap between the Jewish and Arab workers and the Histadruth became concerned with the growing co-operation between Arab workers and the nationalist parties a decision was taken to set up the Palestine Labour League (Brith Poalei Eretz Israel) conceived as a Jewish-Arab trade union federation. In practice, it became an organisation of Arab workers run by the Histadruth. The Arab members of the League could not become members of the Histadruth although they could receive some of its services (health services, loans from co-operative credit societies, etc.). Even so, the league was regarded as the lowest priority in the Histadruth and treated accordingly.[18] It was in the hands of a few individuals (Agassi, Abba Khoushi) who complained of lack of sympathy, interest and understanding on the part of the Histadruth leadership. In these conditions, the League could not compete with purely Arab trade unions and extricate the workers from the orbit of Arab nationalist politics, which skilfully exploited the troubled atmosphere created by the Histadruth's '100 per cent Jewish labour' policy. The evidence of the national solidarity among the Arab members of the League was provided by the burial of the bodies of the followers of Sheikh Izz al Din al Qassam in the cemetery of the Arab workers in the Jewish quarry ('Nesher') near Haifa. At the height of its activities, the League counted 900 members organised in two branches, Haifa and Jaffa. The bulk of Arab workers was totally alienated from the Histadruth. During the biggest Arab strike (in the Iraq Petroleum Company, 22 February to 10 March 1935), when the Histadruth tried to mobilise contributions to the strike funds, Fakhri Nashashibi intervened to negotiate an agreement and persuaded the strikers not to accept it and to cut off relations with Histadruth, using the argument that the Histadruth's intention was to penetrate the company in place of the Arab worker.

The fragility and weakness of the League came to the fore with the outbreak of the Arab rebellion in 1936. Its Secretary-General, Agassi, had to admit that out of many hundreds of members, only a few individuals continued to maintain contacts with the League.[19]

Land

During Ottoman times, the Palestine village was more or less a self-supporting unit, insulated from the fluctuations in the economy of modern capitalist economies and dependent for its prosperity on climate more than on any other condition. Exchange of goods was of minor significance; the use of money was limited. Village crafts produced needed goods and increased its autarchic character. The village was bound by tradition and forms of life and work were passed down unchanged from generation to generation.

The crisis caused by the socio-economic development of Palestine in the Mandatory Period had its roots in the agrarian system which affected the overwhelming majority of the Palestinian population. The system was based on primitive subsistence — agricultural production by the peasants (fellahin) coupled with a land ownership that was both exploitative and unproductive.

As an important government report on the problem remarked:

> . . . one of the main obstacles to agricultural advance is to be found in the existing system of land tenure . . . hardly 20% of the proceeds remains to the cultivator . . . it may almost be said that here landlords are engaged not in exploiting the land but those who cultivate it . . . the owners of large landed property take little interest in the agricultural development of their lands.[1]

Doreen Warriner has defined the 'basic malady' of the agricultural system, which was responsible for keeping the rural population at a low level of income and status, as 'the prevalence of institutional monopoly in landownership linked with a monopolistic supply of capital to agriculture'.[2]

> Large landholdings are generally not in the form of centrally managed farms but were rented out in small holdings, usually through a series of intermediaries, to cultivators who paid high rents and had no security . . . sharecropping: i.e. the division of the crop between the landowner and the cultivator in a fixed proportion, is the main form of tenure. It is a customary form, without any contractual legal basis or any legal protection for the cultivator. The proportion taken by the landowner varies with the density of population, being high near towns and low on the desert rim . . . the system is, of course, a bad one, in so far as the landowner is a pure rent receiver and does not invest in the land . . . the existing land system gives rise to incomes which are not used to improve agricultural production. Large landowners spend conspicuously; or purchase more land; or invest in urban house property; or lend to impoverished cultivators at high rates of interest . . . the cultivators, on a low subsistence level, have neither the means not the incentive to invest; they are labourers, rather than tenants, who work for a variable return, and

cannot increase it by working harder or farming better . . . the system appears to be symptomatic of a static or regressive condition in which the landowner can obtain a higher return by renting the land than by farming it himself.[3]

The landownership system of Palestine was characteristic of this pattern. Only 250 families owned over 4 million dunams of land; among them were the clans of major political leaders (the Husseinis, 50,000 dunams; Abdul Hadis, 60,000 dunams, etc.). The top 116 families averaged over 10,000 dunams each. This small class of landlords (5,300 people in the 1931 census) owned almost as much land as was cultivated by 60,000 farmers.[4] The condition of those at the bottom of the pyramid was summarised by the Johnson-Crosbie report as follows: 35 per cent of the peasants had less than the minimum lot required for subsistence. This situation was particularly acute in the districts of Jerusalem and Nablus, where 77 per cent and 63 per cent of the farmers, respectively, had less than 50 dunams.[5] This situation was characteristic of the other Middle Eastern countries as well. In Transjordan, approximately 30 per cent to 40 per cent of the peasantry was without land; in Iraq in 1932, 35 per cent were landless; in Egypt in 1952, 1.5 million out of 4.5 million peasant families had no land, and 6 per cent of proprietors owned 65 per cent of the land.[6]

Land ownership was not only unequal, but investment in individual farms was deterred by the periodic redistribution of village holdings called Mu'usha, in order to equalise different plots. Furthermore, land-holdings were divided into many small plots distributed through the village. Rights to grazing land, water and wood were held communally by the village. No systematic registration of land titles was undertaken in Ottoman times, and to avoid taxation or army recruitment, when land was registered, it was often done in the name of dead or fictitious individuals, local merchants, sheiks or family heads, especially those to whom the government had given the responsibility of tax collection.[7]

The agricultural credit system was an integral part of the exploitative land system. Many large proprietors originated as money-lenders to poverty-stricken villagers. Rates of interest were usurious — 30 per cent to 50 per cent per year.[8] By 1930, the average debt of the Palestinian fellahin was put at £27 per year, a sum equal to his annual income, and the debt charges alone amounted to one-third of his income. It was only in the 1930s that the first agricultural bank was opened, providing an alternative service of credit. The extent of the crushing debt burden may be seen by comparing it with the short-term indebtedness of

Table 6.3

	Average indebtedness per 100 dunam	Ratio of indebtedness to average annual produce
USA	£94	1:6
England	£15	1:20
Palestine	£27	1:1

agricultural small holders in Western countries in the 1930s.[9]

The crushing burden of absentee landownership and money lending was borne out by the estimate by the Johnson-Crosbie Report, based on a survey of one-quarter of the villages of Palestine, that less than a third of the villages were economically solvent and could afford to pay the rent and interest charges demanded from the outside. Considering the absentee rent alone, only half the villages were solvent.[10] 'It is generally alleged that the Palestinian fellahin is born in debt, lives in debt, and dies in debt . . . his life has been made miserable by his creditors, and his moral and material progress severely hampered.'[11]

This type of system must be distinguished from classic European feudalism. The landlord class did not originate from a political grant of land in return for service to the state, but from a tribal sheik's claim to a crop as revenue or from the city merchant's demand for repayment of debts. Thus, the landlord class was often urban based, with little attachment to the land or interest in agriculture. 'A plough never enters the house without bringing degradation.' Turkish rule was hostile to the large landowners as rival sources of power; consequently, land-ownership was based not on military power and political obligation, but money lending, tax collecting or tribal authority.[12]

During the Mandatory Period the traditional social fabric of the village was invaded by the introduction of capitalist relations in the countryside. This was the result of the combination of the impact of British policies and infrastructure works, of the rapid growth of Jewish settlement, and of the development of the Arab economy. This process was anticipated by Zionist theorists, who believed that the break-up of the feudal system of relations would weaken the large landlords who were the centre of political opposition to Zionism, and lead to the emergence of a more moderate class of Arab small farmer. The capitalist relations did reach the countryside. Improved means of transportation and communication during this period drew the agricultural economy into a national and a world market. But their effect was the opposite expected by these theorists. The fellahin could not hold their own in a world of competition, or vie with goods produced overseas by modern methods. Money became the sole medium of exchange, and the Mandatory Government began collecting taxes in money rather than in tithes of crops. As the fellah's need for cash increased, he became more dependent on the usurer who was often at the same time the landlord and the grain dealer. This resulted in the increased exploitation of the peasant. The large landowners did not hesitate to take advantage of the situation by buying out the small-holders. Large landowners and landless peasants co-existed in the same village.

The amount of land purchased by Arabs from other Arabs rose steadily throughout the period. In 1940, for example, Arab land purchases were 33,000 dunams and in 1944, 64,000; the value of the land purchased had increased five times in that period.[13] Some of this land was purchased for speculative purposes and resold to Jews, but there is no doubt that this statistic demonstrates the continuing pace of social stratification in the countryside. Not only did small proprietors lose their land, many were reduced to wage labour which was insecure. Zionist theorists claimed that wage labour paid a higher return than the miserable existence possible on a reduced small-holding,[14] but they disregarded the problem of unemployment due to economic recessions and the excess of labour supply over demand.

Arab agriculture as a whole developed during this period, stimulated by the expansion of the urban market for foodstuffs (the urban population, spurred by Jewish immigration, doubled between 1922 and 1936). Poultry production, for example, doubled in five years. Agricultural machinery was increasingly adopted, cash crops for export (especially citrus) were increasingly cultivated, and some were able to take advantage of government loans.[15] Arab agriculture increased six-fold in fifteen years. But all these developments benefited only the small minority of well-to-do agriculturalists, while landlessness increased for the majority of peasants.

Landlessness was the major cause of the flow of population to the cities, more than could be absorbed by employment there. This ultimately provided the social base for the most extreme opposition to Zionism.

The character of the transformation of Arab rural society under the impact of Zionist colonisation is illustrated by the situation around Petah Tikva. The majority of the land for the colony — some 14,000 dunams — was bought from two Christian merchants who had received the land from the owners for debts the latter owed them. Additional purchases were later made from the neighbouring villages until the colony had 32,000 dunams, of which 14,000 were orange groves. The money from the sale of these lands was used by the few Arabs who were in a position to do so to plant orange groves themselves. Over 8,000 dunams were planted, but there were only 131 proprietors, thus averaging over 60 dunams per proprietor (much larger than the average Jewish holdings). Only 18 proprietors owned 2,000 dunams of orange groves. On the other hand, 2,000 Arabs from the neighbouring villages became permanent workers in Petah Tivka.[16] Thus, though the old type of landlordism had disintegrated, it did not lead to the emergence of middle-class farmers. Instead, a few got rich from investment of proceeds from the sale of land to Jews; the rest were reduced to wage labourers or share croppers.

While the feudal system was being replaced by a cash crop system in the areas of Jewish colonisation, paradoxically the same trends were strengthening the hold of the large landowners in the purely Arab areas. The landlords and money lenders were able to increase their exploitation of the peasants in those areas which had no alternative sources of employment. One estimate was that in the hill country one-third of the land passed over from the peasants to landlords in one decade (1920-30) alone.[17]

The actual number displaced by Jewish colonisation was limited. After 1930, the government carried out a careful investigation of claims as part of the new Land Compensation Ordinances, and found only 350 peasant families with legitimate claims to compensation for displacement by sale of land to Jews, out of 3,500 who applied.[18] The magnitude of the problem was much less than even the British officials assumed. It is clear that 35 per cent of landlessness was not caused by the 7 per cent of land owned by Jews, much of it formerly uncultivated and concentrated in a few areas.

As a political issue, however, land sales to Jews became the focal point of the campaign by Arab nationalists against Zionism. The landlord class, especially those sections less integrated into the newly emerging bourgeoisie, was threatened as a ruling elite by the economic transformation of the country and the possibility of Jewish rule, even though as individuals they were gaining economically from the sale of land to Jews at inflated prices.

Though the Jewish National Fund (in contrast to the earlier colonisation efforts of PICA in the Galilee) was buying large tracts mainly from absentee landlords (in order to gain a contiguous area), rather than assembling many small plots of villages, the resulting forced evictions of tenants accompanied by much publicity and legal suits were damaging to Jewish-Arab relations, and created a highly explosive issue.

By the 1930s, the Arab leaders attempted to organise a fund to buy land and prevent its sale to Jews. This was largely unsuccessful, as most of the leading figures in the Arab national movement (nearly all of whom were large landlords) sold land secretly to the Jews through brokers (who became the subjects of assassination attempts in later years). The reason for the sale of land to Jews was economic; in the vicinity of Jewish settlement, which was for the most part concentrated in a few connected areas, the feudal land system was in a state of collapse, as the tenants left the land in search for more profitable employment in nearby towns. The rising land prices supplied much of the capital for the expansion of the Arab sector, particularly for reinvestment in citrus groves by landlords. (In absolute terms, the amount of money transferred by Jews to Arabs through land purchase was £10 million in the whole Mandatory period.) But very little of this money reached the tenant farmers themselves, contradicting the Zionist propaganda about the benefits of Zionist colonisation, as admitted by Dr Arthur Ruppin, the Director of the Settlement Department of the Jewish Agency.

The Zionist leaders ignored the effects of modernisation on the peasants: the transition to a cash economy and wage labour, though raising the absolute standard and income of many, was painful as it involved the disintegration of the traditional structures which provided a measure of security and protection for the peasant. George Antonius, in his testimony to the Peel Commission,[19] emphasised how serious the loss of the traditional fabric of social life was to the villager, despite the economic gains that might or might not accrue to him by being a wage labourer in the cities:

> The problem of the exodus from the villages to towns is one which has bothered and has been a factor in almost every civilized country . . . because it is an unhealthy sign and a movement which brings with it a lot of undesirable consequences. Here in Palestine the policy followed hitherto has been to accentuate that exodus, in fact to make it necessary for certain people. Apart from the material loss, it brings with it also the loss of the moral values and moral characteristics which people acquire when they live on the land and live an

agricultural life, with all that implies, from father to son. The fact that they are suddenly uprooted from that life and driven to seek their living elsewhere, in the towns, or on the roads, or in casual labour, is a very serious loss from a moral point of view . . . the moral deterioration which overtakes people in their own characters when they are uprooted and forcibly driven to the towns or away from the villages and the land upon which they had their root is a thing the Government should do a great deal to avoid . . .

The rural crisis led to a flood of under-employed population which could not be absorbed in public works or the Arab sector of the urban economy, and which was increasingly excluded from the Jewish sector.

One index of the crisis of landlessness was rapid urbanisation, which was especially pronounced in the larger towns. The Arab urban population increased from less than 200,000 in 1922 to over 400,000 in 1944, when almost half the Arab urban population was concentrated in the three cities of Jaffa, Haifa, and Jerusalem. The Moslem population of Jaffa grew by 126 per cent between 1922-31 alone. It was due only in part to the expanding opportunities for employment in trade, industry, construction and public works, in all sectors (Jewish, Arab and government) of the economy; the migration of thousands of villagers into the port cities and major towns, was due to the landlessness in the rural areas which left them little choice but to seek employment in towns. The growth of population was greatest in the mixed Jewish-Arab towns, as opposed to the purely Arab towns. Municipal revenues increased 3½ times between 1920 and 1935 in the mixed towns, and only 1½ times in the purely Arab towns.[20] The search for new employment opportunities drew workers from outside Palestine as well, especially from the Hauran of Syria. The authorities did nothing to prevent the influx of wage labourers from abroad. A census of Haifa workers in 1943 revealed that only 30 per cent of Arab workers were permanent residents of the city: 20 per cent were from other countries and 50 per cent from a semi-rural background. Many of these workers were only in casual or seasonal employment, as unskilled labourers in orange groves, civil engineering projects or local industries. Their living conditions were often appalling.

The social and economic conditions of the Arab worker were grim. His hours of work were long (from 9 to 16 hours a day), wages were low, and there was no trade union protection, security of employment or health and social security benefits for most. Wage levels were about one-third of the level of Jewish wages, and unequal rates were paid to the Jewish and Arab workers in government employment (unskilled Arab workers received around 100 mills a day or less — £2 a month — while unskilled Jewish workers received 200 to 300 mills a day); unemployment was endemic and fluctuated between seasons and with changing conditions in Palestine. In 1935, some 5,000 were idle in Jaffa alone, with massive Jewish migration becoming one of the precipitating factors in a violent strike. During the Second World War full employment returned, but with demobilisation it was estimated that 30,000 out of 54,000 were idle.[21] With such a large reserve army of labour, strikes were infrequent (averaging less than 5 per year compared to 100 per year in the Jewish sector during the 1930s) and labour leaders were forced to appeal to political leaders — British or Palestinian — for help in strikes.[22]

Social conditions were just as bad:

Thousands of unskilled workers in Jaffa cannot afford a house to sleep in — they sleep in tin huts or in the open. The rent of a decent room in Jaffa amounts to about two thirds of the wages of an unskilled worker. The fellah in his own village is spared this expense; he does not have to sleep in the open and he does not pay rent. For 18 years past, hardly a single house has been built for the labourer or the poor; the municipality does not build them and no one feels that it pays to build for them commercially . . . I am not exaggerating if I say that in some seasons in Jaffa, when the oranges are being loaded, some 10-15 thousand people live in the city and its suburbs without a single proper latrine. That may pass unnoticed in a village, but in a city it becomes sickening. Thousands live in tin huts without the most elementary accommodation and without any water supply except what they can carry in small jars from a far distance. I observed that in many of the hut colonies, they hardly use more than a cubic meter of water a month.[23]

The disintegration of village society and the emergence of vast shanty towns in the large cities created the social base for the emergence of the Arab terrorist movement in the 1930s.

Paradoxically, it was in Haifa, where economic opportunities and industrial development were greater than in the rest of the country, and where Jewish-Arab relations were better than anywhere else, that violent extremist groups first emerged. This was because of the existence in Haifa of a large floating population of villagers who had come to the city to earn their living. Many drifted from job to job, without a stable economic base, or fixed address, yet in daily contact with the possibilities, temptations and the larger social contrasts of urban civilisation. The villagers were ready to turn to violence because of their rootlessness. For spiritual guidance they turned to the one fixed ideology they knew — Islam. The fusion of their emotional climate and religious fervour created the Qassam movement, which turned on the person (and later the myth) of Sheikh Izz-al-din al Qassam, a Moslem preacher from Jebble near Lataquiya in Syria.

In his sermons to the poor worshippers in a popular mosque in Haifa, he sometimes spoke out against the wealthy Arab leaders, but he called for an armed struggle to drive out the foreigners — the British and the Jews. As secretary of the Young Men's Moslem Association, he recruited a hard core of between 40 and 100 followers to carry out his programme of indiscriminate terrorism. These Moslems included quarry workers who had access to explosives, railway workshop employees who could fashion primitive bombs, and villagers from Tira, Balad ash Sheikh, Yagur and other villages. Their activities began in April 1931, with the murder of three members of Kibbutz Yagur, and continued with some breaks until November 1935 when the Sheikh was killed in a fight with the police. He became a martyr, a model of a brave fighter for Islam, in the eyes of the new generation of militants who despised the talkative Arab politicians and their political solutions.[24]

The quasi-social character of the movement was demonstrated by the fact that its leadership came from the lower orders. For example, the commander of the Haifa section, Yussef Abu Durra, was formerly a farmhand who worked as a porter and soda peddler. Such people had nothing to lose, and combined the old peasant anti-government, lawless attitudes with religious fervour.[25]

Despite the warnings of Ahad Ha'am and Martin Buber, the Zionist movement was from the outset uninterested in the question of the economic development of Arab agriculture and the improvement of Arab social conditions; at best, regarding these as the task of the British Government Administration and, at worst, siding with the landlord class in its eagerness to protect the rights of free property transfer. The Zionist movement never put forward a programme of agrarian land reform, for aid to Arab agriculture through seed banks, credit or cooperative institutions, or for special agricultural training or aid programmes. On the contrary, at every juncture where the government attempted to do something for the fellahin, the Zionist movement opposed the legislation.

This began with the Military Administration, even before Britain had formally gained the Mandate over Palestine. The Military Government proposed a loan to small cultivators to tide them over the next harvest, because many had lost a lot during the war conditions and had not planted that year. Weizmann objected to this suggestion as likely to give a formal title to the land to small peasants whose claims were often not very well registered. (Under Ottoman Law, land registration had been haphazard and often falsified; at the insistence of the Zionist Organisation, the Land Registers from Ottoman times were frozen when Palestine was conquered by the British.)

A Jewish Agency Memorandum commenting on the Draft Ordinances on the Protection of Cultivators, 1930, prepared by the government, reveals some interesting attitudes. The draft stipulated that the High Commissioner must approve sales of land with regard to the availability of other land for the tenants to work. The Jewish Agency argued the case of the money lender: that these would 'discourage the lending of money on mortgage and prevent the securing of capital by land-owners for the improvement of their property and agricultural development'. 'It undermines existing contracts and discourages making loans to landowners.' The Agency objected on the further ground that it gave the existing tenants something like 'the right of perpetual undisturbed eternal occupation of the land'. This would prevent the landowner from removing 'tenants either in order to replace them with more efficient cultivators or to cultivate the land more efficiently himself'. It 'prevents the development of land and of agriculture by maintaining in their present holdings a mass of tenants who are without the capital to improve their holdings'. The recommendations of the Jewish Agency were that there 'should be the minimum possible interference with the free flow of capital into agriculture, and that the execution of transfers, mortgages and leases should be rendered as easy as possible'.

What kind of programme was possible if the Zionist Organisation had been interested? It is noteworthy that the Zionist leaders did propose development schemes outside Palestine for the development of Arab agriculture, and even the transfer of displaced Arabs to Transjordan in order to free the country for Jewish development. The types of schemes that might have been suggested include:

1. Agricultural credit schemes for farmers. This was the crucial problem: indebtedness to usurers was what made peasant production not economically profitable for the peasant.

2. Alternative marketing organisations for grain, then the monopoly of the landlords.

3. Agricultural training programmes.

4. Reforms to defend the interest of the small cultivators, such as anti-eviction ordinances, rent control and redistribution of the large estates. (It is noteworthy that the British legislation only protected those tenants evicted as a result of Zionist land purchase, not the larger number evicted by the Arab landlords. A small-scale agricultural credit scheme was established in later years by the Administration.)

Boycott and Counter-Boycott

The policy of economic separation initiated by the Zionist movement found unexpected help and encouragement from the Palestinian leaders who thought to block the development of the Zionist enterprise by means of violence and economic boycott. From the earliest days of Zionist colonisation, Arabs – Bedouins in particular – incited by local leaders, tried to harass and intimidate new Jewish settlement by theft, robbery and assaults on their members. There was hardly a Jewish settlement that did not experience this danger. It is in this atmosphere that there emerged the first organisation of self-defence, 'Hashomer', whose members later became the backbone and cadres of the (illegal) 'Haganah'.

The riots that broke out in 1920 and 1921 in mixed towns caused the dissolution of the many partnerships and commercial relations between Jews and Arabs and stimulated the tendency towards physical separation between their living quarters. In the 1929 riots, Jewish communities left Arab towns in which they had lived for centuries (Hebron). The 1936-9 disturbances completed the process of physical separation.

In all the mixed towns, Haifa, Tiberias, Safed, etc., Jews moved out from Arab quarters and so did the Arabs who lived in Jewish quarters. The Jewish population from Jaffa moved to Tel Aviv and Jaffa became a purely Arab town. The port of Jaffa, which had served the Jewish population, nearly closed down and the Jews started to develop a port of their own in Tel Aviv. During the General Arab Strike in 1936, all economic contacts between Jews and Arabs were broken. Arab workers disappeared from Jewish plantations, Arab agricultural produce did not reach the Jewish market. A total boycott of Jewish goods in the Arab sector was imposed and Arab merchants who remained in contact with Jews had their life threatened. In particular, the Arab 'land brokers' engaged in mediation or speculation in land transactions became the target of terror and a number of them were assassinated. Thus, the call for an economic boycott of Jews played into the hands of the Jewish policy to build a close economic circuit and facilitate the implementation of the policy of 'Hebrew labour' and 'Hebrew goods'. The opposition of the few economic circles in the Jewish community, who were interested in cheap Arab labour and cheap Arab produce, became feeble in conditions of rising tension, and disappeared entirely during riots and disturbances. Consequently, Arab boycott and Jewish counter-boycott complemented and fed each other, preventing the emergence of a common Palestinian economy. There was, however, an important difference in motivation as well as results.

For the Arabs, the boycott was mainly a political weapon, used in order to restrain the development of the Yishuv. It did not reflect the economic interests of the Arab people. It harmed the Arab more than the Jew. It spelled economic ruin for the landowners, citrus growers and merchants. It brought unemployment for Arab workers and caused great losses to the peasants who depended on the Jewish market. As a political weapon, it was effective at least in the short run, bringing the whole Arab population under the control and authority of nationalist leaders, and forcing the British to review their policy towards the Jewish national home.

For the Jews, the Arab boycott brought many advantages: it liberated the labour market from Arab workers; it gave a boost to Jewish farming and stimulated the investments in the creation of a totally autarchic and independent economic structure. The building of the Tel Aviv port was symbolic of this turn of events. Politically, however, the Arab General Strike turned to the disadvantage of the Zionist cause as it contributed to the nomination of the Royal Commission of Enquiry (Peel) in the autumn of 1936, to reconsider the British policy in the application of the Mandate. This was a crucial moment for the Jewish Agency, calling for long-term decision on whether to continue the policy of economic separation or make an effort to bridge the gap of disruption caused by the General Strike. With the termination of the strike in October 1936, the possibility of return of Arab workers to the Jewish sector, resumption of trade, re-opening of the Jaffa port, and normalisation of economic relations was there. The decision fell in favour of separation.

When the Jewish Agency met to consider what measures to take in preparation for the visit of the Royal Commission to Palestine in the Fall of 1936, following the termination of the Arab General Strike, two issues emerged as paramount in the debate: the land problem and the problem of Arab labour. On 22 July and 21 August 1936,[1] the Mapai Political Committee discussed the issue of the return of Arab workers, and the resumption of economic relations with the Arab population after the termination of the General Strike.

A strong current of opinion emerged in these meetings against the return of Arab workers to the Jewish sector and against the normalisation of economic relations. Ben-Zvi (later President of the State of Israel) called for the mobilisation of the whole Jewish community to strengthen its economy and to make it entirely independent of Arabs: 'Whether we call it boycott or not – the name doesn't matter.' What was important was not to allow Arab labour to come back, not to buy Arab produce, not to renew tenancy of Arab houses in order to boost up Jewish construction. He even suggested a stop to buying land from the Arab, for the time being, as there was enough reserve (150,000 dunam) for new Jewish settlements. 'Let the Arabs know that not a single pound from the Jews will flow into the Arab economy.' The General Secretary of the Histadruth, Remez, too, called to intensify the campaign against the return of Arab workers and against trade with the Arab sector.

As it would be difficult to explain the boycott to international public opinion he proposed to take these measures in protest against the stoppage of Jewish immigration, by the Mandatory power. Tabenkin – the leader of the socialist Ahdut Avoda (at the time, the Left wing of Mapai) – thought that a declaration of boycott would have negative moral and political consequences and would be ineffective as a protest against the policy of British Administration, but he postulated the principle of 'Jewish economic independence'. 'I aspire for maximum of Jewish-Arab co-operation but I oppose Arab labour in the Jewish sector, because there is a boycott of Jewish labour in the Arab sector.' Berl Katznelson – the ideological leader of Mapai – favoured a break-off of economic relations with the Arabs (including non-purchase of lands, evacuation of Arab houses, etc.) though he opposed a declaration of boycott. He thought there was some logic in regarding these measures as protest against the British immigration policy: 'the Arabs should suffer, too, from the stoppage of immigration'. Ben-Gurion took a similar line: 'Boycott was never our policy – Zionism is in favour of Jewish-Arab co-operation and a [declaration] of boycott will harm us abroad. The Arabs prepare now to declare an economic boycott against the Jews – I pray to God that they should do it [to us].' Though not in favour of a declaration of a full-scale boycott, the majority of labour leaders was in favour of seizing the opportunity presented by the Arab strike in order to renew the campaign for exclusive Jewish labour. This applied among others to the new port in Tel Aviv, which had been built and opened when the Jaffa port was closed by the strike.

On 12 October 1936, it was decided to organise a campaign against any Jew using the port at Jaffa, and against paving the road from Jaffa to Tel Aviv. It was agreed that Jewish workers would go back to work in Jaffa only if they were given equal job rights, and also allowed to use the port at Tel Aviv. Ben-Gurion called this the symbol of the whole struggle to preserve the gains that had been won by the Jews during the Arab General Strike. Thus the Zionist leadership was still unconcerned about the political implications of the segregation policy.

Even more serious was their appraisal of the land situation, which also emerged in the debates of the Jewish Agency Executive in preparation for the Peel Commission in October-November 1936.[2] At an early meeting, Ussishkin proposed that if the government would agree to free land acquisition on both sides of the Jordan, the Jewish Agency would not oppose the proposal for a minimum plot size which could not be alienated from the fellahin – on condition that it could negotiate to give him the same size plot in another part of Palestine or Transjordan. Sharett opposed any legal restrictions on land sales or land reserves in Palestine, arguing that Transjordan was the reserve for all Palestine; Jews and Arabs alike. He did suggest, however, that the rights of the fellahin could be protected by a special commission which would investigate transactions and dispossession claims. Ruppin proposed a plan for development of Jewish and Arab agriculture and argued that the minimum plot size was meaningless because it depended on irrigation and development of farming methods. He suggested that the concentration of peasants in one part of a village would allow the sale of other parts – but he proposed that the share croppers' interests should be defended.

Ben-Gurion argued that there was no danger of Arabs being landless; they could be transferred to Transjordan and no injustice would be done. He opposed Sharett's commission proposal, arguing that all opposition to Zionist land acquisition was politically not economically motivated.

On 1 November 1936, the Jewish Agency Executive continued its discussion of Arab agriculture. Ben-Gurion opposed a proposal that it submit a plan to the government for Jewish and Arab resettlement. Ben-Zvi maintained that they should not be arguing to improve the conditions of the fellahin – that was the job of the government. Senator, nevertheless, objected that 'we can not pass over in silence the conditions of the fellahin' but the other Mapai leaders (Kaplan,

Sharett) joined in opposing the government plan – to guarantee by law, the minimum viable lot for the fellaheen.

This approach to the question of landlessness in Palestine led directly to the concept of population transfer, perhaps the most explosive addition to the Arab-Jewish conflict, rather than to any concrete proposals for an improvement of the economic conditions of the vast majority of the Arabs. (See also 'The Debate on Transfer', pp. 259-66).

The Impact of Zionist Colonisation on Arab Society

Zionist economic theorists and ideologists pinned their hopes on economic development and social differentiation within the Arab community. They believed that the Arab effendi (landlord) class was the mainstay of opposition to Zionism, and that with the collapse of the semi-feudal economic system, the emergence of new classes (Arab bourgeoisie and working class, a capitalist sector in agriculture), and improvements in the standard of living and public services, Arab opposition to Zionism would substantially weaken. Their prognosis with respect to the developments in the Arab sector was, on the whole, correct; a process of socio-economic differentiation did take place and the general conditions of life improved.

The Arab population benefited from better conditions in sanitation, health, education, transport and other public services. This factor was stressed by official Zionist spokesmen and conceded also by those who criticised Zionist policy and fought for a bi-national solution. Between 1922 and 1941 the Arab population grew from 660,000 to 1,098,000; that is, by 66.3 per cent as compared with the growth of 35 per cent in Syria and Lebanon; 25 per cent in Egypt; and 20 per cent in Iraq. In this period, the emigration of Arabs from Palestine stopped altogether while 125,000 emigrated from Syria and Lebanon.

Tens of thousands of Arab workers and landless peasants from Hauran and even Egypt flocked to the developing areas in Palestine, especially during the years of Jewish mass immigration in the early 1930s. Improved health conditions in Palestine produced the highest rate of natural increase of the population in the entire Middle East. During this period (1922-41), 325,000 Jews came into Palestine and nearly £115 million were invested in urban development, industry, agriculture, etc., creating a growing internal market and increasing labour opportunities. Nearly £30 million passed from the Jewish to the Arab sector in payment for land, agricultural produce, rent and wages.[1] This capital stimulated the growth of the Arab urban sector with a large

number of commercial and industrial enterprises and the rapid development of Arab citriculture, which increased from 20,000 dunam in 1922
to 147,000 dunam in 1935.[2] Also, Arab society underwent a profound
social transformation with the emergence of capitalist entrepreneurs in
industry, commerce and agriculture, and a class of wage labourers.

All this did not, however, lead to the results expected by Zionist
economists: the disappearance of the feudal effendis and their replacement by moderate bourgeoisie middle-class farmers and class-conscious
workers failed to materialise. The main reason for this was the deepen-
ing separation of the two national economies (Arab and Jewish),
accompanied by a total break in social and cultural contacts between
the two. This separation allowed the transformation of the rapidly
developing socio-economic conflicts within the Arab sector into an
economic competition at every class level between the two communities, without any common interests cutting across national lines.[2]

The new social forces in the Arab society were not any less militant
in their urge for national independence and opposition to Zionism.
Arab industry was on a small scale and suffered from the competition
of the much more modern Jewish industry.[4] Construction of houses,
small businesses and speculation in land were the main areas of Arab
investments. The Arab average firm had only six workers in 1942.
During the Second World War, which provided vast opportunities for
investment to supply the Allied forces in the Middle East, Jewish
industries increased their output five-fold, while Arab industries
expanded only four times. The average size of the Arab firms actually
decreased while the average number of employees in Jewish establishments increased.

The structural weakness of the Arab bourgeoisie and the fear of
Jewish competition comes out clearly in the testimony to the Peel
Commission in 1936. Because of the fear of Jewish competition, the
Arab bourgeoisie (businessmen, contractors, citrus growers, etc.), which
centered mainly around the 'Defence Party' of the Nashashibis, pressed
for a legislative council and treaty of independence with Great Britain,
before the Jews would become the dominant force in the country.
Actually, the 'Defence Party' possessed considerable potentialities for
co-operation both from the point of view of representing a more
moderate attitude towards Zionism and exhibiting strength in the
struggle for leadership inside the Arab society. Arab businessmen,
especially in towns where the population was growing at a rapid rate,
were drawn into partnership with Jews. Arab merchants were also
marketing industrial products manufactured by Jewish firms (for

instance, 'Shemen' oil, etc.). Citrus-grower Jews and Arabs had a common interest in export facilities. Some observers saw the feud between the Nashashibis' Muaradiyun (oppositionaries) and the Husseini's Majlisiyun (the councillors — because the Mufti controlled the Supreme Moslem Council) as purely a family and clan affair, which cut across Arab society from top to bottom and split villages into two, as each group organised rival youth movements, trade unions, cultural clubs, etc. A deeper examination would show that the Muaradiyun attracted more the new elements which were emerging in the wake of the economic development of the country. First organised in the coastal plain and other areas of the growth of capitalist agriculture and intensive farming, like the Jordan Valley, they installed themselves in the cities where the new class of entrepreneurs, merchants and industrialists was growing. Both the Husseinis and Nashashibis were members of a ruling class based on landlordism combined with commerce and money lending, but the percentage of the capitalist elements — plantation owners, bankers, wealthy farmers, town bourgeoisie, etc. — was considerably higher in the Muaradiyun.

The Nashashibis demonstrated their strength by winning the municipal elections in 1927-8. This was one of the reasons why, despite the fact that Zionism was then (1929) at its lowest ebb, the Mufti engaged in a violent religious campaign against an alleged 'Zionist plot' to gain control of the Harem al Shariff. He did this to reassert his position. The Nashashibi faction could maintain its hold only in conditions of progress towards self-governing institutions and growing co-operation between the Arab and Jewish economy. Self-government was blocked by Zionist opposition to the establishment of a legislative council, while the policy of economic separation and the rapid progress of the Jewish enterprise in the 1930s increased the fears of the Arab bourgeoisie of losing out and drove it to join the fervent nationalist campaign in 1935 to stop Jewish immigration and acquisition of land and to press for national government. In this, to cover up for their essentially moderate programme, the Nashashibis resorted to the tactics of outdoing the Husseini in extreme anti-Zionist propaganda. By 1935, the internal conflicts between the Nashashibis and the Husseinis were subsumed in the larger national struggle, when tensions had increased in reaction to massive Jewish immigration, spread of Arab unemployment, discovery of a large Jewish arms cache, and the rejection of the legislative council proposal by the House of Commons and the House of Lords in March 1936. The Arab workers, excluded from joint trade union organisations and constantly harassed by the 'Hebrew labour' picketing, and the masses of landless peasants unable to find work in the weak Arab sector, became the main driving force in this campaign. It was among them that the guerilla bands based on the Qassamite movement (Sheihk Qassam was killed) emerged. It was one of these groups of 'bandits' who were responsible for the precipitating incident of the Arab Revolt and General Strike. Thus by the mid-1930s, the whole of Arab society was involved in a mass mobilisation against Zionism.

Paradoxically, it was precisely the increasing social differentiation in Arab society which provided the basis for a national movement of resistance to Zionism. The new Arab bourgeoisie was too weak, in competition with the technologically superior Jewish industry, to absorb the abundant Arab labour force which was excluded from the autarchic Jewish economy. It was this Arab lumpen-proletariat which provided the political base for extreme nationalist and anti-Jewish propaganda. It is significant that the Arab Revolt of 1936 originated in shanty towns outside Jaffa and Haifa. While the new bourgeoisie and the landlords were profiting as individuals from the rapid economic development, they saw themselves as a class losing their hold over a rapidly changing society and being deprived of the prospect of self-government and political power by a new and dynamic factor (Zionism). The nascent conflict between the new bourgeoisie — as reflected in the more moderate, urban elements rallied behind Nashashibi's National Defence Party and the more radical and pan-Arab elements supporting the Husseini party and the Istiqlal — could not develop fully in the absence of democratic, self-governing institutions. The moderates too shared the general aspiration for independence, but lacking a social programme for the masses had no popular base, while the Husseinis had the advantage of their religious appeal which served as a substitute for social justice. The Istiqlal raised the standard of anti-imperialism. But it was above all the impoverished masses who pushed the political parties beyond their original intentions into a radical nationalism and an armed struggle. Could this development have been prevented?

The only possible way to increase the popular base of the more moderate forces in the Arab camp would have been for Zionist policy to create from the beginning, *in addition* to the Jewish sector of the economy, a joint sector in which co-operation between both capital and labour would be possible and would form a community of economic interests. Complete integration of the two economies would have meant the reproduction of classical colonialism, but complete separation led to the strengthening of the anti-Zionist opposition to a far greater degree than the Zionist movement anticipated.

Such proposals for a *modus vivendi* with the Arabs in Palestine, came from the Jewish side. This was in the spring of 1936, at the outset of the Arab General Strike against the British pro-Zionist policy. The approaches were made by an influential group of Jewish businessmen and civil leaders known as 'The Five', who were in touch with moderate Arabs and were concerned that the continuation of the Arab General Strike would jeopardise the Jewish national home in Palestine. Emerging from these negotiations were very serious and comprehensive proposals for an agreement with the Arabs. The reaction of the official Jewish Agency (mainly Sharett) to the negotiations was to discredit the authority of the negotiators on both sides. The Jewish Agency strategy was to give the appearance of interest in an agreement in order to prove that the Arabs were intransigent.

The economic proposals of 'The Five' contained the following points:

Land: A joint Arab-Jewish Committee of experts must survey the land held by Jews and Arabs, with a view to agreement on the future purchase of land, as follows: (a) The area in Palestine and in which Jews could buy land; (b) The minimum land area that may not be sold should be fixed, so as to avoid landless fellahin selling their land to Jews or Arabs. The committee may specify cases where the sale of land is absolutely prohibited and also permit exchange of land areas.

Work: (a) In all Jewish settlements and industrial enterprises, except those financed by Jewish national bodies, Jews as well as Arabs must be employed. The proportion of Arab labour must be 25 per cent in Palestine and 50 per cent in Transjordan; (b) Every government department, public works, post and telegraphy, railways, etc., must employ Jews at least proportionately to their numbers (now 30 per cent of total Palestine population).

Joint Activity in Commerce and Industry: (a) Arabs must be enabled to invest in any new industrial, commercial or transport enterprise of more than £25,000, and to take part in the management in proportion to their investment; (b) In any enterprise with a capital of more than £25,000, a seat on the Board of Directors must be offered to an Arab; (c) Where established companies decide to increase their capital, they must allow Arabs to participate and assure them representation in the management of the company in proportion to the capital they invest, and one seat on the Board of

Directors even if they have not participated in the investment; (d) Any commercial industrial or transport enterprise of £25,000 capital, save such as are financed, directly or indirectly by Jewish public bodies, must employ up to 25 per cent Arabs; at the same time, Arab enterprise shall be required to employ Arab and Jewish officials in proportion to their number in the country; (e) Some method of join effort must be found for both existing and prospective Arab and Jewish co-operative measures; (f) The government must find a way to treat Palestine as a Dominion for the purposes of tariff preferences in all markets of the British Empire.[5]

The proposals of 'The Five'[6] were first made in private contacts in April 1936, when an agreement was suggested to both Frumkin and Smilansky which would limit Jewish immigration for a number of years. 'The Five' approached Musa Alami, who was crown counsel and an associate of the Mufti. 'The Five' decided that when they could reach common agreement, they would present their proposals to the Jewish Agency and take no action without its approval. Sharett had been disparaging the negotiations, warning Rutenberg that such proposals would weaken the will of the High Commissisoner 'who was disposed to fluctuations in regard to suppressing the riots with force'.[7] Nevertheless, Magnes and Musa Alami drew up a tentative outline of a proposal, which included political parity, an immigration limit of 30,000 a year for ten years, and restrictions on Jewish purchase of land.[8]

In May 1936, Rutenberg submitted his own detailed memorandum to the Jewish Agency, along with the report of 'The Five'. This was a detailed scheme for co-operation between Jews and Arabs in all spheres, with a major effort to integrate the two national economies of both Arabs and Jews in all establishments. The memorandum of 'The Five' asked that they be given authority to negotiate on behalf of the Jewish Agency, and a conference between them and members of the Jewish Agency Executive was scheduled for 1 June 1936. The Agency members continued to delay until 24 June, when they finally stated:

(a)   the Agency welcomes the offer of assistance in negotiations;
(b)   the proposal to fix an immigration quota for 10 years is acceptable only on the basis of the 1935 quota (i.e. 62,000/year);
(c)   the question of immigration certificates already issued should not be raised;
(d)   'The Five' can continue negotiations, but must act only on the

lines determined by the Agency.[9]

The Jewish Agency issued no instructions that were more specific and on 14 July 1936, 'The Five' submitted an additional memorandum, expressing their 'great concern and sorrow at the stand of the Executive' and lamenting that once again a last-minute opportunity to have a path for the unhampered development of a Jewish national home had been missed.[10] Four months later, the proposals had not yet been circulated among members of the Jewish Agency.

Meanwhile, at the end of June,[11] Sharett had gone directly to Musa Alami and, in effect, told him that 'The Five had no authority to negotiate an agreement'. In his discussion with Alami at the King David Hotel, Sharett warned him not to take Magnes too seriously. He described Magnes as a 'charming person eager to see Jewish-Arab differences settled but representing no one and having no right to speak for the Jews', and added that only the Agency could speak for the Jews. Sharett then asked Musa Alami for whom he spoke and whether he could 'deliver the goods', since the Agency would have to be assured that he 'would have the backing of permanent leaders of Arab affairs before any understanding could be reached'. Sharett stated that he could not make any definite proposals without such assurance as he might be exposed to criticism by other Jews if the Arabs repudiated an agreement.

It thus appears that on the one hand, Sharett ruled out private initiative, and insisted on formal negotiations with authorised proposals from both sides; on the other hand, he indicated that it was too early for any substantive agreement. Sharett did not seem to realise that the negotiations were only feelers, in which Musa Alami had agreed 'to act as a guinea pig . . . if he [a moderate] could not be satisfied, the others surely would not be'.[12] Therefore, private, informal talks were essential for *exploration*.

The Jewish Agency did not pursue these suggestions, which had the support of important Arab figures because the Arab Revolt had by then broken out. Had these proposals been accepted as the guidelines of Zionist policy from the very beginning, an area of integrated economic activity could have developed alongside the separate national economies. But coming as they did at the time of turbulence over the political future of Palestine, they were too late to affect the mortal struggle of the two national movements.

The response of the Zionist leadership to their proposals, at the time when the Arab General Strike was threatening totally to segregate the two economies, reveals that it did not understand the political implications of its socio-economic policies. In particular, the problem of the crisis of landlessness in the Arab agricultural sector was not seen as one of the contributing factors to the movement against Zionism.

The crucial period which determined the evolution of Jewish-Arab relations was 1917-36, and the decisive factor in this period was the growing separation between the Jewish and Arab economies. The process started with the initiation by the Zionist movement of a policy of 'economic segregation' from the earliest days of Zionist activity in Palestine. Already in 1913 Dr Arthur Ruppin, Director of the Palestine Office, stated at the Eleventh Zionist Congress: 'The objective we have in view is the creation of a closed Jewish economy, in which producers, consumers, and middlemen will all be Jewish.' This policy was not directed against the Arabs but aimed to prevent the moral decay of Jewish settlers into a class of colonialists, exploiting cheap Arab labour instead of 'redeeming' themselves by creating a working class and a 'productive society'.

However, the implication was a boycott of Arab labour in the expanding Jewish economy. The struggle for 'Jewish labour' became the official policy of Yishuv and the Jewish labour movement, and together with the prohibitions of Arab workers on land acquired by the Jewish National Fund, set the course for segregation of the two societies enforced by nationalist propaganda, picketing and intimidation on both sides. The trend for segregation was reinforced by the British policy of limiting Jewish immigration on the basis of 'economic absorptive capacity', as the exclusion of Arab labour from the Jewish economy seemed necessary for the creation of more job opportunities for Jews. Finally, the general strike and economic boycott proclaimed by the Arabs in 1936, too, necessitated urgent measures to make the Jewish economy independent of the Arab population.

Conclusions

Counter-factual questions are almost impossible to answer in history. The question of whether an alternative orientation was possible for the Zionist movement begs many questions about the reaction of the Arabs, the British and the Diaspora, and it is easy to see, given the constellation of forces at the time, why the Zionist movement crystallised the way it did. Nevertheless, while one can make only putative judgements about possible reactions, it is possible to postulate what strategy would have maximised the chances for peace and reconciliation with the Arabs of Palestine, without necessarily being out of harmony with the main needs of the Zionist movement at the time.

The question of a different economic policy adopted by Zionism was of crucial importance from the beginning. Given the rapid change in socio-economic conditions to Palestinian political development, if the strategy suggested by Ben-Gurion in the 1930s *in relation to the other Arab states* — help with economic development and the modernisation of agriculture — had been applied conscientiously from the beginning to relations with the Palestinian Arabs (without political preconditions), the whole evolution of Jewish-Arab relations in Palestine might have been different.

Proposals by 'The Five' in 1936 came too late to have any effect. This strategy was not in contradiction to the development of a separate Jewish sector of the economy, where Jews would be workers as well as middlemen, but meant the creation of a joint sector where the scope for Arab-Jewish co-operation could be realised. It also meant help to the small farmers who were suffering from landlessness and the burden of debt. In all these aspects such an approach might have had the support of the British Administration. The Zionist leadership preferred to 'force the pace', devoting all efforts to the creation of Jewish employment and land ownership, and was afraid to jeopardise these goals by agreeing to any joint economic programme. But the political costs of such an approach in the end outweighed the advantages of dealing from strength. The desire to create a *fait accompli*, rather than accept limited gains through an agreement with the Arabs, was a fundamental choice of the Zionist movement which preferred the option of a Jewish state to a concrete agreement which would have slowed down the pace but also reduced the price and the risks as well as the legacy of an escalating conflict.

The unwillingness to initiate a policy of economic co-operation had far-reaching consequences at the end of 1936 and the beginning of 1937. After the general strike and economic boycott of Jewish goods was called off, the Arab economy had been ruined. Both bourgeoisie and workers were eager for a renewal of work and feared the possibility of economic competition from Jews. Rather than seeing this as the moment to put into effect the proposals of 'The Five' for joint economic co-operation, the Zionist leadership viewed the occasion as an opportunity finally to realise its long-sought policy of complete economic separation between the two communities. Not only did they try to supplant Arab with Jewish workers in all services that had depended on the former (transport, ports, agriculture), but even considered organising a counter-boycott of Arab goods to accelerate the creation of a completely autarchic Jewish economy. The attitude of the leadership seemed to be that the Arabs should be punished for their rebellion.

Economic co-operation alone, of course, would not automatically have led to peace, but it might have created a congenial climate for the Arab peace feelers, based on a temporary agreement and an agreed quota of immigration, for at least some specified period. It might have been possible to reach some agreement which would have allowed the transfer of hundreds of thousands of Jews from Europe during this most tragic period in Jewish history. But the Zionist leadership was not fundamentally interested in an agreement with the Arabs, because it had made the fateful decision as early as February 1937 to stake everything on partition, regardless of warnings that it would not be implemented over Arab opposition. Despite internal doubts, all resources of the Jewish Agency were mobilised for the promotion of partition in British circles, including the concept of using the British army to effect the compulsory transfer of Arabs out of the Jewish state.

In the circumstances, the partition proposals galvanised Arab opposition and led to a second, more serious guerilla war against the British (1937-9), which reached its peak just when the Partition Commission arrived in Palestine to consider frontiers. The partition plan had frozen political attitudes of both Palestinians and Jews.

Notes

INTRODUCTION

1.   For example, Maxime Rodinson, in *Israel et le Refus Arabe* (Paris, 1968).
2.   Samir Amin (for the Maghreb), *L'Economie du Maghreb*, Editions Minuit (Paris, 1966), pp. 114, 118; for Palestine, Edward Asfour, *Backdrop to Tragedy: the Struggle for Palestine* (Boston, 1957), pp. 330-1. Jewish land-holdings in Palestine were 180,000 hectares, of which 72,000 were cultivated in 1944. This represented 6.6 per cent of the total land area of Palestine, 12.0 per cent of the total land under cultivation, and approximately 20 per cent of total cultivable land. The last figure is uncertain depending on estimates of how much uncultivated land had the potential for cultivation; John Ruedy, in 'Dynamics of Land Alienation' in *The Transformation of Palestine* (Evanston, 1971), pp. 119-20, estimates at a minimum 975,000 hectares of cultivatable land, plus an uncertain amount of the Negev (total area 1.26 million hectares). Approximately 600,000 hectares were cultivated in 1946.
3.   Amin, *L'Economie du Maghreb*, p. 185.
4.   Algeria, in Samir Amin, ibid., p. 187. Palestine: population, Janet L. Abu-Lughod, 'The Demographic Transformation of Palestine', in *The Transformation of Palestine*, pp. 139ff; agricultural revenue per head, Asfour, *Backdrop to Tragedy* pp. 324-30. All prices are constant prices.
5.   Asfour, *Backdrop to Tragedy*, p. 323; Amin, *L'Economie du Maghreb*,

p. 179.
6.   Amin, *L'Economie du Maghreb*, p. 188.
7.   Asfour, *Backdrop to Tragedy*, pp. 319-23.
8.   Amin, *L'Economie du Maghreb*, pp. 126, 119.
9.   Amin, ibid., p. 189.
10.   Asfour, *Backdrop to Tragedy*, p. 323.
11.   Aharon Cohen, *Israel and the Arab World* (London, 1970), pp. 212-13.
12.   Peel Commission Report, p. 129, Cmd 5479, London, July 1937.

JEWISH AND ARAB LABOUR

1.   Example by Maxine Rodinson, *Israel et le Refus Arabe* (Paris, 1968).
2.   Chaim Weizmann, *Trial and Error* (London, 1949), p. 327.
3.   Edmund Asfour, 'The Economic Framework of the Palestine Problem'
in *Backdrop to Tragedy* (Beacon Hill Press, Boston, 1957), p. 333. Total Jewish
private investment was double this sum — the bulk of investment (40 per cent)
was in construction.
4.   Chaim Weizmann, *Trial and Error* (London, 1949), p. 327.
5.   Quoted from Anita Shapira, *The Futile Struggle — The Jewish Labour
Controversy* (Hakibutz Hamcuchad, Israel, 1977), p. 33. The following pages
draw heavily from this excellent and very important study.
6.   Submitted by S. Kaplanski, later Head of the Haifa Technion.
7.   A. Shapira, *The Futile Struggle*, p. 25.
8.   Ibid., pp. 56-7.
9.   All details concerning joint Jewish-Arab trade unions are drawn from
an unpublished research paper by Joseph Vashitz. The IURW (International
Union of Railway, Postal and Telegraph Workers) was founded by the Poalei
Zion Left in 1921.
10.   A. Shapira, *The Futile Struggle*, p. 72.
11.   Ibid., pp. 25 and 35 ff.
12.   Ibid., p. 78.
13.   Ibid., p. 45.
14.   Ibid., p. 164.
15.   Ibid., p. 165.
16.   Ibid., pp. 167-8.
17.   Ibid., pp. 195-213.
18.   Ibid., pp. 174-5.
19.   See report of E. Agassi, Secretary of Labour League, Minutes of
Political Committee of Mapai, 16.1.1937, file 23/37, Mapai Archive, Beit Berl.

LAND

1.   Johnson-Crosbie Report on the Condition of Agriculturalists in
Palestine, 1930, Cmd 3686, Jerusalem 1930.
2.   Doreen Warriner, *Land Reform and Development in the Middle East*
(London, 1962), pp. 6-8.
3.   Ibid., pp. 58-60.
4.   Naji Aluche, *Arab Resistance in Palestine, 1917-48* (Beirut, 1967), p. 18.
5.   Johnson-Crosbie Report; Doreen Warriner, *Land Reform*, pp. 24-5.
6.   R. Patai, *The Kingdom of Jordan* (Princeton, NJ, 1958), p. 122; Zaki
Hairi, *Problems of Peace and Socialism* (Prague, 1959), no. 4, p. 59.
7.   John Ruedy, 'The Dynamics of Land Alienation' in *The Transformation
of Palestine* (Evanston, 1971), pp. 122-4.
8.   Johnson-Crosbie Report, para. 66.
9.   Memoranda prepared by the Government of Palestine for the Palestine

Royal Commission, 1936, p. 42.
10.   Johnson-Crosbie Report.
11.   Memoranda by the Government of Palestine, p. 41.
12.   Doreen Warriner, *Land Reform*, pp. 60-63.
13.   Government of Palestine, Statistical Abstract 1944-45.
14.   Horowitz and Rinden, *Economy Survey of Palestine* (Economic Dept. of Jewish Agency, Jerusalem, 1947), p. 205.
15.   Ibid., pp. 207-8 (government loans to agriculture totalled £169,000 in 1936, out of a proposed development loan of £ 2.8 million).
16.   Report on Petah Tikvah and the neighbouring villages, Central Zionist Archives, S25/7447, n.d.
17.   M. Assaf, *ArabJewish Relations in Palestine, 1860-1948*(Tel Aviv, 1970), p. 192.
18.   L.Y. Andrews, Minutes of Evidence to the Peel Commission, 1937. It should be emphasised however that the investigation used very narrow criteria in defining displacement.
19.   Minutes of Evidence, Palestine Royal Commission, CO 134, 1937, p. 364.
20.   Memoranda submitted by the Government of Palestine to the Anglo-American Committee of Enquiry, 1946, p. 153, Table 9a; Statistical Abstract of Palestine, 1944-5, pp. 21-2.
21.   D. Horowitz and R. Hinden, *Economic Survey of Palestine*, p. 208.
22.   Government of Palestine, Statistical Abstract 1944-5; George Mansur refers to the intervention of the District Commissioner and of the Husseinis ('The Arab worker under the Palestine Mandate', Minutes of Evidence to the Peel Commission, CO134, July 1937).
23.   George Mansur, ibid., Government of Palestine, Employment and Payrolls Bulletin, 1936, Sami Taha speech, Minutes of Evidence to the Peel Commission, 1937.
24.   J. Vashitz, unpublished paper, pp. 10-11.
25.   Ibid.

BOYCOTT AND COUNTER-BOYCOTT

1.   Minutes, Political Commitee Mapai, 22.7.1936; 31.8.1936; 12.10.1936.
2.   Minutes of Jewish Agency meetings in Jerusalem, 12.10.1936; end Oct. 1936; 21.10.1936; 25.10.1936; 29.10.1936; 1.11.1936; 9.11.1936.

THE IMPACT OF ZIONIST COLONISATION ON ARAB SOCIETY

1.   All figures drawn from Aharon Cohen, *The Jewish Problem and Arab Question* (Arabic) (Tel Aviv, 1945).
2.   Royal Commission on Palestine, Cmd 5479, 1937 p. 125.
3.   For example, Dr Judah L. Magnes, in his diary, reported that young Arab intellectuals told him, they have not met a single Jewish young man.
4.   A Government Census of Industry in 1942 revealed the following facts:

	Arab Industry		Jewish Industry	
	1934	1942	1939	1942
No. of establishments	339	1558	872	1907
Capital invested (000's) LP	703	2131	4390	12094
Output per establishment LP	4559	3631	6932	15230
Employed per establishment	11	56	14	19

5.   Ben-Gurion, *My Talks with Arab Leaders* (Jerusalem, 1972), pp. 74-5.

6.   'The Five' were Judah Magnes, President of the Hebrew University; Pinchas Rutenberg. Director of the Palestine Electric Co; Moshe Smilansky, Head of the Citrus Growers Federation; Gad Frumkin, Justice of the Palestine Supreme Court; and Novomejsky, Director of the Palestine Potash Co.

7.   Ben-Gurion, *My Talks*, p. 71.

8.   Aharon Cohen, *Israel and the Arab World* (London, 1970), pp. 269-71.

9.   Aharon Cohen, ibid., pp. 265-8, 271.

10.   Ibid., p. 272.

11.   Ben-Gurion, *My Talks*, p. 93.

12.   The entire conversation in Ben-Gurion, ibid., pp. 93-7.

7 THE ARAB REVOLT OF 1936 AND THE POLICY OF PARTITION

Introduction

The years 1936-9 mark a turning point in Jewish-Arab, Arab-British and Jewish-British relations. During this period, the Palestinian national movement gained momentum as it moved from a six-month general strike into fully-fledged guerilla warfare against a reinforced British garrison. The British proclaimed martial law, dissolved the Arab Higher Committee, arrested activists, and took punitive measures against Arab villages as the country convulsed with terror and chaos.

The previous disturbances might be ascribed to the anti-Jewish agitation of religious propagandists. The events of 1936-9 showed all the features of a popular struggle characteristic of fully mature national movements: a general strike, economic boycott, demonstrations, political actions and guerilla warfare. All the existing Arab political parties united in a common platform calling for an end to Jewish land purchases and immigration, the termination of the British Mandate and the proclamation of an independent state.

The uprising flared up suddenly in the wake of an incident on 15 April, in which two Jews were killed, but the air was already saturated with fumes that needed only a spark to provoke the explosion.

Many commentators view the Arab Revolt in Palestine as a corollary of the fervent nationalist struggle for independence in Syria and Egypt, spurred on by the Italian thrust in the Mediterranean and Africa. While the international atmosphere undoubtedly encouraged the re-awakening of Arab nationalism, the roots of the revolt lay in Palestine. Both the Zionist and Arab leadership realised that the conflict was approaching a climax, and that the quickened pace of Jewish immigration and settlement would lead to the Jews becoming the dominant economic and political factor in the country. This awareness had led Ben-Gurion and Sharett to renounce their previous acceptance (in 1931) of parity as a step to political development towards self-government.

It is perhaps the belief in the probability of a Jewish majority and statehood in Palestine, as a product of the dynamic pace of Zionist settlement, that prompted Ben-Gurion to undertake two initiatives in 1934-5. One was to start negotiations with pan-Arab leaders on a project similar to the Weizmann-Faisal Agreement in 1918, of Zionist support for an Arab Federation in return for Arab recognition of a Jewish Palestine, including Transjordan.[1] The other was an attempt to reach an agreement with Vladimir Jabotinsky, his greatest adversary against whom he launched a short time before a vicious campaign, fully exploiting the murder of Arlozoroff[2] in June 1933, suspected to have been committed by members of a Revisionist group. The agreement purported to put an end to the violent clashes between the Histadruth and the Revisionist National Labour Federation. But, significantly, the talks between Ben-Gurion and Jabotinsky centered around the issue of political co-operation between the Zionist and the dissident Revisionist movement to combat the proposal of a legislative council in Palestine (unless Jewish representation was based on the population of world Jewry and Arab representation on the Arab population in Palestine). The draft proposals for an agreement submitted by both Jabotinsky and Ben-Gurion included a preamble stating the identity of views on the ultimate goal of Zionism, on the future political status and the territorial dimensions of the Jewish society in Palestine. Ben-Gurion presented to Jabotinsky his project of an Arab Federation within the framework of the British Empire.[3]

The agreement caused a sharp controversy in Mapai, Ben-Gurion's party, and was rejected in a referendum of the Histadruth in March 1935. The stormy debates on the Ben-Gurion-Jabotinsky agreement centered, however, on the proposals to regulate trade union relations and ignored the political background of Ben-Gurion's initiative.

While Ben-Gurion was sanguine about the Zionist prospects, the Arab leadership was gripped by fear of rapid transformation of the country, and pressed for a stoppage of Jewish immigration and land acquisition and for the creation of a legislative council to which the Colonial Office and British Cabinet had committed themselves in 1931. The High Commissioner also pressed for the implementation of the project despite the hedging tactics of the Jewish Agency. The proposal was finally adopted by the Cabinet but defeated in the British Parliament in March 1936, by a pro-Zionist majority. The frustration of the Arabs at their utter helplessness to overcome the powerful Zionist lobby in London, contributed to their taking recourse to violence.

The mass character of the Arab opposition is reflected in the report of the Mandatory Administration. Between 1936 and 1939, nearly 10,000 violent incidents were perpetrated by Arab nationalists, including 1,325 attacks on British troops and police, 1,400 acts of sabotage on rail lines and telegraph wires, 153 acts of sabotage of pipe lines, and 930 attacks on Jewish population and settlements. Nearly 2,850 Arabs were killed, and many thousands more wounded in riots put down by British troops, and over 9,000 Arabs were interned. Nearly 1,200 Jews and 700 British were killed or wounded in the disturbances.[4]

The Zionist leadership under-estimated the strength of Arab national feeling in Palestine, and ascribed the General Strike proclaimed on 21 April 1936 to the machinations of the Mufti, encouraged by the 'tolerance' of the Mandatory Administration and by events outside Palestine: the increased Axis power and propaganda in the Mediterranean and the Middle East. It was believed that a 'strong arm' policy by the British could have nipped the revolt in the bud. The Zionist leadership ignored the fact that the revolt originated with the Arab masses, which forced on the Arab political leaders ever more violent forms of struggle, though this spelled economic ruin for the Arab upper classes. Actually, the General Strike started spontaneously in Arab towns at the instigation of local committees. Under the pressure of the masses, the five Arab political parties overcame their feuds and united on common strategy – to form the Arab Higher Committee and to endorse the call for a General Strike, which was to last until the Mandatory Administration stopped immigration and committed itself to the formation of a national government in Palestine. Throughout the strike the pace was set by the local strike committees, not by the Arab Higher Committee, members of which, concerned about their financial interests and official position, were interested in terminating it as soon as possible.[5]

The vehemence of the strike; the deep echoes it aroused in the neighbouring countries, where a fervent nationalist campaign for independence was already well under way; the indecisiveness of the British Government in using harsh measures and large military forces in a tense international situation (at the beginning of German and Italian intervention in the Spanish Civil War); the fear of Arab leaders, who were mostly pro-British (Abdullah, Nuri Said, Ibn Saud), of the spreading unrest,[6] as well as the Arab Higher Committee's and British Mandatory's search for a face-saving formula to end the strike – all combined to create the background for the mediation and the intervention of the Arab states in the Palestine problem. This phenomenon was henceforth to remain a permanent feature of the situation. The problem of the Palestinians, which had been insulated since the collapse of Faisal's Kingdom in Syria, again became a general Arab issue and added a new dimension to the Jewish-Arab conflict.

The face-saving formula was the appointment (on 18 May 1936) of a Royal Commission on Palestine, to investigate the causes of unrest. After eight months of enquiries and deliberations this Commission declared that the Mandate's obligations to the two communities were irreconcilable and recommended the partition of Palestine into a Jewish and an Arab state (to be united with Transjordan).[7] Though this particular plan failed, the principle of partition became the axis around which all future attempts at a solution revolved, until the UN partition resolution of November 1947.

The Partition Plan 1937

The partition proposal was based on the Commission's conclusion that since 'an irrepressible conflict [had] arisen between two national communities within the bounds of one small country . . . with no common ground between them, and their separate national aspirations [were] the greatest bar to peace' then 'Partition seems to offer the only chance of ultimate peace'.[1] The Commission rejected proposals for a legislative council of the parity type as being likely to increase conflict through deadlock, and besides, no 'moderate Arab opinion' could be found to support such a proposal. Cantonisation was likewise rejected as posing all the problems of partition with none of its advantages. 'The problem cannot be solved by giving the Jews or the Arab everything they want . . . While neither race can justly rule all Palestine we see no reason why, if it were practicable, each race should not rule part of it.'[2]

The territorial boundaries of the two new proposed states (and certain territories which were to remain under permanent British mandate) were such as to include a substantial Arab minority in the Jewish state, and only a few Jews in the Arab state. This was primarily because the proposed Jewish state was to include the whole of the Galilee as well as the Valley of Esdraelon and the coastal plain south to a point below Tel Aviv. The British would maintain enclaves at the port of Haifa, the religious holy places of Jerusalem, Bethlehem, Nazareth and Tiberias, the Arab city of Acre, and a communication corridor from Jerusalem to Jaffa. The Arab state would include all the rest of Palestine, including the Negev. It was also the suggestion of the Commission that this state should become part of Transjordan:

> The British Mandate for Palestine should terminate and be replaced by a treaty system . . . treaties of alliance should be negotiated by the Mandatory with the Government of Transjordan and representatives of the Arabs of Palestine on the one hand, and with the Zionist Organization on the other . . . these treaties would declare that two sovereign independent states would be established – the one an Arab

state consisting of Transjordan and the Arab part of Palestine, and the other a Jewish state.[3]

The report showed concern about the potential imbalances in the new states. It was feared that the Jewish state would be stronger economically and, therefore, it was recommended that the Jewish state pay an annual subvention to the Arab state. The most vexing problem however, was the question of the Arabs remaining in the Jewish state, some 296,000. The Peel Commission suggested that the two countries arrange for a transfer of populations following the Greece-Turkey precedent, in order to avoid endless conflict.[4] This would overcome the cardinal question of how to separate the two communities territorially.

The Commission also expressed the hope that their plan might have the support of Arab statesmen who would be willing to concede a little of Palestine provided that the whole Arab nation were to be free (which was virtually accomplished by now).[5] In fact, much more effort was spent in answering Arab than Jewish objections to the scheme. Some external Arab support was vital for its success; for example, the transfer of population envisaged in the scheme could take place only in an enlarged Arab Palestine which included Transjordan.

The fate of the partition proposal is well-known. The Jewish Agency attacked partition officially, as a breach of the Balfour Declaration but privately negotiated with the British Government along the lines of a Jewish state in an area adequate to satisfy the needs for immigration and settlement. The British Cabinet approved the recommendation of the Royal Commission but the House of Commons, at the suggestion of Winston Churchill, adopted a resolution requiring the preliminary approval of the League of Nations before the presentation of a definite plan to the Parliament. Further delay was caused by the League of Nations: the League's Permanent Mandates Commission demanded a period of tutelage for the proposed new states before the granting of independence while on 16 September 1937 the League's Council requested a further study of the status of Palestine. The Arab leaders in Palestine denounced partition and, after a period of relative quiet, between the end of the General Strike (October 1936) and the publication of the report (July 1937) the popular uprising flared up again, this time more fiercely than before. Despite harsh measures employed by the government — deportation of Arab leaders, disbandment of the Arab Higher Committee and local strike committees, introduction of military courts and collective punishment — the Arab revolt grew into a nationwide guerilla action which at times controlled whole town-ships and villages, despite the massive increase of the British garrison.

The technical commission (the Woodhead Commission) whose establishment was announced in January 1938[6] and whose function was to work out the details of the partition scheme, arrived in Palestine in April and engaged in its task in conditions of rising violence and chaos. Its terms of reference indicated from the outset a tendency on the part of the British Cabinet to retreat from the partition plan: they included a dissociation from the idea of a compulsory transfer and required the Commission to study boundaries that would prescribe respective areas to the two groups to include the smallest numbers of people of the other nationality.

The Commission was also enjoined to report on whether the whole scheme was workable. In November 1938 the Commission reported that the Peel plan was unrealisable, because of the large number of Arabs (300,000) included in the area assigned to the Jews. It proposed two alternatives that whittled down the Jewish area to a size unaccept-able to even the most enthusiastic Zionist supporter of partition. One member of the Commission declared that no practicable scheme of partition could be devised.[7]

The Zionist Leadership and Partition

The British retreat from partition is attributed to the government's hesitancy and vacillation in the face of Arab opposition and the deteriorating international situation. Very little has been written about the share of Zionist policies in both the crystallisation of the scheme and in its collapse. The fierce and passionate debates that threatened the unity of the Zionist movement more than once, provide the lens through which Zionist policies in this most turbulent period in the evolution of Jewish-Arab relations may be examined.

Not realising the depth of the popular character of the Arab Revolt, the Zionist leadership (with the exception of Sharett) grasped at a casual suggestion of Professor Coupland of the Royal Commission (in January 1937) to partition Palestine. The leadership viewed this as an historic opportunity to realise the centuries-old dream of a Jewish state, albeit only in part of Palestine, although before then, in their testimony before the Commission, Weizmann, Ben-Gurion and Sharett had solemnly declared that Zionism had no aspirations for statehood. Actually, the ultimate aim of most political Zionist leaders was state-hood, but until the partition plan was proposed, this concept was not considered politically practical. It was something to be realised in the distant future. To speak of a Jewish state prematurely would have served only to mobilise opposition. When it was realised that Jewish sovereignty was being proposed by a high-powered British Commission, the Zionist leadership reacted spontaneously and enthusiastically. It was an emotional reaction: an age-old dream was suddenly, unexpectedly near realisation! When, in a secret meeting in January with Professor Coupland Weizmann learned that the Royal Commission was seriously considering partition, he exclaimed: 'today we have laid the foundations of the Jewish state!'[1]

From the very start, Weizmann liked the idea of partition. When Professor Coupland first mentioned the idea at an 'in camera' session, on 23 December 1936, Weizmann asked for concrete suggestions. Two weeks later he volunteered that the scheme could be considered in perhaps five or ten years as 'we don't have enough tracts of land in one bloc' but to his private secretary he said, 'the long toil of his life was at last crowned with success. The Jewish state was at hand.'[2] Later the same month he observed that, 'the Jews would be fools not to accept even if it were the size of a tablecloth'.[3] He set out immediately to persuade Zionist leaders and British, French and American statesmen to support the idea. On 1 February 1937, he reported that Leon Blum, the French Prime Minister, was favourably disposed. He also solicited the support of Rappard, head of the Permanent Mandates Commission of the League of Nations, and William Bullitt, American Ambassador in Paris.

Ben-Gurion's response was equally positive. In his view, the Arab Revolt of 1936 posed the question: 'Will Palestine become a Jewish state or will it remain an Arab country?'[4] The answer was linked to the fate of Jewish immigration. Would it continue at the present rate (60,000 a year) or would it be stopped under pressure of Arab violence? Already at the beginning of February 1937, Ben-Gurion had arrived at the conclusion that only partition would permit the continuance of large-scale Jewish immigration. He even worked out a plan for partition and submitted it to the Central Committee of Mapai.[5] What he envisaged was a Jewish state comprising the districts of Safed, Nazareth, Tiberias, Haifa (except the port, which would remain British for a specified period), Beisan, Tulkarem (up to the mountain ridge), and half of the Negev. The districts of Jaffa, Ramle and Lod would be within the Jewish areas but the towns would remain Arab and be joined by a corridor to the Arab state. Jerusalem, Bethlehem and Nazareth would have an international regime under British control. The districts of Acre and Gaza, densely populated by Arabs,[6] would become autonomous and acquire a status similar to that of Alexandretta in Syria. They would, however, be open to Jewish settlement. In all, the Jewish state would consist of 6,177,800 dunams and half of the Negev (the western part from north of the Dead Sea to Aqaba), while the Arab state would have 6,500,000 dunams and the remaining half of the Negev. Under this plan, there would be 300,000 Arabs and 313,000 Jews in the Jewish state.

Ben-Gurion was convinced that the Jewish people and British public opinion would welcome this solution. He proposed then the immediate despatch of all the principal Zionist and Labour leaders to Britain and the United States to promote the plan. At the same time, he claimed that the proposal would be defeated *ab initio* if it appeared to have originated with the Jews and that only as a proposal emanating from the British would it have a chance to succeed. He therefore suggested the formation of a group of British statesmen (Churchill, Chamberlain, Lloyd George, Amery, Greenwood, Attlee)[7] which would present the proposal as their own. The strategy would be that the Zionist movement would assume the posture of accepting the proposal reluctantly, under pressure, by way of a compromise and would at the same time, protest against the violation of the Mandate and the Balfour Declaration. In this, Ben-Gurion differed sharply from Weizmann who was in favour of prompt acceptance of the principle of partition and of serious negotiations on its geographical dimensions. Ben-Gurion was afraid of Weizmann's immediate acceptance of partition, expressing strong reservations about Weizmann's competence as a negotiator: 'In negotiations he is the greatest danger to Zionism [because] he would begin with the plan and end up with land reserves [vague promises]'.[8]

Ben-Gurion followed through on his approach: within the Mapai and the Jewish Agency, he fought vigorously for the partition solution; outside, in order to achieve a more satisfactory partition scheme, he encouraged criticism of the plan. He left no doubt about his strategy:

> ... this report ... gives us a wonderful strategic basis for our stand, for our fight ... the first document since the Mandate which strengthens our moral and political status ... it gives us control over the coast of Palestine; large immigration; a Jewish army; a systematic colonization under state control; the possibility of a large state loan; the chance of an ally on our northern border ...

> ... but there is the politico-strategic factor ... we have to consistently

pursue the fight for the continuation of the Mandate, without tying our hands in negotiations with the government . . . woe betide us if the English come to think they are doing us a favour – they have to be made aware that they took upon themselves a larger and more difficult obligation towards the Jewish people, and we must not let them off lightly from this obligation . . .[9]

In the end, the strategy proved counter-productive when in July 1937 partition came for approval to the British Parliament. The pro-Zionist lobby, which took the pleas for full implementation of the Mandate literally, launched a campaign of sharp criticism of the British withdrawal from the commitment to build a Jewish national home in Palestine. Following the line of the official and public Zionist state-ments, they criticised the restriction of the areas of Jewish immigration and settlement. But the criticism backfired in that instead of pressing the government to improve the plan, it caused the government to hesitate. Winston Churchill, who was a staunch supporter of Zionism, but who did not share Weizmann's belief in partition and warned him that he was pursuing a mirage, himself delivered a blow to the partition policy, by an amendment which made the adoption of the scheme conditional upon preliminary approval by the League of Nations' Mandates Commission.[10] This meant a delay of three months (until September 1937), during which the Arab uprising in Palestine acquired a degree of violence that forced the Cabinet to consider a retreat from partition.

Up to this point, however, Weizmann and Ben-Gurion, each in his own way, used all their authority and persuasive powers to have the project for a Jewish state in part of Palestine approved by the Royal Commission, the British Cabinet, and, subsequently, by the Zionist movement. Ben-Gurion in his own party and in the Jewish Agency, and Weizmann and Sharett in contacts with British politicians, invested an enormous amount of effort on the crystallisation of the partition plan. Members of Parliament, Cabinet Ministers, senior officials of the Foreign and Colonial Office were approached and advised on the demands and acceptance of partition. This effort was of such magnitude and intensity that it is legitimate to pose the question whether the idea of partition, originally made by Sir Stafford Cripps,[11] would have become a British policy recommendation without the active encourage-ment and support of the Zionist movement. When Professor Coupland first mentioned the idea of partition[12] to Weizmann, it was a feeler on the part of an individual member of the Royal Commission. It took many months of debates and all manner of pressures to induce the Commission unanimously to adopt it. Even then, the Commission was assailed by doubts and 'second thoughts', reflected in the 'palliative proposals' to restrict immigration and settlement, proposals which in fact foreboded the White Paper of 1939.

It was the active involvement of the Zionist movement in shaping the proposals, by submitting memoranda and by discussion with government officials involved in the work of the Royal Commission which made the Commission propose partition and choose between the different territorial concepts of the plan ('northern-oriented' versus a 'southern-oriented' Jewish state). In fact, all the questions of unification of the Arab state with Transjordan, British rule in certain areas, and transition from the Mandate to independence were subjects of discussions and negotiations with the Zionist leadership. These discussions were effective in that they enabled the Jewish Agency to play an important role in shaping the concrete plan for partition finally recommended by the Commission.

When Ben-Gurion compared the Commission plan to his own, formulated in February 1937, he concluded that the advantages outweighed the disadvantages. The latter were: the Negev was included in the Arab state instead of being divided between the two states; only part of the whole coastal plain was given to the Jews; the towns of Haifa, Tiberias and Safad were to remain temporarily under British Mandate instead of being part of the Jewish state; the northern part of the Jordan valley with the Electric Power Station and the northern part of the Dead Sea with the potash works were not included in the state. On the other hand, Ben-Gurion found the Peel project better than his own on a number of points: the whole district of Acre and part of Gaza district were included in the Jewish state, which Ben-Gurion dared not propose because of its large Arab population; instead of an Arab corridor from Jaffa to the Arab state, as envisaged by Ben-Gurion, the Commission proposed a British corridor from Jaffa to Jerusalem, thus leaving the door open to Jewish settlement.[13] Ben-Gurion derived the greatest satisfaction from the Commission's recommendation to transfer the Arab population from the coastal plain, the Valley of Esdraelon, and the Jordan Valley, to Transjordan or any other Arab state for resettlement.

'Thus', wrote Ben-Gurion:

[the Jews] will get [these areas] vacant from an Arab population and the prospects for Jewish settlement will be increased manyfold

> ... We could not and had no right to propose transfer of the Arab
> population, because we did not want to dispossess the Arabs. But as
> the British propose to give to the Arabs a part of the country – they
> promised to us, it is only fair that the Arabs in our state should be
> transferred to the Arab part.[14]

Actually, the transfer proposal emanated from the Jewish Agency. In
his diary entry[15] of 12 June 1937, Sharett reported that the American
Consul in Jerusalem, Wadsworth, told him that the (British) Government
'was very impressed with our memorandum to the Royal Commission
dealing with the transfer of the Arab population from Western Palestine
to Transjordan in order to make place for new Jewish settlers. They
thought it a very constructive proposal'. Little did Ben-Gurion in his
elation envisage that it was precisely this 'constructive proposal' that
would play a decisive role in the collapse of the whole partition plan.

A considerable share of the 'success' in producing a partition plan
which could serve as basis for further negotiations with the British
and induce the Zionist movement to accept is due to Sharett, the one
man in the leadership who was least enthusiastic and most sceptical
about the idea. In an address to the Mapai Central Committee on 5
February 1937 – the same session in which Ben-Gurion outlined his
plan for partition – he expressed grave doubts about the plan: there
was no guarantee that the proposal of the Peel Commission would
conform to Ben-Gurion's expectations, and there would be the serious
problem of 300,000 Arabs in a Jewish state. It would be difficult to
persuade them to leave their orchards in the coastal plain and resettle
in the Arab state, and to remove them by force would cause terrible
bloodshed, making the Revolt of 1936 seem like child's play. In any
case, this could only be done with the help of the British Army, at least
in the transitional stage, and it was doubtful whether the British would
agree to such a proposal. And if they did, they might decide to narrow
down the area of the Jewish state so much that it made it doubtful
whether unlimited immigration to this small part of Palestine was
preferable to limited immigration to the whole country. Finally, the
British Government might decide to withdraw from the whole scheme
because it was too radical (which is what actually happened).[16]

Despite his doubts, Sharett was ready to co-operate in bringing
about a satisfactory partition plan. In the middle of February he went
to London to join Weizmann in his activities to help promote the plan
for partition. These included visits to a great number of British statesmen whom the Peel Commission was likely to consult before making

its final recommendations, Cabinet Ministers, Members of Parliament, and senior officials of the Foreign and Colonial Office, Vansittart, Boothby, Churchill, Lloyd George, Cazalet, Herbert Samuel and the Archbishop of Canterbury. He warned the Colonial Secretary that partition was acceptable only if it meant real independence and offered prospects for development.[17]

Sharett continued to develop a campaign to inform the leaders of the Labour Party about the Zionist position (he contacted Tom Williams, Strickland, Brailsford, Middleton and Gillis). Since his informants told him that public opinion in Britain would not stand for military intervention to enforce partition, especially with the mounting danger of a European war,[18] he tried to allay fears that there would be a violent Arab reaction to partition. Sharett argued that the threat of outside Arab intervention had diminished, and that many Palestinians now despaired of any solution and looked to the government to solve the situation.

In a meeting with the High Commissioner for Palestine, Arthur Wauchope, in London on 14 March, Weizmann and Sharett detailed the areas which should be allotted to the Jewish state. Weizmann thought that the whole coastal plain to the Egyptian frontier, and the Negev to Eilat, should be included. Sharett demanded the whole of the Galilee (except Acre and its environs) and both sides of the North Jordan Valley and parts of the South Jordan Valley. Weizmann added that Haifa, which the British wanted to retain for strategic reasons, presented no problem if it were included in a Jewish state since such a state would in any case be part of the British Empire.[19] Weizmann later wrote to the Colonial Secretary, presenting the 'minimum demands' for a Jewish state, which must include the Galilee and the Negev in order to give sufficient area for settlement of new immigrants.[20] After the plan was published, the Zionist leadership continued to ask for the Negev, which could support a large population, it was argued, with modern methods of irrigation. British interests could be protected in the area.[21]

When the High Commissioner asked Sharett and Weizmann about the possible opposition of the Arab minority of 300,000 in the new Jewish state, they expressed confidence that they could deal with the situation. Weizmann stated that they would deal severely with those violating law and order, while giving full civil equality to all. Sharett agreed that they might need British help in the transition period, but that increased Jewish immigration would soon reduce the weight of the Arab minority and consequently its influence.

In the same conversation, they also objected to the idea that the Jewish state should subsidise the Arab state. They insisted that even without this, there was likely to be great opposition to partition within the Zionist movement, which would regard it as a renunciation of their historic claim to the whole of Palestine. Weizmann even hinted that partition might be only a temporary arrangement – for the next 20-25 years.[22]

Strikingly, Jerusalem was not included in the territorial demands. It was accepted that Jerusalem should be under international or British control for some time, and the fact that it was not included in the Arab state gave hope that ultimately it could be incorporated into a larger Jewish state.

In a debate by Zionist leaders in London,[23] on 15 March 1937, Sharett was the only one to express pessimism about the prospects of partition. The transfer of Arabs from the fertile orchards in the coastal plain to dry-farming in Transjordan could not be enforced, the Arab minority might become irredentist and the British would be forced to intervene and gradually deprive the Jewish state of its sovereignty. Nevertheless, Sharett did his best to dispel British fears of hostile reaction to partition in Palestine and in neighbouring Arab countries. He tried to convince senior Foreign Office officials that pan-Arabism was a myth. The new states of Syria and Iraq had concentrated on political independence rather than on the pursuit of the pan-Arabist aims. He also suggested that it might not be in Britain's interest to support pan-Arab aims: this only encouraged adventurous elements in the Arab world and antagonised non-Arab Moslem states (Iran, Turkey) as well as non-Arab minorities (Christians in Lebanon, Syria and Palestine). Britain could encourage the development of co-operation between individual states without creating a single political framework.[24] As to the Arabs in Palestine, Sharett claimed that they did not support the guerillas but were afraid of them and would welcome energetic measures by the government.[25]

Sharett used a different approach in his talk with Liddell-Hart, the well-known military expert who at that time was a correspondent for *The Times*. Sharett emphasised the 'war.potential' of the Jewish community in Palestine, which could mobilise 50,000 men to carry out mobile, mechanised warfare. He stressed the strategic importance of the Aqaba-Haifa land route in case the Suez Canal was unavailable, and pointed out that the Jews could develop the port of Aqaba and defend the land corridor.

Typical of Sharett's equivocal attitude was his debate with the opposition, ranging from Hashomer Hatzair on the left to Revisionists on the right. He rejected the argument of 'historical frontiers' sanctified by religion and mystical sentiment: 'The mystical Land of Israel stretching from the Egyptian Desert to the Euphrates was never wholly Israeli. The real Land of Israel underwent many changes and trans-figurations.'

> I can't accept opposition to partition for mystical reasons . . . The criterion for us Jews is what is the appropriate framework and political regime which will allow us to grow rapidly, to consolidate and maximalize our strength . . . And by strength I don't mean a standing army of 500,000 maintained by the Diaspora. That is not strength. Strength means the maximum number of Jews settled on the land and rooted in the economy, as well as armed forces for defense . . . Partition offers us rapid growth, the utilization of our potentialities for development, maximum possibilities for us to reveal our creative forces, a new status and new political weight in our eyes and in the eyes of the world. But these advantages are for the time being theoretical. All depends on what kind of partition will be offered to us.[26]

But when he went on to analyse the concrete problems of partition, he left no doubt concerning his reservations in this solution.

> The new State would have long and twisted borders which would be difficult to defend and guard against Arab opposition. And the Arabs would lose a great deal and gain nothing. They would lose forever the richest part of the country which they regard as their own. The Jews would receive a part, but they are a force in the ascent with a chance to gain more. The Arabs would lose their orange plantations and industrial areas, their major sources of national income, and most of the coast, which is also a loss for other Arab states. They would be driven back to the desert. A Jewish State with fewer Arabs means a Procrustian bed for us, while a larger territory means more Arabs in the Jewish State. For at least ten years the possibility of transfer of the Arab population will be excluded. Do not forget who will have to migrate: those who possess the richest villages, with irrigation and pumping stations, orange and fruit plantations, and easy access to markets. Where will they go? What will they receive in return? What is there to offer them in return? These are not the conditions that existed between Greece and

Turkey when they exchanged populations with assistance from the outside . . . Would the Jewish State be able to subdue the revolt without the help of the British Army? And does recent experience suggest that the British will be willing to use force against the Arabs until the new state can defend itself?[27]

Sharett warned of illusions both in regard to partition and the status quo, but he offered no solutions.

Sharett's pessimism grew from day to day. In a meeting in Jerusalem on 8 June, he stated prophetically that he did not believe that the Jews would get the desired areas. 'Until I see such a report signed by Peel, I don't believe he will sign; and if he signs I don't believe the British Government will approve. And if they approve, I don't believe that they will implement the report, because there will be an Arab revolt against it on an unprecedented scale.'[28] Sharett was prophetic, for this is precisely what happened after the publication of the report. Yet, it was the same Sharett who was the inspiration behind the strateggic plan of the 'Stockade and Watchtower' settlements in remote areas that was put in operation in May and June 1937 in order 'to hurry and create facts' and to influence at the last moment the territorial configuration of the partition scheme.

In retrospect the Zionist movement views the 1937 partition plan as a great lost opportunity which, if implemented, would have saved many Jews in Europe. Golda Meir, who opposed the plan at the time, comments in her autobiography, 'Ben-Gurion, in his greater wisdom arguing that any state was better than none, was right . . . Thank God it was not because of me that we did not get that state in 1937 . . . if we had had even a tiny little mockery of a state only a year before the war broke out, hundreds of thousands of Jews, perhaps millions might have been saved.'[29] And Nahum Goldmann, who had many political disagreements with Golda Meir, made the same point in his autobiography.

If there has been a tragedy in the history of Zionism, it is the fact that largely through our fault, partition was not put into effect the first time it was suggested, in 1937 . . . The Zionist Movement's attitude towards partition was a major sin of our generation.[30]

A spirit of optimism pervaded the Zionist leadership when it became known in June 1937 that the Royal Commission finally adopted the partition scheme in principle and that its territorial outline corresponded essentially with Weizmann's and Ben-Gurion's proposal.

The optimism and the sense that the Zionist movement stood on a threshold of an historic moment is captured in an anecdote recorded by Eliahu Eilat concerning Weizmann's reactions on the day partition was proclaimed as policy:[31]

> From the beginning of our struggle for a Jewish state in Palestine, we have found in Emile Edde [the President of Lebanon] an ardent supporter of the plan for partition . . . When I heard that Emile Edde would be in Paris, I immediately proposed to him that he meet Dr. Weizmann in June 1937. The meeting took place on June 22 in the Hotel Lutetia. After the exchange of the usual greetings, Dr. Weizmann took out his watch and remarked casually that in about half an hour the Royal Commission report which had recommended partition and a Jewish state in Palestine, would be signed. At first Edde did not react . . . He talked about the problems of Zionism and Lebanon . . . but in the middle he suddenly interrupted his speech, looked at his watch, and rose to his feet. He approached Dr. Weizmann and said: 'Now the half an hour you mentioned has elapsed and the Peel Report has become an official document; and therefore I have the honor of greeting the first President of the Jewish State that is about to be born.' Both were moved by this dramatic moment. The feeling of historical importance was signified when both men raised glasses in honour of the future friendship between the two neighbouring states possessing common ideals and interests.

The Failure of the Partition Policy

Why did the state not come into being? Why was the partition plan abandoned by the British although the British Cabinet accepted it as 'the best and most hopeful solution to the deadlock'? The British retreat from partition is attributed to three major factors: the deterioration of the international situation which pointed to the acute danger of the war; the resistance to partition within the Zionist movement and the Jewish Agency, which engaged in passionate debates and handicapped the Zionist leadership; and the violent opposition of the Arabs, who renewed and intensified their campaign of terrorism and guerilla warfare in Palestine and mobilised all Arab states to prevent the implementation of the plan.

No doubt, the international situation figured in British considerations of the plan. But it was not German or Italian pressure that led to its abandonment, as Jon Kimche has convincingly proved.[1] In July 1937, the German Foreign Office was persuaded that Britain would implement the plan and had the power to do so and so informed their Arab clients. It was the vacillation of the British which led the Axis to agitate against partition, not the reverse. As to Italy, its anti-British propaganda in the Arab world had toned down after Italy concluded its agreement with Britain in April 1938.

Zionist opposition played a more important role. Goldmann has maintained that:

> If the Zionist Movement had accepted the proposal then, spontaneously and without delay, it is quite conceivable that it might have been implemented . . . At the 1937 Zionist Congress . . . a motion hedged with restrictive clauses was finally passed expressing willingness to consider partition. But it was already too late. The acceptance was too vague and the British Government itself had begun to waver in the face of categorical Arab rejection. The plan died.[2]

Actually, it was the time factor rather than the opposition within the Zionist movement which played the more important role. The Zionist leadership did not refrain from presenting the movement with *faits accomplis*, as shown by intensive efforts to induce the Royal Commission and British Cabinet to opt for partition. The interval during which partition might have had a chance for success was very brief — from July 1937, when the partition recommendation was published, until the end of the year. In 1938, world war was already on the horizon. Dr Goldmann, who understood that time was running out, called for a clear-cut, straightforward policy in favour of partition. Ben-Gurion's double game of encouraging criticism of partition in the hope of obtaining a more favourable proposal, caused a delay, during which the impact of mounting Arab opposition and of the international situation increased considerably.

Arab rejection of the plan, the new wave of terror and sabotage in Palestine and the protests and warning of Arab governments were undoubtedly decisive factors. Two questions however, are relevant: one, what led the Royal Commission and the British Cabinet to assume that the plan would meet with some degree of acquiescence if not co-operation by the Arabs? Two, if the assumption was valid, what caused the Arab change in attitude?

No doubt the Royal Commission and the Palestine Administration made attempts to ascertain Arab opinion and to determine areas of possible Arab support for partition. In this regard, the main British and Zionist hopes were pinned on Emir Abdullah and the Nashashibi National Defence Party in Palestine. When the Royal Commission was in Palestine it secretly visited Abdullah and was favourably impressed by him. During the period before the report was published, Abdullah was careful not to commit himself publicly to support partition, which had been widely condemned within Palestine. However, his statements (such as the one to the Peel Commission that he would 'prefer to reserve his personal opinion until a later time') gave rise to the assumption that, as the person who stood most to gain from partition, he would not oppose it. It was believed that Abdullah's alliance with the British and his territorial ambitions would lead him to support the plan.

In June 1937, Abdullah wrote to a Palestine group: 'since the people of Palestine have confined themselves to making protests, I consider it my duty to strive to ward off the calamity by bringing about the union of Palestine and Transjordan.' At the League of Nations, the British Colonial Secretary, citing Abdullah's support for the partition plan, said that he 'had every reason to believe that for national and other reasons, the Arabs of Transjordan would like a larger state, would like independence, and regarded the proposal favourably'.[3]

Abdullah's support was conditioned upon the unification of the projected Arab state with Transjordan, under his rule. This union was not at first embodied in the concept of partition. In fact, the Royal Commission and the Colonial Office hesitated a great deal and weighed the pros and cons of the proposal in view of Abdullah's unpopularity among Palestinians and in the Arab world in general. He was both hated and distrusted and the fact that he had most to gain from partition was in itself an argument against partition, as it was bound to provoke the opposition of other Arab states and of the Mufti. The distrust hearkened back to the end of World War I when the British 'gave' Abdullah the Emirate of Transjordan, to compensate for their failure to set up an Arab kingdom ruled by the Hashemites, and their inability to prevent the humiliating expulsion of Faisal from Damascus in 1920. Since 1920 Abdullah had been regarded as a British pawn totally dependent on the Colonial Office. Abdullah's effort to develop his desert and thinly populated country with the help of Jewish capital and settlers increased his unpopularity among all Arab states adjoining the Transjordan. Abdullah continued to nurture dreams of a 'Greater Syria' under his rule but the nationalist leaders in Syria and Iraq viewed this as British-inspired and not as a desire to promote Arab independence. The most independent leader in the Arab world, King Ibn Saud, who fought the Hashemites in the 1920s and united Saudi Arabia under his political and military leadership, never forgot nor forgave the unilateral inclusion of Aqaba and Maan within Transjordan. The leaders of all Arab states adjoining Transjordan feared and distrusted Abdullah and opposed any idea of increasing his political status and territorial base in the Middle East.

The British knew all this and many regarded Abdullah as more of a liability than an asset and none viewed him as a decisive factor.[4] In March 1937, it was not certain that the Royal Commission would propose the unification of the Arab state with Transjordan.[5] L.Y. Andrews, a British senior official in Palestine, acting district commissioner and the government's liaison officer with the Royal Commission,[6] admitted as late as June 1937 that had the Mufti favoured partition, the British would have preferred an Arab state under his rule than under Abdullah's.[7]

The decision in favour of Abdullah was due to two factors. Already in 1936, the Mufti entertained ideas about an independent pan-Arab movement which would exploit the tense international situation to further its aims. During a visit in Mecca in March 1937, he was reputed to have asked King Ibn Saud to assume the leadership of this movement, employing the argument that the approaching war might signal the salvation of the Arabs or spell disaster.[8] Second, the Mufti's attitude was uncompromising in his opposition to partition. This facilitated the Zionist initiative to persuade the Royal Commission to accept the Abdullah option.

As opposed to Sharett, who had doubted Abdullah's usefulness as an ally and was sceptical about British readiness to support him at the price of antagonising all his opponents[9] (as proved by subsequent events), Ben-Gurion threw all his weight and fervour in favour of Abdullah, exploiting Rutenberg's negotiations with Abdullah on the creation of a development company with a capital of PL 2 million to finance Arab and Jewish settlements in Transjordan. The plan, agreed to by Abdullah, was to provide him with PL 1 million for settlement of Arabs, in return for which one million dunam in Transjordan would be placed at the disposal of Jewish settlers who would become citizens of Transjordan with internal autonomy, though not under the provisions of the Jewish national home embodied in the Balfour Declaration. In May 1937, Ben-Gurion went to London, accompanied by David Hacohen and Dov Hoz, to negotiate with Rutenberg and Abdullah, the application and use of the plan in promoting the idea of partition, though Rutenberg's plan was originally no part of the scheme. Ben-Gurion helped Rutenberg draft a memorandum to the Royal Commission[10] and to arrange contacts for him with Professor Coupland of the Royal Commission, Ormsby-Gore, the Colonial Secretary, Jewish financiers (Rothschild and Horst) and Abdullah, who agreed to the plan.[11] Ben-Gurion, briefing his associates on the approach to be used in negotiations with Abdullah,[12] suggested that they make the following points: Abdullah's total dependence on Great Britain made his rule and independence fictitious; the country stagnated; the population did not increase; and that Jewish capital and investment for resettlement of Palestinian Arabs (if not for Jewish colonisation) would develop the Jordanian economy and liberate it from financial dependence. A Jewish state would co-operate economically and militarily with Abdullah against those who intrigued to replace him in the Arab world by the House of Saud.[13] It is interesting to note Sharett's criticism of this move. He counselled Ben-Gurion that Abdullah 'cannot deliver the goods' and would under no circumstances enter any binding agreements with the Zionists without British consent.[14] Ben-Gurion replied that there was no reason for pessimism. Ormsby-Gore and Coupland favoured the plan, though they suggested that in view of the forthcoming partition, the two states about to be created would have to agree upon the scheme.[15] As events have proved, Ben-Gurion was right in the short term: the Commission recommended the unification of the Arab state with Transjordan to which the Arabs from the plains in the Jewish state would be transferred either by agreement or by a compulsory exchange of populations.[16]

Sharett was right in the long run. The objections of Arab states were so unequivocal that Britain concluded that in the tense and dangerous international situation, she could not afford to jeopardise her friendly relationship with other Arab countries and, in particular, Saudi Arabia, for the sake of a loyal but unimportant ally like Abdullah.

Sharett himself contributed to the British decision in favour of Abdullah. In the period preceding the Peel Report, Sharett developed a campaign of information to prove to British public opinion and decision-makers that it need not worry too much about the reaction of the Arab states, which were too much involved in their own affairs to be concerned about Palestine; in fact, they had a vital interest in terminating the Palestinian revolt and in restoring peace.

He further maintained that Syria was eager to resume agricultural exports to Palestine and to receive Zionist support in her negotiations on independence with Leon Blum, the incumbent French Prime

Minister. According to Sharett, Iraq was not concerned with pan-Arabism but with her strained relations with Britain. Both Syria and Iraq were facing the problem of Turkish pressure on their borders. The Jewish Agency maintained intensive contacts with the Syrian and Iraqi Government which repeatedly offered their good offices to mediate between Zionism and the Arab Higher Committee in Palestine. The Colonial Office headed by Ormsby-Gore, Weizmann's liaison officer during the Balfour Declaration period (1917-20), listened to Sharett's reports and evaluations attentively. The sharp Arab reactions to the report of the Royal Commission therefore came as a surprise.

When the Peel Commission report was published, the Iraqi Prime Minister, Hikmat Suleiman, immediately issued a warning against Abdullah: 'Any person who would serve as the head of such a [Arab] state would be an outcast in the Arab world . . . and I would always oppose him.' Although the British, who had strong influence in Iraq, succeeded in getting the Prime Minister to withdraw this statement, it nevertheless had a major impact on galvanising Arab opposition to partition, both within and without Palestine. In this context, the Syrian opposition to Abdullah may be explained by the fact that before the partition plan was published, the Iraqi Prime Minister secretly proposed to Britain the unification of both Transjordan and Palestine with Iraq; in which event he would agree to unlimited Jewish immigration.[17]

But the most crucial factor for Britain was the opposition of Saudi Arabia. For strategic reasons, Saudi Arabia was very important to British interests in the Middle East (at that time not so much for the oil, but the strategic-military position on the peninsula guarding the sea route) as the Foreign Office was eager to point out. Ibn Saud had suggested to the Royal Commission that Jewish immigration should be ended, and hinted that he was duty-bound to support his Arab brothers in Palestine. But his actions showed that he was motivated mainly by his concern over Transjordan. In July 1977, it was reported that arms were being smuggled across the Transjordan border 'though not for use in Palestine' and Ibn Saud gradually increased pressure on the (undefined) border with Transjordan. By August, this pressure was considered significant and there was concern whether military action was being contemplated. In addition, Ibn Saud announced to the British that if Transjordan expanded, he would have to renew his claim to Aqaba, which, at British urging, he had reluctantly given up in the late 1920s.

Arab reactions spurred an attack on the partition scheme by the

Foreign Office, which had already criticised the plan when it was presented for the Cabinet's approval. Anthony Eden then managed to formulate the approval 'in principle' without commitment to a specific scheme.[18] In October 1937, Sir George Rendel, Head of Middle East Department of the Foreign Office, proposed the abandonment of partition.[19] One of his arguments was that the Zionists made no secret of their intention to use the Jewish state as base for expansion, which would eventually necessitate the intervention of British troops. A similar argument against partition was raised by Winston Churchill[20] though he attributed the danger to objective strategic reasons, not to Zionist intentions. In fact, Zionist leaders themselves supplied material for these accusations: in seeking to gain acceptance of the plan by the opponents within the Zionist movement, they stressed not only considerations of political realism but also the view that partition was a temporary expedient (Ben-Gurion: 'this is only a stage in the realization of Zionism';[21] Weizmann: 'in the course of time we shall expand to the whole country . . . this is only an arrangement for the next 25-30 years'[22]). Referring to Churchill's article, Ben-Gurion wrote: 'He supposes (and rightly so) that the Jews will create a strong army, equipped with the best weapons, and the Arabs will not be able to face it; the Jews . . . not satisfied with their narrow boundaries, will spread into undeveloped areas — and cause troubles to the British . . .'[23]

The delay in the nomination of the second partition commission which was to work out the technical implementation of the plan was caused by struggle between the Colonial Office and the Foreign Office over the terms of reference. The latter insisted that the Commission be allowed freedom to consider alternatives to the recommendations of the Royal Commission whilst Ormsby-Gore objected to any deviation from the government statement of July 1937, which embodied the recommendations for partition over the terms of reference. This indicated the reappraisal and retreat from the partition policy. When, in January 1938, 'the terms of reference were finally announced, they included the significant sentence that the Government was in no sense committed to the boundaries of the plan outlined in the report and in particular . . . not to the compulsory transfer in the last resort of Arabs from Jewish to the Arab state'.[24] By then, partition was actually a dead issue and the despatch of the second partition commission was only a face-saving device to avoid a premature announcement of the abandonment of the plan, inviting the charge of Cabinet surrender to Arab threats and violence. The Cabinet forced Ormsby-Gore to inform the Commission that if it concluded that partition was impracticable it must say so.[25]

The transfer proposal was one of the stickiest points in the entire plan. It caused the defection of the one factor in Palestine that might have considered a compromise between Jews and Arabs: the National Defence Party of the Nashashibis. For the Mufti, the leader of the Husseini clan, the partition and the unification with Transjordan meant political death. No wonder, therefore, that he set out to fight it tooth and nail.

The reactions of the other leading political faction in Palestine, the Nashashibis, were more complex. This faction had been counted on by the British to support partition. In general, this group was more moderate in orientation and had sought a limited self-government such as the British had proposed in 1935. The Nashashibis were also in close touch with Abdullah and in favour of unification with Transjordan. Two days before the publication of the report, the National Defence Party withdrew from the Arab Higher Committee. This was widely believed to be in order to support partition but the support never came. The High Commissioner complained[26] that, while a week ago Raguib Nashashibi told him he was in favour of the principle of partition, now the Nashashibis had openly declared their opposition to it. They proposed instead, 'a sovereign democratic state with fully-guaranteed minority rights to the Jews, immigration so limited as not to change the existing ratio between Jews and Arabs, and prohibition of Jewish land purchase in areas allocated to the Arabs under the Royal Commission'.[27]

What caused the volte face of the Nashashibis? Sharett regarded the National Defence Party as an unstable and unreliable political grouping, lacking in courage and out of weakness yielding to popular trends. He was always reluctant to help them and accept them as partners in political struggles ('money will not help if courage is lacking'[28]). Actually, the economic interests which prompted the Nashashibis to adopt a more moderate attitude towards the British and Zionism were the same interests that made them oppose partition. They were not against partition in principle, but the particular plan which allocated the richest parts of the country with fertile lands, orange groves and urban areas, to the Jews, struck at the centres of their power and influence. They were horrified at the thought of transferring the people to a poor Arab state, leaving behind rich lands, orange groves, wells, houses, etc. Thus, it was the transfer idea that killed any prospect of Arab support for partition. The proposal, in the eyes of the Arabs, was the best proof that Zionism aimed at the dispossession not only of individual tenants but of a whole people. The call to avert this danger galvanised into action the whole people, and the rebellion in Palestine flared up with unprecedented violence. The Nashashibis were unable to stem the tide; their own supporters would have turned against leaders who would try to defend a project from which they would have been the first to suffer. The road was thus clear for the Mufti, who, having nothing to gain and everything to lose from partition, declared war under the battle-cry 'death to partition'.

The Debate on Transfer

The concept of transfer was as old as the beginnings of Zionist colonisation. Even before the First World War, leading Zionists had toyed with the idea. Arthur Ruppin, the director of Zionist settlement in Palestine, proposed in 1911 a limited population transfer, with the Zionists purchasing land near Aleppo and Homs for the resettlement of Arab peasants dispossessed in Palestine.[1] In 1912, Leo Motzkin suggested that the Arab-Jewish problem was soluble if considered in a wider framework; if the Arabs would be willing to resettle in the uncultivated lands around Palestine, using the money they had received from the sale of land to the Zionists.[2]

One of the most important early proponents of transfer was Israel Zangwill, who, during and after the First World War, was so persistent in his advocacy of the proposal, that he alarmed Faisal. Zangwill argued that there had been many such migrations in history, including the transfer of Boers to Transvaal. He believed that unless an 'Arab trek' took place, a Jewish state would remain in a constant state of friction with the Arabs. He hoped that when their own state would be established, the Arabs would be magnanimous enough to allow Jews, their kinsmen, to have Palestine.[3]

The concept of population transfer, as a facile solution to the twin problems of the Arab landless peasants and the creation of land reserves for Jewish settlement was for some time in the back of the minds of the Zionist leadership. In fact, in private discussions with the British, the Zionist leadership put forward population transfer as a tentative suggestion but stopped short of formulating it into a proposal for action. Only once – after the riots of 1929 – did Weizmann formally present the idea in discussions on Arab landlessness and its impact on Jewish-Arab relations. However, he did not press the point when Lord Passfield, the Colonial Secretary, indicated that he was strongly opposed to the idea. (See 'Weizmann and the Palestinians', pp. 69-70.)

The origin of the transfer proposal submitted by the Jewish Agency in 1937, may be traced to the debates of the Jewish Agency in October and November 1936, when it discussed the main policy lines to be presented to the Royal Commission. It was inevitable that the problem of landless Arab peasants and land purchases for Jewish settlement should figure prominently in these debates. The Mandatory Administration was pressing for legislation to preserve minimum holdings for Arab owners, to establish a land policy to save 'viable plots' and land reserves for Arab peasants, and to restrict the purchase of land by Jews to certain areas, embracing no more than 10 per cent of the country. The problem for the Jewish Agency was whether to concentrate only on Jewish needs for settlement or also to submit suggestions for the development of landless Arab peasants, and the right of Jews to buy land and settle in Transjordan, occupied a central place in the discussions. The views expressed in the course of the debates reflected, *inter alia*, the attitudes towards the Palestinian problem which at the time, prevailed in the Zionist movement.[4] Nearly all members of the Jewish Agency were against legislation designed to secure minimum holdings for Arab tenants and to restrict land sales, as these provisions would make land transactions burdensome, if not impossible.

Ben-Zvi maintained that the alternative to the proposed legislation aimed to help Arab peasants, is to transfer landless peasants to other places, including Transjordan, on a voluntary basis. Sharett also favoured Jewish settlement and Arab resettlement in Transjordan which offered large land reserves. Ben-Gurion and Ben-Zvi opposed Ruppin's idea that the Jewish Agency should propose a development plan to improve conditions in Arab agriculture; this was the task of the government. Ussishkin opposed Ruppin's scheme because the 'whole of Palestine is ours and ours only' and if there was no place for Jewish settlement the Government should move out the Arabs.

This approach was sharply criticised by Senator and Hexter, members of the Jewish Agency who represented non-Zionist groups. They vehemently opposed the transfer idea: 'there are Arabs in this country. The more we take them in consideration, the more we will succeed ... A constructive policy on land policy is necessary, not only opposition and criticism.' Senator considered transfer as fraught with danger: 'We can't say that we want to live with the Arabs and at the same time transfer them to Transjordan.' In summing up the debate, Ben-Gurion stated that he was against the view of both Ussishkin and of his opponents. He argued that the population exchange between Greece and Turkey could not serve as a precedent since it was a pursuant to voluntary agreement between two states: 'We are not a state and

Britain will not do it for us . . .' In Ben-Gurion's view, the proposal would alienate public opinion, including Jewish public opinion, 'but there is nothing morally wrong in the idea'.

In justification of his position, he maintained that 'if it was permissible to move an Arab from the Galilee to Judea, why is it impossible to move an Arab from Hebron to Transjordan, which is much closer? There are vast expanses of land there and we are over-crowded . . . Even the High Commissioner agrees to a transfer to Transjordan if we equip the peasants with land and money. If the Peel Commission and the London Government accept, we'll remove the land problem from the agenda.' In a final vote, on 29 October 1936, the proposal for the 'opening' of Transjordan for a voluntary transfer was accepted, with only Senator and Hexter dissenting. This debate would indicate that the transfer idea was already at the back of Ben-Gurion's mind and that the contention that Ben-Gurion was consistently opposed to the transfer of the Arabs from a Jewish Palestine, as claimed by Walter Laqueur, is demonstrably untrue.[5] In private debates over partition in 1936-7, and at the Eighteenth Zionist Congress at Zurich in August 1937, Ben-Gurion emerged as one of the most energetic advocates of transfer, which he justified morally and ethically as nothing more than a continuation of a natural process already taking place.[6] Ben-Gurion secretly but actively promoted the idea of transfer with the Peel Commission and participated in securing Abdullah's support for the plan.[7]

At this stage, however, there was not the slightest mention of a compulsory transfer. The transition from voluntary to compulsory transfer was a natural outcome of the partition scheme; there was no sense in having a small Jewish state containing 294,000 Jews and nearly 296,000 Arabs,[8] with the latter owning 75 per cent of the land, unless enough reserves of land were made available in the Jewish state by reducing the Arab population. Thus compulsory transfer became an essential and integral part of the whole partition scheme. Ben-Gurion declared unequivocally that sovereignty of the Jewish state, especially in matters of immigration and transfer of Arabs, were the two condi-tions *sine qua non* for his agreement to partition.[9] He was ready to entertain the renunciation of transfer, in return for the inclusion of the Negev within the Jewish state. Since partition envisioned a Jewish state, his early views on the inapplicability of the example of the Greece-Turkey arrangement were no longer relevant, and in his eyes that precedent was not only valid for exchange of populations but even a model of great statesmanship.

At the Zionist Congress in Basle which considered the partition proposal, the question of the transfer of Arabs from the proposed Jewish state became one of the main debating points. The transfer proposal came under fierce attack from both left and right. In general, difficulty or impracticability of transfer was used as an argument against partition, while the leadership, which favoured the partition proposal, tried to justify the transfer of Arabs as both possible and essential to the state. Rabbi Hillel Silver, for example, in attacking the partition plan, claimed that the plan was unworkable because of the difficulty of transferring 300,000 Arabs. He held that the transfer was 'impracticable and cannot be justified on moral grounds'.[10] Gruenbaum replied for the leadership that 'those who maintain that a Jewish state with 300,000 Arabs cannot maintain itself must surely also admit that a Jewish state in the whole of Palestine with a million Arabs, would be incapable of existence . . . the alternative is either a Jewish majority in a Jewish state or a Jewish minority in an Arab Palestine'.[11]

Ben-Gurion supplied the main rationale for the transfer proposals. He maintained that 'they would never dispute the rights of the Arabs in Palestine, and there was no contradiction between this and the principle that as many Jews as wished could come to Palestine'. He added that the decisive advantage of a Jewish state was that it would allow large-scale immigration, and that 'also the possibility of Arab-Jewish understanding would be greater'. But in the next sentence he went on to justify transfer:

> Was the transfer of Arabs ethical, necessary and practical? . . . Transfer of Arabs had repeatedly taken place before in consequence of Jews settling in different districts, and they would have to provide the transfer of Arabs with the means of setting up their own government.[12]

Some maintained positions that cut across the line suggested above. Golda Meir, for example, was opposed to partition but in favour of transfer 'as the Arabs had vast territories in which the Arabs of Palestine could settle'. Dr Ruppin, on the other hand, favoured an even reduced area for the Jewish state in order to avoid the problem of a large Arab population in that state. He believed that with modern irrigation such a state would still be economically viable.[13]

Dr. Weizmann thought that the Arabs could easily be transferred in the course of time. Others believed that the Arabs would not leave the Jewish state, and besides, it would be difficult to provide the money necessary for this purpose. The analogy of exchange of populations between Turkey and Greece did not apply [Rabbi Brickner and Dr Glickson].[14]

Sharett posed the most pertinent question: 'Will the establishment of the Jewish state lessen the possibility of peace with the Arabs?' His reply was: 'We choose the road not of the least resistance but of the greatest progress, even if it is more difficult. Our future bristles with uncertainties and unknown difficulties . . . in proportion as we consolidate our position, we secure our future.'[15]

The debate on transfer was also a major topic in discussions with the Woodhead Commission, which arrived in April 1938, to discuss partition frontiers, without being committed to the plan of the Peel Commission and in particular to the proposal for a compulsory transfer. Ben-Gurion reported to the Jewish Agency the new situation on 12 June 1938:

I am for a compulsory transfer; I don't see anything immoral in it . . . Since we can't execute it ourselves, we shouldn't propose it; this would be a dangerous course when the British Government has declared that they won't implement a compulsory transfer . . . There are two central issues — sovereignty, and a reduction of the number of Arabs in the Jewish state, and we must insist on both of them, without using the formula of compulsory transfer . . . There are many formulas which might replace compulsory transfer and which we have discussed before — such as citizenship and a state development policy . . . With a state development plan, say with a maximum plot of 20 dunams, with water, tractors, and machines, if you force the Arabs to do this, and they cannot they will starve. We cannot say this is not our concern; therefore we must introduce such a programme gradually, and those who cannot adapt will have to leave the country . . . We cannot allow the present state of cultivation, where an Arab owns 300 dunams and cultivates only 50, leaving the rest to the goats.

. . . We have to state the principle of compulsory transfer without insisting on its immediate implementation . . . We are against the principle of a tribute from the Jewish to the Arab state, but we are willing to make some financial provisions . . . in connection with transfer . . . but without obligations [Jewish Agency Executive minutes, Central Zionist Archives, Jerusalem, 12 June 1938].

Members of the Executive were in favour of the transfer. Ruppin for example, presented at the same meeting, a memorandum on transfer with the following points:

1. Transfer must be voluntary and based on an agreement with both the British and an Arab state. The British must release government lands in Transjordan and give a large loan.
2. One must distinguish between owners and tenants. Owners will willingly sell land at a good price, which is four to five times higher than the price of land in Transjordan. As for the tenants, we must help with the costs of resettlement through loans and a Development Company, which will build model villages so that the Arabs can see exactly what their new conditions will be. I don't believe at once, but in 10 to 15 years some 20,000 families (100,000 individuals) might be resettled.[16]

Ben-Zvi proposed a compulsory transfer in the framework of co-operation with the Arab state.[17]

The more right-wing circles in Zionism supplied the main arguments against transfer — not on the basis of morality but impracticability. Menahem Ussishkin argued:

I am not saying that the transfer is immoral, but that it can't be implemented. The moment you start the whole world will be up in arms and the Arabs will be their favoured child and we the stepchild. We shall not be able to force them and they will not go. The first to oppose the use of force will be the Jews, because of the fear that Poland will say, 'see what the Jews are doing to Palestine' . . . it must be done by the British, and before we take power because otherwise the British promises to do it will be worthless.[18]

Parallel with the transfer issue, the Jewish Agency also discussed the status of the Arabs in the proposed Jewish state. Werner Senator argued that there were only two ways to deal with a large Arab minority in the Jewish state: (1) to oppress it; or (2) to educate it to make it feel at home in the state.

Even if some Arabs emigrate there will still be a large Arab minority in the state. I reject the policy of oppression — it will not succeed. I cannot conceive a Jewish state maintaining over a long period two economic organisms, without hurting the state itself. Until now we have been forced to do it, but in a state in which we are the decisive factor we shall not be able to pursue a policy of separate economic entities for Jews and Arabs. We ought to find a way to full equality. As the Arabs are less developed, formal equality is not enough . . . if the state sets up a bank to help co-operatives it will have to provide help to both Jewish and Arab co-operatives.[19]

Ben-Gurion again was the main advocate seeking to delay making such a commitment to the Arabs. 'We cannot discuss the status of a minority without knowing the political and territorial framework of the State . . . the Zionist mission will determine all its policies . . . the starting point to the solution to the Arab problem is to prepare the conditions for a Jewish-Arab agreement on the assumption that after we become a strong force, as a result of the creation of a state, we shall abolish partition and expand to the whole of Palestine.'[20]

When asked if he meant expanding by force, Ben-Gurion replied that he meant that the Arabs would come to an agreement with Zionism only when faced with a *fait accompli*.

As long as we are small and weak, the Arabs have no interest in allying with us . . . The state will only be a stage in the realization of Zionism and its task is to prepare the ground for our expansion into the whole of Palestine by a Jewish-Arab agreement. This means that we must run the state in a way that will win the friendship of the Arabs both in and outside the state. Therefore, the problem of the Arab minority is a fundamental issue of the Zionist movement. The state will have to preserve order not only by preaching morality but by machine guns, if necessary. The Arab policy of the state should not only aim for equality of rights but should aim for cultural, economic and social equality, and the elevation of the standard of living of the Arabs to that of the Jews [Jewish Agency Executive minutes, Central Zionist Archives, Jerusalem, 7 June 1938].

Ben-Gurion then proposed a programme for the future Jewish state. The state would approach Arab states with regard to the voluntary transfer of Arab farmers to neighbouring countries and would organise a campaign to buy land for this purpose in those countries. The Arabs would be given three years to decide whether they wanted citizenship in the Jewish state; those who refused would have to leave. There would be equal voting rights to Parliament; until that time (for the transition period) the Jewish Agency would control the government. Ben-Gurion was also ready to accept Arab language and religion as having equal rights, and to guarantee universal social and educational services, and a percentage of employment in government services for Arabs.[21] Ben-Gurion's concept of 'abolishing' partition by a Jewish-Arab agreement seems to be a 'contradiction in adjectio', but it acquires some logic if one keeps in mind that by a Jewish-Arab agreement he meant an agreement with Abdullah, not with the Palestinians. He believed that, in need of Jewish capital and technical aid, Abdullah would in the end acquiesce in ceding the West Bank to a strong and highly-developed Jewish state.

All these debates took place in the middle of 1938,[22] when it was clear that Britain had already abandoned the idea of enforcing partition and, confronted with the deteriorating international situation and drift to war, was trying to improve her relations with the Arab world. Against the backdrop of the international crisis — the Austrian *Anschluss*, the Sudeten crisis and Munich — these discussions had a dreamlike air of utter unreality.

The British offically abandoned partition in November 1938, but their decision to do so was known already in August. On 17 May 1939, the White Paper was published which signalled the end of British commitment to the establishment of a Jewish national home in Palestine and the abrogation of the Balfour Declaration. However, the White Paper recommendations on immigration (15,000 a year for five years, then only with Arab consent), land purchases (prohibition to sell land to Jews in 90 per cent of the country) and on a national government and independence (after ten years), correspond to the 'palliatives' suggested by the Royal Commission in 1937.

In summing up the 1936-8 period, J.C. Hurewitz suggests[23] that 'The Arab revolt has won two major political victories. It proved that the Mandate was unworkable and it defeated the partition scheme.' The Zionist strategy in this period was a strange mixture of wishful thinking, fallacious assumptions, lack of realism, and counter-productive manoeuvres. It raised messianic hopes and failed miserably. At root of the failure lay the under-estimation of the Arab factor in general, the ignorance and negation of Palestinian nationalism, the illusions attached to the orientation of British imperial interest, and on an alliance with the Hashemites.

Abortive Negotiations

Before the Arab Revolt, the day-to-day contacts in economic relations and the physical proximity in mixed towns served as brake on the creation of an atmosphere of fear and hatred. The turbulent events of 1936-8 destroyed this mechanism and separated the two communities to a point where it was impossible for either side to have a realistic evaluation of the other. The field was wide open for emotions, passions, vicious propaganda, and the spread of wild and panic-producing rumours. Nevertheless, in the very midst of riots, there were Jews and Arabs who attempted to prevent the drift to complete chaos and total war. Perhaps more than in any other period serious negotiations on a possible alternative to war and partition took place between 1936 and 1939.

Essentially, these contacts fall into two categories. Until the arrival of the Royal Commission (November 1936) the focus of the talks was the search for a formula which would put an end to the General Strike and open the way to a normalisation of economic life and to negotiations on the political future of the country (see Chapter 6). The initiatives in this respect came from Jews; from the opposition to the Mufti in the Arab camp; and from the neighbouring countries, particularly Syria.

The second phase of negotiations started with the emergence of the partition proposal (officially in July 1937 but unofficially already in February 1937). The initiative came from opponents to partition on both sides: the bi-nationalists and the 'maximalists' (partisans of the 'undivided Eretz Israel') in the Zionist camp; the non-Zionist elements in the Jewish Agency, who supported the Zionist enterprise in Israel but opposed the idea of a Jewish sovereign state; and the leading faction among the Palestinians, headed by the Mufti, for whom partition plus unification with Transjordan meant political death.

An interesting aspect of Jewish-Arab negotiations during the General Strike was the contacts between the Jewish Agency and the leaders of the neighbouring Arab countries. While Syria, Egypt, Iraq and Lebanon made no secret of their sympathy for the Palestinian Arabs, they were worried about the danger of a violent confrontation in Palestine, and on more than one occasion offered to mediate. These countries were preoccupied with the advance of their political independence and economic development and were engaged in intensive negotiations with Britain and France, two countries in which the Zionist movement enjoyed public support and wielded considerable influence.

At this stage there was no conflict between Zionism and the Arab states. Zionist leaders and Palestinian Jews were able to travel freely to

Egypt, Syria, Lebanon and Iraq and to discuss openly with political leaders there, the future of Palestine. Jews from these countries were at liberty to settle in Palestine. In some Arab capitals Zionist organisations and youth movements operated as freely as any other political movement. In Cairo, Beirut and Damascus, Zionist representatives maintained regular contacts with Arab leaders, while these leaders themselves visited Jerusalem for talks with the Jewish Agency, and sometimes toured Jewish areas accompanied by Zionist guides.[24]

The Jews and the Arabs also maintained cultural contacts: an Egyptian soccer team visited Palestine and the Jewish Philharmonic Orchestra gave concerts in Cairo. Thousands of Jews took their summer vacations in Lebanon, where hotels and restaurants had Hebrew menus. Jewish manufactured goods were sold in Arab capitals, and Arab agricultural produce from Syria and Lebanon reached the Jewish market.

Ben-Gurion himself met and discussed solutions to the conflict with the future Lebanese Prime Minister, Riad al Sulh,[25] and Weizmann did the same with the Iraqi Prime Minister, Nuri Said (June 1936). The Arab section of the Political Department of the Jewish Agency (directed by Sharett and including Eliahu Sasson and Eliahu Epstein) maintained a large network of contacts with Arab leaders while relations between Jews and Arabs in Palestine deteriorated into civil riots and bloodshed. The main proposal put forward by Arab leaders was that, as a gesture of goodwill, the Zionist Organisation agree to a voluntary cessation of immigration pending the arrival and enquiry of the Royal Commission. In return, the Palestinians would call off the strike and co-operate with the Commission. Weizmann was inclined to accept this proposal and intimated his accord to Nuri Said[26] and to a Quaker friend of the Mufti. However, the proposition was categorically rejected by all the Zionist leaders as well as by the Mufti, who insisted that the stoppage of immigration must come from the British Government and not as a voluntary gesture of the Zionists.

The negotiations took a different turn when it became known that the Royal Commission was recommending partition. Both sides resorted to tactics to achieve their objectives: the Zionist leadership, who staked everything on partition, to have it approved and implemented by the British Government, and the Mufti to prevent it at all costs. The attitude towards talks and negotiations swung like a pendulum from approval to sabotage, according to what the parties thought were the chances for partition. When events did not augur well for a satisfactory partition plan, the Zionist leadership thought of an agreement with the Arabs as an alternative solution, exploiting Arab opposition and fear of partition. Thus, at the end of April 1937, Sharett told Auni Abdul Hadi, the leader of the Istiqlal party that partition was a very real danger, that the Jews did not want it either and that only a common Jewish-Arab front against the British could prevent it.[27]

Auni answered that the Arabs would fight partition to the last and would also oppose further Jewish immigration. He emphasised that the Arabs must remain a two-thirds majority, and that without further Jewish immigration, the Jews already constituted one-third of the population of Palestine. He further stated that he had no faith in political parity, for a Jewish majority would change the character of the country. According to him, the Palestinians would not be satisfied with joining neighbouring Arab states in a federation. 'It is not in your power to give me an Arab Federation; it is also not in my power to bring it about now; the Federation is hidden in the future. My task concerns this country; even if a Federation will emerge some day, this country should join it as an Arab country. We have no interest in a Jewish Palestine joining the Arab Federation; thus, there is no basis for agreement. The Arabs have no alternative but to fight both the British and the Zionists. Maybe they will lose the battle, but they are obliged to fight if only for the sake of honour.'[28]

The Arabs became more flexible when, in subsequent weeks, the issue of partition seemed to be settled. Now it was from the Arabs that several proposals for an agreement filtered through. They were conveyed by Colonel Newcombe, who was the Arab League's representative in London. In May 1937, he, together with A.M. Hyamson, the former Chief Immigration Officer in the Palestine Administration, drew up a proposal for a bi-national, independent Palestinian state, with special British interests guarded. The most important point was immigration. The proposed draft set a maximum Jewish population of Palestine at some figure to be negotiated, but not exceeding 50 per cent of the total population. This proposal was then circulated on both sides.

At this point (July 1937) an Arab intermediary of the Mufti (Dr Tannous) made direct representations to Jewish leaders in London. This related to the imminent arrest of the Mufti for continuing to oppose the British authorities. Almost weekly the High Commissioner was agitating with the Cabinet for his arrest and deportation. Only this report of the negotiations led to a momentary hesitation.[29]

With partition being proposed, the Jewish Agency was in no mood to accept in its place an agreement with the Arabs. Weizmann cabled

Sharett in Jerusalem:

> Felix Warburg, Stephen Wise request joint Jewish Arab intervention
> enable postponement Mandates Committee meeting/as result conver-
> sation with Tannous who propose ten years agreement at end which
> Jewish population not exceed 40 percent/Have replied: not prepared
> to intervene Mandates Committee no final decision possible Geneva/
> until end of September. This gives time for negotiations which can
> only be . . . with fully authorized representatives.[30]

In August, Dov Joseph, Sharett's aide, reported that an Arab notable
had approached Kalvarisky with a proposal to negotiate. Dov Joseph
was very critical of such unofficial contacts: 'there was no point in
talks . . . before Arab leaders evinced an attitude of serious respect
towards elected Jewish representatives'.[31] This theme was to be the
leit-motiv of the long and fruitless discussions around the Hyamson-
Newcombe proposals, which continued and increased in intensity
through the autumn and winter of 1937-8.

 On both sides the official leadership was interested mainly in the
effect of the negotiations on the British view of partition, and engaged
in tactical manoeuvres designed to strengthen one side's position and,
as such, any initiative was immediately suspected by the other side. The
Mufti wrote to Shuqri al Quwatli, the head of the Syrian National Bloc
(later Vice-President of the United Arab Republic) who was negotiating
with Sharett:

> The Zionists pretend they want a common front against the British,
> but in fact they worked to initiate and realize partition. Goldmann
> — the official representative of the Jewish Agency in Geneva —
> declared in a speech that Zionism wants partition, but with an
> adequate area.[32]

Reacting to the Hyamson-Newcombe proposals, Ben-Gurion stated:

> It seems to me the whole thing was meant simply to frustrate the
> plan of the British Government to establish a Jewish state in the
> country . . . After the plan for a Jewish state failed, I was sure that
> the same Arabs who approached us with this offer — if Hyamson
> was in fact speaking in the name of the Arabs — would approach
> us in a quite different tone . . . I was for continuation of negotia-
> tions, but first we must make sure there was no trap.[33]

Hyamson and Newcombe claimed to have been authorised by members of the Arab Higher Committee close to the Mufti, to submit proposals as a basis for negotiations with representatives of the Jewish Agency. They sent a copy of the proposals to Magnes who, with the support of his bi-nationalist friends and non-Zionists (Felix Warburg, Maurice Hexter, etc.) and the Zionist opponents to partition (Ussishkin), tried to obtain the Jewish Agency's consent to negotiations.[34] The Hyamson-Newcombe draft, purported to be approved by the Mufti, proposed an agreement for an unspecified period but renewable, on the establishment of an independent sovereign Palestinian state, with full equality for all citizens, complete autonomy to all communities, but without jurisdiction over members of another community, thus providing for a Jewish national home but not a Jewish state and a maximum Jewish population to be less than 50 per cent of the total.

The Zionist Executive considered the Hyamson-Newcombe proposals on 21 November 1937, and again political considerations in regard to the British were uppermost: 'We should not give our enemies, particularly in England, a pretext for saying that the Jews refuse to negotiate with the Arabs.' But — 'first of all we should find out who was conducting the negotiations'. It was this latter question which was to preoccupy the Executive, which, in the final analysis, was more concerned with who was active on the Jewish side than with the attitude of the Arab side. There probably was no basis for agreement; the Jewish Agency would not have accepted the minimum demands of the Arabs that would have left the Jews a permanent minority in Palestine.

Magnes was asked by Sharett to clarify certain clauses of the draft and to identify the members of the Arab Higher Committee who authorised Newcombe to draft the proposals. (The latter claimed to have the authorisation of the Mufti and Jamal Husseini.) Magnes went to Beirut (11 January 1938) and through intermediaries[35] learned that the Mufti and his friends disavowed the Newcombe draft and disclaimed having seen or approved it. The Mufti submitted another draft which contained no mention of a Jewish national home and fixed as the maximum for the Jewish population its present size. A few weeks later, Magnes went again to Beirut to meet Nuri Said who tried to salvage the contacts by a compromise formula that the maximum Jewish population should be X per cent until there be further agreement between the two peoples. An acrimonious exchange of letters developed between Magnes, who thought that the new formula could still serve as a basis for informal discussion, and Sharett, who accused him of unauthorised independent forays. Sharett wrote of 'willful deceit, lying and unrepresentation'. At the Jewish Agency meetings in January 1938, Ben-Gurion commented: 'Obviously some monkey business is afoot here . . . the mediators had deceived us . . . purportedly in the name of Arabs . . . we must not permit these men to continue their damaging and harmful game.'[36] In response to the criticism, Magnes attributed the change in Arab proposals to Ben-Gurion's attempt to 'torpedo' the talks by a statement (21 December 1937) that 'the demand for a Jewish minority status as a prerequisite for any agreements voids the possibility of any negotiations'.

> The search for a formula that would enable the calling of a preliminary meeting should be continued in every possible way . . . not just to achieve a tactical victory . . . but as an effort to gauge the temper of the other side in the conflict. It should be sought only if the Jewish Agency has an honest desire to sit down and discuss terms . . . the fact that members of the Arab Higher Committee were prepared to meet with the Jewish Agency . . . is of no little importance.[37]

Actually, the change of Arab attitude was due to the change in circumstances. In January 1938, the situation was different from that of October 1937. Rumours spread about the forthcoming retirement of Ormsby-Gore, who was the main driving force in the Cabinet for partition. The terms of reference for the Woodhead Commission indicated British withdrawal from the plan. There was, therefore, no need for flexibility and negotiations with the Jewish Agency.

These contacts show how partition had poisoned the atmosphere. Once the Jewish Agency had decided to go for statehood, it had very little patience with the idea of an agreement on limited immigration or on a maximum percentage for the Jewish population, amounting to a status of permanent minority even if it were near the 50 per cent line. When Herbert Samuel first proposed an agreement for the period of 15 years in which the Jewish immigration would be limited so that Jews would constitute 40 per cent of the population, Ben-Gurion branded him as a 'coward, traitor, and slave'.[38]

Herbert Samuel's project was clearly not an acceptable solution though it enjoyed considerable support in many Jewish circles in the Diaspora and was taken up by the Mufti and Nuri Said, not so much as an alternative to partition, but as a weapon to combat it. Zionism could not accept the status of a permanent minority even if it were not far from the 50 per cent line. It is very doubtful whether this formula could have served as a solution to the urgent needs of the Jewish people threatened by the Nazi regime spreading over Europe. It is no less doubtful whether it would have satisfied the determination of the Mufti to rule in Palestine and to prevent at all costs the growth of the Yishuv. The bid for statehood even in part of Palestine left no place for a constructive alternative, which could have emerged only as a result of a long-term socio-economic policy that would have made the Palestinians partners to the development of the country and satisfied their yearning for self-government and independence, and at the same time would have left the doors open to Jewish immigration and settlement. Such a policy could have been initiated only before the Arab Revolt. As it was, the partition policy of the Zionist movement experienced a bitter end.

The Mufti's Fatal Decision

In May 1939 the Arabs were near total victory in their struggle against Zionism. Had they accepted the White Paper of 1939, and co-operated with Britain on its implementation, it would have been most difficult for the Zionist movement to put together again the shambles of its broken strategy. What saved Zionist chances was the fatal decision of the Mufti to stake the future of the Palestinian people on the collapse of Britain's rule in the Middle East and on Nazi military victory in the approaching World War II. The moderates of the National Defence Party were in favour of co-operation with Britain and its White Paper policy. The Mufti, however, was already engaged in preparing for an Arab revolt against Britain in the forthcoming war. A civil war ensued between the two factions, causing thousands of casualties, destruction, chaos and flight from the country. The Palestinian people were left without a leadership or an authoritative and realistic policy and in that state drifted, disorganised and confused, down the road to national calamity.

The switch from strategy based on a treaty with Great Britain to a gamble on Hitler's victory in the approaching war had its origin in 1937 when the Mufti escaped to Lebanon to avoid detention by the British. Even before, in September 1937, he urged the all-Arab Conference of Committees for the Defence of Palestine, which issued a warning to Great Britain that the continuation of its pro-Zionist policy would compel the Arabs to ally themselves with the powers opposed to Great Britain. Immediately afterwards he engaged in all-Arab campaigns to form an alliance between the Arab world and the Axis powers. To understand his predilection for the anti-British powers in Europe one has to bear in mind that unlike Raguib Nashashibi, the leader of the Defence Party, the Mufti was concerned not only with the future of Palestine Arabs but with Arab politics in general. He was a mediator in the war between Saudi Arabia and Yemen in 1934, he was President of the World Islamic Conferences in Jerusalem in 1931 and of subsequent conferences in Karachi and Bagdad and played an important role in Iraq, where, after his exile from Palestine, he wielded a considerable influence.[1] His position in Palestine and in Arab politics brought him to rally with Arab leaders dominated by the feelings of frustration and resentment against Britain and France which prevented Arab unity in 1918 and divided among themselves the Arab countries in the Middle East and later impeded and obstructed their independence. Hitler's spectacular rise to power and his prestige in the wake of his conquests in Europe, and Mussolini's penetration into Africa and occupation of Libya and Ethiopia, had generated hopes for a collapse of British rule in the Middle East and intensified anti-British feelings. The social background of the Mufti and his followers facilitated the transformation of these feelings into sympathy for the authoritarian and military dictatorships in Germany and Italy and their policies. The speculation on a new Arab revolt in the approaching war, this time against Great Britain, began to occupy the minds of many Arab politicians in Syria, Iraq and Egypt and the Mufti was one of the first to embrace this idea. Already in January 1938, he was reported as having said (raising his finger) to the intermediaries in the negotiations with Dr Magnes: 'I see the independence of Palestine as I see my finger.'

He was not swayed from his pro-Nazi orientation even by the White Paper of 1939, which gave to the Arab Higher Committee in Palestine most of its demands. The Mufti forced through a decision to reject the White Paper and its recommendations. A desperate attempt was made by the Defence Party to have them accepted. In July 1939, a number of commanders of Arab rebel groups issued in Damascus a manifesto calling for the acceptance of the White Paper which 'forms [a] good basis for the realization of natural aspirations in the cause for which we have fought'. The manifesto accused the Mufti and his adherents of having rejected the White Paper because 'they aim at serving some foreign interests in consideration of fixed remuneration'.[2]

The manifesto was widely circulated in Palestine and given large publicity but amounted to no more than a feeble and abortive attempt to undermine the Mufti's authority. In the civil war that raged in Palestine between the two factions in 1937-9 the 'Peace Bands' organised by the Nashashibis, with British (and some Jewish) aid, managed effectively to assert themselves and repel the attacks of the Husseini gangs, though a number of prominent leaders of the Defence Party were assassinated in the process.[3] Among the exiled politicians and members of the Arab Higher Committee the Mufti wielded the power and remained the undisputed leader of the Palestine Arabs. His policy appealed to many Arab leaders abroad and brought him increased prestige and popularity.

On 9 May 1941, the Mufti declared a 'Jihad' against Great Britain and after the failure of the Iraqi revolt in 1941, he proceeded to Berlin, where until the end of the war he offered his services in mobilising Moslem populations in Europe for Hitler's armies, in fostering pro-Nazi elements in the Arab countries, and even in collaborating with Himmler and Eichmann, the planners of the 'final solution' of the Jewish problem.[4] This policy resulted in disaster for the Palestinian Arabs. Though a fatal adventure, at the time it could hardly be classified as such. The prospects of an Allied victory in 1941 and 1942 seemed so gloomy and those of the Axis so promising that orientation towards the latter appeared a reasonable risk, carrying the promise of success.

The Mufti's pro-Nazi orientation was not an isolated phenomenon. Hitler's spectacular rise to power and his prestige in the wake of his conquests in Europe; the subsequent collapse of France, which left Syria and Lebanon in the hands of the pro-Nazi Vichy Government; and General Rommel's successful offensive in Africa, which brought German troops to within 50 miles of Alexandria – all these events seemed to justify the reluctance of the Arab governments to declare war on the Axis powers and to encourage the tendency of some politicians and military men to establish contacts with Germany. This mood was particularly felt in Iraq, where it culminated in the pro-German policies of Rashid al Gaylani and in Egypt (where the Egyptian Chief of Staff Aziz al Masri and some officers, among them the present President, Anwar al Sadat, conspired to contact General Rommel).

The prestige of the Mufti began to disintegrate when it became apparent that he was backing the wrong horse. The moment the wheels of fortune in the war turned in favour of the Allies, the Arab governments declared war on the Axis, and were thus able to salvage some prestige and bargaining power for post-war arrangements. However, the Mufti's alliance with the Nazis caused confusion and demoralisation in the Palestinian movement. At the end of the war, the Palestinian Arabs had no leadership capable of launching a realistic and effective policy.

Notes

INTRODUCTION

1.   Ben-Gurion, *My Talks with Arab Leaders* (Jerusalem, 1972), p. 15.
2.   Then head of the Political Department of the Jewish Agency as from 1931.
3.   Ben-Gurion, *Memoirs*, vol. II (Tel Aviv, 1974), pp. 181, 202, 206 (Hebrew).
4.   Summary from the Survey of Palestine prepared by the Government of Palestine for the Anglo-American Commission of Enquiry, 1945-6, pp. 37, 38, 46, 49.
5.   The Mufti requested the intervention of Ibn Saud already at the end of April, imploring his aid; on 1 May, Abdullah was requested to mediate by the Arab Higher Committee members who went to Amman; they went again to Amman in June 1936.
6.   Discontent spread to Transjordan. See A. Mahmoud, 'King Abdullah and Palestine', PhD thesis, Georgetown University, 1972, pp. 63-70 (University microfilms no. 72-34185).
7.   The Royal Commission headed by Lord Robert Peel arrived in Palestine on 11 November 1936, after the Arab Higher Committee called off the strike on 11 October, in response to a pre-arranged appeal for its termination by King Ibn Saud, King Ghasi and Emir Abdullah. The Report was delivered on 8 July 1937.

THE PARTITION PLAN 1937

1.   Peel Commission Report, Cmd 5479, 1937 p. 376.
2.   Ibid.
3.   Ibid., p. 381.
4.   Ibid., pp. 389-91.
5.   Ibid., p. 395.
6.   The official policy statement published in January 1938 along with instructions to the Woodhead Commission confirmed that the internal policy debates had finally been resolved by a 'resolution to be irresolute': 'I wish to make it clear that HMG are in no sense committed to that plan [outlined in the RC report], and in particular that they have not accepted the recommendation of the Commission for the compulsory transfer in the last resort from the Jewish to the Arab area of Arabs . . .' (Cmd. 5634, January 1938.) This is in sharp contrast with the reception the British Government accorded the Commission's recommendations at the outset:

Her Majesty's Government believes that a scheme of partition on the general lines recommended by the Commission represents the best and most hopeful solution to the deadlock . . . and propose to take such steps as are necessary and desirable to obtain freedom to give effect to a scheme of partition, to which they earnestly desire that it may be possible to secure an effective measure of consent from all parties concerned.

7.   Appendix to Palestine Report – Historical Background – Middle East Library, St Anthony's College, Oxford DS. 126.4.

THE ZIONIST LEADERSHIP AND PARTITION

1.   Walter Laqueur, *History of Zionism* (London, 1972), p. 517.
2.   Norman Rose, 'The Debate on Partition, 1937-8', *Middle Eastern Studies*, November, 1970, January 1971.
3.   Ibid.
4.   Letter to his son, Amos, 7.7.1937, *Memoirs*, vol. II, p. 327.
5.   On 5-6 February 1937, ibid., p. 57.
6.   At the time there were 153,000 Arabs and 2,250 Jews in Acre and Gaza, ibid., p. 61.
7.   Ibid., p. 64.
8.   Ibid., p. 65.
9.   Ben-Gurion to Sharett, May 1937, CZA, 525/10,066.
10.   The Permanent Mandates Commission was not very enthusiastic about immediate implementation of partition:

While declaring itself favourable in principle to an examination of a solution involving the partition of Palestine, the Commission is nevertheless opposed to the idea of the immediate creation of two new independent states. The Commission therefore considers the prolongation of the period of political apprenticeship constituted by the Mandate would be absolutely essential both to the new Arab state and the new Jewish state. [Permanent Mandates Commission, Resolution of the 32nd Session, quoted in Cmd. 5634, Jan. 1938 1938.]

11.   In *Manchester Guardian* of 8 September 1936. Stafford Cripps took up the suggestion made by a former official of the Palestine Administration, Archer Cust, to divide the country into a number of Jewish and Arab cantons and proposed to set up two cantons, one Jewish and one Arab, to become in due course independent states free to decide on problems of land and immigration.
12.   In a closed session of the Commission, 23 December 1936.
13.   Ben-Gurion, *Memoirs*, vol. II, pp. 330-1.
14.   Ibid., pp. 330-1.
15.   Sharett, *Diary*, vol. II (Tel Aviv, 1971), p. 188.
16.   Sharett, ibid., p. 15.
17.   Ibid., p. 41.
18.   Ibid., pp. 48-9.
19.   Ibid., p. 65.
20.   Public Record Office, CO 733/348/75550/69, 15 June 1937.
21.   PRO, CO 733/349, Mander to Ormsby-Gore, 8 July 1937, Memorandum of Theodore Zissu, November 1937.
22.   Sharett, *Diary*, vol. II, p. 67.
23.   Sharett, ibid., pp. 69-71. The participants were Professor Brodesky, Professor Namier, Leonard Stein, Mrs Dugdale, A. Lurie, Maurice Perlzweig, Weizmann and Sharett.
24.   Sharett, ibid., p. 83.
25.   Sharett, ibid., p. 87.
26.   Speech at the Zionist Actions Committee, 22 April 1937, ibid., pp. 105-10.
27.   Ibid.
28.   Sharett, ibid., p. 179.
29.   Golda Meir, *My Life* (London, 1975), p. 126.
30.   Nahum Goldmann, *Memories: Autobiography of Nahum Goldmann* (London, 1970), pp. 179, 181.
31.   Eliahu Eilat, *Zionism and the Arabs* (Hebrew) (Tel Aviv, 1974), p. 311. Eilat was then member of the Jewish Agency's Arab Department and developed a

wide range of contacts with Arab statesmen and intellectuals.

THE FAILURE OF THE PARTITION POLICY

1.　Jon Kimche, *The Second Arab Awakening* (London, 1970), pp. 85-6.
2.　Goldmann, *Memories*, pp. 180-1.
3.　A. Mahmoud, 'King Abdullah and Palestine', p. 74.
4.　Sharett, *Diary*, vol. II, pp. 113 and 200.
5.　Sharett, ibid., p. 100.
6.　Assassinated later by Arab terrorists on 22 September 1937.
7.　Sharett, ibid., p. 184.
8.　Reported by Ben-Gurion, *My Talks*, p. 103, who conveyed the information to Abdullah and the Iraqi Government.
9.　Sharett, *Diary*, p. 387.
10.　Ben-Gurion, *My Talks*, p. 207. The memorandum includes a paragraph about the transfer and resettlement of Arabs from Palestine.
11.　Ben-Gurion, ibid., pp. 200-2.
12.　Ben-Gurion, ibid., pp. 177-8.
13.　Ben-Gurion, ibid., pp. 177-8.
14.　Sharett, *Diary*, vol. II, letter of May 25.
15.　Ben-Gurion, 3 June 1937, *My Talks*, pp. 201-2.
16.　Report of the Royal Commission Command Paper 5479, p. 391.
17.　CO 733/344/75550/A9/56 (11 February 1937).
18.　Cab 23/88, 28 June 1937.
19.　FO 371/20816. E.5964/22/31.
20.　On 23 July 1937 in the *Evening Standard*.
21.　R. Isaac, 'The Land of Israel Movement', a doctoral dissertation, University microfilms, no. 72-5804, p. 97 (quotation the *New Judea*, Aug.-Sept. 1937).
22.　To the High Commissioner A. Wauchope on 14 March 1937, Sharett, *Diary*, p. 67.
23.　Letter to his son, 28 July 1937, Ben-Gurion, *Memoirs*, vol. II, p. 332.
24.　Cmd. 5634, January 1938.
25.　The debates in the Cabinet and the exchanges of notes between the Colonial and Foreign Office, see Cab 23/90a 22.12.1937; FO 371/20822 and FO 371/21862 E 1529/1/31.
26.　On 14 July 1937.
27.　J.C. Hurewitz, *The Struggle for Palestine* (New York, 1950), p. 79. On 11 July 1937, the National Defence Party rejected partition and sent protests to the League of Nations and the Colonial Office claiming that the most fertile and developed part of the country was awarded to the Jews.
28.　Sharett, *Diary*, vol. II, p. 387.

THE DEBATE ON TRANSFER

1.　Memorandum to the Zionist Executive, May 1911, quoted in Laqueur, *A History of Zionism*, p. 231. The proposal was rejected as likely to increase Arab suspicions.
2.　*Judische Rundschau*, 12 July 1912.
3.　Quoted in R.N. Salaman, *Palestine Reclaimed* (London, 1920), pp. 175-6. Nor were such suggestions limited to Zionists. Brigadier Clayton wrote in 1918: 'the districts east of Jordan are thinly populated and their development would allow considerable emigration from Palestine thereby making room for Jewish expansion' (to Balfour 18 Nov. 1918, FO 371/3385/f747.191229).
4.　The following were the members of the Jewish Agency: Ben-Gurion,

Sharett, Ben-Zvi, Kaplan of Mapai; Weizmann, Brodetsky, Rotenstreich, Gruubaum, Ussishkin of the General Zionist Federation; Fishmann of the religious party Mizrahi; Ruppin (head of the Settlement Department of the Jewish Agency) and Werner Senator and Maurice Hexter, representatives of the non-Zionists.

5. Walter Laqueur, *A History of Zionism* (London, 1972), pp. 240 and 248-9.

6. *The New Judea*, Aug.-Sept. 1937, p. 220.

7. Ben-Gurion, *Memoirs*, vol. II, p. 173.

8. 225,000 without the mixed towns of Safed, Tiberias, Acre and Haifa which were to remain temporarily under British Mandate.

9. Ben-Gurion, *Memoirs*, vol. II, p. 365.

10. Reported in *New Judea* (London), Aug.-Sept. 1937, p. 222.

11. Ibid.

12. Ibid.

13. Ibid., p. 222.

14. Ibid., pp. 224 and 225.

15. Ibid., p. 225.

16. Jewish Agency Executive Minutes, 12 June 1938.

17. Minutes of the Political Committee of Mapai, 8 June 1938.

18. Jewish Agency, 12 June 1938.

19. Jewish Agency Executive minutes, 7 June 1938, Central Zionist Archives.

20. Ibid.

21. Ibid.

22. The Zionist leadership had staked everything on partition and were bitter when the British Government abandoned it. The British had given clear signs of their hesitancy and reluctance to implement partition. Yet, as late as July 1938, Weizmann was complaining of the 'delaying tactics' of the Commission, pointing out that the Commission's report had been promised for before the end of 1937 and that, instead, the Commission was still meeting, with no report in sight. Weizmann to Woodhead Com., 10.7.1938. (Tegart Papers, Box IV, File 3, Oxford University Archives.)

23. J.C. Hurewitz, *Struggle for Palestine*, p. 93.

24. E.g. Fakhri al Baroudi, of the Secretariat of the Syrian Bloc toured settlements accompanied by E. Eliat, Sharett, *Diary*, vol. I, p. 218.

25. Ben-Gurion, *My Talks*, p. 17.

26. Report of the Jewish Agency, 20 July 1936, S25/3234 CZA and Sharett, *Diary*, vol. I, pp. 112, 118.

27. Sharett, ibid., pp. 112, 118.

28. Ibid., p. 113.

29. Cab 24/270 C.P. 193 (37), letters from Sir Arthur Wauchope to Cosmo Parkinson 10, 14, 19, 29 July 1937; PRO, FO 371 E 4708/24/37.

30. Ben-Gurion, *My Talks*, p. 141.

31. Ibid., p. 142.

32. Sharett, *Diary*, vol. II, p. 147.

33. Ben-Gurion, *My Talks*, p. 146.

34. A detailed analysis of the Hyamson-Newcombe episode is given by Herbert Parzen in 'A Chapter in Arab-Jewish Relations during the Mandate Era', *Jewish Social Studies*, vol. XXIX (1967), pp. 203-33.

35. The Anglican Bishop Graham Browne and Dr I. Tannous, the authorised representative of the Arab Higher Committee.

36. Ben-Gurion, *My Talks*, pp. 174-5, 181-2.

37. Ibid.

38. Ibid.

THE MUFTI'S FATAL DECISION

1.   'The arrival of Haj Amin al Husseini opened a new phase in the development of pan-Arabism in Iraq. The Mufti's General Staff was a non-official government and the Mufti himself was the spiritual leader of the anti-British movement whose executors were Rashid Ali al Gailani and Naji Shawkat, who organised the revolt against the British in 1941. The Mufti's secretary, Osman Kemal Haddad, was sent on a mission to Von Papen in the name of an Arab committee comprised of Iraquian, Syrian and Palestinian politicians, to propose a plan for an uprising against the British and the French.' Majid Khadduri, *Independent Iraq* (Oxford UP, 1960), p. 162.

2.   Public Record Office CO 733/406 (8529), 3 July 1939. The signatories claimed to be Section Commanders 'of Jaffa, Ramleh, Nablus, Tiberias and Lyda'. Two signatories gave their titles as 'Chief Editor of the Arab Rebellion' and 'Secretary of the Rebellion'.

3.   Among them Hassan Bey-Shukri, Mayor of Haifa; Fakhri Nashashibi, Chairman of of the Jaffa Chamber of Commerce; Nasr-al Din-al Din, Mayor of Hebron; Dr Taha Khalel Taha, well-known physician and public worker in Haifa; Abdul Salem Barkawi, National Committee of Jenin; Said al Shanti, rich merchant and land broker in Jaffa. (Public Record Office CO 733/332 55529.)

4.   Marek Gdanski, *Arabski Wschod* (Warszawa, 1962). p. 284.

THE WAR OF 1948

From Biltmore Back to Partition

In spite of the collapse of the 1937 partition proposal, the idea of
partition became the main axis around which attempts at the solution
of the Jewish-Arab conflict revolved until it became the basis for the
UN Resolution in November 1947 and for the creation of the state six
months later. It is interesting to note, however, that the Zionist leadership underwent serious debacles and stormy debates on strategy before
it finally accepted this solution. With the abandonment of the plan by
the British in 1938, and the proclamation of the White Paper in 1939,
the Zionist leadership pinned its hopes on a radical change as a result of
events in World War II.

At the outbreak of the war, the Jews were engaged in a sharp
conflict with Britain, but the war found the Jews and Great Britain
facing the same enemy. The White Paper of 1939 closed the doors of
Palestine to the masses of Jews in Europe suffering incredible persecution by the Nazis. But, unlike the Arabs, the Jewish people had no
choice. Hitler was the greatest enemy of the Jewish people in all their
history of martyrdom. Though nobody at the time could foresee the
holocaust and imagine the possibility of cold-blooded plans for the
extermination of millions, it was clear that the struggle for survival
demanded the mobilisation of all Jews in support of the Allied powers.
Ben-Gurion's famous utterance: 'We shall fight against the White Paper
as though there were no war and we shall fight the war against Germany
as though there were no White Paper', was more a rhetorical formula
than a guideline for action. In fact, the Yishuv concentrated on an all-
out war effort to help Britain in her fight against Germany and on
preparing for defence in the event of a successful German offensive in
North Africa. However, the military effort of the Yishuv was not
undertaken without long-range political aims. The Jewish war effort
was considered not only as a contribution to the war effort of the Allies
to ensure their victory and the survival of European Jewry, but also as
a solution to the political impasse in Palestine.

During the war, the Zionist movement faced strategic options of
great importance. The main strategic decision was made at the Zionist
conference at the Biltmore Hotel held in New York, 6-11 May 1942.
This decision reflected the changed mood of the Zionist leadership

in the midst of global conflagration. The Biltmore programme had a paralysing effect on any last minute attempts at Arab-Jewish reconciliation. The strategic calculations on which the programme was based, and the resulting maximalist demands, left the Zionist movement in a trap at the end of the war. The descent from the Biltmore programme to a more realistic one was a difficult task which was accomplished largely through the initiative of Dr Goldmann to revive the partition proposal and to make it accepted by the movement.

Held in the United States, the Conference, attended by some 600 delegates, signalled the new importance attached to American Zionism in the struggle for a Jewish state. The Conference also marked the rise of Ben-Gurion to the unchallenged leadership, supported by this new force.

The Biltmore programme's optimism was based on several fundamental miscalculations yet its slogans established the political momentum of Zionism, particularly in the Yishuv and in the United States. The programme demanded the fulfilment of 'the original purpose' of the Balfour Declaration, and rejected the British White Paper policy of restricted immigration. It called for autonomous Jewish military force to play its full part in the war effort and set forth the Jewish demands upon a post-war world of 'Peace, Justice and Equality'.

> The conference urges that the gates of Palestine be opened; that the Jewish Agency be vested with control of immigration with Palestine and with the necessary authority for upbuilding the country, including the development of its unoccupied and uncultivated lands; and that Palestine be established as a Jewish commonwealth integrated into the structure of the new democratic world.[1]

The term 'Jewish commonwealth' was a thinly veiled call for a Jewish state in all of Palestine.

The programme, formulated *before* the news of the systematic extermination of millions of Jews in the Nazi concentration camps had leaked abroad, was based on the assumption that the war would leave in Europe millions of destitute Jews living in utter misery and in need of immediate relief and rescue.

Britain had just lost most of its Eastern Asian empire to the Japanese, she was retreating before Rommel's powerful offensive in North Africa and fighting a heroic battle for survival in Europe. The United States had declared war only a few months before (December

1941) and was preparing to throw its powerful human and industrial potential into the struggle. The Soviet Union was still bleeding heavily from the crushing thrust of German armies besieging Leningrad and Moscow and advancing rapidly towards Stalingrad. As yet, there was no sign of the counter-offensive which would, within two to three years, destroy the Nazi armies, reconquer Soviet territories and reach Berlin. The future of the world seemed to depend on the inexhaustible economic and military reserves of the United States, where an organised and influential Jewish community, alerted by the situation of Jews in Europe, would play a decisive role in shaping the political future.

The dramatic changes that occurred in Eastern Europe in the wake of Soviet victories, the developments in Asia and Africa as a result of the Chinese Revolution, and the emergence of national liberation movements, were neither considered nor foreseen.

The Biltmore programme signified a basic change in relation to the Arab factor; it ignored it completely. In contrast with the period preceding the White Paper of 1939, when some efforts were made to ensure a degree of Arab acquiescence or, at least, to reduce the degree of Arab opposition, the Zionist movement now considered an agreement with the Arabs as unnecessary, if not harmful. This was evidenced by the sudden change of attitude towards attempts by certain Jewish circles in Palestine to establish contacts with Arab leaders and discuss with them the future of the country and Jewish-Arab relations. The defection of the Mufti and his friends to the enemy camp, the pro-German feelings in Iraq and in Egypt, and the feeble contribution of the Arab governments to the war effort were considered by the Zionist leaders as an indication of declining influence of the Arab world, while the impressive war effort of the Yishuv and world Jewry carried the promise of its increased weight in international decisions. In a letter from Moshe Sharett to the 'League for Jewish-Arab Rapprochement', which during the war years was developing intensive relations with Palestinian leaders and with Arab statesmen abroad, there appears the following statement:

The most crucial time for Zionism is the period of transition from a Jewish minority to a majority. In this period not the Arabs but the British and the Americans will be the decisive factors. It is not the Arabs who will have the final word, neither in the world nor here; let us not adopt the view that one has to go to the Arabs and agree with them.[2]

Moshe Sharett, then the political secretary of the Jewish Agency, feared that any proposal for a compromise would become 'a Jewish maximum, with the result that the practical solution will be far removed from it'.[3] In view of the British determination to continue with the policy of the White Paper, any restrictions on immigration agreed to by Jews in search of a compromise with the Arabs, would only strengthen the British White Paper policy.

The assumptions underlying the Biltmore programme proved to be wrong. The significance of the Arab factor was not reduced because of their poor war record. Post-war settlements were not a system of punishments and rewards for conduct during the war. They were determined by the economic and strategic importance of certain regions soon to become areas of confrontation in the cold war between the Soviet Union, which emerged from the war as the second power in the world, and the United States.

Moreover, the pro-Nazi tendencies in the Arab world were neither typical nor dominant. They were pronounced mainly in the early stage of the war and disappeared as soon as the advance of German armies came to a halt in North Africa and in the Soviet Union. With the succession of Allied victories, the counter-offensive of the Soviet Army, and the Allied landing in North Africa, the Soviet and its anti-fascist ideological campaign began to exert a considerable influence on Arab society. Socially alert clubs, discussion groups, periodicals, professional associations and trade unions, with a desire for far-reaching democratic reforms, began to make their appearance. Though still illegal, communist groups attracted larger audiences and introduced into the Arab society ideas and opinions hitherto regarded as sacrilegious. They organised trade unions, which demanded higher wages and better conditions, peasant associations which insisted on a radical agrarian reform and redistribution of land, and intellectual clubs, which agitated for freedom of expression and parliamentary reform. The social change was most pronounced in Egypt where a movement for National Liberation, Democracy and Freedom (HADITU) was able to launch a daily newspaper and in Syria and Lebanon, where the Communist Party had exerted some influence even before. Palestine was also affected by this ferment. The stationing of considerable military forces in the country, which had become an important centre for supplying military needs, changed the economic face of the country beyond recognition. The army of unemployed, dispossessed peasants was absorbed by the growing labour market, higher prices enabled the peasants to pay off their debts, and a general prosperity[4] changed the political mood.

Most of the leaders left or were deported from the country in 1938-9, and the civil wars and political terror which ravaged the country subsided. Arab Communists organised themselves in the League for National Liberation, which tried to build up a base among the workers and intellectuals. Social contacts and relations between Jews and Arabs, severed almost completely between 1936-9, could now be resumed. For the first time, the League for Jewish-Arab Rapprochement, comprising a large variety of people in search of compromise, and even political parties such as Hashomer Hatzair, Poalei Zion Left, and Aliya Hadasha (a party of liberals from Central Europe), in addition to the Magnes group, were now able to visit Arab villages, meet Arab students and organise lectures and debates. This activity brought to light the existence of a group of Arabs in favour of the bi-national solution. An agreement between this group and the League for Jewish-Arab Rapprochement was signed calling for common action and the publication of an Arab magazine to propagate the idea of Jewish-Arab co-operation. Also, in the neighbouring Arab countries, in which the idea for Arab unity was gaining ground, the interest in a compromise formula for a Jewish-Arab agreement was growing.[5]

The years 1943-6 are rich in Arab proposals and plans for a settlement. In January 1943, Nuri al Said, Prime Minister of Iraq, proposed in his *Blue Book*, a Federation of the Fertile Crescent with autonomy for Jews in an Arab state. The same year, Emir Abdullah of Transjordan, in his conversation with Zionist personalities, expressed his fear that Jewish insistence on the realisation of the Biltmore programme would lead to the partition of Palestine and would indefinitely divide Jews and Arabs. He suggested the formation of a Palestine state with proportional representation in government by Jews and Arabs which would join in four-state federation with Syria, Lebanon and Transjordan, with the proviso that Jewish immigration would not be controlled by the state but by a special two-member committee whose decisions on Jewish immigration would be governed by the absorptive capacity of the country. All these proposals, however, found no interest within the Zionist movement which, under the shock of the Nazi holocaust, was determined to achieve full sovereignty at whatever cost.

At the meeting of the Zionist Executive in Jerusalem in November 1942, Ben-Gurion gained the support of the majority of his colleagues for the Biltmore proposals, though some expressed the view that they were utopian or mere slogans. Ben-Gurion asserted his undisputed control and argued against compromise, stating that every Jewish concession would become the new maximum programme which the

Arabs would seek to whittle down.

> [It is argued] that the British and Americans will accept neither the full Arab demands nor the full Jewish demands, and so we must propose some middle course. Since the middle is only a relative concept, determined by the extremities, the middle course we would propose would become the maximum immediately, and compromise would have to be made at a new middle point, between our middle which has become an end and that of the Arabs.[6]

The main opposition to the Biltmore programme came from the bi-nationalist Hashomer Hatzair and its allies. They warned that the claim to the whole of Palestine would not be realised after the war, and this would lead to another partition of Palestine, with increased bitterness between the two communities. Secondly, the programme assumed that the Arabs would not be a factor after the war, because of their support of Hitler; on the contrary, Hashomer Hatzair argued, the emerging forces of national liberation in the Arab world would be even more important after the war. Finally, they disputed the assumption that the British and Americans were the main allies of Zionism, while the Arabs were the main enemy and demanded a common front with the Arabs against imperialism.[7]

The immediate outcome of the Biltmore programme was a refusal to develop contacts with the new forces that were emerging in the Arab world after 1943, which were not as hostile to the Zionist enterprise as the pre-war leadership had been. They were interested more in political independence and economic development rather than engaging in war against Zionism.

In the summer of 1943, a group of Arab notables approached the League for Jewish-Arab Co-operation and Rapprochement with proposals for negotiations with the Jewish Agency. These included for the first time proposals for free immigration up to numerical parity and possible compromise after that point had been reached.[8] The Jewish Agency publicised these secret proposals but wielded them only as a weapon against the British White Paper. Other attempts to reach a modus vivendi, suggested by other Arab states (such as the leader of Egypt, Nahas Pasha) were not acted upon. At the same time, the Jewish Agency sought to discredit the advocates of a bi-national solution, attacking the proposals of the Hashomer Hatzair group (the so-called 'Bentov Book') which had been privately submitted for internal policy discussion in the Zionist movement, and generally tried to ignore the special Zionist committee that had been set up to consider the Arab problem.[9]

The fundamental assumption of this strategy — that the Arabs were no longer an important factor in post-war Palestine, because of their poor war record and pro-Nazi elements — was a moral, not a realistic political judgement. The war had shown that the oil reserves of the Middle East, whose scale had for the first time been revealed, were of decisive strategic and economic importance. Furthermore, Great Britain's weakness left a vacuum in the area where the United States and USSR, the two Great Powers to emerge from the war, were struggling for supremacy.

The second and related strategic miscalculation of the Biltmore programme was the belief that the United States would have undisputed hegemony in the world after the end of the war. The Zionist movement correctly understood that the United States would succeed Britain as the centre of power in the Middle East, but did not foresee the important role the Soviet Union would play after the war. Indeed, before the decisive battle of Stalingrad in early 1943, there was little likelihood that the Russians would emerge from the war strengthened politically and militarily, and that their prestige would affect the nationalist and anti-imperialist movement in the Arab world. The Biltmore strategy was that with American backing, the success of Zionism was assured.

The final and most tragic miscalculation of the Biltmore programme was the belief that there would be millions of European Jews after the war in urgent need of immigration to Palestine. At the Biltmore conference, Weizmann estimated that 75 per cent of European Jews would survive the war. He and Ben-Gurion envisaged the immediate transfer of millions in a few years to the new Jewish state. Within a year after the Biltmore programme it was known that very few Jews would survive.[10] But, understandably, 'the emotional appeal of the plan grew all the stronger . . . just at the moment when the politico-diplomatic value of the Biltmore programme crumbled, the heart-touching summons on which the programme rested, grew stronger'. It was inconceivable that justice would be withheld from the Jewish people.[11]

The insistence of the Jewish Agency on full implementation of the Biltmore programme inevitably led to conflict with Great Britain. In her weakened state after the war, Britain, under a Labour government, was seeking to disengage herself from her colonial commitments throughout the world; most dramatically, in India. Exhausted militarily and financially from the war, Britain could no longer play the role of a Great Power on a par with the United States and the Soviet Union. She was dependent on American loans to sustain her economy, and she sought to have the Americans shoulder her commitments in the Eastern Mediterranean, culminating in her withdrawal from Greece and Turkey and her replacement by the United States (the Truman Doctrine, 1947). Britain's reluctance to satisfy Jewish demands in Palestine was due fundamentally to her war exhaustion and military and economic weakness.

Reeling under the impact of the holocaust, the Zionist movement saw the British attitude as a shameless betrayal. The new Labour government had adopted resolutions in favour of the Biltmore programme when it was in coalition in 1943 and 1944. As late as April 1945, the Labour Party executive adopted a resolution in favour of a large Jewish immigration to Palestine so as to become a majority; it recommended even a transfer of the Arab population to neighbouring countries and extending the present boundaries of Palestine by agreement with Egypt, Syria and Transjordan.[12]

On 27 May 1945, three weeks after the war ended, the Zionist movement petitioned the UN and the British government to set up a Jewish state in Palestine. It was clear that this demand would produce no immediate results. Meanwhile, there was the pressing problem of the plight and fate of the displaced persons, survivors of the holocaust, who were in camps in Europe awaiting transfer to Palestine. To appease the Arabs, the British were still enforcing the provisions of the 1939 White Paper severely restricting immigration. During the war, the Haganah had been organising illegal immigration of refugees from Europe. In June 1945 the Zionists demanded immediate entry of 100,000 displaced persons to Palestine.

In response to this request, Bevin told Weizmann that only 1,500 immigration certificates would be issued — 'the last available under the White Paper which would remain in force'. With his notorious bluntness Bevin accused the Jews of trying to 'push to the head of the queue'. He argued that to depart from the White Paper would 'inflame the Middle East' and jeopardise vital British interests there.

The British obstinacy was extremely frustrating to the Zionist leadership. During the last stages of the war, the dissident 'Irgun' and its 'Lehi' (Stern) splinter group had been engaged in terrorist warfare against the British. Now the Haganah, transformed into an underground 'Jewish resistance army', began to resort to widespread military activity and sabotage in Palestine and large-scale illegal immigration in defiance of the British naval blockade, and of the military authorities in Palestine. At the same time, the Zionists in America also began to apply pressure against Britain, and gained the support of President Truman for the admission of 100,000 refugees. The British replied that if the Americans advocated a revised policy in Palestine, they would have to take their share of responsibility in carrying it out.

At a meeting of the Inner Zionist Council in October, Moshe Sneh, the Commander of the Haganah, stated that the British would have to pay a high price for implementing the White Paper policy. Rabbi Silver, the militant leader of the American Zionists, had already called for 'fighting them with whatever weapons are at our disposal'.[13] Weizmann could not sanction a policy of violence and terrorism, though he was for every form of pressure on Britain short of this. Weizmann was increasingly out of step with Ben-Gurion who, in alliance with the American Zionists, advocated and pursued a policy of 'active resistance', which meant walking a thin line between legality and terrorism.

The deterioration of Jewish-British relations led to the appointment on 11 May 1946, of the Anglo-American Committee of Enquiry which met through the winter of 1946. Its report unanimously recommended that the Mandate be continued, ultimately through the UN, but that 100,000 immigration certificates be granted immediately. The Zionist leadership was divided about the acceptance of the report, but the British were totally opposed. Bevin exacerbated the situation with a characteristically undiplomatic remark that the Americans were putting pressure on him because 'they did not want too many Jews in New York'.

In Palestine, the situation deteriorated rapidly. The Haganah continued its 'active resistance'. On 29 June 1946, the British arrested all the leaders of the Jewish community and sealed the offices of the Jewish Agency. Over 2,000 persons were interned in Latrun detention camp, including Moshe Sharett and religious leaders. Ben-Gurion had escaped arrest only because he was abroad. On 26 July 1946, the Irgun blew up the King David Hotel, headquarters of the Mandatory Administration, with great loss of life. The British began house-to-house searches in Tel Aviv, and General Barker stated that they 'would punish the Jews in the way this race dislikes most, by striking at their pocket and showing our contempt for them'. Matters had reached an impasse from which there was no way out.

At the end of July 1946, a joint US-UK Cabinet Commission on Palestine prepared its report. In the Morrison-Grady Plan, Palestine was to be cantonised, with the British retaining large sections. Truman stated that he was not in favour of a Congressional resolution endorsing a Jewish state in Palestine. The American acceptance of what seemed to be British suggestions indicated that the Zionist movement had reached a dead end. The eruption of the cold war in the Middle East (in November 1945 a Communist uprising took place in the Azerbaijan province of Iran and troops sent to quell it were stopped by the USSR forces at Kazvin) prompted the State Department to support British policy in the area. Ben-Gurion's strategy to obtain American endorsement of the Biltmore programme drew a blank. However, the bid for leadership in the Zionist movement necessitated an alliance with American Zionists, who vehemently opposed what seemed to provide the only issue out of the impasse: partition.

Goldmann's Mission to America

In the prevailing situation, the Zionist Executive met in July-August 1946 in Paris, in a mood of despair.[14] The Americans were threatening to withdraw from involvement in affairs in Palestine, while Zionist relations with Britain had reached their lowest ebb. It fell upon Dr Nahum Goldmann to put forward what he had believed since 1945 to be the only viable solution. Goldmann argued that partition was the only way to assure American involvement and to prevent a violent confrontation with Great Britain.[15] The time before the November 1946 elections in the USA was, in his view, the last propitious moment to take some action to prevent a deterioration of Zionist American relations.[16]

Goldmann's analysis was supported by two American members of the Executive, Rose Halperin[17] and Stephen Wise, the greatest opponent of partition in 1937. Wise feared an American approval of the Morrison-Grady Plan, as the Americans were now determining policy in the context of the cold war.[18]

> The two terrible alternatives facing us − the degradation of assent and the bitterness and bloodiness of revolt against Great Britain − are equally tragic. I have not changed my mind about Partition . . . but after what has happened in Europe, I confess to a sense of guilt.
>
> We must take our courage in our hands . . . We are not facing a theory of Partition any more, but a condition, and we have got to make our choice. President Truman is sick and tired of us. If we go to him with another 'No', he will think and perhaps say, 'to hell with you Jews', and he will act upon it.

Wise proposed to send Dr Goldmann, without delay, to negotiate a proposal for partition.

Ben-Gurion's reaction was ambiguous: 'we must demand one thing only, and that is a Jewish state in Palestine, or in part of Palestine . . . I don't think there should be any negotiations as long as our people are under arrest . . . On the other hand, if there is any one member of the Executive who wants to go to the US Government and negotiate, I will not stand in his way. Everybody must decide that for himself.'[19]

Goldmann, however, asked for a definite vote. He stated:

> I refuse to go to Washington merely to ask for a Jewish state . . . I cannot possibly go to the President with such a proposal . . . His Cabinet Committee has signed the [Morrison-Grady] Report, and the State Department does not want a break with Great Britain . . . It takes years to establish a state. In the meantime, what should happen to the 100,000 in the camps? We must tell the President what immediate action is to be taken.[20]

Goldmann's resolution (after rejecting Morrison-Grady) read:

> 2. The Executive is prepared to discuss a proposal for the establishment of a viable Jewish state in an adequate area of Palestine.
> 3. For the immediate implementation of Paragraph 2, the Executive submits the following demands:
>   (a)   The immediate issuance of 100,000 immigration permits and an immediate start on the transportation of 100,000 Jews to Palestine.
>   (b)   The immediate granting of all administrative and economic autonomy to the area of Palestine designated to become a Jewish state.
>   (c)   The right of the Jewish administration of the area of Palestine designated, to become a Jewish state to supervise immigration.

On the crucial second paragraph, which signified the end of the Biltmore programme and the revival of the partition plan, the vote was 10 to 1 in favour, with one abstention.[21]

From 6 August to 11 August, Goldmann conferred with members of the President's Palestine Committee: Acting Secretary of State, Dean Acheson; Secretary of War, Robert Patterson; and Secretary of the Treasury, Snyder. In the crucial meeting with Acheson on 7 August,[22]

Goldmann stated that the Executive would be willing to accept a plan which would: (1) provide for immediate partition (Jewish state: Peel Plan plus the Negev; Arab state: the remainder, except Holy Places; Galilee negotiable); (2) terminate the Mandate and provide for a Jewish state in two to three years; and (3) allow immediate Jewish administration and grant control of immigration to that administration.

Goldmann argued that a continuation of the present situation would lead to Jewish terrorism gaining the upper hand, and to instability in the region and in Anglo-US relations for years to come. He stated that the Jews would be prepared to join in a Middle East Federation, that moderate Arab opinion would support this plan, and that Abdullah would, too, if the Arab state were united with Transjordan.[23] Goldmann's mission became the subject of stormy debates in American Jewry[24] and the Zionist movement. Rabbi Silver, the head of the American Zionists, resigned from the Zionist Executive and launched an intense press campaign to discredit Goldmann's initiative.[25] The Vice-President of the Zionist Organisation of America accused Dr Goldmann of deceiving his organisation and argued that the result had been an American retreat from support for immigration, without positive commitment to a Jewish state.[26] The *New York Post* ran articles entitled 'Another Zionist Munich?' and 'The Amazing Deceit of Nahum Goldmann'. The *Post* maintained that the partition scheme was another excuse for Britain stalling and an escape for the Americans.[27]

Official American documents and memoirs confirm the importance of Goldmann's initiative.[28] The American Zionists did not understand how close the Americans were in the summer of 1946 to washing their hands of the whole affair despite intense Zionist pressure.[29]

There was strong opposition to Zionist demands in the American cabinet. The Joint Chiefs of Staff were interested in securing Middle Eastern oil supplies and military bases. The campaign in the Cabinet was led by James Forrestal, the Secretary of the Navy. He confided to his diary his dissatisfaction with Truman: 'Unfortunately the President has gone out on a limb and endorsed the Bartley-Crum report [of the Anglo-American Committee of Enquiry] for admitting 100,000 Jews.'[30]

Goldmann's initiative offered the Americans a way out of an impossible situation. The insistence on the Biltmore programme and the total severance of Zionist relations with the British did not allow for American support of the Zionist cause, as it would entail an American clash with Britain. Reporting on his meeting with Goldmann, Acheson cabled the American Ambassador in London:

> I said to [British] Ambassador that this resolution [on partition]
> and interpretative talks seemed to me a definitely hopeful develop-
> ment . . . if discussions could be broadened in scope to include . . .
> proposal of Jewish Agency, situation might change so this Govt.
> might lend sympathetic moral support and . . . might also be able,
> with hope of success, to recommend to Congress assistance.

Now, Truman wrote to Attlee suggesting that the London talks be
broadened to include alternative suggestions made by Dr Goldmann,
and stating that the United States would not support the Morrison-
Grady Plan.[31]

The Americans withheld a public statement about the plan in order
not to antagonise the British and the Arabs,[32] and the State Department
was hopeful that some agreement would be worked out between the
contending parties. It soon became clear, however, that the differences
with the British were irreconcilable. Bevin objected to partition, maintaining that it would alienate the Arabs and increase British difficulties
in the Middle East.[33] He was unwilling to take action unless he could
get concrete American economic and, perhaps, military support, which
the Americans were not ready to give. The Zionist leadership kept
pressing Truman for a formal statement in favour of partition, until
finally, on Yom Kippur, 4 October 1946, a few weeks before the
American elections, Truman issued a statement that came close to
endorsing the partition plan:

> the Jewish Agency proposed a solution of the Palestine problem by
> means of the creation of a viable Jewish state in control of its own
> immigration and economic policies in an adequate area of Palestine
> instead of in the whole of Palestine . . . This proposal has received
> widespread attention in public forums and the press in the United
> States. From this discussion which has ensued, it is my belief that a
> solution along these lines would command the support of public
> opinion in the United States. I cannot believe the gap between the
> proposals which have been put forward is too great to be bridged by
> men of good will and reason. To such a solution our Government
> should give its support.[34]

The American position had an influence on Britain. On 17 November,
Goldmann discussed the partition plan with Lord Inverchapel, the

British Minister in Washington, who hinted for the first time that 'the British government is definitely moving towards Partition as a solution . . . [however] there was a definite decision of the British Cabinet to give up the Mandate and transfer the matter to the UN if no solution to the problem will be reached at the forthcoming London Conference.'[35] Ben-Gurion, however, was playing another double game. Eager to gain the support of the American Zionists in his bid to replace Weizmann as the leader of the Zionist movement, he avoided coming out in favour of partition, which the American Zionists vehemently opposed. But he, too, was afraid of the loss of American Government support, and was grateful to Goldmann for securing this support and for absorbing the public criticism for making the necessary concessions to accomplish this.

Ben-Gurion's tactic of furthering partition and unseating Weizmann was reflected in his opposition to negotiations with the British at the Round Table talks, asserting that the Goldmann plan for a Jewish state in part of Palestine represented the minimum demands on which the Jewish Agency was prepared to negotiate.[36]

Matters came to a head at the Twenty-second Zionist Congress in Basle in December 1946, where a formal decision was to be made concerning the London Round Table talks. Weizmann was strongly in favour of participating in the talks and not breaking with the British.

Ben-Gurion's rejection of negotiations with the British at the Round Table allowed him to avoid the embarrassing question of whether he supported partition. He stated that the Jewish Agency would not itself propose partition and demanded a Jewish state in the whole of Palestine and full Jewish immigration. He defended Goldmann's mission to America, however, as 'undertaken with the full approval of the Executive'.[37]

In his own defence, Goldmann stated that:

> The Biltmore idea was a good one, but it was based on the hope that a different world would emerge after the war, one in which just claims would be recognized and honoured. If they could get unlimited immigration, they would not demand Partition, but immigration in the Mandate was likely to be a continual struggle over Arab opposition. There had to be a short-cut . . . partition means compromise. If the British reject our proposals, we shall have to bring the matter to the UN.[38]

Goldmann was opposed by both the right (Revisionists) and the left

(Hashomer Hatzair), by the former as defeatist,[39] and by the latter for renouncing co-operation with the Arabs.[40] The conference rejected participation in negotiations with Great Britain and deposed Weizmann. The British abdicated on the problem by referring it to the UN which eventually, due to Soviet support and at US urging, recommended partition.

The Zionist movement accepted the partition plan and exerted its efforts to assure its passage by the UN when it was presented for a vote on 29 November 1947. The Palestinian Arabs, supported by the other Arab states, opposed the UN partition resolution and began an armed struggle to undermine its implementation. Thus, the Jewish state was born in flames.

Israel's 'Original Sin'

The War of 1948, which started with the entry of Arab armies on 15 May into Palestine, irrevocably shaped the course of Israeli-Arab relations for at least a generation. While 1937 was the decisive moment in the conflict between Jews and Arabs in Palestine itself, 1948 transformed this conflict into a confrontation between the entire Arab world and Israel. At the same time, the success of Israel's strategy confirmed her bias in favour of relying on military options for the solution of her long-range political problems.

One of the most distinguished Zionist leaders, Dr Nahum Goldmann, suggests that this course was not inevitable, and that the birth of the state of Israel could have taken place under more favourable circumstances:

> The Zionist movement had conceived the creation of the Jewish state on the basis of amity and understanding with the Arabs . . . our ideas contained two points of principle: the demand for a Jewish state in part of Palestine, and the participation of that state in a confederation of Near Eastern states.[1]
>
> When it came to the founding of the State, I was against the proclamation of the State despite the fact that I was one of the main fighters for Partition . . . I felt that after the vote at the UN – where both the Communists and the democratic bloc, East and West, voted for a Jewish state leaving the Arabs in desperate isolation – it may have been the time to reach some agreement with the Arabs, even if only a temporary one. At that time I had some hints from Egyptian diplomats that we should meet . . . not to get the Arabs to accept the idea of Partition or a Jewish state, which they wouldn't have

done at that time, but at least to get them not to react by a war. President Truman, who was also very much afraid of an Arab-Jewish war, offered us his private airplane. The only one to side with me was Moshe Sharett who was in New York at the time . . . we decided to send him over to convince Ben-Gurion — but the enthusiasm in Israel was so great and Ben-Gurion's determination to proclaim the State immediately so strong that our suggestion to postpone it for a month, to try to avoid a war if possible, was rejected . . . in a sense it was the original tragedy of Israel because, as the Talmud says, one sin leads to another — aveira goreret aveira; that's what I was afraid of, that there will be another war and another.[2]

The proclamation of the State and the ensuing invasion by the Arab armies naturally ruled out reconciliation . . The basic and tragic fact is that no agreement was reached and that the State of Israel made its entrance into history with a war, albeit a defensive war, against the Arabs. How to overcome the consequences of this is the central problem of contemporary Israeli politics and will be for many years to come, for that first war and the Israeli victory produced inescapable consequences, for both Israel and the Arabs. As far as the latter were concerned the breach with Israel had been widened enormously . . . The unexpected defeat was a shock and a terrible blow to Arab pride. Deeply injured, they turned all their endeavours to the healing of their psychological wound: to victory and revenge.

On the other hand, success had a marked psychological effect on Israel. It seemed to show the advantage of direct action over diplomacy . . . The victory offered such a glorious contrast to the centuries of persecution and humiliation, of adaptation and compromise, that it seemed to indicate the only direction that could possibly be taken from then on. To brook nothing, tolerate no attack, but cut through Gordian knots, and to shape history by creating facts seemed so simple, so compelling, so satisfying that it became Israel's policy in its conflict with the Arab world.[3]

This was the basis of a whole wrong development of Israel because, first of all, I have always thought of Israel as a neutral state between the two blocs in the world. We are the classic people who have to be neutral, as a people or as a State, because millions of our people live in the Communist world, millions in the Western world, and we must have a State that any Jew living under any regime can be emotionally attached . . . But in the long run, we have had to depend on arms we got mostly from the West; so we became more and more members of the Western bloc and so the whole policy of Israel — not only its relationship with the Arab world — was determined by it.

The second consequence was that, being threatened by the Arab world, being a small minority, we were absolutely committed to mass immigration, and naturally had to depend on numbers of people — not only for the army, but for the economic development of the country. So we organized a great mass immigration which had to weaken all the ideals of kibbutzim and [of] creating a new society in Israel . . .

To sum up, Israel was forced, from its beginning, into a situation where it can only become a State like all other States and I don't believe such an Israel will survive.[4]

Goldmann in effect argues that the postponement of the declaration of the State of Israel could have led to a negotiated truce with the Arab states, with incalculable consequences for Israeli-Arab relations and the development of Israeli society generally. In the following pages we shall endeavour to trace the origin of the truce proposal, Israeli and Arab reactions and the reasons for its failure.

The War of the Palestinian Arabs 1947-8

The war between the newly proclaimed State of Israel and the Arab states was preceded by a bitter and bloody struggle between Jews and Palestinian Arabs from November 1947 to May 1948. The Arab states rejected the UN November Resolution on partition and supported the Palestinians with money, arms and volunteers but the latter had to bear the brunt of the struggle.

It ended in the total collapse of the Palestinians, militarily and politically. By 12 May 1948, the Jewish forces controlled nearly all the territory assigned to the Jewish State by the UN resolution, and were moving into Arab areas (Jaffa, Tiberias). The lines of communication to the Negev settlements and Jewish Jerusalem were still precarious, but effective Jewish civil administration and a well-organised political structure existed, headed by a Provisional Government. In the Arab areas the military setbacks and the flight of the refugees caused a collapse of all public services and administrative bodies. Not one leader of the Arab Higher Committee remained in Palestine.

During the month of April the Haganah had won military superiority over the indigenous Palestinian forces, who no longer posed a serious threat. On 8-9 April in pitched battle the Palestinian Liberation Army of Fawzi Qawakji (made up of volunteers trained in Syria and with artillery and tanks) had been decisively defeated at Mishmar Haemek. Meanwhile, the other major Arab guerilla force which was loyal to the Mufti and had been lodged in the hills to the east of Jerusalem, threatening communications with the Jewish community in the city, was attacked in Operation Nachson. This manoeuvre was designed to open the Jerusalem-Tel Aviv road. When, on 10 April, the commander of the Arab forces, the popular Abdul Qader Husseini, was killed in the battle for the village of Kastel, the Arab forces lost their cohesion and disintegrated.[1]

These two military defeats proved that the Palestinian Arab irregulars were no match for the Haganah. Ill-trained, ill-equipped and numbering no more than 5,000-7,000 men in each region, without defined or co-ordinated command or support structures, the Arab irregulars could, at best, mount only a harassing operation against the Jewish settlements. But with the turn of the military tide, Jewish forces went on the offensive; they actively established Jewish control over most of the Arab areas which were within the boundaries of the proposed Jewish state. Tiberias was the first major town to be controlled by the Haganah. After Arab attacks from Haifa, the Haganah retaliated with the approval of the British and were allowed to control all but the British enclave. The Arab population fled despite Jewish pleas to stay. In Tel Aviv the Irgun had launched an offensive against the neighbouring Arab city of Jaffa. Most of the inhabitants fled and the villages leading out of Tel Aviv were secured. In Jerusalem Jewish forces captured the adjoining Arab sections of the New City (Katamon and the German Colony). In the Galilee communications between Haifa and Tiberias were secured by the capture of Safad on 10 May, and the Beisan Valley was completely occupied by the Haganah on 12 May.[2] A total of over 200 Arab villages had been captured.

Thus, by 12 May, the Jews controlled a continuous area from Rehovet and Hulda northwards as far as Zichron Yaa'qov, including Tel Aviv; all the territory from Haifa to Acre; the Plain of Esdraelon; the Beisan Valley; and the whole of the upper Galilee to the Lebanese and Syrian borders. The Haganah had nine brigades consisting of 18,900 men mobilised to hold these positions; three brigades in the Galilee (one poised to capture East Galilee and two to hold the west); two in the centre; two in Jerusalem; and two in the south to take the Negev (which was then unoccupied no man's land). In addition there were 15,000 men in the settlements who were capable of defending them.[3]

On 13 May, partition was more or less a *fait accompli*. 'The successes of the Haganah have given Jews new hope and courage. Proclamation of [the] Jewish state, following [the] termination of the mandate [15 May] is awaited by Yishuv with greatest excitement and jubilation. Jewish national administration, which is already functioning in wholly Jewish areas and partly in Jerusalem, will become government of [the] new Jewish state', cabled the American Consul in Jerusalem, Wasson.[4]

The Palestinian struggle against the Yishuv and against the UN Resolution on Partition 1947 had a very different character from the Arab Revolt in 1937, reflecting the changes in economic and social conditions that had occurred in Arab society, the crisis of leadership and the new political mood of the population in 1947. The initiative of the uprising in 1936 was taken by the local committees in towns and villages and the immediate response of the population set the pace of events. The leadership was hesitant and trying to avoid a direct confrontation with the mandatory power. The Arab Higher Committee, formed under popular pressure, issued resounding and belligerent declarations, but tried, at the same time, to stem the tide, appealing to the heads of Arab states to mediate and offer a face-saving formula. The Arab masses, both in the towns and in the country, gave enthusiastic support to the rebels, supplying volunteers, food and cover, notwithstanding the severe 'collective punishment' on the part of the British armed forces. In 1947 the situation was reversed. The leadership, most of them in exile, viewed the struggle against partition as a matter of life and death and beseeched the masses to fight to the last. The masses were in no mood to respond. The number of volunteers to the fighting groups was considerably smaller[5] than in 1938 though the population had increased since then in leaps and bounds. The Arab Commanders had to round up arms and men, and to requisition food and money by force. In 1937 the whole country was engulfed by the flames of the rebellion. In 1947 many areas remained quiet and kept aloof from the fighting. In this respect it is of interest to note the opinion of Jewish security and intelligence officers on the Palestinian struggle in 1947, contained in the minutes of the Yishuv's Security Committee[6] meetings in which the Chiefs of Staff, representatives of the Yishuv and the Jewish Agency, among them Ben-Gurion, Sharett, etc., were taking part. In the meeting on 1-2 January 1948, we find the following:[7]

The Arabs were not prepared for the fighting when they started it. The majority is reluctant to join. [There are] no authorities;

community leaders [are] passive, police non-existent. [There are] only a few hundred fighters – but free trade with arms. The Opposition to the Mufti exists and is even stronger but does not plan to take the initiative. The only factor troubling the Arabs is our own preparations – which they view with anxiety. The Opposition waits for the Partition to take place in order to make a bid for power. It is strong in Nablus, Jenim, Tulkarm. Officially, the Opposition is against partition, but prepares itself for this eventuality. We exaggerate about the armed strength of the Palestinians – they don't have enough arms. [Though] trade is free, the supply [of arms] is limited and prices high . . . The Mufti has now only 500-600 people but the problem is how to prevent his growth. Can we find an Opposition leader to come out against the Mufti? In 1936-9 Fakhri Nashashibi organised his 'Peace Troupes' only when the Mufti attacked the Opposition, killing its leaders. Now the Mufti has an interest in creating a united front with the Opposition. The number of volunteers from abroad is small and even if it increases they are less dangerous than the Palestinians because they don't know the terrain. The Arab community as a whole – the peasants, merchants, citrus growers, workers – did not respond to the Mufti's appeal to rise in arms, but the vicious circle of killings and reprisals draws an increasing number of innocent people, even those who don't want troubles, into the fighting.

The many villages in the South and in the North that did not join the uprising presented a more difficult strategic problem than those which were up in arms: should one leave them intact or forestall the volunteers of the Arab Army of Deliverance and the regular Arab armies, by overrunning the villages in spite of their inaction?

The basic difference between the 1937 and the 1947 Palestinian struggle was reflected in the flight of hundreds of thousands of Arabs from their homes and villages which led to the creation of the tragic and intricate problem of Palestinian Refugees. In 1937 too, a considerable number of Palestinians sought refuge in the neighbouring countries, in Lebanon and Syria. But they were in the main political leaders and members of the rebel units, escaping from the law, and security forces, and the rich who preferred to pass their time at a safe distance until the storm was over. This phenomenon repeated itself also in the early stage of war in 1947: nearly 30,000 Palestinian merchants, landowners, community leaders and their families left the country as 'self-displaced' persons, between November 1947 and April

1948. The massacre of Deir Yassin (April 1948) caused a panic which spread like wildfire causing a mass flight of unprecedented dimension.

The Palestinian refugee problem does not come within the scope of this study, concerned mainly with the problem of Arab invasion in the 1948 war. However, the impact of this problem on the evolution of the Israeli-Arab conflict was so decisive that a few comments are required. The Zionist and the Arab versions of the origin and causes of the mass flight of Palestinians are diametrically opposed and equally inadequate. The Arabs attribute the flight to a deliberate Zionist design to drive the population out of the country by means of intimidation, terror and forceful expulsion. The Zionists place the responsibility for the flight on the Arab Higher Committee which called upon the civilian population to clear the way for the Arab armies and stay out of the battle areas until the war was over and the Zionists defeated. The Arab version ignores the flight of the 'self-displaced' persons – the economic elite and community leaders who left Palestine at the outset, leaving the community leaderless, without an administration and even public services except on a local level. It also ignores the fact that thousands of Palestinians, who resigned themselves to the fact of partition and did not wish to live in a Jewish state, chose to emigrate to Arab environs. This applied in particular to Arab officials in the government and free professions, who occupied a privileged position in Arab society under the British Mandate. Also many thousands simply ran away from the battle areas looking for safety. There were also instances of Jewish appeals to Arabs to remain in place, with the assurance of protection of their lives and property. There remains, however, the hard core of refugees deliberately intimidated into a panic flight, or driven out by force even after the war was over. The Zionist version glosses over this fact, although the forceful expulsion of Arabs was the subject of heated debates inside the leadership, the political parties and in the press. The expulsion was explained in many cases on the grounds of military exigencies but, as later events have shown, the argument of security was often wilfully employed and without foundation.

The Zionist version of an Arab appeal to the population to leave their homes in order to return later with the victorious Arab armies was a very successful weapon in political warfare. But the authenticity of the appeal has never been proved beyond doubt and, as we shall see later, it was highly improbable that such an appeal was made by those in office. In spite of their boastful propaganda, the Arab leaders, far from believing in a victory, had a feeling of an impending disaster. The Mufti opposed the intervention of regular Arab armies in the war.[8] All

Arab leaders viewed the flight of refugees as a hindrance to war. The Political Committee of the Arab League decided, in its meeting in Cairo, 11-14 May 1948, to grant refuge to children, women and old people among the Palestinian refugees but to send back to Palestine all able-bodied men fit for service.[9]

There is no evidence of a Zionist deliberate design to expel the Arab population. The magnitude of the flight phenomenon took the Yishuv leaders by surprise. They were, however, quick to recognise the potential benefits from the chaotic disintegration of the Arab community for successful warfare and for the ethnic composition of the Jewish state in the future. Weizmann did not disguise his feeling of relief, describing the flight of the Palestinians as a 'miraculous simplification' of the problem.[10] Sharett rushed to declare that there can be no mass return of Palestine Arabs to Israel until a general political settlement was achieved and that after the war only those acknowledging Israel's authority and sovereignty would qualify for application to return.[11] While Sharett left open the prospect of return under certain political conditions, the Israeli authorities took steps to reduce this prospect to a minimum by levelling to ground a great number of villages deserted by the population.[12] The flight of the Palestinians was subsequently presented as part of a population transfer although there was no connection between this flight and the mass immigration of Jews from the Arab countries, in terms of time, country of origin or motivation. Jewish immigration came in the main from Morocco, Iraq and Yemen, countries not involved in the fighting (except Iraq, in an insubstantial way) while the Palestinian refugees fleeing from the war, concentrated in the immediate neighbourhood of Israel, in the West Bank, Gaza Strip and the adjoining Arab states. The old idea of 'transfer' was thus revived and used to explain and justify *a posteriori* an event of an entirely different nature.

The American Truce Proposal

On 13 May 1948 the US Consul in Jerusalem cabled that: 'So far with exception of [the] Irgun attack on Jaffa and Hagana occupation of certain areas of Jerusalem — Tel Aviv road — Jews have strictly observed territorial limits imposed by UN Resolution of 29 November.'[1] The future of Palestine and peace in the region depended now on whether the Arab states would accept the *fait accompli* or whether they would try to prevent partition, as they committed themselves to do, by military invasion, following the termination of the Mandate and withdrawal of the British forces from Palestine.

It was known that the Jewish Agency would regard invasion of Palestine by Arab armies as releasing it from the obligations of the UN Resolution, and justifying the acquisition of more territory.[2] For the US, the danger of a major war in the Middle East was alarming. The support for the UN November Resolution on Partition 1947 created the dilemma of conflicting interests for the American Administration. The State Department and the Chiefs of Staff viewed with growing concern the spread of anti-Western sentiments and propaganda in the Middle East and the penetration of the USSR as an active factor in Middle Eastern affairs, in the wake of their support for partition and a Jewish state. An Arab invasion of Palestine would grant the Soviets a legitimate basis for political and military intervention in defence of a UN Resolution and pose a threat to vital Western interests in the region as well as to pro-Western Arab regimes.[3]

The White House, however, had to take cognisance, in a year of Congressional elections, of the feelings of a large and powerful Jewish community which, tantalised by its own guilt complex rooted in its inability to prevent the Nazi holocaust, was now engaged in feverish campaign to rescue its survivors. These conflicting tendencies were reflected in the vacillation of American policy regarding the implementation of the Partition Plan approved by the UN. In March 1948, the Americans began to recoil from supporting the plan. On 30 April, President Truman, alarmed by the news of an impending Arab military intervention in Palestine, gave his approval to the proposal of 'truce in Palestine' as the only way to prevent a war. 'Go and get a Truce', he told Dean Rusk, Director of the Office of the UN affairs, 'there is no other answer to the situation.'[4] The issue of war and peace centred on the prospects of a truce being accepted by the parties to the conflict as the only alternative to war.

The proposal to postpone the declaration of Israeli statehood, in return for a truce with the Arabs, originated in the American retreat from full support of partition at the UN, which climaxed in an American proposal for a temporary trusteeship over Palestine. But since trusteeship was exposed as politically unacceptable to all parties concerned, an attempt was made to separate the truce proposal from the trusteeship issue, and to put pressure on both Israel and the Arabs to agree upon a truce.

The American retreat from partition first formally emerged at the meeting of the United Nations Security Council on 24 February 1948, less than three months after the US had been one of the main supporters of the partition of Palestine resolution in the UN General

Assembly. Now the US argued that the General Assembly vote had been only a 'recommendation' and not a 'decision' and, as such, was not binding on the Security Council (which had the sole power to enforce UN decisions). The new US view was that the Security Council was not empowered to enforce a political settlement against the will of the inhabitants of a country and that only external aggression was within the legal powers of the UN. This was a reversal of the US position at the time of the General Assembly resolution, when the US representative stated that the General Assembly was 'the effective voice determining the new forms and structures of government which should prevail in Palestine'.[5]

The shift in American strategy represented the reassertion of the supremacy of the State and Defense Departments which urged that support of a Jewish state was detrimental to US interests in the Middle East. James Forrestal, the Secretary of the Navy, was particularly vociferous in warning against alienating the '300 million Moslems'. The professional diplomatic experts and military planners were worried about jeopardising US military bases in the strategic Middle East and US investments in oil (which was also vital militarily and economically for the US-sponsored recovery of Europe).[6]

On 19 March 1948, the US made its formal trusteeship proposal at the UN. It suggested that the activities of the Palestine Partition Commission be suspended and that a special session of the General Assembly be convened to consider a temporary trusteeship without prejudice to the rights or claims of the parties concerned or to the character of the eventual political settlement. Secretary of State Marshall explained that the reason for the proposal was that the original UN resolution could not be peacefully implemented. After the British left, a breakdown of law and order would occur in Palestine. Trusteeship would be ended as soon as a peaceful solution could be found, and was necessary for a political and military truce. Reacting to intense public criticism, President Truman added that the trusteeship proposal had been made only after the US had exhausted every effort to find a way to carry out partition by peaceful means.[7]

The US had already made the decision at the urging of the Joint Chiefs of Staff, not to intervene in Palestine with troops. At this time it was feared that if partition went through and the Jewish state was defeated by the Arabs, there would be irresistible pressure for US troops to intervene to save the Jewish community. President Truman's version was that the trusteeship proposals were seized upon by those elements in the State Department hostile to Zionism, contrary to 'my attitude and the policy I had laid down'.[8] Truman had met Weizmann the day before the trusteeship proposal was announced, and secretly had assured him that the US would continue to support partition.[9]

Together with the trusteeship proposal presented on 30 March, the US also made a formal proposal for an immediate Arab-Jewish truce in Palestine. This called for the suspension of political as well as military activity, and asked for both the Arab Higher Committee and the Jewish Agency to send representatives to arrange truce terms with the Security Council. At this point the truce proposal was merely tactical, in that the US wanted to explore with the Security Council the actual content of any trusteeship proposal before presenting it to the General Assembly.[10]

The trusteeship proposal received a cold reception from the parties involved — the Arabs and Jews — as well as from the majority of the UN. The Jewish Agency called trusteeship a 'political reward for violence' and defiance of the UN resolutions. Zionists in the United States mobilised mass demonstrations and Congressional pressure against the plan and in favour of a Jewish state in Palestine.[11]

The Arabs were no less suspicious of the proposal. Jamal Husseini of the Arab Higher Committee told Warren Austin of the US UN delegation that 'the Arabs had grown to distrust the words mandate and trusteeship' and were determined not to continue to be pawns of the 'vicissitudes of British policy'. He thought that a 'temporary' trustee-ship of 'indefinite' duration was a contradiction in terms and would merely give the Zionists time to strengthen their position. In addition, he was opposed to the introduction of additional foreign troops in the area, as he believed they were likely to be pro-Zionist.[12] Other Arab states were ready to discuss the proposals if they were not a cloak for partition.[13]

The Security Council failed to reach a consensus on the trusteeship proposal. The proposal and the plan were then buried in committee in the UN General Assembly and were never voted on.[14] The US had also failed to reach agreement with the other Western powers — France and Great Britain — on its secret proposals jointly to enforce trusteeship; by military force, if necessary.[15]

By mid-April, therefore, the US State Department was considering the possibility of separating the truce proposals from the trusteeship plan. On 8 April Dean Rusk of the US UN delegation informally cir-culated a 14-point truce proposal to representatives of the Jewish Agency and the Arab League in New York. The draft read:[16]

The Arab Higher Committee and the Jewish Agency for Palestine accept the following articles of truce for Palestine effective April 30 – 1 May 1948, and accept responsibility for insuring compliance by the Arab and Jewish communities therewith:

Article 1: All military or para-military activities, not authorized by the Security Council Truce Commission, as well as acts of violence, terrorism and sabotage, shall cease immediately.

Article 2: Armed bands and fighting personnel, groups and individuals, whatever their origin, shall not be brought into Palestine nor assisted or encouraged to enter Palestine during the period of truce.

Article 3: Weapons and war materials shall not be imported into Palestine by the Arab Higher Committee or by the Jewish Agency for Palestine, nor shall any assistance or encouragement be given to the importation or acquisition of such weapons or war materials.

Article 4: All Jewish and Arab armed elements in Palestine shall be immobilized and their activities during the truce under the supervision of the Security Council Truce Commission.

Article 5: Any person or group of persons found by the Security Council Truce Commission, after proper investigation, to have committed acts of violence, terrorism, or sabotage contrary to the terms of this truce, shall be immediately expelled from Palestine or placed in custody under arrangement to be made by the Security Council Truce Commission.

Article 6: During the truce, and without prejudice to the future governmental structure of Palestine, existing Arab and Jewish authorities shall accord full and equal rights to all inhabitants of the area in which such authorities are functioning; further, no steps shall be taken by Arab or Jewish authorities to proclaim a sovereign state during this truce.

Article 7: The Arab Higher Committee and the Jewish Agency for Palestine accept the Security Council Truce Commission as a mediator to maintain by mutual collaboration public order and essential services and to adjust administrative problems.

Article 8: All persons, groups, and organizations in Palestine pledge their maximum effort to preserve the holy places and to protect all activities connected therewith.

Article 9: All traffic and communications throughout Palestine of the nature declared by the Security Council Commission to be peaceful and non-prejudicial in character shall be allowed complete freedom of movement and operation by all parties in Palestine.

Article 10: During the period of the truce, 4,000 Jewish displaced persons shall be allowed to enter Palestine each month. The selection and administration of such immigration shall be assumed jointly by the International Refugee Organization and the Jewish Agency for Palestine, in consultation with the Security Council Truce Commission and the Arab Higher Committee. The Security Council Truce Commission and the Arab Higher Committee shall determine, in consultation with the Jewish Agency for Palestine, the quotas and selection of all non-Jewish immigrants.

Article 11: The Security Council Truce Commission shall institute or arrange patrols both by land and sea to ensure that immigration into Palestine does not exceed the agreed number and conforms with the selection requirements set forth in Article 10, above.

Article 12: The Arab Higher Committee and the Jewish Agency for Palestine undertake to assist the United Nations in the establishment of a temporary international zone, as a matter of emergency, for the protection of the city of Jerusalem.

Article 13: The Arab Higher Committee and the Jewish Agency for Palestine undertake to participate in the establishment of a Palestine truce council, composed of three representatives of each, to effect the joint action necessary for the execution of this truce and to assist the Security Council Truce Commission in the carrying out of its functions.

Article 14: This truce shall remain effective for three months, and thereafter unless either the Arab Higher Committee or the Jewish Agency for Palestine gives at least 30 days notice of termination to the Security Council Truce Commission. The Security Council Truce Commission shall immediately notify the Security Council of the receipt by it of any such notice of termination.

Rusk added that the proposals in this draft 'except for Article 10 dealing with immigration have been provisionally agreed upon, subject to approval by their principals, by representatives of the Jewish Agency and the Arab League in New York'.

At this point Rusk still appeared to be thinking of this proposal as preliminary to trusteeship, and cabled Lovett:

> If truce can be agreed along lines these articles, result may have substantial bearing upon our trusteeship proposals. Both JA and AHC dislike trusteeship and may prefer some *ad hoc* arrangement of a more flexible nature. US delegation's position thus far has been sufficiently flexible to permit adjustment to any alternative preferred by Arabs and Jews.

Rusk also mentioned that at this point the main pressure was being exerted by the Jewish side:

> Proskauer [head of American Jewish Committee] was most helpful with Shertok . . . unfortunately short time limit [of truce] in draft was attempt meet Jewish objections . . . Proskauer drafted Articles 6 and 7. My estimate is that once Arabs can confess their willingness to accept immigration, final agreement will then turn on the wording of article 6 [provisional authorities].[17]

This prediction proved accurate; immigration was the sensitive point in the truce proposals from the Arab standpoint, while the question of sovereignty in civil administration was crucial to the Jewish side. Two days later, on 29 April, Rusk took special cognisance of the immigration issue when he submitted a revised set of draft truce articles.

> Prospects for a truce now turn on dealing with the question of immigration on which there is a very wide gap between the parties . . . There is little hope that we can get formal agreement in advance on immigration, but some chance that we could get acquiescence in an arrangement 'imposed' from the outside that would keep their respective records clear . . .[18]

Rusk's revised truce terms eliminated Article 4 of the first draft, which placed Jewish and Arab forces under UN command, and also Article 9 (freedom of movement). The crucial revision, however, was in the provision regarding immigration. The new draft article read:

> Article 8: During the period of the truce, the AHC and JA for Palestine accept, as a matter of emergency, the authority of the SC Truce Commission to adjust administrative problems such as

the repatriation of Arabs and Jews displaced from their homes in Palestine, immigration, the applicability of existing laws, and similar questions.[19]

Meanwhile, Secretary of State Marshall had given an off-the-record press briefing during which he stated that agreement had been reached on the proposed truce on 13 of the 14 articles with representatives of both sides (all except immigration). This immediately drew a reply from Sharett in a letter (29 April 1948) to Marshall:

> I hasten to clear up a serious misunderstanding which seems to have arisen. I understand that you are reported to have said that an agreement for truce has virtually been reached between the Jewish Agency and the Arab League, the outstanding point on which a reply from the Arab League is yet due, being that of immigration.
> I regret to say that this is not the case . . . The main objections to the draft as I saw them are: First, the proposed truce entails the deferment of statehood and renders its attainment in the future most uncertain, thereby gravely prejudicing our rights and position; second, that an effective operation of the truce obviously involves the presence and use in Palestine of force, we cannot but assume that the intention is to keep the British forces in occupation and control of Palestine.
> I was also greatly concerned about the gross inequality under which we would be placed as regards arms and military training: the Arab states would be entirely free to acquire arms and stock-pile them for eventual use in Palestine against us; Palestine and other Arabs would be free to train in neighboring Arab countries; we would be precluded from either acquiring arms abroad or from any large-scale training; training which we could only organize in Palestine.[20]

Meanwhile, American representatives had been meeting with Arab leaders to assess their reactions to the truce proposal. Rusk reported that in meeting with the Egyptian and Saudi Arabian delegates to the UN, he had 'the distinct impression that it will be most difficult to gain Arab acquiescence to anything like the rate of 4,000 a month during period of truce'.[21]

At the same time the US Secretary (Ireland) in Damascus had been urging Azzam Pasha, secretary of the Arab League, to accept the truce. Azzam was reported to have replied that:

1. He must reject any mention of immigration in truce terms.

2. Purpose truce was maintenance status quo until definite solution could be made. Immigration could not be accepted as it means alteration of status quo.

3. Arabs would not agree to right of Jews to immigration. Would however, accept exisiting conditions whereby 1,500 Jews per month were permitted [to immigrate].

4. [But] subject to provision that such immigration during truce would represent cross section displaced persons and not merely fighting men.[22]

Other reports also indicated that Arab acceptance of truce terms depended on 'immigration of fighting personnel both by land and sea to stop'[23] and 'entry Jewish reinforcements, arms and ammunition stopped and provided Arab sections seized by Jews were handed back'.[24] Ambiguity, therefore, had to remain built into the truce proposals on immigration and Rusk's compromise formula was retained in the final draft.

Harold Beeley of the British Foreign Office had meanwhile told the State Department that the British Government 'would probably permit the Jews in Cyprus to leave for Palestine' and would take no responsibility to prevent the entry of illegal immigrants into Palestine after the expiry of the Mandate except as the normal responsibilities of all members of the UN. This secret conversation was also the final death knell for trusteeship, which Beeley declared was 'too late to obtain without prejudicing the rights, claims, and positions of the Jews and Arabs because, in his opinion, the Jewish community in Palestine would not consent to such a trusteeship, and neither the United States nor any other Western power would be willing to fight the Jewish community in Palestine to impose a trusteeship by force.'[25]

Secretary of State Marshall's letter of transmittal of the final version of the truce proposal contained the following qualifications:

Crucial articles are 5 and 11. Latest text Article 5 was intended to give somewhat greater recognition to existing Jewish regime by reference to 'temporary truce regime' without going so far as 'provisional government'. Shertok apparently thought 'Temporary Truce Regime' weakened the article, hence those words could be dropped.

Article 11 merely states that the Truce Commission would deal with question of immigration during period of truce. Actually we have in mind that SC Truce Commission would be concerned with existing quota of 1500 monthly, but all parties would be aware that British are determined to empty their Cyprus camps into Palestine during truce. Article 11 would thus permit Arabs to take status quo in theory but acquiesce in fact to substantial Jewish immigration during truce, Jews on other hand would get 4,000-6,000 per month into Palestine during truce, a figure on which they would never hope to get Arab agreement.[26]

The final version (Third Provision Draft) of the truce proposal reflected the reduced supervisory role that the UN Security Council Truce Commission would play as compared to that provided in earlier drafts. No mention was made of an SC force, nor specific instructions for it to enforce provisions on matters such as immigration. Azzam Pasha's assertion that 'UN guarantees were worthless', was not answered.[27]

Marshall met with Sharett on the eve of his departure to Palestine on 8 May to urge him to accept the American truce proposals. The American Secretary of State warned the Jews that they could expect no assistance from the US if they were defeated militarily as a result of rejecting the truce. He also suggested that the UN Security Council would, in any event, force a cease-fire in order to prevent a threat to peace, if no agreement was reached. Sharett replied that the 'basic and crucial question was what does the US government want? . . . Does it really fundamentally want the establishment of a Jewish state? . . . It is demanded of us that we delay independence with our very own hands . . . the dominant government shall not be in our hands but again in the hands of strangers who would be obligated to give honourable privileges. Furthermore, all the existing laws will remain in force. All the preparations that we made for transfer of rule to our hands would be eliminated . . . How can we agree to all this?' Marshall replied: 'If you are right and establish a Jewish state, I will be happy. However, you are taking a very grave responsibility.'[28]

Marshall cabled Bevin his view of the reason for the hardening of the Jewish position: 'Shertok, in reporting conversation with Creech-Jones, gave the definite impression (which was apparently strongly influencing Jewish Agency attitude) that Abdullah would move his Arab legion into Palestine but occupy only the Arab section . . . as a result of this conversation, there was a very limited possibility of Jewish Agency accepting truce. Objections to truce expressed by Shertok today took a substantially different line from that taken by him in negotiations of past three weeks.'[29]

Strong American pressure did not seem to affect either Jewish or Arab attitudes. At the end of April, the Americans had attempted to persuade the Arabs to accept the trusteeship and truce proposals by threatening to withdraw all economic assistance to the Middle East until the Palestine problem was settled. Azzam Pasha of the Arab League had replied that this was 'childish' and would force him to turn to the Russians for assistance.[30] This reply was effective and the threat of economic reprisals was dropped; the US was now tacitly relying on Britain to influence the Arabs while the US handled the Jews. The US made indirect threats to members of the Jewish Agency: no money would be allowed to be sent from the US to Israel and all goods would be embargoed if a war broke out. At a meeting with Rusk on 29 April, Goldmann was instrumental in persuading Rusk to separate the truce proposals from the trusteeship plan.

Goldmann apparently supports truce along lines we have indicated and is most anxious for some special arrangement for Jerusalem. He is opposed to trusteeship and believes that truce and trusteeship must be dealt with separately . . . From things he said, together with similar information from other sources, it is clear that Silver leads the intransigent school and is primarily responsible for our difficulties on a truce. Goldmann concluded by saying that at the right moment the US should crack the whip and insist upon a settlement, using its powerful position with regard to both parties to force them to take a reasonable truce.[31]

In a conversation between Dr Goldmann and Robert Lovett, Under-Secretary of the State Department, the problem of truce was discussed from the point of view of Russian support for Israel:

Goldmann: If there is no agreement on truce and the Jewish state will be proclaimed on the 16th of May, the Soviet Union may immediately recognize it — the USA won't — then the position of the Jewish State will be exactly the same with regard to the Soviet Union as the position of Transjordan is towards England. The USA has not recognized Transjordan. The UN has not admitted them. Only England and the Arab States recognize them, and still, based on this recognition, England has signed a treaty of alliance with Transjordan, giving them money, personnel, weapons, etc. Don't you realize the danger in case the Jewish State abandoned by you and Great Britain, will in desperation turn to the Soviet Union for help?

The Soviets would have exactly the same legal right to come to Palestine as the British have in being in Transjordan.

Well [he (Lovett) said in great excitment] if the Jewish people want to commit suicide nobody can prevent them from doing so. Do you really think that we didn't contemplate such a possibility? You have no high opinion of our diplomacy, but don't believe for a moment that we will sit quietly and see the Russians coming into Palestine, directly or indirectly — legally or illegally. There are certain measures we can take, although it is not this department, but another one which will have to do it. [meaning War Department] . . . Still, I said, even if you will still take measures against a Jewish-Russian alliance, it is not in your interest to create a legal basis for the Soviets to come in.

Well, that is why [he said] we insist on a truce and will do everything to obtain it.[32]

The American fears of Russian gains from a Middle East war were outlined in a memorandum from Dean Rusk to Robert Lovett on 4 May:

The refusal of the Jewish Agency last night to agree to our proposal for on-the-spot truce negotiations in Palestine reveals the intentions of the Jews to go steadily ahead with a Jewish separate state by force of arms . . . it seems clear that in light of Jewish military superiority which now obtains in Palestine, the Jewish Agency would prefer to round out its State after May 15 and rely on its armed strength to defend that state from Arab counter-attack . . .

There will be a decided effort, given this eventuality, that the United States will be called upon by elements inside this country to support Security Council action against the Arabs. To take such action would seem to me to be morally indefensible while, from the aspect of our relations with the Middle East and the broad security aspects in that region, it would be almost fatal to pit forces of the United States and possibly Russia against the governments of the Arab world.[33]

The Israeli Rejection of the Truce

The British believed that since the beginning of May 'the Jews were [now] in a more intransigent position than the Arabs' in regard to the truce[1] and that 'US is only power that can bring effective pressure to bear upon the Jews'.[2]

There was a manifest split within the Jewish Agency, with strong opinion, particularly in Israel, centring around Ben-Gurion, against the truce proposals. Dr Leo Kohn of the Jewish Agency in Jerusalem said that they did 'not find in the draft agreement even a basis for discussion since it does not provide for the establishment of a Jewish state'.[3] Nevertheless, Sharett, in his formal reply to the truce proposal on 4 May, was careful not to reject an 'unconditional agreement for an immediate cease-fire' which 'we are ready forthwith to agree to', while rejecting the suggestion of a special mission to fly to Palestine.[4]

Two days later the American UN delegation met Sharett and Silver. This delegation found 'willingness for the first time to forego proclamation of Jewish state May 15, and their statement — accepting an immediate unconditional cease-fire for an indefinite period, despite in both cases impractical conditions attached'. Even Silver stated that 'if they could establish provisional government they could forego establishment sovereign state provided there was a guarantee that at the end of truce period they could go ahead and establish their state'. The chief worries were cited as (1) sovereignty and (2) impairment relative military position.[5]

Thus, Jewish objections were motivated by the fear that during a truce the Americans would abandon their support for partition and statehood as well as by the fear of impairing the military position as a guarantee for better boundaries for partition. These considerations also appear to be crucial in the provisional cabinet debate. The first fear, related to the original American trusteeship proposal, had no basis in the American intent. In the conversation with Goldmann the Under-Secretary of State, Robert Lovett, assured Goldmann that 'they still want partition, even if it will come a little later . . . And the truce we think of', he said, 'leads to partition de facto, and a little later de jure.'[6]

The Americans reiterated their position to Arab statesmen — that they ultimately favoured partition. In conversation with the Egyptian representative, Fawzi Bey, and Prince Faisal of Saudi Arabia, the American diplomat (Ambassador to the UN Austin) stated, 'I would not be frank if I did not say that the President considers partition a fair and equitable solution for Palestine.'[7]

Despite American assurances, the National Administration, which met on 12 May 1948, voted six to four to reject the truce proposal. The decisive vote was that of Moshe Sharett, who had brought the proposal back with him from the United States after meeting Secretary of State Marshall. Sharett had favoured the truce while in the US but

at Ben-Gurion's urging changed his mind. The minutes of this debate
have not yet been declassified. However, what transpired can be recon-
structed from a number of leaks and the carefully-censored account
by Zeev Sharef, secretary of the Cabinet. Dr Goldmann in New York
pressed for acceptance of the American proposal, but the decision had
to be taken by the National Administration (provisional Cabinet).

The four ministers who voted against the immediate proclamation
of the State and for acceptance of the truce proposal were Eliezer
Kaplan and David Remez of Mapai, Pinhas Rozen (Rosenbluth) of
the Progressive Party, and Moshe Shapiro of the Religious Party. The
six for rejection of the truce were: Ben-Gurion and Sharett of Mapai,
Behor Shitrit of the Sephardi List (later Mapai), Aharon Zisling and
Mordechai Bentov of Mapam, and Peretz Bernstein of the General
Zionists. Thus even Mapai was split 3-2 with the deciding vote being
Sharett's.

The reason the four ministers voted in favour of the truce proposal
is not surprising. The Chief of Staff of the Israeli Defence Forces, called
in for his opinion, reported that from the purely military point of view
the truce might be advisable. They were also concerned mainly with the
risk that the nascent state would jeopardise American aid and political
support.

Political considerations were decisive also for those who rejected the
truce proposal. At the meeting Ben-Gurion read the list of arms the
Yishuv had accumulated abroad and assured the ministers that if these
weapons could be received they need have no doubt about ultimate
victory. The real fear was that a truce would pave the way for the
Americans to retreat from the support for a Jewish state, as they had
in March 1948. At the same time there was the threat of a deep psychological crisis within the Jewish community eagerly awaiting the historic
moment. There was also the danger of a revolt by the extremists who
warned they would proclaim a state unilaterally in defiance of the
authority of the national institutions. (Katz of the Irgun had told
Rabbi Silver late in April that the Irgun maintained its separate
organisation in order to prevent a 'postponement' of statehood.[8])

The fear of an American sell-out also comes across in Sharett's
account of his last minute talk with Marshall on 8 May, when he asked:
'The real question is: What does the US Government want? Does it
really fundamentally want the establishment of a Jewish state?'[9] But
on close scrutiny these fears had little justification, regardless of
American intentions (which we have seen were at that stage recover-
ing already from trusteeship towards partition). In March 1948, the

American proposal for trusteeship could have affected the shape of a settlement in Palestine, as at that time the Jewish forces did not effectively control the Jewish areas. However in May 1948, US plans could not change the new realities established in Palestine and cancel or dissolve Jewish authority and effective control of the *de facto* existing state. This was evidenced by the inability of UN efforts (through the Palestine Commission, the Consular Truce Commission, etc.) to control the situation. Only a military intervention by the United Nations or the United States – both unlikely in the extreme – could have reversed the situation. The truce proposal recognised the existing *de facto* political and military situation, including a functioning Jewish Provisional Cabinet (National Administration).

The reconstruction of the actual debate in the Provisional Cabinet shows the difference in the assessment of the situation. Sharett introduced a compromise resolution calling for a proclamation of a provisional government instead of statehood. He argued that this was in keeping with the letter and spirit of the UN resolution on partition, which had established a progressive schedule: provisional governments should be established on 1 April, the complete British withdrawal was to be completed by 1 August, and independent states were to be proclaimed on 1 October. Since the British had refused to co-operate in the establishment of a provisional government and had moved up their date of departure, the time table ceased to be applicable. But adherence to the UN procedure on the part of the Jews would allow a Jewish state to come into existence *de facto* and would prevent the charge that Jewish independence had been proclaimed unilaterally.[10] Ben-Gurion presented reasons for an immediate declaration of independence. He brushed aside Sharett's proposal with the argument that the impending British withdrawal would leave a vacuum which must be filled, and that the imminent invasion by Arab armies called for immediate decision.

In fact, he stated that the Arab invasion had already begun with the attack of the Arab legion on the Etzion block of Jewish settlements situated near Jerusalem. Since this bloc was not to be a part of the proposed Jewish state, Ben-Gurion was thus disregarding the question of the Army Chief of State as to whether the Israeli forces should fight the Legion when it crosses the Jordan into Palestine, or only when it crosses the boundaries of the Jewish state, as designated by the UN.[11]

Ben-Gurion's major argument was that a truce would *reduce* the chances of a *military victory* over the Arabs. The proclamation of the state would allow the full mobilisation of the manpower and resources of the Yishuv in Palestine and the immediate transfer of the large military stores and experienced personnel abroad. A truce agreement which prohibited the importation of arms or men (probably enforced by a naval blockade by the Great Powers on behalf of the UN) would cripple the vital Jewish external aid, while nothing could prevent the Arab states from purchasing arms and supplying them to the Palestinians across their contiguous frontiers.[12] This argument, which proved convincing at the time, was disproved less than a month later when a similar UN cease-fire was accepted with the same conditions, and did not prevent the large-scale reinforcement of Jewish forces from abroad — to such an extent as to alter permanently the military balance of power *vis-a-vis* the Arab armies.

It appears that it was precisely the deep conviction of victory which motivated the majority to reject the truce proposal. Ben-Gurion possessed an accurate knowledge of the relative strength of the military forces and had no doubts about ultimate victory.

Ben-Gurion was afraid only of the psychological effect of setbacks in the first stage of the war — when the Israeli forces would still lack artillery, armour and aircraft — but believed that this stage would not last more than one to two weeks.[13] He also feared risk of a political set-back — the loss of American support for Israeli statehood — in view of their persistent tendency to fall back on the trusteeship proposals. In this, Ben-Gurion was strongly supported by the two representatives of Mapam, Zisling and Bentov. Paradoxically, it was Mapam, which had been most opposed to partition and in favour of a bi-national state, and had even proposed an international trusteeship over all Palestine in 1946, which now supported Ben-Gurion in his fears of trusteeship as the greatest danger. This was due to two factors: first, the national mood of elation and enthusiasm for statehood in the Yishuv after the UN resolution in November 1947, and secondly, the exuberance caused by the fact that the Soviet Union and its allies were supporting partition. Mapam, a militant left-wing party at that time, was deeply influenced by the Soviet victory over Nazi Germany and by Soviet support for a Jewish state and viewed with distrust British and American policies in the Middle East.

The Military Balance of Forces on 12 May 1948

In view of the 'David and Goliath' legend surrounding the birth of Israel, it may seem surprising to assert that the Cabinet decision was based on the conviction of Israeli military superiority. Even at that time, Jews and non-Jews believed that one community of 600,000 with local defence confronted five regular armies of the Arab states. This image was to a large extent deceptive. The Arab regular armies were not combat-trained and prepared for real warfare. As they were intended to symbolise independence and to preserve internal security, they lacked the experience of Jewish soldiers, battle-hardened in Allied armies, in partisan activity and in the many civil wars in Palestine. The Arab armies were ill-equipped for long lines of communication and prolonged warfare (especially the Egyptians and Iraqis). Most importantly, they lacked a unified command structure or a co-ordinated plan of operations, because of their mutual distrust. While the Jewish forces were inferior in big weapons, they had formidable quantities of heavy weapons and ammunition acquired and stored in Europe, especially in Czechoslovakia. Even from the point of view of numbers, the Jewish defence forces exceeded those of the Arab invading armies.[14] Those factors allowed the Israeli high command to use its interior lines of communication for concentrating at every decisive point against the unco-ordinated Arab forces. After the first truce (June 1948), when massive arms shipments reached Israel, she had the military advantage. Above all, the psychological aspect played a decisive role. For most of the Arabs it was a political war, instigated by autocratic rulers to serve their interests. For the Jews it was a war for survival, a matter of life and death – the only chance to secure their future as an independent nation. The military balance could not be understood by the public at large, but was known to the members of the Israeli Cabinet when it considered its crucial decision. There is also evidence that responsible observers on all sides – British, American and Arab – believed that the Arab states would be militarily defeated in a conflict with the Jewish state.

British and American experts had no illusions about the relationship of forces and outcome of the war. On 8 May 1948 Austin reported to the Secretary of State, Marshall, that the British are pessimistic about the possibility of guiding events through peaceful channels and take for granted Abdullah's invasion and effective partition of Palestine. Their hypothesis was that intervention of Arab states, aside from Transjordan, would be of negligible importance.[15] On 13 May 1948 the Secretary of State, Marshall, in a circular letter to US diplomatic offices, described the situation in the Middle East:

> Internal weaknesses in various Arab countries make it difficult for them to act. The whole government structure in Iraq is endangered by political and economic disorders and the Iraqi government cannot,

at this moment, afford to send more than a handful of troops it has already despatched. Egypt has suffered recently from strikes and disorders. Its army has insufficient equipment because of its refusal of British aid, and what it has, is needed for police duty at home. Syria has neither arms nor army worthy of name and has not been able to organize one since the French left three years ago. Lebanon has no real army while Saudi Arabia has a small army which is barely sufficient to keep tribes in order. Jealousies between Saudi Arabs and Syrians on one hand, and Hashemite Governments of Transjordan and Iraq, prevent Arabs from making best use of existing forces.[16]

The Palestinian leader — Musa Alami — reportedly felt even in February, after a tour of Arab capitals, that the Palestinian cause was lost inasmuch as the Arab states were not preparing for war or giving any real aid to the Palestinian cause.[17] American diplomatic reports indicate that both Syria and Egypt 'feared defeat' in May 1948.[18]

The British adviser on Palestine, Harold Beeley, stated in a conversation with American experts: 'It was his opinion that for some time at least the Jews, strengthened by recruits entering by sea, could withstand and possibly defeat the poorly organized and badly equipped Arab armies.'[19] The Americans cautioned Israel 'not to be too sure of their military advisers', but their private assessment was also that the Jews would be victorious.[20] At the outbreak of the war the Israeli forces, numbering 30,000 men, had experience and enthusiasm but lacked equipment. Over one-third of the soldiers were without rifles. The Israeli forces had very little long-range armament, neither cannon nor mortars, few anti-tank weapons, and only light aircraft. However, there were massive stores of modern weapons, including tanks, aircraft, artillery and small arms, that had been purchased abroad and were awaiting transfer to Palestine. The two Israeli arms purchasers had acquired 30,000 rifles, 5,000 machine guns, 200 heavy machine guns, 30 fighter aircraft, several B-12 Flying Fortresses, 50 65mm cannon, 35 anti-aircraft guns, and 12 heavy mortars, all with large stores of ammunition.[21] In addition, trained men from Eastern Europe and from the displaced persons camps were awaiting transfer to Israel. The Czechs even trained an entire brigade force composed of Jewish displaced persons (DPs) and others.[22]

The best fighting force in the Arab world was the Arab Legion of Transjordan. But in May 1948, it consisted of 6,000 men, of whom only 4,500 were available for combat. The Legion consisted of two brigades, each having two semi-mechanised regiments. Each regiment had one squadron of twelve armed cars, three motorised rifle squadrons, and one headquarters squadron. The Legion's arms included 6-pound anti-tank guns, 25-pounder field guns, and 3-inch mortars. Disciplined and trained by British officers, the Legion inspired respect in its opponents. However, the Legion was dependent on the British for its operational efficiency. Its commander was a British officer, John Glubb (Glubb Pasha), and 45 of its 50 officers were British. The British covered all expenses of the Legion and it was dependent on them for resupply of ammunition.[23] In addition, the staff of the legion had made agreements with both the British and the Jews in regard to its operational plans. On behalf of Glubb Pasha, Colonel Goldie had met with Shlomo Shamir of the Haganah to promise the Legion's co-operation in the peaceful partition of the country between them, and that the Legion would occupy only the Arab areas. They would even delay their advance across the boundaries for several days in order for the Haganah to arrange things on their side.[24] This promise related to an earlier agreement between Abdullah and the British. The latter agreed to acquiesce in the annexation of Arab Palestine by Transjordan so long as 'they keep out of the Jewish areas'.[25] The British threatened to withdraw their officers if the Arab Legion became involved in a fight.[26]

While the Jordanian forces were strengthened militarily but hampered operationally by their connections with Great Britain, the second most important military force — that of Egypt — had the reverse problem. Egypt's Prime Minister, Nuqrashi Pasha, was afraid that the British, who held the Suez Canal, could cut off his forces attacking Palestine from their lines of communication. Egypt was pressing for a revision of the Anglo-Egyptian treaty of 1936 and for the evacuation of the Suez Canal by the British. Nationalist elements agitated for an armed struggle against British troops. In addition, there was the question whether the Egyptian army was ready for a campaign. This question was raised by the former Prime Minister, Sidki Pasha, when the motion to go to war was being debated in the Egyptian Parliament on 11 May.[27]

Of 40,000 men, the Egyptians had concentrated 15,000 in two brigades in El Arish in the Sinai. Their state of preparation is shown by the fact that just a few weeks before, they had to obtain road maps of Palestine to know where they were going. The deputy commander of the force, Mohammed Naguib, warned that only four battalions of the two brigades were ready and that they were courting disaster.[28] Nevertheless, the 4,000-5,000 men of the main Egyptian force, supported by aircraft and tanks, was a substantial force. (The second Egyptian brigade, mainly made up of volunteers of the Moslem Brotherhood – an extreme nationalist group – moved into purely Arab held areas to contest Abdullah's control of the West Bank.[29])

The other Arab armies – of Iraq, Syria and Lebanon – were in varying states of preparedness as well, and were much smaller than the Egyptian forces. The Syrians would commit 3,000-4,000 men, half their army, to the Galilee, with tanks and artillery. Iraq offered a mechanised brigade of 3,000 men for the North, and Lebanon had smaller detachments.[30] However, none of the Arab states except Transjordan had made serious preparations for the war. Egypt had voted its appropriation for the war only on 11 May, and Syria likewise voted £6 million for 5,000 additional recruits only at that time. The Arabs had no stockpiles of arms and ammunition. Of the war chest of £4 million voted by the Arab League, only 10 per cent had been collected.[31] But the most serious weakness of the Arab side was the lack of a unified command structure. Nominally it had been agreed that King Abdullah of Transjordan would be the overall commander of the Arab forces; however, as his compatriot states mistrusted him they refused to place their troops under his operational control. The Iraqi appointed to lead all the troops, Safwat Pasha, resigned on 13 May, stating that he was 'firmly convinced that absence of agreement on a precise plan can only lead to disaster'.[32]

The main cause of the confusion in Arab plans was that both Abdullah and the Egyptians, subordinating military to political considerations, did not intend to adhere to the strategy agreed upon in the Arab League plans drawn up in April for the invasion. These called for the Egyptian army to advance up the coast to Tel Aviv, while the Syrians and Lebanese armies would move south towards Nazareth, to join with Arab Legion and the Iraqi army arriving from the east towards Afulah. Thus the whole of East Galilee, Tiberias, Safed, Nazareth, Afulah would be cut off from the sea and the Jewish state considerably reduced to a narrow strip in the coastal area. In the second stage of the war the Arab armies would cut the Jewish state in half by attacking across the 'narrow waist' north of Tel Aviv (see Figure 8.1) and seizing seaports to prevent reinforcements from reaching the Jews. Instead of a joint command, each army was to send a liaison officer to Arab League military headquarters near Amman. The Egyptian liaison officer arrived at HQ on 12 May and said that he did not know what his army's movements would be. The Iraqis, who were supposed to spearhead the north, only reluctantly committed their forces, consisting of 2,000 men

Figure 8.1: The Plan for Arab Invasion of Palestine 1948 (the Damascus Plan) Compared with Actual Campaign

PLAN

IMPLEMENTATION

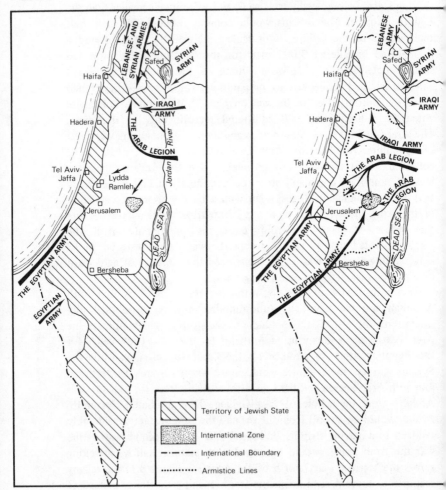

Territory of Jewish State

International Zone

International Boundary

Armistice Lines

commanded by a man described by the British resident as 'an incompetent incapable of commanding a squad of infantry'.[33] (The Iraqi forces were, in fact, inactive during much of the war.) The main changes in the plan were made by the Egyptians and Jordanians. The Arab Legion was determined to secure its position on the West Bank, and not to advance to the sea near Tel Aviv but commit its main forces to Jerusalem. Likewise, the Egyptians divided their forces rather than advance on Tel Aviv, and sent one part towards Jerusalem to deny control to Abdullah. Glubb later said he had never been shown the Arab invasion plan.[34]

Dr Meir Pa'il's version of the Arab plan of campaign differs considerably from that of J. and D. Kimche, Collins-Lapierre[35] and many others who claimed that the Arab objective was much more ambitious: to reach, with a pincer-movement, the port of Haifa and the coast north of Tel-Aviv (in the 'narrow waist', near Nathanya) thus cutting the Jewish state into two and depriving it of its major seaport. Pa'il's version seems more plausible and reliable: it is based on Arab military documentation and conforms with the Arab military experts' more realistic appraisal of the relationship of forces. The limited objective of the 'Damascus Plan' was perfectly attainable with the existing Arab forces, which were to move in purely Arab areas in the Galilee and the West Bank; it was also in the long run more dangerous to Israel because it would have deprived it of essential areas of colonisation (the whole of Galilee, the Jordan Valley and the Eastern part of the Izreel Valley) and would have created for the Arabs a solid base for further operations. The conquest of Haifa and cutting the state into two was possible only through mortal combat in Jewish areas, with superior Israeli forces; the Arabs simply did not possess enough men and arms to stage such a dangerous operation. The Arab Legion, 4,500 men strong, was too small to undertake and carry out this task, apart from the fact that Abdullah's political objective was to annex the West Bank *in the wake of* partition, rather than prevent partition. This explains the last-minute change in the plan of invasion, ordered by Abdullah, and amounting, virtually, to a complete rejection of the 'Damascus Plan' and to a confusion with disastrous consequences for the Arab invading armies.

The military agreement between the Haganah and the Arab Legion had an important effect on the Israeli attitude to the truce, proposed by Secretary Marshall on 8 May. But there was another aspect of the situation which prompted Ben-Gurion to argue for the declaration of statehood. On 8 May, Emir Abdullah had requested a meeting with a member of the Jewish Agency and three days later met Golda Meir in Amman. At this meeting Abdullah seemed to repudiate the secret agreement to divide up Palestine with the Jewish Agency on the basis of the UN partition frontiers – though he still was ready to abide by his agreement not to attack the Jewish state.[36]

The apparent withdrawal of Abdullah from the secret agreement he made with Israel in November 1947, on the partition of Palestine, freed the Jewish state, which now had military superiority, from adherence to the frontiers fixed in the UN partition resolution. Ben-Gurion was eager to seize the chance to improve the borders of the new state, with his original frontiers secure from attack by the Arab Legion. Ben-Gurion was opposed to having the Israeli declaration of statehood delineate frontiers based on the UN partition plan boundaries, citing the American Declaration of Independence as precedent. This was accepted by five votes to four. Ben-Gurion argued:

> We don't know if the UN will insist on their resolution and whether this will be a factor in the situation. If the Arabs start a war and we defeat them, we shall take Western Galilee and both sides of the road to Jerusalem. If we have the power to do this, why should we commit ourselves in advance to frontiers?

Ben-Gurion rejected the draft declaration of statehood produced by Sharett which included (in Para. 10) a reference to the UN decision 'for partition with economic union'. He deleted all reference to partition, and changed it to read 'on the basis of the UN resolution creating a Jewish state in Palestine'. Also deleted from Sharett's draft (Para. 16) were the words 'we are ready to co-operate with the institutions of the UN and work for the establishment of an economic union'.

Even Dr Goldmann, the chief advocate of the truce proposal and the postponement of statehood, shared the leadership's view of the importance of an agreement with Abdullah as the best way to peace. Goldmann conferred with the British in London on 13 May. His views were reported as follows:

> G. remarked that recent British behaviour are all in favour in Jewish state . . .
> G. said everything depends on where Abdullah stops, and this poses delicate problems for JA. Abdullah has completely eclipsed Mufti and AHC 'which is all to the good'. Moreover, 'our relations with Abdullah are excellent and he would make the best possible

neighbour for us' . . . If Abdullah stops at Jewish frontier Jews should immediately begin negotiations with him for a truce. Any truce signed between Jews and Abdullah, G. said, will be more valuable than one between Jews and AHC.

G. said he and Shertok are agreed that it would not only be foolish but illegal under old resolution for Jews to declare state May 15. Better plan would be to announce provisional government for internal affairs Jewish Palestine and wait until October to ask UNGA for recognition as sovereign state. Among advantages of course would be that Soviet bloc could not recognize Jewish state 'thus damning us before world' . . .

Asked why Jews were being so intransigent re truce, G. explained at length technical points truce proposals making it difficult for Jews to agree. He made it clear, however, that since Abdullah is still uncertain factor at same time best Jewish hope on Arab side, technical objection of Jews might alter with circumstances especially if truce is negotiated directly with Abdullah and not AHC . . .[37]

Yet, it was precisely the agreement with Abdullah that prevented the success of the truce proposals. Abdullah needed a war to legitimise his territorial ambitions and the Arab states could not accept unilateral action by Transjordan.

Arab Attitudes to the Truce

The Arab League and the Palestinians

In April 1948, the tension and excitement in the Arab states caused by the situation in Palestine had reached fever pitch. Since the creation of the Arab League in March 1945, the Arab states solemnly committed themselves to struggle for the independence of Palestine as an Arab state. A delegate of the Arab Higher Committee was nominated to represent the Palestinian people in the League's Council. In November 1945 the Arab League decided to demand the termination of the British Mandate and the recognition of the right of the population democratically to elect its government and legislative body based on proportional representation of Jews and Arabs.

A Conference of Arab heads of state in Inschass, 26-28 May 1946, issued a statement demanding immediate stoppage of immigration, prohibition of land transfers to Jews and proclamation of independence. The Conference decided also to 'defend the Arab character of Palestine' with every available means, to set up a propaganda machinery on behalf of the Palestinian cause and to recruit funds for the Palestinian Higher Committee. A special session of the League's Council in Bludan a few weeks later, 8-12 June 1946, decided to reorganise the Arab Higher Committee and to set up a permanent Palestine Commission in Cairo composed of representatives of all Arab states. The new Arab Higher Committee consisted of two members of the former Mufti-dominated, Higher Committee (Jamal Husseini and Emil Ghouri) and two members of the National Front (Ahmed Hilmi Pasha and Dr Tewfik al Khaldi) with the Mufti as its Chairman.[1] The Bludan Conference formulated a detailed programme for action: boycott of Zionist goods, the creation of a fund to counteract the sale of Arab land to Jews, the establishment of 'Palestine Defence Committees' all over the Middle East, and issued a warning that the Arab states would not be able to prevent their peoples from volunteering to the defence of their brethren in Palestine, threatened by the 'Zionist terrorist' organisations. The 'Palestine Defence Committees' launched a feverish campaign of propaganda and mobilisation of funds, arms and volunteers. The call for arms and volunteers was intensified when the London Round Table talks (end of 1946 and beginning of 1947) failed to find an agreed solution and Britain decided (in February 1947) to hand over the Palestine problem to the United Nations. The meeting of the Arab Foreign Ministers in Sofar (16-19 September 1947) which faced a rapidly deteriorating situation in Palestine reinforced the call for arms and volunteers but the British announcement (in September 1947) on the termination of the Mandate forced the Arab states to consider seriously the problem of military intervention in Palestine. The Council of the Arab League in Alya (7-9 October 1947) decided that in view of the British decision to withdraw its administration and armed forces from Palestine and of the threat presented by the Zionist terrorist forces, to the Arabs of Palestine, the Arab states were obliged to consider *military measures* along Palestine's frontiers. A Military Commission was set up, headed by the Iraqi General Ismail Safwat, to recommend these measures. It is interesting to note that the Mufti strongly opposed the decision on the Arab states' intervention fearing this would impair Palestine's right to determine its own future.[2] His fears proved to have been completely justified. The meeting of the Arab heads of state in Cairo, 8-17 December 1947, resolved to set up an army of volunteers under the command not of the Arab Higher Committee, but of the Arab League's Military Commission.

The number of volunteers was fixed at 3,000 men, of whom only 500 were Palestinians and the Military Commission was charged with

the organisation of their training in Qatana (Syria) as well as with the
procurement of 10,000 guns to be distributed to the volunteers and to
the Palestinians. Safwat (an Iraqi) was nominated as the Commander-
in-Chief of the 'Jeish al Inqad' (Deliverance Army). The setbacks
suffered by the Palestinians precipitated the growing involvement of
the Arab states in the Palestine war, and the decrease of the Palestinians' role and influence over the events. The League's Political
Committee decided (in Cairo, February 1948)[3] to transmit the command of military action in Palestine to a Committee of Arab Chiefs-
of-Staff and rejected the demands of the Mufti to co-opt a Palestinian
representative to the Committee, to establish without delay a Palestinian government-in-exile and to nominate Palestinians as military
governors in Palestine. Also his demand to provide a loan for a Palestinian Administration and for relief funds for the families of Palestinian
fighters was rejected on the grounds that an administration was premature and relief was a matter for the Palestinians themselves to deal
with. The Political Committee of the Arab League meeting in Cairo
(12 April 1948) decided on the intervention of the Arab armies in the
Palestine war, upon the termination of the British Mandate on 15 May,
and confirmed this decision at a special session in Damascus on 11-14
May, which nominated the Iraqi Brigadier Nur-al-Din Mahmoud as
Commander-in-Chief of all Arab forces in Palestine, including regular
armies and volunteers.

The total collapse of the Palestinian fighters and of the Army of
Deliverance, in May 1948, and the terrifying news of the massacre in
Deir Yassin, spread by thousands of refugees fleeing in panic from
Palestine, had an electrifying effect on the Arab masses, inflamed
by the bellicose posture of their governments but unaware of the discrepancy between the resounding resolution and the actual preparations
for intervention in the Palestine war.

The unanimous decisions and proclamations of the Arab League
to oppose, by force, the partition of Palestine and the creation of a
Jewish state were not an expression of the Arab states' readiness for a
co-ordinated political and military effort to defend the Palestinian
cause, but a screen set up to conceal diverging and contradictory
tendencies as regards the future of Palestine. Abdullah, supported by
the Hashemite rulers of Iraq and encouraged by the British, clearly
pursued the old vision of 'Greater Syria' for which the partition of
Palestine and an arrangement with the Jewish state was to serve as a
stepping-stone. An independent Palestinian state headed by his arch-
enemy Haj-Amin al Husseini was to Abdullah like a nightmare and he

was determined to prevent it at all cost.

In the deliberations of the Arab League, Transjordan and Iraq pressed for the most radical line and demanded direct military intervention of the regular armies, knowing that the major role in this case would be given and played by the Arab Legion, the best-equipped and trained of all the Arab armies. Syria, Egypt, Saudi Arabia and the Palestinians, each of them for reasons of their own, opposed this tendency, suspicious of Abdullah's designs, but disguised their opposition to the deployment of regular armies with extremist political declarations and proposals. The US representative at the UN (Jessup) wrote about Syrian extremism: 'The real reason for present Syrian extremism is not so much fear of Israel as fear of the expansion of Transjordan and increase in Abdullah's prestige in the light of his former Greater Syrian ideas. In other words a fear that a settlement based on arrangements between Israel and Abdullah would be only a stepping-stone for the latter, his next step being attempted expansion into Syria.'[4]

Ahmed Shuqairi, at that time member of the Palestinian delegation to the Arab League, reported in his memoirs that when the delegation met the President of Syria and asked him to allow Iraqi arms, promised to Palestinians, to pass through Syria: 'President Quwatli's face became very pale; he was enraged and said in anger: "you want to destroy Syria; Nuri [General Nuri Said, at the time a minister in the Iraqi government] does not want us to rest in peace . . . The Hashemites harbour evil [designs] toward Syria. Why do they not send them through Transjordan . . . Our situation in Syria is very precarious . . ." ' (In the event, Quwatli changed his mind and agreed to the transfer of arms saying 'God be with Syria'.)[5]

Egypt was suspicious of Abdullah's connection with the British and suspected his designs to be part of British policy, aiming to maintain its military hold over the Suez area by placing the south of Palestine and the Negeb under Abdullah's rule. Of all the members of the Arab League, Egypt was least interested in an armed intervention and tried to parry Iraqi and Transjordanian pressure by putting off as long as possible the resolution on military intervention and by disregarding most of the operative decisions. It did not send a representative to the Military Committee, formed by the Arab League in October 1947; of the 2,000 rifles it was supposed to place at the disposal of the Military Committee, it gave over only 800, the rest were handed over to the Mufti; it opposed the decision of the Arab League's Political Committee in Cairo, February 1948, to call a meeting of Arab Chiefs of Staff for

15 March, with the argument that such a meeting could not be held while the Security Council was discussing the proposal for trusteeship in Palestine.[6]

The Mufti, in his memoirs, reported that at the crucial meeting in Alya which decided on the deployment of Arab armies along the frontiers of Palestine, the Egyptian Prime Minister, Nuqrashi Pasha, declared: 'I want you all to know that Egypt, while agreeing to take part in this military demonstration, is not ready to go further than this.'[7] He explained to Shuqairi that Egypt could not fight because of its problems with Great Britain and that volunteers from the Moslem Brothers and Yemen were enough.[8] While stalling Iraq's and Transjordan's pressure for military intervention, Faruq was keeping an eye on Abdullah's contacts with Britain. Egypt was, at the time, engaged in an intense struggle for British evacuation of the Suez Canal. A powerful anti-British propaganda was sweeping the country. While the left-wing 'HADITU' (Democratic Movement for National Liberation) called to concentrate on the struggle against British colonialism,[9] the Moslem Brothers presented the support for the Palestinian cause as an integral and essential part of the fight against the British. The change of the Egyptian positions occurred when growing domestic troubles posed a threat to the government, and the failure of negotiations with Britain on evacuation forced the Egyptian Government to undertake drastic measures to break the deadlock.[10] 'Among the reasons that led to entry into war was the King's eagerness to establish for himself Arab leadership in rivalry with the ruling Hashemite family in Iraq and Transjordan. It was also said that King Abdullah and King Faruq raced with each other to see who would be the first to perform the Friday prayer in the Al-Aqsa mosque.'[11]

Against this background it was inevitable that most of the Arab League's resolutions, in particular those threatening cancellation of all US and British concessions in Arab countries, economic boycott of British and American goods and interests, would remain without implementation. 'The various [Arab] delegations left [Bludan] for their capitals leaving behind them a trail of resounding statements. But when Arab diplomats met the Ambassadors of Britain and the US in the comfort of their offices, they were apologetic and the conversation would end with the Arab diplomat saying: "You know how Arab public opinion feels and it was necessary to say something. Nevertheless we will remain friends." '[12]

The fate of the resolutions on military preparations was no better. The supply of volunteers and ammunition lagged behind the schedule.

No agreement could be reached on the nomination of the military command, and on the size of Arab forces necessary for the invasion. Military experts estimated the required Arab forces at five or six divisions with air support. The politicians said this was too much and that the military had over-estimated the Zionist strength.[13] Abdullah demanded to be nominated General Commander of the Palestine operation and threatened to withdraw from the war[14] when some Arab governments refused to hand over the command of Arab armies to him. At the last moment (29 April 1948) it was agreed that Abdullah should be appointed 'an honorary General Commander'. The fiercest opposition to the intervention of Arab armies came from the Mufti who, rightly, suspected that this would lead to the 'removal' of the Palestinians from the command of the operation in Palestine. He insisted on retaining the control over the funds for arms and volunteers in Palestine, and suspected the resolution on deployment of Arab armies to be instigated by the British.[15] 'In Damascus there was a fierce conflict between Haj Amin and the Military Committee over the control of the various regions in Palestine. It was only God's mercy that this had not turned into an armed conflict' (between the Palestinian units and the volunteers of the 'Army of Deliverance' under the command of Fawzi al Qawukji).[16] In May 1948, 'Abdullah was making resounding military statements to the effect that he would fight to preserve Palestine Arab, even if this meant he would be alone in the battlefield . . . Arab official meetings followed one another in an attempt to find a way out of the predicament . . . and confront the flagrant challenges which King Abdullah had thrown in their faces . . .'[17]

The Arab governments were now facing a 'moment of truth'. The masses demanded immediate action while the governments hesitated, paralysed by the fear of the effects of a popular outburst in case of inaction and of a military defeat in Palestine. They were looking, desperately, for a formula which would save them from both. The American Ambassador cabled from Cairo:

1. Arab morale almost totally collapsed in Palestine.
2. Depression and frustration rampant in most countries as a result of (a) Jewish military successes everywhere; (b) ineptness of Arab military leaders; (c) failure of Arab League and member states, notwithstanding endless conferences, to agree on concerted program and unified command; (d) failure to acquire arms abroad.
3. Informed circles inclined to agree that Arabs would *now welcome almost any face-saving device* if it would prevent open war. Might

even accept *de facto* partition through acquiescence to march of Abdullah troops to Jewish-Arab frontier.

4. Also feared that Arab armies will probably be soundly defeated by Jews and that such defeat together with already high resentment of masses for what they hold to be failure of League and Arab governments may have severe repercussions in Arab countries with fall governments generally and possible change of regime as in Iraq . . .

5. Such reactions for alleged mishandling of Palestine may also result in renewed resentment of local Jews and Western powers.

6. Situation may also be exploited by interested elements seeking to come to power through agitation that poverty, unemployment and other current economic and social ills are also attributable to present governments.[18]

Other Arab governments (Syria and Lebanon) also feared defeat and the pressure of mass resentment and supported or were leaning towards a face-saving device of truce.

From Lebanon it was reported 'President says Lebanon has supported and will continue to support US proposals for truce'.[19] In Syria the atmosphere was bordering on hysteria in the top leadership:

British Minister Broadmeed delivered fourteen-point truce terms to President Quwatli and Prime Minister Mardam last night . . . Broadmeed prior delivery indicated British approval . . . Broadmeed plans to defend terms as best if not only way out of tragic situation. He said 'its tragedy Arab league meeting in Damascus instead of calmer city . . . most important Arab leaders are near exhaustion, frustrated, and desperate . . . Barazi [Foreign Minister] today talked to me abour how 'Arab faith' would soon conquer 'brutal Jewish materialism'.[20]

In fact, Syrian desire for war was greatly fanned by the fear of neighbouring Transjordan enlarging herself and being able to dominate them:

Those advocating intervention express doubts re ability Syria to handle job alone and insist on Arab unity while fearing Abdullah in fact will only effect partition and avoid fight.

Government appears to have led public opinion to the brink of war and is unable to retreat.

Some, fearing defeat, desperately hope if war begins Russia will intervene Jewish side and blindly assume US will automatically support Arabs.[21]

Barazi said seemingly fantastic story, now widely believed here, that Abdullah has made deal with the Jews 'not without foundation'. According story Haganah will counter-invade Syria after crushing Syrian Army then return quickly to Jewish Palestine as Abdullah rushes to rescue. Abdullah would receive plaudits of grateful Syrian population and crown of Greater Syria ... Barazi added Syria would not tolerate Abdullah with his royal airs and his black slaves ... he added 'We must invade, otherwise the people will kill us.'[22]

Even Iraq accepted the truce proposal informally.

King Abdullah's Double Game

The major Arab opposition to the truce proposal came from the one person who had a secret agreement with the Jews — Abdullah of Transjordan: 'When Transjordan Foreign Minister telephoned Amman for Abdullah's approval, Abdullah asserted truce impossible because he publicly committed liberate Palestine.'[23]

The Americans also heard the same reply from a member of the Arab Higher Committee who had just returned from Amman:

Dr Tannous had just returned from Amman where he had seen Abdullah. He stated (one) that there was no basis for discussion of draft truce articles (two) that truce at this time would only postpone decision for three months while the UN wrangled leading to further strife (three) that Arab armies will move into Palestine starting midnight Friday May 14. He stated unequivocally that only thing which would stay the invasion was unconditional acceptance by Jews to form a unitary state with proportional representation. Following this, question of immigration would be settled by the representative body as in any democracy.[24]

Abdullah's rejection of the truce was confirmed when the Security Council Truce Commission visited Amman on 13 May.[25] In a radio broadcast monitored by the BBC, Abdullah announced that he had rejected the US truce proposal 'supported by Syria' and that if the Arab league accepted the truce proposal, he would not do so but advance with his army into Palestine after 15 May.[26]

Abdullah's attitude towards the truce was determined by the fact that he planned to annex the West Bank to Jordan, and was going to do this regardless of the attitude of the other Arab states. Only a war could give legitimacy to this annexation.

As early as March 1947 the Jordanian delegation to the Arab League reserved to itself the freedom of independent action in its policy towards Palestine. The Palestine delegate objected and claimed that Jordan was merely a pawn of Britain, and an argument ensued.[27] At the December 1947 meeting of the Arab League, Abdullah asked to be allowed to conquer Palestine alone on behalf of the Arab League, but this was rejected.[28] On 24 April 1948 a meeting took place in Amman to discuss the military situation in Palestine. Abdullah again demanded to be Commander of Palestine Operations. When the other Arab states opposed his appointment, he threatened to withdraw from the fighting; on 29 April he was appointed honorary general commander.[29]

Abdullah's secret agreement with the Jews also led him to believe that he could seek a pseudo-military solution without a truce and to the exclusion of the other Arab states. On 14 May he changed the invasion plans to prevent the Syrian Army from attacking south of Lake Kinneret (and thus operating in or near the West Bank); this caused consternation in Syria and made impossible the main Arab invasion plan – to cut off the whole of East Galilee.[30] Syria asked for a postponement of the invasion, while the forces of the other Arab governments were poised on the border not knowing what to do. Only Transjordanian and Iraqi troops were already moving to war.[31]

The other Arab states and the Palestinians had good reason to fear the ambitions and plots of Abdullah. The most important question of the political situation in May 1948 was what was to become of the informal political alliance forged over 40 years between Zionism and the Hashemites. Abdullah had, in fact, been meeting secretly with the Jewish Agency for years, and had agreed in 1937 and 1948 to divide Palestine. Abdullah's first contacts with the Jews followed closely on the agreement signed between Chaim Weizmann and Abdullah's brother, Faisal, in 1919. When Faisal's kingdom in Syria collapsed and the British created Transjordan in 1922, Abdullah went to London where he met Zionist leaders, to seek their support for the enlargement of the Emirate over both sides of the Jordan, in return for implementation of the Balfour Declaration.[32] The plan was dropped due to British opposition, but Abdullah persisted for many years in seeking Jewish colonisation and capital investment in Transjordan. In 1924 he met Colonel Kisch of the Zionist Executive in Amman, where he declared: 'Palestine is one unit . . . We, the Arabs and the Jews, can live together peacefully in the whole country, but you must make an alliance with us . . . We are poor and you are rich. Please come to Transjordan. I guarantee your safety. Together we will work for the benefit of the country.'[33]

Early in the 1930s Abdullah again tried to promote Jewish settlement in Transjordan, offering to sell some lands to Zionist agencies and to send tribal leaders to meet Dr Weizmann in Jerusalem to discuss this (8 April 1933). It was rumoured that Abdullah was trying to reduce his dependence on the British treasury by encouraging settlement, but more importantly he was building up his contacts with Zionist leaders to gain their support for his ambitions for a Greater Syria. Again nothing came of these colonisation plans due to British and Arab opposition: the British did not want to allow anything which would antagonise other Arab states by increasing Abdullah's power.[34]

The turning point in Arab-Jewish relations in Palestine, signalled by the Arab Revolt of 1936, was seen by Abdullah as an historic opportunity for him to realise his aims, and led to a strengthening of the informal alliance with the Jewish Agency.

Abdullah's convergence of interest with the Zionists over a partition plan in Palestine, and his willingness to put off his final aim of a Greater Syria in order to increase his power immediately, were again repeated in 1947-8. Abdullah wanted to control all or part of Palestine, and was not hostile to the Zionist endeavour so long as this could help him.

In November 1947, while the UN was considering the resolution to partition Palestine (which was uniformly opposed by Arab states), Abdullah met Golda Meir, head of the political department of the Jewish Agency in Pinhas Rutenberg's house at Nahariya. Abdullah assured Mrs Meir that he would not attack the partitioned Jewish state but that he would annex Arab Palestine. He spoke disparagingly of the other Arab states and stated that he would allow no other Arab army to cross his territory. They also agreed that the Mufti, Haj Amin, leader of the Palestinians, was their common enemy who had to be prevented from disrupting their plans.[35] The meeting ended with an agreement to maintain contact and meet again after the UN had voted on partition. Because of disturbances, no further meetings were held until May 1948. Contact, however, was maintained through emissaries, principally the King's personal physician, Dr Mohammed el Saty, who gave assurances that the agreement still stood.[36]

At the first meeting Abdullah had asked what the attitude of the Jewish Agency would be to the incorporation of the Jewish state into his kingdom with full autonomy, and had also mentioned that he did not want to be embarrassed by too small an area in the Arab state.[37] Now he renewed this suggestion, first asking through his emissary whether the Jews would make territorial concessions from the UN partition frontiers. When this was answered negatively, he requested another meeting with Mrs Meir. As news of his contacts had leaked out, he insisted that this time she must come to Amman. On 10 May 1948, dressed as an Arab woman and accompanied by an Israeli, Ezra Danin, Mrs Meir was driven by the King's personal chauffeur to a house in Amman.[38] At this meeting Abdullah announced that because of changed circumstances, he could not honour his former pledges. The recent events in Palestine, like the massacre in Deir Yassin, had in-flamed Arab opinion, and he was now only one of five commanders of Arab armies. He therefore proposed that he be allowed to occupy all Palestine unpartitioned and merge it with Transjordan after one year. The Jews would have autonomy, 50 per cent representation in the Jordanian Parliament, and possibly half the ministers as well.

Mrs Meir rejected these proposals and rested on their previous agreement. She stated that if the agreement was abrogated the Jews would not abide by the frontiers but try to take what territory they could. She pointed out that the Jews were Abdullah's only real friends, and that they had inflicted important defeats on their common enemy the Mufti. She suggested that Abdullah stay out of the Arab League war plans and make peace with the Jews. In return, he could send a governor for Arab Palestine and merge it with his kingdom. Abdullah refused to accept this, but promised that the armies of Transjordan and Iraq would stay within the boundaries of Arab Palestine.[39] This agreement had been confirmed a week earlier by the meeting between the operations chief of the Arab Legion, Colonel Goldie, and Shlomo Shamir, the commander of the Haganah in the Jordan Valley.

During the war, Abdullah honoured the agreement. The main fighting occurred in or around the approaches to Jerusalem, which had not been allotted to either state by the UN partition plan. The Arab Legion force at Latrun was under strict orders only to defend its position and not attack the new road the Israelis were building to Jerusalem. In July, the legion withdrew from Lydda and Ramla without a fight, thus abandoning the most dangerous Arab salient into Israeli territory near Tel Aviv. Abdullah tried to sign a truce and a peace agreement with Israel as soon as he could after he had occupied the West Bank.[40]

Abdullah's plans were tacitly encouraged by the British, who already agreed to his partitioning the country, in a meeting with the Jordanian Prime Minister in London in March 1948. Now they confirmed this by supporting a *de facto* partition of Palestine. They even thought that Abdullah would gain, or should get, a corridor to the sea, as this would appease the Arabs and give him leeway to solve his problems with other Arab states. In a conversation between the chief British and American advisers on the Middle East, the British expert, Harold Beeley, stated:

> It was his personal opinion that if the United Nations could find a way out, its best course would be to encourage the partition of Palestine between the invading Arab forces and the Jews. Such partition, of course, would only be a temporary measure since it was clear that whenever the international situation would permit, the Jews on their part would try to enlarge their state, and the Arabs on their part would try to overwhelm the Jewish state . . .[41]

The British UN Ambassador had a more precise concept of partition; when asked if Abdullah contemplated annexation of the West Bank to Transjordan, he replied:

> 1. Relations between Ibn Saud and Abdullah on the one hand, and Abdullah and Mufti on the other hand were very strained; Abdullah's growing prominence in Arab world and threat to Ibn Saud's position; Mufti feared losing his position in Palestine to Abdullah;
> 2. Abdullah in very strong position within Arab League because of organized force at his disposal;
> 3. Quite conceivable that Abdullah after May 15 would invade Palestine with backing Arab states, effectively partitioning country along line running across to and including Jaffa;
> 4. He would settle his differences with the Mufti by liquidating latter;
> 5. He would settle his differences with Ibn Saud by ceding him port of Aqaba;
> 6. Any differences with Syria would be settled by ceding to Syria northeastern corner Palestine.

Parodi asked Creech-Jones whether this would be a good solution and Creech-Jones replied that he thought it would.[42] The American State Department was inclined to accept such a solution, as Dean Rusk's memorandum stated:

> Given this almost intolerable situation [of war], the wisest course might be for the United States and Great Britain, with the assistance

of France, to undertake immediate diplomatic action to work out a modus vivendi between Abdullah of Transjordan and the Jewish Agency. This modus vivendi would call for, in effect, a de facto partition of Palestine along the lines traced by Mr Arthur Creech-Jones . . . In effect, Abdullah would cut across Palestine from Transjordan to the sea at Jaffa, would give Ibn Saud a pòrt at Aqaba and appease the Syrians by some territorial adjustment in the northern part, leaving Jews a coastal state running from Tel Aviv to Haifa. If some modus vivendi could be worked out peaceably, the UN could give its blessing to the deal.[43]

But the British promotion of their main client state in the Middle East (confirmed by Kirkbride's recollection of 'waving a green light' at Abdullah)[44] had serious repercussions among the other Arab states. It was especially Egypt, increasingly anti-British and supporting the Mufti, at whose expense a new partition would be made.

Egypt's Entry into the War

The actions and intentions of Jordan, with the tacit consent of the British and Israelis, had a crucial impact on Egypt's decision to enter the war. Egypt was the most important Arab state, with the largest army and through the Arab League was attempting to assert her hegemony in the Arab world. Therefore, her attitude to the truce proposal was crucial. There is substantial evidence that Egyptian intentions were not to invade Palestine, but to find a diplomatic solution to the conflict. But Egypt could not afford to lose prestige to Abdullah in the Arab world at a time when its own internal position was so weak. Both America and Britain were pressing Egypt to agree to the truce. On 30 April the American Embassy in Cairo reported the following information from a 'controlled source citing an informant' high in Egyptian government circles regarding the Egyptian government's attitude to military intervention:

Nevertheless, it is believed that Egyptian attitude continues to oppose participation of Egyptian troops in Palestine, prior to British evacuation . . . the informant states that as far as the despatch was concerned, Egypt would permit volunteers to go to Palestine, but had no plan or intention of sending units of its regular army to join the battle . . . the Government was pursuing officially a hands-off policy and had no intention of jeopardizing its position in the United Nations by taking independent action perhaps in defiance of UN decisions . . . the various representatives seemed in agreement that the time for official action on the part of Arab governments had not yet come. They all felt they must await the outcome of the debate in the Security Council.[45]

The fact that Egypt made no war preparations confirms the view that she had expected a diplomatic solution, and thus may have been prepared to accept the truce proposal to allow for a new round of negotiations.

As we have seen before (p. 329), Egypt was reluctant to join the war. Egypt reported to the Arab League Council in October 1947 that 'in agreeing to take part in a military demonstration they are not willing to go farther than that'.[46] In March 1948 Egypt vetoed a meeting of Arab League military commanders on the ground that she was not prepared to discuss military intervention when the Security Council was considering the situation (the trusteeship proposal).[47] At a private meeting of the Arab League early in May 1948, Nuqrashi Pasha, the Egyptian Prime Minister, declared that Egypt could not fight because of its problem with England, and would send only volunteers from the Moslem Brotherhood.[48]

When the Egyptian Parliament met in secret session to authorise war and to vote war appropriations (for the first time) on 12 May 1948, Nuqrashi Pasha assured them that no large scale operations were contemplated.[49] This was based on the assessment by the General Staff of the war preparedness of the Egyptian Army. It was only on 13 May that King Faruq gave a direct order for the Army to march into Palestine without the knowledge of the Prime Minister. Only three of its nine battalions were anywhere near the frontier when the order was given, and the first Egyptian communique described this as a 'punitive operation against Zionist gangs', i.e. not a serious military operation.[50] The deputy commander of the Egyptian force did not conceal his fear that such an unprepared intervention would lead to disaster.[51]

During the secret session of Parliament on 12 May, the Minister of Defence assured Parliament that despite an official declaration of war, 'we shall never even contemplate entering the war officially. We are not mad. We shall send our men and officers to volunteer for service in Palestine and give weapons but no more'.[52] The former Egyptian Prime Minister, Sidki Pasha, also questioned the army's readiness to fight:[53]

. . . Doesn't the Prime Minister think that by participating in this war, we are lighting a fire that will engulf the whole Arab world?

. . . Is Egypt economically and militarily ready for a confrontation that may be of long duration?

. . . Is it true that the Egyptian army is not sufficiently well equipped, and that its stocks of ammunition will only suffice for a few days?

. . . Doesn't the Prime Minister think that a continuous war, which will cost many millions of pounds, may endanger the economic development of Egypt at a time when social and national reform is badly needed?

. . . If the Arab armies are insufficiently prepared to destroy the adversary and we have heard of its strength — what will happen then?

While Parliament was meeting, it was reported that the Egyptian Under-Secretary of State for Foreign Affairs, Kames Abdul Rahim Bey, was meeting Mr J. Paterson, Counsellor of the American Embassy, to discuss the truce proposals.[54] It is significant that the Egyptian Government — alone among the Arab states — did not broadcast its intention to invade Palestine, and reported 'without comment' the US proposal to extend the Mandate for ten days.[55]

There were other groups in Egypt who were opposed to, or sceptical about, the prospects of war. The Democratic Movement for National Liberation supported the partition resolution and strongly opposed Egypt's entry into the war. It thought a religious war over Palestine was one 'from which only colonialists could benefit' and that the struggle should be against Great Britain. The Movement issued a statement on 21 December 1947 saying that unity of the Jewish and Arab masses against colonialism was needed, not a diversion of the struggle for a better living standard by external war.[56] 'We do not want to take Palestine away from the Arabs and give it to the Jews; we want to take it away from colonialism and give it to the Jews and Arabs. We approve of partition because we have no choice as a basis for independence . . . to be followed by a long struggle to bring the viewpoints of the Arab and Jewish state closer.'[57]

From a purely professional viewpoint the Army was also opposed to the Egyptian military intervention. General Headquarters reported early in 1948 to the Egyptian Cabinet that the army was operationally and logistically unprepared for war.[58] Both the military and the politicians believed that only a demonstration of force, not a real war, was needed. As Nasser put it: 'This could not be a serious war. There was no concentration of forces, no accumulation of ammunition and equipment. There was no reconnaissance, no intelligence, no plans. Yet we were actually on the battlefield.'[59]

Two factors influenced the Egyptian decision to intervene militarily, despite their obvious reluctance. The first was the grave social and political crisis that Egypt was undergoing at the time. The Nuqrashi Government was threatened by unrest and disorder at home. The extreme nationalist and religious Moslem Brotherhood had been terrorising Egyptian society with a campaign of political assassination since 1946, bombing courthouses and theatres and killing the Chief of Police and Chief of Justice.[60] The Moslem Brotherhood organised a campaign to recruit volunteers for an armed struggle in Palestine and agitated against the policy of the government to confine itself to diplomatic means. The campaign, however, had only a limited appeal as other problems, particularly the relations with Britain and the economic crisis, had priority. The Egyptians were investigating the Anglo-Egyptian Treaty of 1936 with a view to getting the British military presence in Egypt removed and the UN had rejected this claim to the Suez Canal.

In addition to political tension, there were many large strikes and growing economic demands, culminating in the strike of the police force in May 1948. Major strikes had occurred in 1946 and 1947, including textile works, ports, etc. Pressed from the left and the right, the king saw the war as a way out of the crisis. Martial law was declared when the Parliament voted to go to war: all political activity against the government, strikes and demonstrations were suspended.[61]

The fear of the internal consequences of non-intervention in Palestine was emphasised in most of the counsellor reports, and admitted publicly by Azzam Pasha, when he broadcast to the Arab people 'to consider these informal questions in light of war conditions'.[62] In a private conversation with an American diplomat, he was reported as saying 'Failure of the League to invade might lead to mutual recriminations among the Arabs . . . and there was also the fear that Arab governments themselves might be overthrown'.[63] In fact, Nuqrashi Pasha was to be assassinated in October 1948 by extremists of the Moslem Brotherhood.

The factor that prompted the king to order intervention was, paradoxically, the tacit and secret understanding between Emir Abdullah and Ben-Gurion dividing Palestine between themselves, and the apparent American and British support for the arrangement. Egypt could not accept the increased power and prestige in the Arab world that would accrue to Transjordan if she seized Arab Palestine; in particular, Egypt had to oppose the plan for Jordan to recover part of the Negev and a port and corridor to the Mediterranean, which the British and later on, Count Bernadotte, were pressing for. Egypt waited to see what Transjordan's intentions were before intervening.

Faruq's aim was to prevent his rival dynasty, known for its close association with the British, from increasing its power and prestige. In fact, the Egyptian forces, which invaded Palestine, were divided into two, and one half advanced through purely Arab territory towards Jerusalem and the West Bank.[64] It is also suggested that the major event that precipitated the Egyptian decision, was that Abdullah had, on 13 May, gained the agreement of the Arab League that the Arab armies, not the Arab Higher Committee, would constitute the actual civil authority in liberated areas of Palestine.[65] This foreshadowed Abdullah's intention to exclude Egypt's client, the Mufti, from Palestinian affairs. Abdullah's plan forced the Egyptian hand. The Egyptian troops, concentrated on the border to Palestine were, at first, unsure of what they were going to do, even on 15 May, and the Egyptian Prime Minister, Nuqrashi Pasha, was known to be hesitant. They invaded only when King Farouk issued a direct order to do so, and this determined the attitude of the other Arab states (Iraq and Transjordan had already begun to occupy the West Bank before 15 May).[66]

Conclusions

We found no evidence to support Dr Goldmann's version that Nuqrashi Pasha was willing to meet the Jewish Agency. This is no proof that such a document does not exist. Most of the material related to secret contacts between Arab statesmen and representatives of the Jewish Agency remains classified. The papers of the members of the Arab Department of the Jewish Agency which played a role there (Eliahu Sasson, Shiloach (Zaslani), etc.) are still awaiting declassification. However, Dr Goldmann's statement is corroborated by the logic of the situation and the pattern of behaviour of the Arab states, especially Egypt. It is beyond doubt that from November 1947 until 11 May 1948, the Egyptian authorities initiated no steps to prepare for war and staked everything on a last-minute diplomatic solution. It is inconceivable that they awaited such a solution passively without exploring its prospects in contact with the State Department and possibly with the Jewish Agency. As the American Ambassador reported, the main difficulty was in finding a 'face-saving formula'.

But what even Dr Goldmann did not consider was the impact of the 'Hashemite connection' on the prospects for a truce. It was the determination of Abdullah, assured of Jewish acquiescence in his plan to annex the West Bank, which prevented the other Arab states from accepting the truce proposal. Egypt, with the only other significant military force, was vitally affected by this. In particular, Egypt could not accept the British-sponsored plans for Jordan to receive part of the Negev, and a port and a portion of the Mediterranean, which would have destroyed the credibility of Egyptian foreign policy against a British threat to the Suez Canal.

Dr Goldmann played a significant role in trying to prevent the war with the Arab states. It was he who suggested to the Americans that Marshall should talk with Sharett on 8 May and he made every effort to get Jewish support for the preservation of peace and ultimately to gain support for a Jewish state.[1]

It is futile to speculate about the 'ifs' but it is relevant to list the range of possibilities that existed had the truce proposal been accepted. Possibly, the truce would only have postponed the fighting until after a new round of negotiations, as the Arab states would have refused to accept partition and the *de facto* Jewish state. This could hardly have affected the essential military co-ordinates of the situation as revealed by the war of 1948. The determination of the Jews to have a state, the Soviet Union's political and military support of Israel as well as the inter-Arab rivalries and their grave domestic problems, were not likely to change perceptibly within a short period. Perhaps Israel might have been in an even stronger position since America might have found it more difficult to impose an embargo on war material to the Middle East while Britain continued to supply arms to the Arabs.

The possibility of preventing the escalation of the conflict into a generalised Israeli-Arab conflict should also not be excluded. For Egypt the problem of relations with Great Britain took precedence over opposition to the partition of Palestine. This was shown in March 1949 when Egypt preferred to sign an armistice with Israel rather than accept a British offer of military support (based on the 1936 Anglo-Egyptian Treaty) when the Egyptian forces in Palestine were near collapse. The Armistice Treaty was conceived as a prelude to negotiations for a peace settlement. These negotiations took place within the framework of the Palestine Conciliation Commission from 1949-51. They failed to produce a peace settlement because of the disagreement on the problem of frontiers and the rights of the refugees to return to their homes.

The other feature of the truce proposal was that it implied the re-establishment of the Arab Higher Committee as the civil authority in the Arab areas of Palestine. This could only have been brought about by the support of Egypt and against the wishes of Abdullah. It would certainly have started open conflict between them, transferring the focus of tension from the conflict between Israel and the Arabs. As a matter of fact, the later annexation of the West Bank by Transjordan was violently opposed and never formally approved by most of the other Arab states and a considerable part of the Palestinians.

Rival Palestinian governments were actually set up during the first and second truces in 1948 — one in the Gaza Strip under the patronage of Egypt (the All-Palestine Government), and the 'National Palestine Congress' in Jericho which voted to join Transjordan. This decision was denounced by Egypt, which attempted to have Transjordan expelled from the Arab League.

The war of 1948 between Israel and the Arab states was a decisive turning point in the relations between Israel and the Arab world. Its psychological impact was enormous: for the Israelis, the euphoria of victory gave them exaggerated belief in their power; for the Arabs, the trauma of defeat and the complex of humiliation led to a deep desire for revenge, rehabilitation, and restoration of lost prestige. It had also a decisive influence of the strategic outlook of Israel's policy-makers. The war was a vindication of Ben-Gurion's doctrine that peace with the Arabs was an unattainable, though noble, aim so long as the Arabs believed that they would be able, one day, to destroy Israel. The only way for the Jewish state to survive is by developing such military and technological superiority as to demonstrate to the Arabs the futility of this hope. Accordingly, the achievement of peace, as an objective in Israeli policy, was relegated to a lower rank in the scale of national priorities than security, military power, immigration and economic and technological development.

What followed from this doctrine was the subordination of foreign policy and socio-economic development to the aim of building up a military deterrent, the strategy of massive reprisal as a periodical demonstration of the efficiency of the deterrent, and ultimately a pre-emptive war to prevent a change in the military balance in the Middle East. A corollary of this was Israel's belief in its role as a 'mini great power' able to match the combined strength of all the Arab states and to prevent any substantial unfavourable changes in the region's political structure.

The war of 1948 had one other decisive consequence on Zionist views of the Arab problem. Before 1948, Zionist leaders favoured the concept of Arab unity as a way to bypass the Palestinian problem.

But the realisation that their victory in 1948 was due primarily to Arab disunity and lack of co-ordination led them from now on to regard pan-Arabism as a mortal danger to Israel.

The war of 1948 seemed to vindicate the Zionist policy of non-recognition of the Palestinians, whose intransigent leadership brought upon its people disaster. The Palestinians became a people of refugees, dispersed all over the Middle East and their territory taken over, divided and annexed by Jordan, Israel and Egypt. It seemed at first that the Palestinian people had ceased to exist and only the problems of refugees and frontiers stood between the Armistice Treaties signed by the Arab states and a final peace settlement with Israel. The Palestinians were deprived of the right to speak on behalf of themselves.

Nearly thirty years had to elapse before it came clear that the continued anomaly of the Palestinians as a politically homeless people had bred a movement of radical nationalism, characterised by desperation and terrorism which has become a detonator for internal Arab conflicts and a major cause of an ever more dangerous escalation of the Israeli-Arab conflict.

Notes

FROM BILTMORE BACK TO PARTITION

1.   Quoted in Laqueur, *History of Zionism* (London, 1972), p. 546.
2.   Yehuda Bauer, *From Diplomacy to Resistance* (Philadelphia, 1970), pp. 216-17.
3.   Ibid., p. 217.
4.   J.C. Hurewitz, *The Struggle for Palestine* (New York, 1950), pp. 188-90.
5.   A detailed report of these contacts is given in Aharon Cohen, *Israel and the Arab World* (London, 1970).
6.   Quoted in Aharon Cohen, ibid., p. 204 (Zionist Executive, 5 July 1943).
7.   Cohen, ibid., pp. 291-2.
8.   Ibid., pp. 310-12.
9.   Ibid., pp. 305-8.
10.   Laqueur, *History of Zionism*, p. 542.
11.   Yehuda Bauer, *From Diplomacy to Resistance*, p. 243.
12.   Full text in 'Problems of World War II', Part 2, p. 348, US House of Representatives.
13.   Laqueur, *History of Zionism*, pp. 566-7.
14.   Laqueur, ibid., p. 572.
15.   Nahum Goldmann, *Memories: The Autobiography of Nahum Goldmann*

(London, 1970), pp. 321-2.

16.   Goldmann's informants included David K. Niles, an adviser to
Truman and good friend of Zionism (David B. Sacher, 'David K. Niles and US
Palestine Policy', Harvard BA Thesis, 1959, p. 36). Truman himself called the
situation 'insoluble', letter quoted in Harry S. Truman, *Years of Trial and Hope
1946-1953* (London, 1956), p. 163.

17.   Draft Minutes of the Meeting of the Executive of the Jewish Agency in
Paris, on Friday, 2 August 1946, at 10.30 am, pp. 3-10 (mimeographed copy).

18.   Ibid., Sunday afternoon, 4 August 1946, pp. 1-3.

19.   Ibid., Sunday evening, pp. 5-6.

20.   Ibid., Monday morning, 5 August 1946, 10.15 am, p. 1.

21.   Goldmann, *Memories*, pp. 232-3.

22.   *Foreign Relations of the United States*, 1946, vol. XII, *The Near East*,
p. 679.

23.   Goldmann, *Memories*, p. 234; *Foreign Relations of the US*, vol. XII
pp. 679-89.

24.   Joseph Proskauer, *A Segment of My Times* (New York, 1950), pp. 242-3.

25.   Dr Leon Feuer, 'The Truth Will Out', *National Jewish Post*, Vice
President, ZOA, 13 September 1946, p. 3; *New York Post*, 26 September 1946.

26.   *National Jewish Post*, 13 September 1946, p. 3.

27.   *New York Post*, 13 September 1946.

28.   The belief that the Goldmann mission was a failure and did not reverse
American hesitancy to support Zionist aims is shared by a number of scholars,
including Walter Laqueur (*A History of Zionism*, p. 573) and Michael Brecher,
The Foreign Policy System of Israel (London, 1972).

29.   David K. Niles papers, quoted in David B. Sacher, 'David K. Niles', p.
36.

30.   James V. Forrestal, *Diaries*, ed. by Walter Millis (New York, 1951),
p. 189.

31.   *Foreign Relations of the United States*, vol. VII, *Palestine and the Near
East*, p. 682 (12 August 1946).

32.   Truman to Acting Secretary of State Clayton, 12 September 1946
(Niles Papers, quoted in Sacher, 'David K. Niles', p. 43).

33.   Quoted in Sacher, 'David K. Niles', p. 45.

34.   Report of conversation sent to David K. Niles, Niles Papers, quoted in
Sacher, 'David K. Niles', p. 48.

35.   Minutes of conversation at Dorchester Hotel, London, 29 August 1946.

36.   Draft Minutes of the Executive, Thursday evening, 15 August 1946,
8.30 pm, pp. 2-3.

37.   22nd Zionist Congress, reported in *New Judea*.

38.   *New Judea*, 22nd Zionist Congress.

39.   Ibid., speeches by Mordechai Bentov, Rabbi Rabinowitz.

40.   Ibid.

ISRAEL'S ORIGINAL SIN

1.   Dr Nahum Goldmann, *Memories*, p. 287.

2.   'Israel's Original Sin', an interview of N. Goldmann by S. Flapan,
New Outlook, vol. 17, no. 9, Nov.-Dec. 1974.

3.   Dr Nahum Goldmann, *Memories*, pp. 288-90.

4.   'Israel's Original Sin', *New Outlook*.

THE WAR OF THE PALESTINIAN ARABS 1947-1948

1.   Larry Collins and D. Lapierre, *O Jerusalem* (Simon and Schuster, 1973), pp. 288-95.
2.   Zev Sharef, *Three Days* (New York, 1962), pp. 91-100; also Collins-Lapierre, ibid., pp. 288-95.
3.   US National Archives, 13 May 1948, 599, 867N 01/5-1348.
4.   Ibid.
5.   Evidence for this comes from both Arab and Jewish sources: Naji Alluche in his *Arab Resistance in Palestine 1918-1948* (Arabic) (Beirut, 1967); Samuel Katz in *Days of Fire* (London, 1968) estimates the number of Palestinian volunteers at 4,500. Ben-Gurion in his speech in the Knesseth (1956) affirmed that the overwhelming majority of the Palestinian people did not take part in the war.
6.   Minutes of the Yishuv's Security Committee, Zionist Archives, Jerusalem, S25/9345.
7.   The minutes give only nicknames of the participants and though their identity can be easily verified, I chose to withhold their names.
8.   Meir Pa'il, 'The Problem of Arab Sovereignty in Palestine 1947' in *Zionism*, vol. III, p. 440 (Tel Aviv University, The Institute for Zionist Research) (Hebrew).
9.   Meir Pa'il, ibid., p. 457.
10.   Rony E. Gabbay, *A Political Study of the Jewish-Arab Conflict*, (Geneva 1959), p. 110.
11.   Sharett to John MacDonald, US Consul in Jerusalem, 27 June 1948, *Foreign Relations of the US*, 1948, vol. V, part 2, p. 1151.
12.   M. Bar-Zohar, Ben-Gurion's biographer, wrote in *Ben-Gurion – Le Prophete Arme* (Paris, 1966):

Ben-Gurion n'a jamais cru a la possibilite d'une existence avec les Arabes.
Moins il y'aura d'Arabes dans les limites du futur Etat, mieux cela vaudra. Il
ne dit pas explicitement, mais l'impression que se degage de ses interventions
et de ses remarques est nette: une grande offensive contre les Arabes
ne briserait pas seulement leurs attaques mais aussi reduirait au maximum le
pourcentage de la population arabe dans l'Etat qu'on prepare. On peur l'accuser
de racisme, mais alors on devra faire le proces de tout le mouvement zioniste
qui est base sur le principe d'une entite purement juive en Palestine. Les appels
qu'addressent alors diverses institutions zionistes aux Arabes de ne pas quitter
le pays et de s'integrer dans l'Etat juif comportent une forte part d'hypocrisie
[p. 146] ... Il fera tour pour que dans les territoires deja conquis les Arabes
soient convaincus de ne pas revenir [p. 175].

THE AMERICAN TRUCE PROPOSAL

1.   US National Archives, 13 May 1948, 599 867N 01/5-1348.
2.   Z. Sharef, *Three Days*, p. 132; M. Bar-Zohar, *Ben-Gurion – Le Prophete Arme*, pp. 175 f.
3.   Western, Arab and Israeli politicians were agreed as to the aims and motivations of Soviet policy to support the creation of a Jewish state in Palestine: (1) to accelerate British withdrawal from Palestine and weaken British positions in the Middle East; (2) to drive a wedge between the British Government pursuing a pro-Arab policy and the White House, inclined to support the Zionist cause; (3) to obtain a foothold in the Middle East by supporting and defending a UN resolution and winning the sympathy of a dynamic Jewish state, run by a socialist movement originating in Eastern Europe; (4) to weaken semi-feudal and

reactionary and pro-Western Arab regimes emphasising their inability to confront the rising new factor in the Middle East (see *Foreign Relations of the US*, 1948, vol. 5, Part 2: Jessup to Marshall, pp. 1180-6; Naji al Asil, Iraq representative to UN to Austin, US representative to UN, pp. 1055-6; Hurewitz, *The Struggle for Palestine*, p. 307; A. Krammer, *The Forgotten Friendship – Israel and the Soviet Union 1948-1953* (New York, 1974).

4.   US National Archives, 501BB Pal. 4-3048.
5.   Quoted in D. Golding, 'United States Foreign Policy in Palestine and Israel', unpublished dissertation, New York University, 1961 (University Microfilms, no. 66-9694).
6.   Golding, ibid., pp. 260-4.
7.   Ibid., pp. 283-8.
8.   Harry S. Truman, *Years of Trial and Hope* (Hodder and Stoughton, 1956), pp. 172-5.
9.   Larry Collins and D. Lapierre, *O Jerusalem*, p. 228.
10.   Golding, 'United States Foreign Policy', pp. 296-7.
11.   Ibid., pp. 292-3.
12.   Austin to Henderson, 7 April 1948, US National Archives, State Department, 501BB, Palestine/4-948.
13.   UN General Assembly Records, 21 April 1948, in Golding, 'United States Foreign Policy', p. 300.
14.   Golding, ibid., pp. 297-301.
15.   National Archives, Lovett to American Ambassador in London, 9 April 1948, 501 BB Palestine/4-948.
16.   National Archives, McClintock (US-UN) to Lovett, 27 April 1948 501 BB Palestine/4-2748.
17.   Rusk to Lovett, 511, 27 April 1948, US Nat. Archives, 500 BB Pal.
18.   Rusk to Lovett, 526, 29 April 1948, US Nat. Archives, 500 BB Pal./4-2948.
19.   Ibid.
20.   US Nat. Archives, 501 BB Palestine/4-2948.
21.   Rusk to Lovett, 554, 3 May 1948, US Nat. Archives 501 BB Pal./5-348.
22.   Tuck to Henderson, NIACT 471, 5 May 1948, US Nat. Arc. 501 BB Pal./5-548.
23.   Kopper to Henderson, 589, 6 May 1948, Nat. Arc. 501 BB Pal./5-648.
24.   Beirut to Sec. of State, 160, 3 May 1948, US Nat. Arc. 867N 01/5-348.
25.   Memorandum of conversation, 2 May 1948 (Beeley-Henderson), Nat. Arc. 867N 01/5-248.
26.   Marshall to American Consul, Jerusalem, 377, 9 May 1948, National Archives 501 BB Pal./5-948.
27.   US State Dept. outgoing telegram control 1486 to certain American diplomatic and consular officials, Nat. Arc. 501 BB Pal./5-748, 7 May 1948:

Articles 1-4 (on the cessation of hostilities) and 13-14 (on the terms of the truce) were again identical with the original truce proposal. The remainder of the final draft read:
The President today approved the following draft of the proposed articles of truce which USUN handed today to Representatives in New York City of JA and AHC.
QUOTE The AHC and JA for Palestine accept the following articles of truce for Palestine effective midnight, May 12-13, and accept responsibility for insuring compliance by the Arab and Jewish communities of Palestine therewith.
Article 5: During the period of the truce, and without prejudice to the

future governmental structure of Palestine, existing Arab and Jewish authorities are now exercising control and shall accord full and equal rights to all inhabitants of such areas.

Article 6: During the period of the truce, and without prejudice to the future governmental structure of Palestine, no steps shall be taken by Arab or Jewish authorities to proclaim a sovereign state in part or all of Palestine or to seek international recognition therefor.

Article 7: During the period of the truce, the AHC and JA for Palestine accept, as a matter of emergency, the authority of the SC Truce Commission to arrange the necessary collaboration between Arab and Jewish authorities required for the maintenance of public order and essential public services.

Article 8: During the period of the truce, freedom of movement and communications shall be accorded to all persons and traffic throughout Palestine except as may be declared by the SC Truce Commission to be in violation of the truce or prejudicial to a final political settlement.

Article 9: All persons displaced from their homes in Palestine by recent disorders shall be permitted to return to their homes and resume their normal occupations unless the SC Truce Commission shall decide in specific cases that such repatriation shall jeopardize these truce arrangements.

Article 10: During the period of the truce, existing Arab and Jewish authorities shall continue to apply to existing laws of Palestine unless otherwise authorized by the SC Truce Commission.

Article 11: During the period of the truce, and without prejudice to future decisions on the question of immigration, the AHC and JA for Palestine accept as a matter of emergency, the authority of the SC Truce Commission to deal with the question of immigration into Palestine.

Article 12: All persons, groups, and organizations in Palestine pledge their maximum effort to preserve the holy places and to protect all activities connected therewith; to this end the AHC and JA for Palestine accept, as a matter of emergency, the authority of the SC Truce Commission, to establish special security arrangements for the protection of the city of Jerusalem and of the holy places.

28.   Moshe Sharett, *The Gate of Nations* (Tel Aviv, 1958), pp. 226-8.
29.   Marshall to American Embassy, London, NIACT 1672, 8 May 1948, Nat. Arc. 501 BB Pal./5-848.
30.   Tuck to Marshall, Despatch 361A, 'Memorandum of conversation between Azzam Pasha and Philip Ireland, April 28, 1948', US Nat. Arc. 501 BB Pal./4-2848.
31.   Rusk to Lovett, 527, 29 April 1948, US Nat. Arc. 501 BB Pal./4-2948.
32.   Report on conversation with Mr Robert A. Lovett, Under-Secretary of State, Wednesday 28 April 1948, Zionist Archives, Jerusalem.
33.   'Future Course of Events in Palestine', 4 May 1948, US Nat. Arc. 501 BB Pal./5-448.

THE ISRAELI REJECTION OF THE TRUCE

1.   565 from New York, 4 May 1948, US Nat. Arc. 501 BB Pal./5-448.
2.   NIACT 1842 from London, 30 April 1948, US Nat. Arc. 501 BB Pal./4-3048.
3.   515 from Jerusalem, 29 April 1948, US Nat. Arc. 501 BB Pal./4-2948.
4.   Sharett to Rusk, 4 May 1948, US Nat. Arc. 501 BB Pal./5-448.
5.   Report of conversation with John C. Ross, 6 May 1948, 501 BB Pal. 5-648.

6. 515 from Jerusalem, 30 April 1948, US Nat. Arc. 501 BB Pal./4-3048.
7. 554, 3 May 1948, US Nat. Arc. 501 BB Pal./5-348.
8. 585 in a conversation with John C. Ross, 6 May 1948, from New York, US Nat. Arc. 501 BB Pal./5-648.
9. Report on conversation with Secretary of State, George G. Marshall, and Robert A. Lovett, Under-Secretary of State, 8 May 1948, 501 BB Pal./5-848, 501 BB Pal./5-1248, also Moshe Sharett, *The Gate of Nations*.
10. Zev Sharef, *Three Days* (New York, 1962), pp. 69-103.
11. Ibid.
12. Ibid.
13. Ibid.
14. It is interesting to note that the estimates of the armed forces in Palestine on 15 May 1948, by pro-Zionist and pro-Arab authors differ not so much on the total of Arab forces, as on their composition; but they vary largely as regards the Jewish forces. Following are the estimates of J. and D. Kimche (*Both Sides of the Hill* (London, 1960)), Walid Khalidi (ed., *From Haven to Conquest: Readings in Zionism and the Palestine Problem until 1948*) and Glubb Pasha, the British Commander of the Arab Legion (*A Soldier in the Desert* (London, 1958)):

	J. and D. Kimche	Glubb	Khalidi
Palestine Arabs	–	–	2,563
'Army of Deliverance'	2,000	–	3,830
Egypt	10,000	10,000	2,800
Transjordan	4,500	4,500	4,500
Iraq	3,000	3,000	4,000
Syria	3,000	3,000	1,876
Lebanon	1,000	1,000	700
Arab forces total	24,000	21,500	20,269
Israel	25,000	65,000	27,400 + 90,000

Khalidi differentiates between Jewish first-line, fully mobilised troops and second-line troops including defence troops in Jewish settlements, youth battalions ('Gadna'), home-guard and dissident groups of 'Irgun' and 'Lehi'. Ben-Gurion noted in his diary on 15 May 1948 the following figures for the Israeli forces: 24,000 in the brigades, 4,161 in service units, and 1,719 in training – a total of 30,574 of which, however, only 40 per cent were armed.
15. *Foreign Relations of US*, vol. 5, part 2 (Washington, 1976), pp. 936-41.
16. Ibid., p. 983.
17. *Palestine is My Country: A Biography of Musa Alami*, pp. 152-3 (London, 1969).
18. 513 from Cairo, 13 May 1948, US Nat. Arc. 867N 01/5-1378. 266 for Damascus, 10 May 1948.
19. 'British American Co-operation in Palestine', memorandum of conversation with Harold Beeley, 2 May 1948, US Nat. Arc. 867N 01/5-248.
20. 'Future Course of Events in Palestine', 4 May 1948, 501 BB Pal./5-448.
21. L. Collins and D. Lapierre, *O Jerusalem*, p. 410.
22. A. Krammer, *The Forgotten Friendship – Israel and the Soviet Bloc*, Urbana.
23. A. Mahmoud, 'King Abdullah and Palestine', PhD thesis, 1950, p. 129. University Microfilms; Collins, *O Jerusalem*, pp. 390-1.
24. Marshall to Bevin, quoting Shertok, 8 May 1948, US Nat. Arc. 501 BB Pal./5-848; Collins and Lapierre, ibid., pp. 354-5.

25.   Ibid., pp. 211-12.
26.   London (Douglas) to State Dept., 12 May 1948, US Nat. Arc. 867N. 01/5-1248.
27.   *Egyptian Gazette*, 12 May 1948.
28.   Collins and Lapierre, *O Jerusalem*, p. 388.
29.   Ibid., pp. 524-5.
30.   Sharef, *Three Days*, pp. 96-7.
31.   Collins and Lapierre, *O Jerusalem*, pp. 330, 388-9.
32.   Ibid., pp. 424-5.
33.   Ibid., pp. 331-2.
34.   Ibid., pp. 425, 457.
35.   Mahmoud, 'King Abdullah and Palestine', pp. 127-36; Jon and David Kimche, *Both Sides of the Hill* (London, 1960), pp. 149-56.
36.   Mahmoud, 'King Abdullah and Palestine', pp. 96-7.
37.   Goldmann to McNeil; 2081 from London, 12 May 1948, US Nat. Arc. 867N 01/5-1248.

ARAB ATTITUDES TO THE TRUCE

1.   Meir Pa'il, 'The Problem of Arab Sovereignty in Palestine 1947-1949', *Zionism*, vol. III, p. 441 (Tel Aviv University, 1973; Hakilotz Hamenhead).
2.   Ibid., p. 445.
3.   Ibid., p. 448.
4.   *Foreign Relations of the US*, p. 1169.
5.   Ahmed Shuqairi, *Arbau'n 'Aman Fi'l Hayat Al-Arabiya Wad 'Dawliya* (Beirut, 1969), pp. 275-7. It is interesting to note that Musa Alami, member of the Palestinian Delegation, was advised by the people in Jordan not to mention the issue of Iraqi arms for fear that Abdullah would confiscate them and take them for himself.
6.   Maj. Gen. Saleh Sa'ib Al-Juburi (Iraqi Chief of Staff at the time) in *Mihnat Falastin Wa-Asraruha As-Siyasiyah Wal-Askariyah* (Beirut, 1970), pp. 11, 118, 122.
7.   Amin al Husseini, *Haqaeq an Qadiyat Falastin* (Cairo, 1953), p. 174 and Shuqairi, *Arbau'n Aman*, p. 290.
8.   Shuqairi, ibid., p. 289.
9.   'Let us direct the arms against colonization in Fayid, the Suez Canal and Sudan. The liberation of Palestine would be impossible while our backs are exposed to the enemy. Let us liberate the Nile Valley in order to liberate the whole East' (*Al-Jamahir*, 7.12.1947).
10.   Tariq al-Bishri, *Al Harakah Al Siyasiyah Fi Misr 1945-1952* (Cairo 1972), pp. 259-66.
11.   Ibid., quote from Muhammad Husayn Haykal, *Muthakkarat Fi Al-Siyasah Al Masriyah* (Cairo), vol. II, p. 338.
12.   Shuqairi, *Arbau'n Aman*, p. 271.
13.   Salih Sa'ib al Juburi, *Mihnat Falastin*, pp. 116-18, 131-2.
14.   Ibid.
15.   Amin al Husseini, *Haqaeq an Qadiyat Falastin*, pp. 22-3, quoted in Pa'il, 'The Problem of Arab Sovereignty', pp. 446-7.
16.   Shuqairi, *Arbau'n Aman*, p. 269.
17.   Ibid., p. 288.
18.   513 from Cairo, 13 May 1948, US Nat. Arc. 867N 01/5-1348.
19.   167 from Beirut, 10 May, 1948, US Nat. Arc. 501 NN Pal./5-1048.
20.   NIACT 272 from Damascus, 11 May 1948, US Nat. Arc. 501 BB Pal./ 5-948.

21.   263 from Damascus, 9 May 1949, US Nat. Arc. 867N 01/5-948.
22.   266 from Damascus, 10 May 1948, US Nat. Arc. 867N 01/5-1048.
23.   589 from New York, 6 May 1948, US Nat. Arc. 501 BB Pal./5-648.
24.   NIACT 604, from Jerusalem, 13 May 1948, US Nat. Arc. 867N 01/5-1348.
25.   Pablo Azcarate, *Mission in Palestine 1948-52* (Washington, DC, 1958), pp. 88-9.
26.   Extract from Summary of World Broadcasts, part IV, no. 50, period 3 to 9 May 1948, p. 59.
27.   Ahmad Shuqairi, *Arbau'n Aman*, p. 281.
28.   'Rose-el Yusuf', Cairo, 21.12.1947.
29.   Maj. Gen. Salih Sa'ib Al-Juburi (Iraqi Chief of Staff), *Mihnat Falastin*, pp. 128-30.
30.   Ibid., p. 169; Kimche, *Both Sides of the Hill*, p. 153.
31.   Shuqairi, *Arbau'n Aman*, p. 290.
32.   Mahmoud, 'King Abdullah and Palestine', p. 44.
33.   Ibid., p. 45.
34.   Ibid., pp. 48-52.
35.   Marie Syrkine, *Golda Meir: Woman with a Cause* (New York, 1963), p. 196; Larry Collins and Dominique Lapierre, *O Jerusalem*, p. 86; Dan Kurzman, *Genesis 1948* (New York, 1970), pp. 23-4; Zev Sharef, *Three Days*, p. 72.
36.   Sharef, *Three Days*, pp. 72-3; Collins and Lapierre, *O Jerusalem*, p. 395; Syrkine, *Golda Meir*, p. 196.
37.   Syrkine, *Golda Meir*, p. 196; Sharef, *Three Days*, p. 72.
38.   Sharef, *Three Days*, pp. 73-6; Syrkine, *Golda Meir*, pp. 197-202; Collins and Lapierre, *O Jerusalem*, pp. 394-8.
39.   These last proposals are not mentioned by Jewish sources: Cf. Sharef, *Three Days*, pp. 74-6; but Mahmoud, 'King Abdullah and Palestine', pp. 95-6, refers to the Memoirs of Abdullah al-Tall.
40.   Mahmoud, 'King Abdullah and Palestine', pp. 136-7, 143-8.
41.   NIACT 272 from Damascus, 11 May 1948, Nat. Arc. 867N 01/4-1148. British American Co-operation in Palestine, memorandum of conversation, 2 May 1948, US Nat. Arc. 867N 01/5-248.
42.   549 from New York, 2 May 1948, US Nat. Arc. 501 BB Pal./5-248.
43.   Future Course of Events in Palestine, memorandum, 4 May 1948, US Nat. Arc. 501 BB Pal./5-448.
44.   Collins and Lapierre, *O Jerusalem*.
45.   A-279 from Cairo, 30 April 1948, US Nat. Arc. 867N 01.
46.   Ahmed Shuqairi, *'Aman Fi'il Hayat Al Arabiya Wad-Dowliya* (Beirut, 1969).
47.   Maj. Gen. Salih Sa'ib Al Juburi, *Minhat Falastin*, pp. 122-3.
48.   Shuqairi, *'Aman Fi'il Hayat*, p. 289.
49.   Tariq Al-Bishri, *Al-Harakah*, p. 266 (quoting President of the Egyptian Senate), 1972.
50.   'Nasser's Memoirs of the First Palestinian War', translated by Walid Khalidi, *Journal of Palestine Studies*, p. 9 (February 1973).
51.   Mohammed Naguib, quoted in Collins and Lapierre, *O Jerusalem*, p. 388.
52.   Jon and David Kimche, *Both Sides of the Hill*, p. 153.
53.   Quoted in Shimon Peres, *Military Aspects of the Israeli-Arab Conflict* (Tel Aviv, 1975), p. 5.
54.   *Egyptian Gazette*, 12 May 1948.
55.   BBC, Summary of World Broadcasts Received, part III, no. 50, 3-6 May 1948, p. 56.

56.   Al Bishri, *Al-Harakah*, pp. 262-3, quoting *Al Jamahir*, 19.10.1947.

57.   *Al Jamahir*, 22.10.1947.

58.   Collins and Lapierre, *O Jerusalem*.

59.   'Nasser's Memoirs', p. 10.

60.   P.J. Vatikiotis, *The Egyptian Army in Politics* (Bloomington, Ill.) pp. 34-5.

61.   Al Bishri, *Al-Harakah*, p. 266.

62.   Summary of Broadcasts Received, 10-16 May 1948, part IV, no. 51, p. 59.

63.   'Arab League Action Regarding Cease-Fire', US Nat. Arc. 5 May 1948, 867N 01/5-548.

64.   Shuqairi, *'Aman Fi'il Hayat*.

65.   Collins and Lapierre, *O Jerusalem*.

66.   Shuqairi, *'Aman Fi'il Hayat*, p. 290.

CONCLUSIONS

1.   NIACT 587 from New York, 6 May 1948, US Nat. Arc. 501 BB Pal./ 5-648.

IN PLACE OF A SUMMARY

The Mandatory period was characterised by three main features of Zionist policy towards the Arabs. First, the Arab national movement as a whole was viewed *de haut en bas*. There was a dramatic under-estimation of the potential of the Arab world for modernisation, based on its enormous natural resources, and its capacity to mobilise social, intellectual and political ability to exploit them.

The importance of the Middle East, politically, economically and strategically, has increased many times over since 1917 or 1948. The dependence of the Western economies and military operations upon oil is far greater than it was. The weight of the bloc of the 17 Arab states in world councils has no comparison with their position during the Mandatory period.

No Zionist leader foresaw these developments. The Zionist movement believed that the qualitative superiority of the Jewish people, with their highly-educated scientific-technical cadres, would compensate for the superiority in numbers of the Arabs. While originally this had an economic context, during the Mandatory period it developed into a concept of military superiority, which, confirmed by the 1948 war, seemed to place Israel on par with all the Arab states combined. It was only in the wake of the war of October 1973 that a new and more realistic appraisal of the Jewish-Arab relationship began to emerge. It is only beginning because those who determine Israel's policy today are still committed to the old concept of maximising Israel's military potential based on its scientific-technical advantages over the Arabs disregarding the truth that while battles are won by military technology, wars, today, are determined by the economic potential of the combatants. The futility of this strategy today is expressed by Israel's desire for the ultimate weapon — the nuclear bomb — whose introduction into the Middle East can lead only to the mutual destruction of both sides.

The corollary of the military strategy towards the Arabs has been the search for a Great Power ally, the second tenet of Zionist strategy which was initiated in the Mandatory period. Until 1948, the Zionist movement staked its future on British support and strove to integrate itself into the strategic needs of the British Empire. Today it is seeking a similar alliance with the United States, without regard to the fact that the international scene has changed considerably, and that Great Powers can no longer exert untrammelled influence throughout the world. It also ignores the same disparity that existed with respect to Great Britain, that the strategic interests of the Great Power and the Zionist movement may not correspond. Today America is in a process of reappraising its strategic position in the Middle East. Just as with Great Britain, it must assess its interests in the Arab world, and the possible role of the Arab factor in an international confrontation, without regard to Israel's dependence on American support.

The third tenet of Zionist policy, inherited from the Mandatory period, was the non-recognition of the national aspirations of the Palestinians. This was a consistent feature of Zionist strategy, initiated by Weizmann and carried out by Ben-Gurion and his followers (Golda Meir, etc.). This policy has been followed despite the abundant proof of the tenacity with which the Palestinians have clung to their national identity in the most adverse circumstances of dispersion. The Palestinian question was seen as the major stumbling block by even the most far-seeing and intellectual Zionist leaders (Ruppin, Arlozoroff), who were led to pessimism and despair of any solution.

From these strategic tenets certain erroneous policies were derived: (a) a policy of economic segregation of the two national economies; (2) the illusion that the Palestinian problem would disappear through a transfer of population to neighbouring Arab countries; and (3) a belief in the Hashemite connection — that the pro-Western regime of Jordan would solve the Palestinian problem.

All of these policies were realised by the state of Israel. The war of 1948 led to the flight of most of the Palestinians, and Jordan took over the West Bank. Yet, rather than resolving the conflict, these developments intensified it. Today the Palestinian people, though without a state, an army, or an economy, are the most important factor among the powerful Arab states, for one reason — because they alone hold the key to real peace in the Middle East. The Palestinians are a more decisive factor today than they were in 1948, and without a settlement with them on the basis of mutual recognition it will be difficult if not impossible to achieve a comprehensive and durable peace-settlement in the Middle East.

INDEX